WALLABY

ASTROSCOPE
Compatibility
Guide

A WALLABY BOOK

Published by Simon & Schuster

New York

Contents

(I)
Astrology and Love

Can astrology help you find the ideal mate? That all depends on how you describe "ideal" and what you mean by "mate." Each of us has our own notion of the ideal romantic partner, and "mate" can mean husband, wife, or lover—or a combination thereof.

The art of "synastry"—the comparison of two charts in order to determine the quality of relationship possible between two people—is a very complicated and involved process. For the purposes of this book, we have simplified things somewhat and will attempt to give an idea of what *is* possible with astrology in this very complex area of love.

Traditionally, Sun signs of the same element are said to relate the best of any combination of elements because they share many similar qualities. The fire signs, Aries, Leo, and Sagittarius, are usually grouped together as "compatible." The same goes for the air signs, Gemini, Libra and Aquarius; the earth signs, Taurus, Virgo, and Capricorn; and the water signs, Cancer, Scorpio and Pisces.

The second best combinations are the complementary signs: Air gives fire oxygen, and earth gives water shape. So air can work well with fire, and earth works well with water. However, these combinations have not always proved to work as well in reality as they do in theory.

In a relationship between two fire-sign people, both want to be the boss because they both have strong egos. Ideally, they believe in

1

equality, but one always likes to be "more equal" than the other. Their ideals are vital to both of them, and if these ideals should differ, there are sure to be many heated discussions.

Also, all three fire signs have different ways of getting things. For example, the reckless and thoughtless behavior of Aries may embarrass the Leo, who has a more "respectable" and conservative way of behaving. The Leo may also be frightened by the extremes in the Sagittarian, who doesn't mind gambling with his security from time to time.

The relationship between two air-sign people can have trouble getting started because they love to talk and think, but air, by itself, doesn't have the initiative necessary to put the ideas into action. Also, Libra likes to do things properly, but Gemini and Aquarius are both controversial types. Of course, the Aquarian swears by his controversial behavior, whereas the Gemini is easily influenced by other people and will conform.

Earth-sign people care about their physical needs and are not very willing to risk their security. They tend to hold back their trust until they see something that appeals to their senses. If both partners are afraid to make the first move, the relationship doesn't go anywhere. In particular, Taurus's stability is disturbed by Virgo's finickiness and Capricorn's ambitions.

Water-sign people tend to look for somebody to take care of them, so in a relationship between these two, one must be willing to play the mother role and remain the crutch for the other. However, a Cancer can be so self-protective that he cannot put the other person first all the time. A Scorpio's depth and a Pisces' flightiness can frighten the security needs of a Cancer, or even of each other.

A relationship between two people of the same element may be safe, but it's rarely dynamic. Since most people are looking for excitement and challenge (whether they realize it or not), they are usually attracted to the signs whose elements "conflict" with theirs. A relationship of this sort promises anything but complacency.

For instance, the physical needs of earth give fire's conviction a purpose and direction. Fire's ideals may be offended by earth's materialism, but at least they can accomplish something, and the glory is what they are interested in. The emotionalism of water may endanger the air-sign people, who use detachment as a defense for expressing their feelings. But air is curious about and amazed by water's ability to survive and its depth and power. Water can put fire out, of course, but water can serve as a reflection for the fire-sign people, who love to see their own images. Earth challenges air to give its ideas value and definition. Earth can change a blabbermouth air-sign person into a realistic achiever.

Naturally, the entire chart must be considered when evaluating a native's potential for a relationship. Sometimes chemistry is just good timing regardless of the elements. But one thing can be agreed upon: Being in love is usually the happiest time in a person's life. But, when we consider how important love is to us, it becomes a serious issue. Maybe that's why so many people look to astrology to help them find the "perfect mate." Astrology lectures on love and relationships draw the largest audiences. And the question most frequently asked of astrologers is: "What's the best sign for me to fall in love with?"

Before that question can be answered, one must first examine his needs and desires. Love can mean many things to different people: romance, sex, companionship, acceptance, play, security. Before a person starts a relationship with another, he should be sure he is dealing with someone who has the same definition of love that he has. If the prospective mate does not have an acceptable definition, he had better be sure he can handle the consequences.

It may safely be assumed that up until relatively recent times, horoscope comparisons for prospective mates were done as a means of determining the degree of compatibility, especially in terms of common goals. Marriage was, and still is in some quarters, seen as a life-long *partnership*.

We must remember that originally astrology was not used for the general public but rather for powerful people such as royalty and other public leaders. In such situations, it was imperative that there be as little conflict as possible between the couple, since the fate of a city or an entire nation might depend on the degree of marital tranquility enjoyed by those in power! However, in this age of the individual, differences and incompatibilities can and do make for diversity and dynamism in a relationship.

It is surprising only to the uninitiated that so many people of "incompatible" signs wind up being attracted to each other. There is an old verity, "Opposites attract." They do—and so do "squares." Signs that are at a 90° angle to each other are known to be in a square angular relationship, or aspect. Signs that are 180° apart are in opposition to each other. "Square" and "opposition" relationships are traditionally known as incompatible signs, but they aren't hopelessly doomed to be so forever. And even more fascinating is that they are either magnetically attracted or absolutely repellent to each other. More often than not, they are attracted.

The signs that are in opposition to each other are:

Aries–Libra	Cancer–Capricorn
Taurus–Scorpio	Leo–Aquarius
Gemini–Sagittarius	Virgo–Pisces

Signs that square each other are:

Aries squares Cancer, Capricorn	Libra squares Cancer, Capricorn
Taurus squares Leo, Aquarius	Scorpio squares Aquarius, Leo
Gemini squares Virgo, Pisces	Sagittarius squares Pisces, Virgo
Cancer squares Libra, Aries	Capricorn squares Aries, Libra
Leo squares Scorpio, Taurus	Aquarius squares Taurus, Scorpio
Virgo squares Sagittarius, Gemini	Pisces squares Gemini, Sagittarius

Statistically speaking, more marriages occur between opposing signs. Love affairs, or magnetic attraction relationships, most often occur between squaring signs. Friendships and acquaintances occur most commonly between the compatible signs. These are:

Aries—			Gemini—	
Easy:	Leo, Sagittarius		Easy:	Libra, Aquarius
Good:	Gemini, Aquarius		Good:	Leo, Aries
Possible:	Taurus, Pisces		Possible:	Cancer, Taurus
Neutral:	Virgo, Scorpio		Neutral:	Scorpio, Capricorn
Taurus—			Cancer—	
Easy:	Virgo, Capricorn		Easy:	Scorpio, Pisces
Good:	Cancer, Pisces		Good:	Virgo, Taurus
Possible:	Aries, Gemini		Possible:	Gemini, Leo
Neutral:	Libra, Sagittarius		Neutral:	Sagittarius, Aquarius

Leo—Easy:	Sagittarius, Aries		Scorpio—Easy:	Pisces, Cancer
Good:	Libra, Gemini		Good:	Virgo, Capricorn
Possible:	Cancer, Virgo		Possible:	Libra, Sagittarius
Neutral:	Capricorn, Pisces		Neutral:	Aries, Gemini
Virgo—Easy:	Capricorn, Taurus		Sagittarius—Easy:	Aries, Leo
Good:	Scorpio, Cancer		Good:	Libra, Aquarius
Possible:	Leo, Libra		Possible:	Scorpio, Capricorn
Neutral:	Aries, Aquarius		Neutral:	Taurus, Cancer
Libra—Easy:	Gemini, Aquarius		Capricorn—Easy:	Virgo, Taurus
Good:	Leo, Sagittarius		Good:	Scorpio, Pisces
Possible:	Virgo, Scorpio		Possible:	Sagittarius, Aquarius
Neutral:	Taurus, Pisces		Neutral:	Gemini, Leo

Aquarius—Easy:	Gemini, Libra	Pisces—Easy:	Cancer, Scorpio
Good:	Sagittarius, Aries	Good:	Taurus, Capricorn
Possible:	Capricorn, Pisces	Possible:	Aquarius, Aries
Neutral:	Cancer, Virgo	Neutral:	Leo, Libra

Astrology can help to determine the similarities and the differences between people; it can definitely point out the areas of difficulty and the areas of ease. But it is finally up to the individuals to use these energies constructively and to seek the compromises necessary to any deep and fulfilling relationship.

(II)

Signs and Cusps: Positive and Negative Characteristics of the Signs

MARCH 21–APRIL 20

THE POSITIVE SIDE OF ARIES

Aries is the first sign of the Zodiac, and people born under it like to be first in whatever they do. These people are pioneers and inventors. They have leadership ability both because of their tremendous physical energy and because of their ability to inspire others to action. They are always moving forward with enthusiasm and expectation. Each day is a new adventure for them. They do not dwell on the past, as they are too busy moving into the future.

The Aries person has a great deal of physical energy. He requires less sleep than other people and he loves being active. The Aries person accomplishes a great deal because he will rise to any challenge. There is nothing that he will not try, and if he can compete with someone else at the same time, so much the better. He doesn't shy away from difficulties but meets them head on, dealing with them as quickly as he can so that he can get on with his life.

The Aries person has great optimism about any and every venture in which he is involved. He inspires those around him with his optimism and quick wit. He goes after what he wants in life and usually gets it, for he sees anything between him and his goal as a challenge rather than an obstacle.

The person born under the sign of Aries is straightforward and open. There is no deviousness or guile within him. His optimism and enthusiasm together with his vitality keep him young throughout his life. He gets excited about everything around him and wants to experience everything in life. There is nothing that seems impossible for him to achieve. He is popular and has an active social life as he provides an example to others of how life ought to be lived.

THE NEGATIVE SIDE OF ARIES

Swept up by his own enthusiasm, the Aries person can move so quickly toward his goal that he is callous or inconsiderate of those around him. He is impatient with slower-moving people, and in his frustration at being slowed down he can be sharp-tongued. He speaks before he thinks and so is often tactless.

The negative Aries is too impulsive. He jumps into things without thinking and leaves them as fast. Such a person leaves a trail of unfinished projects in his wake. He also leaves behind hurt feelings and bruised egos.

The negative Aries hears only what he wants to hear. He doesn't let fact interfere with his fantasy. He has two ways of viewing things: his way and the wrong way. He can be very destructive if he doesn't get his own way. By being sensitive to the needs of others, he can overcome these negative traits.

APRIL 21–MAY 20

THE POSITIVE SIDE OF TAURUS

The most outstanding qualities of Taurus are his consistency and reliability. He can always be found where you expect him to be, as he is a creature of habit. He is helpful to those around him. A gentle soul, he is quiet and reserved, hiding a romantic center. He is very sentimental and affectionate, and he is shy. He is easy to get along with, as he is tolerant of others. The Taurus person likes his creature comforts and so he will have furniture chosen for comfort rather than style and serve sumptuous meals. Food is important to the Taurus person, especially sweets.

The Taurus person works very hard in his chosen profession and rises to the top through perseverance. He does not change careers frequently, preferring the familiar to the unknown. He is honest with his dealings and expects the same from others. He is thorough in everything he does. He has great patience and will not take short cuts to get a job done faster.

The Taurus person is cautious, preferring to be safe rather than sorry. He will not take risks if he can avoid them. He will deliberate for a long time before making any decision. His decisions are based on as much information as he can possibly gather. He takes a great deal of time to make a decision because he will seldom change his mind once the decision has been made.

The Taurus person loves his home and family and will spend all his leisure time with them. He is an excellent parent, kind, nurturing, reliable, and supportive. He is loyal and steadfast in his relationships. Those people that are his friends are ones he has known for years. He does not make friends easily because he is shy, but he does make lifetime friends. For the Taurean, time is the measure of all things. The longer something lasts, the better it is.

THE NEGATIVE SIDE OF TAURUS

The Taurus person can be stubborn. He dislikes change because it requires risk. He likes to move slowly and becomes quite angry when people try to get him to move fast. He does not like to be told what to do, nor does he deal well with being wrong.

The negative Taurus person can be miserly. He loves money and the things it can buy. He doesn't like to spend money on others. Sometimes his fear of not having enough keeps him from enjoying what he has.

The negative Taurus can be extremely possessive of those he loves, and therefore he can be jealous. He doesn't trust easily because he is afraid people will take advantage of him. He takes himself too seriously, so he gets hurt easily.

MAY 21–JUNE 20

THE POSITIVE SIDE OF GEMINI

The Gemini person is extremely intelligent and very quick-witted. A delightful sense of humor and wit assure his popularity both professionally and socially. He can get along with anyone and has an insatiable curiosity about everything. He keeps an open mind and is always eager to learn new things.

The Gemini person is most satisfied when he is in a situation in which he can make use of his intellect. He is governed more by his mind than by his emotions. He can see both sides of any issue and will argue either side with equal delight. A battle of wits is one of his favorite pastimes.

The Gemini person is very adaptable and can adjust quickly to any situation in which he finds himself. He moves with the times, adapting to the prevailing social structure, so he is regarded as forward-thinking and "with it." His ability to adjust to any condition gives him an ageless quality, so that people think he is younger than he actually is.

The Gemini person tends to be slight in build and has good physical balance, so he is graceful as well as charming. He wins dance contests as well as spelling bees. He may be found on television because of his charisma and communication skills.

The Gemini person is very creative and is attracted to art and literature in any form. He works quickly so he will have plenty of time for socializing. The exchange of ideas is to the Gemini as food is to other people.

THE NEGATIVE SIDE OF GEMINI

The negative Gemini person has trouble focusing his attention. He tries to do everything at once and usually winds up finishing nothing. His concentration span is very short and he is easily distracted. He has trouble distinguishing the essential from the trivial and often puts too much energy in the wrong place.

The negative Gemini person does not like to decide on anything; he prefers to keep his options open to see what will happen. As a result, he is not very reliable and sometimes not even truthful. He can be sharp-tongued and inconsiderate because he is more concerned with his own pleasure in a battle of wits than of the other person's feelings.

JUNE 21–JULY 20
THE POSITIVE SIDE OF CANCER

Cancer is the sign of nurturing, and those people born under it are concerned about feelings. They would never do anything to hurt another and usually go out of their way to help those less fortunate than themselves. They are aware that all of us are part of the large family of humanity and so treat strangers as family members.

The Cancer person is very intuitive, and when he plays his hunches, he is extremely successful in life. When he uses his intuition in business, he can become very wealthy. He has a sixth sense when it comes to speculation. He knows when to buy and when to sell.

The Cancer person has a strong sense of family unity and of tradition. He loves his home, especially the kitchen, and brings all his friends there where he can feed them. In any crisis, he will fill the stomachs of those around him and then deal with what has to be done.

The Cancer person has a great sense of tradition and respect for the past. He loves antiques both for their investment potential and for their fine craftsmanship. Tradition gives him a feeling of security, so he will continue the rituals of his childhood with his own children. The well-being of his family is very important to him, and he is extremely sensitive to their moods.

THE NEGATIVE SIDE OF CANCER

The negative Cancer person tends to overreact to the situations in his life. He can wallow in self-pity. Often life is too hard for him to face, and he resents the fact that others are not sensitive to his feelings. Although the Cancer woman tends to cry more readily when things go wrong than the Cancer man, both tend to eat when they are depressed and so must watch the tendency to be overweight.

The negative Cancer person has a lazy streak. He feels his efforts go unnoticed so there is no point in trying. He needs constant reassurance that he is loved, so he makes heavy emotional demands upon those around him. He tends to cling and sometimes even to emotionally smother the object of his affections in an effort to get his security needs met.

JULY 21–AUGUST 21
THE POSITIVE SIDE OF LEO

The Leo person is a good executive. He is a natural leader, able to manage many people and delegate tasks. He inspires respect and affection from those around him. He has a highly developed sense of responsibility to his employers and employees alike. Once he sets a goal for himself, he has the drive and the tenacity to achieve it.

The Leo person has a sunny disposition. He is loving and generous and has a great capacity for having fun. He loves parties and celebrations and spends time chasing appropriate gifts. He likes to spend money on others, for seeing them happy makes him happy.

The Leo person has a dramatic flair that makes him a wonderful storyteller. Many Leos go into the dramatic arts professionally or into a related entertainment field. They love being the center of attention, and being on stage fulfills that need.

The Leo person has presence, confidence, and style. He appears to be in charge, so he is put in charge. He has a quick and decisive mind and is not afraid of responsibility. Although he can be light-hearted and funny, he is not superficial or glib. He is a person of substance. He is honest and reliable and very giving to those who treat him well. He enjoys entertaining and fills his home with his friends. Very popular, he is seldom alone.

THE NEGATIVE SIDE OF LEO

Sometimes a Leo person can be too arrogant. He assumes that no one can do things as well as he can, so he takes over and alienates people. He can be egocentric, demanding that everyone's attention be focused on him. He has the conceit to think that he is God's gift to the world and resents people who do not share this view.

The negative Leo can be very materialistic and conscious of social status so that he measures everybody by their genealogy or bank account. This kind of Leo feels that the world owes him a living, that he is a prince without a country. He will marry well.

Some negative Leos are bossy to the point of being rude and cutting. They treat their families as slaves.

AUGUST 22–SEPTEMBER 21

THE POSITIVE SIDE OF VIRGO

The Virgo person is very hard-working and reliable. He is extremely well organized and can create order out of chaos. He develops systems. He is not afraid of hard work and will give all he's got to see that the job is done on time. He can always be depended upon to come through when the chips are down.

The Virgo person has a desire to be of service. He is sensitive and observant and will anticipate the needs of those around him. He is always there when you need him. He is unobtrusive and will serve from the sidelines; he doesn't need the limelight.

The Virgo person is straightforward, open, and honest. He says what he means and means what he says. He is without guile and is as good as his word. He is never secretive or underhanded. He is down to earth.

The Virgo person is curious and well informed. He has a good intellect, which he likes to use but tempers with sensitivity. His communication skills are excellent, as are his critical faculties. He criticizes to improve, and his criticisms are usually well founded and accurate. His ability to explain anything he understands makes him a natural teacher.

The Virgo person is moderate in his life. He strives for balance, so he eats well and remembers to exercise. Most Virgos are slim and look younger than their years. Some are health food and vitamin enthusiasts. All Virgos recognize the need for balance and moderation even if they don't practice them.

THE NEGATIVE SIDE OF VIRGO

The negative Virgo person is picky and critical. He thinks that no one can do a job as well as he can, so he is always telling people how things should be done. He can find fault with anything and has a compulsion to tell others about it. He can drive people crazy with his criticisms and can be quite insensitive to their feelings.

The negative Virgo can be very cold emotionally. He feels that emotions are beneath him and make life untidy. He can get very set in his ways and try to force those ways on others. He is intolerant of the weaknesses of others and tends to be extremely judgmental.

The negative Virgo can see life as a trial to be endured and will be a wet blanket whenever others are up. He will undermine their confidence at every turn. If he is unhappy, he doesn't want others to be happy either.

SEPTEMBER 22–OCTOBER 22
THE POSITIVE SIDE OF LIBRA

The Libra person loves peace and harmony. He expends great energy in keeping his environment serene. He is a natural arbitrator and helps other people to achieve a balanced view of a situation. He can see both sides of almost any issue, and his council is sought when people have problems. He makes a good lawyer too.

The Libra person has a keen intellect as well as a sense of fairness. He always tries to put himself in the other person's shoes. He is against injustice and will usually defend the underdog. He will use his intellect to help balance the injustices he sees around him.

The Libra person has a well-developed sense of beauty. He has an innate sense of color, line, and space, so he usually lives in a beautifully decorated home even if he is poor. The Libran may draw, paint, or design clothes. He has a flair for clothes and can make an elegant outfit out of anything. He has impeccable taste both in clothes and furnishings, and his home is always a pleasure to visit. He is a gracious host, making sure everyone feels welcome and at home. He'll remember a guest's favorite drink and have it ready the second time the person visits.

The Libra person gets along with just about everyone and is much in demand socially. He is elegant, witty, well informed, and probably very good-looking. The most handsome men and the prettiest women seem to be born under the sign of Libra.

THE NEGATIVE SIDE OF LIBRA

The negative Libra person will go to any length to ensure peace and is thus often considered insincere. So eager is he to achieve harmony in all relationships that he will even go so far as to lie. He is an escapist and will avoid confrontation at all cost even if it is with himself. He finds facing the truth an ordeal and prefers to live in a world of make-believe.

The love of beautiful things can make a negative Libra person materialistic. He can get so caught up in possessions and luxuries that he has no time or energy left for human relationships. He can be vain and jealous and can regard his mate as a possession rather than a person. His refusal to deal with life makes him difficult to live with. To him it's appearances that matter, not feelings.

OCTOBER 23–NOVEMBER 22
THE POSITIVE SIDE OF SCORPIO

The Scorpio person usually knows what he wants out of life. He is very determined and usually achieves what he sets out to do. The ultimate realist, he sees things as they are and deals with them. He has few illusions about life and thus he is seldom disappointed.

The Scorpio person has tremendous courage and stamina. When others have fallen by the wayside, he'll still be going strong. He rises to any challenge. He will push the limits of anything just to test himself. He is afraid of nothing.

The Scorpio person is wonderful at finding solutions to life's problems. He'll usually manage to find two or three solutions to any one problem. He does very well in positions of responsibility because of his problem-solving capabilities and his memory. Nothing is ever forgotten.

The Scorpio person is very loyal to those he cares about. It takes him a long time to trust someone, but once he does, there is nothing he would not do for the person. He does not take relationships lightly, nor anything else. There is nothing superficial about him; he is profound. His favorite question is "Why?" He wants to know the causes of everything and is not content with the obvious. He digs beneath the surface of things and keeps digging until he gets his answer. He is extremely perceptive and can be very supportive.

THE NEGATIVE SIDE OF SCORPIO

The negative Scorpio person is extremely manipulative. He uses his strong will to get other people to do things for him. He loves the feeling of power and can be ruthless and cruel in wielding it. He is extremely vindictive. He will not get angry, but he will get even. He will seek revenge.

The negative Scorpio is sarcastic and wounding with his tongue. He always knows the other person's weakness and goes right for it. He can be violent. He has no compassion and doesn't care what anybody thinks. He is unforgiving and unforgetting. He will accuse, try, judge, convict, and pass sentence on a person without letting the person know. He uses people for his own needs without regard for theirs.

The negative Scorpio takes himself too seriously; he has no humor. He imagines slights where there are none. He is secretive and will not let anyone know what he is thinking or feeling. He is dishonest when it suits him to be so. He has no scruples.

NOVEMBER 23–DECEMBER 20
THE POSITIVE SIDE OF SAGITTARIUS

The Sagittarius person is honest and open in life. He cannot stand underhandedness or sneakiness. He has a highly developed sense of social justice and will lead the way in social and legal reform. The Sagittarian has a delightful sense of humor and an almost eternal optimism. He brings out the best in people because he sees only the best.

The Sagittarius person is adventuresome and loves to travel. He'll go anywhere because he is interested in how other people live. He has an open mind and gains from every experience he has. He can turn a disaster into an adventure.

The Sagittarius person has high ideals and inspires respect from others. He is dynamic in his speech and can move masses of people because of his charisma and sincerity.

The Sagittarius person is intelligent and witty. He loves a discussion and will adapt his views easily when he hears good reason to do so. He loves to learn and often has a great deal of education, probably more than he needs. He will always be learning something new. Adult education classes are full of Sagittarians.

The Sagittarius person is very popular because he knows lots of jokes and because he is always game for a good time. A party is a guaranteed success when there are Sagittarians present. The Sagittarian is not afraid of looking ridiculous and is the butt of his own jokes.

He is seldom critical and almost always generous.

THE NEGATIVE SIDE OF SAGITTARIUS

The negative Sagittarius is restless and has trouble staying anywhere for long. He tends to be superficial with his relationships. He's the original out-of-sight, out-of-mind person. He will swear eternal love and then disappear.

The negative Sagittarius thinks he can do everything, so he promises more than he can deliver. He has no concept of time and is always late, if he shows up at all. He has no sense of discipline and accomplishes little. He is careless with life. He mismanages his money and may even be a compulsive gambler. He mismanages people, often taking outrageous advantage of his friends. He can be tactless and hurtful out of carelessness rather than malice. His need to be honest is greater than his need to be kind. He puts his foot in his mouth by being too honest at the wrong time.

The negative Sagittarius wastes a lot of energy moving fast and going nowhere.

DECEMBER 21–JANUARY 19

THE POSITIVE SIDE OF CAPRICORN

The Capricorn person is stable and patient. He sticks to his tasks until they are done. Discipline is natural to him, so he can accomplish a great deal. He is reliable and hard-working. He is a serious person and works hard at life. Duty is sacred to him, and he will never shirk what he considers to be his responsibilities. He does not let his feelings get in the way of his work.

The Capricorn person is ambitious and knows how to get what he wants out of life. He is not afraid of hard work to achieve his goals. He pursues a slow and steady course. He likes to keep his feet firmly on the ground.

The Capricorn person has a good business sense and knows the value of a dollar. He understands how to make money and usually is wealthy in later life. He is neither a spendthrift nor a miser. He recognizes value and will spend wisely. He hates waste and unnecessary loss, so he takes care of his possessions.

The Capricorn person is self-reliant. He does not expect others to do things for him. When someone does him a favor, he will return it in kind. He never expects more from others than he is willing to give. As a friend, he is loyal and trustworthy. You can count on him when the going gets tough. He keeps a clear head in a crisis and provides practical solutions to the problems at hand.

THE NEGATIVE SIDE OF CAPRICORN

The negative Capricorn person can be so ambitious that he is blinded to everything else. He can use people unmercilessly to achieve his goal. He can see people as cogs in the machinery of his ambition rather than as feeling beings. He turns a deaf ear to their problems.

The negative Capricorn person can have such a need to be an authority figure that he cannot relate to people as equals. He must always be in a superior position. He may also feel that he is better than others and may behave in a condescending manner. He can be too bossy, assuming that he knows what's best for everyone. He can be narrow in his thinking and closed to anything new.

The negative Capricorn can be too greedy. His need for money and position may keep him from forming successful relationships.

JANUARY 20–FEBRUARY 18
THE POSITIVE SIDE OF AQUARIUS

People born under the sign of Aquarius are the most tolerant and least prejudiced of people. They recognize that everyone has something to contribute, so they seek out those different from themselves to learn new things. The Aquarian person is genuinely interested in other people and in causes of freedom. He is a free spirit and refuses to be confined. Because of his own need to be free of all constraints and conventions, he respects other people's right to believe and live as they wish.

The Aquarius person is always fair. An Aquarian probably wrote the Golden Rule, "Do unto others as you would have them do unto you." He is concerned with humanitarian endeavors, as he regards all men as his brothers. He works hard to improve the quality of life for large groups of people.

The person born under this sign has a keen intellect and a probing mind. Many are scientists and engineers. He is forward-thinking and likes to invent labor-saving devices. He has a mathematical mind and enjoys dealing with abstract concepts.

The Aquarian is a good friend. He is eager to help when others are in need. He has a wide range of friends and belongs to many organizations. He genuinely likes people but prefers being a loner, moving in and out of groups as the mood strikes. He gets along with everyone.

THE NEGATIVE SIDE OF AQUARIUS

The negative Aquarius person is too detached. He has trouble forming emotional connections. He tends to be more helpful to his friends than he is to his family. He can be so busy with his own thoughts that he doesn't notice what is going on around him.

The negative Aquarius person can be so absorbed by abstract ideas that he loses touch with the practical realities of life. He is the true eccentric. His intellectual gifts can lead him to assume he is better than others. He can be very closed-minded and will seldom, if ever, admit that he is wrong. He has a way of convincing everyone else that they are wrong. He lives in a fantasy world and convinces himself (and anyone else that he can) that it is real. He can be a real mind-bender. He can be critical and destructive of others.

FEBRUARY 19–MARCH 20

THE POSITIVE SIDE OF PISCES

The Pisces person is sympathetic and warm. He understands the problems of others and is willing to help. He likes to serve others and is a natural healer. Many Pisces are in the medical profession. The Piscean instinctively knows how to make another person feel good.

The Pisces person is idealistic and sometimes unworldly. He creates illusions for himself and others. He may be an artist who creates fantasies with pen, brush, or film. When the world is too harsh for him, he escapes into a nicer world of fantasy.

The Pisces person is highly intuitive and usually knows what is going to happen before it does. He always knows what someone else is feeling, often before the person himself knows. Sometimes he gets too many perceptions at once and gets confused.

The Pisces person is as sensitive physically as he is creatively. He likes soft lights, soft colors, and soft fabrics. Loud noises are painful to him. Sometimes the world is to bright and too loud for him, and he has to retreat to get his balance. The sea is soothing to his nervous system; the water smooths the rough edges of his personality.

The Pisces person has a great need to be of service to those who are suffering and will try to rehabilitate the most hopeless cases. He really cares.

THE NEGATIVE SIDE OF PISCES

The negative Pisces person has a very gloomy outlook. He feels that he is a victim in life, always being used and never understood. He views life as a punishment and himself as having been born to suffer. All he sees around him is pain. He is easily discouraged and seldom develops the talents with which he was born.

The negative Pisces is a great escapist. He would rather withdraw from life than deal with it. Many Pisceans escape through alcohol or drugs, others through sex. Since they have almost no will power, they seldom resist temptation. They are lazy and drift through life letting the prevailing current take them wherever it is going.

The negative Pisces fantasizes all the time instead of living in this world, but he rarely does anything to make his fantasies come true.

CUSP BIRTHS: DOMINANT CHARACTERISTICS

Being born on the cusp means that you were born between the 19th and the 24th of any month. This is the period during which the signs change. The actual day the sign changes differs from month to month and year to year because the time used to measure planetary motion differs from calendar time. Being born on the cusp means that you exhibit characteristics of two signs.

Cusp of Aries/Taurus

People born between April 19 and April 24 are born on the cusp of Aries and Taurus. These people have some of the drive of Aries and some of the slowness of Taurus. They have wonderful ideas and great energy to implement them as well as tremendous enthusiasm, all of which they get from the Aries side of their personality. The Taurus side gives them a practical, thorough approach and an ability to finish what they have started. Together these energies can be a formidable combination. A person born on this cusp will take risks, but not unnecessary ones. He will try new things but with a practical approach. He has the ability to initiate *and* to follow through. He will start new businesses on a thoroughly practical foundation. The chances of success with this combination are very high.

On the negative side, the person born on the Aries/Taurus cusp can be at war with himself. He may want to take risks but be too afraid. He may feel that his innovative ideas are not practical enough. He may feel that his Taurus resistance to change is at odds with his Aries need to create something new. Taurus wants to be slow and sure, and Aries is too impatient to wait. Taurus wants to be secure and thus will not take risks, while Aries wants new challenges and hates the too familiar. People born on this cusp may feel that they are going through life with one foot on the accelerator and one foot on the brake.

Cusp of Taurus/Gemini

People born between May 19 and May 24 are said to be born on the Taurus/Gemini cusp. They combine strong practicality and a lightning-quick mind. The Taurus brawn together with the Gemini brains make them particularly well suited for athletics. The Taurus energy can make the person not want to move at all, so the restless Gemini energy is a perfect balance. These people are much more open-minded than a Taurus is likely to be and much more practical and patient than a Gemini. They can give practical application to their ideas. They will see a project through and not take the rest of their lives to do it. They are excellent students and probably have more than one degree. They are often found improving their homes and have a whole library of do-it-yourself books. They like all kinds of handy work. Some of them write the books. These people are generally successful in life because they have good mental discipline.

On the negative side, people born on the Taurus/Gemini cusp can be so intent on getting all the information that they need that they never get started. Some of them are professional students, being attracted to learning but afraid of the real world. They spend a lot of time talking about what they are going to do and very little time actually doing it. The Taurus resistance to change can be well supported by the Gemini inability to make a decision. These are people who are mentally agile but never move beyond square one. They spend a lot of time doing crossword puzzles and other brain teasers. They like nothing more than a wonderful dinner and stimulating conversation. They give away many good ideas because they do not have the drive to use the ideas themselves. They also find it easy to think up excuses for not changing. The negative Taurus/Gemini person can be accident-prone because his mind moves faster than his body and he has a tendency to trip over his feet.

Cusp of Gemini/Cancer

People born between June 19 and June 24 are said to be born on the Gemini/Cancer cusp. This combination of energies provides the intellect of Gemini and the intuition of Cancer. These people have tremendous communication skills. Not only do they instinctively know the right words to say, but they also put feeling into those words, so they can move any audience. They are well suited to political speech writing, public relations, and advertising. They know what the public wants to hear. They can also write best-selling novels. Their understanding of people's feelings plus their facility with words makes them particularly well equipped for creating characters and situations. Cancer/Gemini cusp people are social animals. They love to entertain, providing excellent food and scintillating conversation. Some of them do it so well that they make a career of it. Other Cancer/Gemini people are psychologists and teachers, and still others do very well writing cookbooks.

On the negative side, people born on the Cancer/Gemini cusp spend too much time talking about their feelings. They want sympathy so much that they think that if they tell you how bad they feel, you will provide the appropriate amount of sympathy. When they don't get the emotional support they think they deserve, they assume it is because they haven't explained their needs well enough. They will explain and explain, feeling that they have not found the right words, rather than the right person. They go back and forth between their intuitive side and their thinking side rather than integrating these two sides. As a result, they will mistrust their intuition if their logic does not agree, or try to reason out matters when their intuition already knows the answer. Their reasoning tends to be circular because the clarity of their intellect is clouded by their feelings.

Cusp of Cancer/Leo

People born between July 19 and July 24 are said to be born on the Cancer/Leo cusp. These people have excellent dramatic skills. The flamboyance of Leo together with the sensitivity of Cancer makes them award-winning actors and actresses. Even those not involved in the entertainment field create drama in their everyday lives. Their lives *are* soap operas. These people also have a great sensitivity to the feelings of others. They are very generous with time and affection. These are natural nurturers. They will make such a dramatic event out of your being sick that you almost hate to get well. They are particularly sensitive to the needs of children, having the mothering quality of Cancer and the childlike quality of Leo. Cancer/Leo cusp people give memorable parties; they are particularly fond of costume parties. These people provide entertainment for everyone around them.

On the negative side, Cancer/Leo cusp people are extremely demanding emotionally. They must be the center of attention at all times and they throw temper tantrums if someone else has the limelight for even one minute. The Cancer insecurity together with the Leo need for ego gratification can make them very difficult to live with. When they do not receive all of the other person's attention, they feel unloved and they sulk. They can be very possessive and manipulating, and no matter what is done for them, it is never enough. They blame everyone else for whatever goes wrong in their lives. They feel indignant and outraged at what they consider the lacks in their lives, and refuse to take any responsibility for them. They see themselves as tragic figures on the stage of life, and no amount of evidence to the contrary will change their mind. They prefer dramatic suffering to undramatic happiness.

Cusp of Leo/Virgo

People born between August 19 and August 24 are said to be on the Leo/Virgo cusp. These people combine the drama of Leo and the service of Virgo, and so are often teachers of dramatic arts. They produce children's plays, teach in acting schools, and use dramatic expression as a tool in psychotherapy. The precision of organizational ability of Virgo, together with the executive ability of Leo, makes these people particularly well suited to run any business. The Leo/Virgo person appears at home in any situation because the poise and competence of Virgo, together with the Leo confidence and flair, command attention and respect. Because of Virgo's communication skills and Leo's dramatic skills, these people are naturally suited to writing plays, television scripts, and best-selling novels. They are generally wealthy in later life.

On the negative side, the Leo/Virgo person never feels adequately rewarded for his work. The Virgo side of him feels no one could do it as well, and the Leo side demands to be in charge. As a result, he has to do everything and feels that no one appreciates his contribution. He is intensely sensitive to criticism, as he cannot admit his mistakes. In an effort to get a job done, he bosses others around, points out their imperfections, and then wonders why others do not like him; he is therefore often quite lonely. He cannot understand their attitude, because he feels he was only trying to be helpful. Leo/Virgo cusp people tend to overdo everything and are flamboyant with details and showy about the amount of work that they do. They sometimes have trouble distinguishing between the essential and the trivial. They tend to make an opera out of blowing their nose, yet will handle a crisis with perfect ease.

Cusp of Virgo/Libra

People born between September 19 and September 24 are said to be on the Virgo/Libra cusp. The precision of Virgo, together with the artistic quality of Libra, makes them particularly well suited for fine arts. They have an eye for line and color and like to design their own pictures or needlework. Their creations are often meticulous and lovely. They make very charming hosts and hostesses because of the Virgo need to serve and the Libra need to bring peace to the environment. These people are very popular because they listen well and provide adequate solutions to problems without becoming emotionally involved. They are found most often helping other people dealing with their lives. They are fair and unbiased in their dealings with others. They work hard at their relationships and try to help other people work as hard. They are usually very attractive and take great care with their appearance and their surroundings.

On the negative side, they can be too cold and calculating in their relationships. They can find it difficult to be emotionally involved and are often considered to be very distant. This is hard to deal with because they always want to keep everything pleasant, and others find it hard to believe that such an attractive person would have so little feeling. The Virgo inability to accept criticism together with the Libra refusal to confront situations makes it very difficult for these people to deal with the emotional problems of their own lives. It can also be frustrating for those people who have to deal with them. They can be very indecisive, because of the Virgo insecurity and need for perfection and the Libra need to consider both sides of a question before taking action. Their inability to make decisions leads many of them into escapist activities such as living in a fantasy world of perfection and harmony.

Cusp of Libra/Scorpio

People born between October 19 and October 24 are said to be on the Libra/Scorpio cusp. The charm of Libra and the intuitive qualities of Scorpio make these people extremely attractive because the Libra side knows how to please and the Scorpio side knows what others want. They can often achieve prominence in the field of their choice because the Scorpio stamina and persistence together with the Libran ability to create harmonious working conditions enable them to rise at a meteoric rate. There is no one more skilled at drawing people out and finding out what makes the other person tick, often without that other person's realizing what is happening. They have an ability to manipulate others so gracefully that people seldom feel used and actually give them what they want joyously. They can move mountains because they can charm other people into helping them.

On the negative side, the Libra/Scorpio person can be cold and calculating to the point of being insensitive to the feelings of others. He can manipulate those around him to serve his needs with little regard for what they need. Such a person charms others into service, and it isn't until after he is gone that they realize that they have been had. A master at illusion, he will create whatever environment is necessary to achieve his ends. He is secretive in the extreme, hardly letting his right hand know what his left hand is doing. He is conceited, as he truly believes that he is more attractive and brighter than almost everyone. He is possessive of his family and expects them to adhere to his rules. He can be extremely vindictive when his feelings are hurt. He can ruin a career without the victim's ever realizing what has happened. This is one to be wary of. He would never forgive you if you disappointed him.

Cusp of Scorpio/Sagittarius

People born between November 19 and November 24 are said to be on the Scorpio/Sagittarius cusp. These people have the Sagittarian optimism and the Scorpio realism. Such a combination enables them to fulfill their dreams. They are spontaneous and enthusiastic as well as passionate and deep. They accomplish what they set out to do and have unbelievable energy and drive. Their Sagittarian curiosity and their Scorpio need to get to the bottom of things lead them to learn everything possible about the subject of their choice. Their powers of concentration are formidable, as is their physical stamina. They are able to accomplish goals which others aspire to but rarely achieve. The Sagittarian side gives them high ideals and the Scorpio side gives them the fixity of purpose to achieve those ideals. The Sagittarian desire for travel and the Scorpio need for constancy leads them often into careers in which travel is an integral part.

On the negative side, the Sagittarian/Scorpio cusp person has trouble trusting others. The Sagittarian need to believe the world is wonderful, and the Scorpio realization that it is not, make it difficult for them to be open and honest about their feelings. These people can be very immediate in their relationships, and they are the ones who invented the phrase "out of sight, out of mind." Although they are most charming, they can disappear without a trace, leaving people wondering what happened. Their humor can be sarcastic or black, and they are not above destroying somebody for the sake of being funny, a combination of the Sagittarian humor and the Scorpio sting.

Their rapier wit is their greatest tool, and they know how to use it when it will do the most damage. These people are extremely secretive and sometimes have two separate lives, complete with aliases. They are not trustworthy.

Cusp of Sagittarius/Capricorn

People born between December 19 and December 24 are said to be on the Sagittarius/Capricorn cusp. The Sagittarian optimism that everything will work out well is combined with the Capricorn willingness to make things work. The Sagittarian's immediacy is tempered by the Capricorn's foresight and planning. The natural curiosity of Sagittarius to cover as many bases as possible, together with the innate ambitiousness of Capricorn to get to the top, enables these people to achieve professional success early in life. The Capricorn side enjoys working hard, being responsible, and keeping his finger on the pulse of things, while the Sagittarian side is able to deal with multiple factors simultaneously with efficiency and good humor. These people are successful because they can set more far-reaching goals and see possibilities that others would miss, and then design and implement the methods by which the goals can be attained. There is often therefore a fruitful combination of idealism and practicality.

On the negative side, the Sagittarius/Capricorn person has trouble integrating his idealism with his innate practicality. The natural conservatism of the Capricorn side is at odds with the flamboyance of the Sagittarian side. Here is a person with idealism, but his Capricornian pessimism makes him think he can never realize them. He wants the best of all possible worlds, but doesn't think he will ever achieve it. These people resent all authority, whether parental or organizational, because the Sagittarian need for freedom is in conflict with the Capricornian need to be in charge. They are difficult to work with because they are either too bossy or too cavalier, and sometimes alternate between the two. The Sagittarian's belief that he knows the truth and wants to share it, together with the Capricornian's need to be an authority figure, can make these people tyrannical in their dealings with others. They can be extremely self-righteous, even when they are wrong.

Cusp of Capricorn/Aquarius

People born between January 19 and January 24 are said to be on the Capricorn/Aquarius cusp. The Aquarian's ability for abstract thinking, together with the Capricornian's practicality, makes this combination formidable for problem solving of all kinds. Since the Aquarians are usually the most scientifically minded people of the Zodiac, and the Capricorns are the people who deal with the practical details of daily living, people born on this cusp are often very good troubleshooters. They often have mechanical ability and are amateur as well as professional inventors. The Aquarian desire to improve the quality of life plus the Capricorn ability to see practical solutions to problems leads these people into social reform and political organizations. They are clear-thinking and unbiased by the emotional environment in which they are operating. They tend to see life's problems as solvable like a mathematical equation. These people will establish social structures that will guarantee the freedom of each individual.

On the negative side, the Capricorn/Aquarius person can be too detached from the people around him. He can be so busy organizing the community that he neglects his family. He has trouble establishing close emotional relationships and is more comfortable being a friend to all. His natural intellectual gifts may make him arrogant and condescending to those around him. He can run into difficulty because he keeps his eye on the goal and forgets the needs of the people doing the work. Such a person can have a pessimistic view of life and deal with every situation with too much seriousness. Although he can get things done, it is not necessarily enjoyable to work with him. He can push the people around him unmercifully because he has no tolerance for emotional weakness. His lack of success in relationships often leads him into dealing with abstract ideas and mechanical devices.

Cusp of Aquarius/Pisces

People born between February 19 and February 24 are said to be on the Aquarius/Pisces cusp. These people combine the Aquarian ability for logical reasoning and the Piscean ability to fantasize and imagine. Many of these people are talented in the arts, particularly in areas in which they can create an illusion out of time, such as science fiction, fairy tales, or allegories. They have an abiding awe of the universe and a great desire to understand how it works. Many are led into the study of higher physics. They can often envision future events. They are sensitive to the harshness of life and will often turn to music for solace. Basically the Pisces side has faith that things will work, and the Aquarius wants to know how. The Piscean creativity is given expression by the logic and fixity of Aquarius. Many Aquarius/Pisces people are exceptionally fine painters and musicians, and many others are excellent psychiatrists because of the Piscean sympathy and the Aquarian analytical ability.

On the negative side, the Aquarius/Pisces person is caught on the horns of the dilemma of wanting to know, which is an Aquarian quality, and having faith, which is a Pisces quality. Such a person may have trouble integrating the creative and logical sides of his nature. He is likely to have very structured thinking and deny his creative impulses. As a result, he stalls in his progress and accomplishes very little. He can be facile in his talk but lazy in his accomplishments. Such a person will escape into fantasy and abstract thinking. He will construct crossword puzzles and Double-Crostics. He would tend to be a dabbler, rather than pursue anything thoroughly. Because of the Aquarian need for freedom and the Piscean confusion about this world, such a person can have a great deal of trouble surviving in the real world. The problem is that he can be too easily distracted, so that he has difficulty finishing things and therefore has no sense of accomplishment.

Cusp of Pisces/Aries

People born between March 19 and March 21 are said to be born on the Pisces/Aries Cusp. It should be noted that because the Sun moves into Aries on March 21 of each year, this cusp is very small. These people combine the creativity of Pisces with the drive of Aries, so they often achieve renown in some artistic field. The Aries need to be first, coupled with the Pisces ability to generate fresh ideas from the imagination, often puts these people in the forefront of their field. The enthusiasm and energy to initiate is tempered by a sensitivity to the needs of others, so that such a person often has an enthusiastic team working with him. He can encourage others to take risks and is sympathetic to their fears. He appreciates creativity in all forms and encourages his associates to express their own creative urges. He has great compassion and will think of new ways to take care of people's needs. His optimism inspires others to have faith in themselves.

On the negative side, the Pisces laziness together with the Aries impatience can cause this person to give up any creative endeavor before he has completed it. He tries everything once, perfecting nothing. This person wants to be a leader and be respected for his executive abilities, but will get very hurt and upset if this does not happen. He can get arrogant about his own ideas. He has the ability to create a fantasy world for himself and does not let the facts interfere with that fantasy. People on this cusp are past masters at not dealing with issues whenever they so choose. They put the Aries energy into the Pisces fantasy. They are willing to take risks, but are terribly upset when those risks fail. In an effort to overcome the insecurity of Pisces, the Aries side can make these people domineering. They can become angry if others do not share their fantasy. They find it difficult to live with themselves, so naturally it is difficult for others to live with them.

(III)
Your Rising Sign
(Your Ascendant)

The rising star, or Ascendant, is the sign that is on the horizon at the time of your birth. The rising sign indicates how you look to the world, how you appear to the world, and how you interact with the world, or your environment. It is the image you project, the way other people see you, which may be very different from the way you feel inside.

The Earth rotates on its axis completely every 24 hours, placing each of the twelve signs of the Zodiac in turn on its horizon. Thus a new sign rises on the horizon every two hours, approximately. Knowing the exact time of your birth is thus quite important, and many birth certificates today do carry this information. If yours does not, you must try to find out the time of your birth as closely as you can.

Depending on your Sun sign, the Ascendant will add complementary traits or disclose internal disturbances. For example, a Cancer with Sagittarius rising is apt to come across as a carefree, sociable, funny extrovert. This may completely mask the sensitivity of Cancer's deeper and truer feelings. A Cancer with Cancer rising would most likely come across as a quieter, more emotional, insecure introvert. Even though both these examples are Cancer, they express their energies differently through the rising sign.

To approximate your own rising sign, follow this procedure:

Construct a circle as shown in the first illustration below, based on the chart showing the houses. Draw a horizontal line; the Ascendant is on your left at the point it touches the arc of the circle, the Descendant on the right. Divide the interior area of the circle into twelve equal segments as shown. These are the twelve houses, starting with 1 at the first segment on the left, or East, below the horizontal line and continuing counterclockwise until all twelve houses are numbered.

Each house is allotted its two hours, with midnight beginning on the cusp of the fourth house. Thus, moving counterclockwise every two hours, midnight to 2 A.M. is in the third house, 2 A.M. to 4 A.M. in the second house, 4 A.M. to 6 A.M. in the first house, and 6 A.M. to 8 A.M. in the twelfth house, above the Ascendant line. Continue until all 24 hours are placed on the chart.

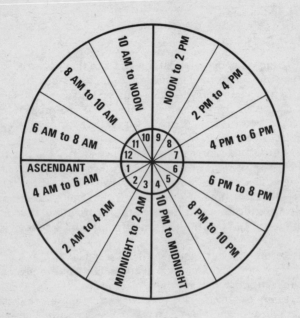

Assume, for example, that you were born at 10:30 A.M. and that your Sun sign is Leo. Leo, then, would be placed on the cusp of the tenth house since the hour of your birth falls within that house.

Moving counterclockwise, place the rest of the signs in order on succeeding cusps, as in the illustration. With Leo as the sign on the tenth house, Virgo would be on the eleventh house, Libra on the twelfth, and so on.

The sign appearing on the first house cusp is the rising sign, or Ascendant. In this example, Scorpio is the sign on the first house cusp for a Leo born at 10:30 A.M.

As another example, consider a Virgo born at 9:15 P.M. Virgo would be placed on the cusp of the fifth house. Placing the remaining signs in order counterclockwise around the circle, Libra would follow on the cusp of the sixth house, Scorpio on the seventh, Sagittarius on the eighth, Capricorn on the ninth, Aquarius on the tenth, Pisces on the eleventh, Aries on the twelfth, and Taurus on the first house cusp. This Virgo would have Taurus rising.

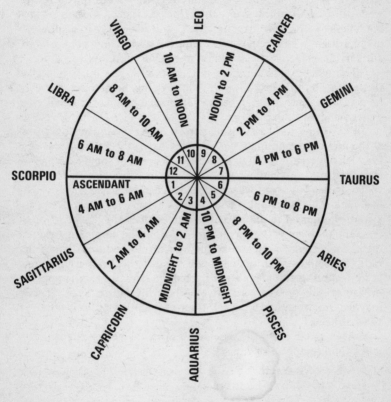

To get a better understanding of yourself, draw a circle like the one shown above and label it. Then turn to the Ascendant Tables at the end of this chapter and find your rising sign.

YOUR ASCENDANT PERSONALITY: DOMINANT CHARACTERISTICS

Aries

Aries on the first house indicates a person who is assertive, direct, and impulsive. This person projects the image of a go-getter who will stop at nothing to achieve his goals. He appears to have boundless energy, absolute confidence, and the ability to inspire others to action. Such a person is adventurous and spontaneous, and has a highly developed sense of humor about himself as well as others.

The Aries Ascendant person appears to be in a hurry and gives the impression that he knows what he is doing. Sometimes, however, he gets his mouth in gear before his brain becomes aware of what he is saying, or doing.

Physically, the Aries-rising person may exhibit a widow's peak at the hair line, denoting the symbol for Aries, the Ram's horns. The fire of Aries comes through in rosy cheeks and, in some cases, an extremely flushed complexion. When the person with Aries rising walks, he tends to lead with his head and in his haste trips over his feet. You can always tell if your friends have Aries rising if you feel a compelling need to put away breakables when they come to visit.

The problem with this placement is that the dominant Aries energy is so strong that it masks the insecurities and sensitivities that may also be present in the personality. Since the Aries-rising person is seen as being confident and directed, he seldom gets the opportunity to express the more sensitive parts of his nature. Such a person may feel fraudulent, since what other people respond to is only part of what he is.

Aries rising is a great asset, as it gives the person the ability to make things happen for himself.

Taurus

People with Taurus rising project an image of sensitivity and warmth. These people are natural nurturers and are usually seen as parent figures. They are quiet and shy. They are extremely hard-working and dependable. Their consistency and loyalty make them valued friends.

People with Taurus rising tend to be cautious, considering the consequences of their actions before they act. They would rather be safe than sorry.

Physically, the Taurus-rising person is square or stocky in build. He tends to put on weight, for he loves food. He moves slowly and generally suffers from a lack of exercise. Taurus rising gives the individual grace in his movements and a lovely singing voice.

Taurus rising indicates a person who is unwilling to initiate action and will go to great lengths to maintain a status quo. If your Sun is in a fire or air sign, Taurus rising can give stability to those energies. If your Sun is in an earth or water sign, Taurus rising can complement the energies so that a person appears as he actually is.

Because of the steadfastness that Taurus rising lends to the personality, the person is cast in a parental role more frequently than he wishes. It is assumed that he will accept responsibility for other people at their, rather than his, discretion. As a result, he tends to be used. His wish to be kind and helpful often makes him the patsy. Taurus-rising people must learn to set limits on their giving, and learn to say no when it is appropriate.

Gemini

Gemini on the first house lends to the personality a quickness of movement and of thinking. This person is constantly in motion and finds it difficult to sit still for more than ten minutes at a time. A person with Gemini rising is seen as a gifted and witty conversationalist with an outrageous sense of humor.

The duality of Gemini makes these people very adaptable to whatever comes their way. It also makes it difficult for them to make choices. The Gemini-rising person would rather talk about the options than choose one.

Gemini rising is particularly advantageous for anyone involved in speech making, debating, or any other verbal activity in which he must think on his feet. This is a fine placement for anyone who has political aspirations.

Physically, Gemini-rising people are slim and wiry. The highly developed nervous system of some keeps them from putting on weight. Others simply move too fast to waste time on eating. The Gemini-rising person is high-strung and appears to have all his nerves exposed. There is a sense of rhythm and balance to his body. His face is delicate and angular and has a mischievous expression. Because he looks impish, he can get away with things for which others would be castigated.

The Gemini-rising person is the original idea kid. He generates more ideas per minute than others do per day. He's a great generator of ideas, but has trouble implementing any one of them. He delights in acting strangely, for he doesn't want others to think they know who or what he is.

People with Gemini rising view life as an adventure and thus retain their youthful looks longer than their contemporaries do.

Cancer

Cancer rising indicates a person who is very aware of the feelings of those around him. The immediate environment of this person is of critical importance, as he will reflect the prevailing mood. If those around him are cranky, then he'll be cranky. If he is surrounded by happy people, then he'll be happy. He appears to be shy and will not venture into a situation unless he is sure his feelings will be protected. When he feels protected, he can be quite aggressive in getting what he wants. This masked aggression always fools people. Cancer is, after all, a cardinal sign.

The Cancer-rising person is the chairman of the chicken soup committee. He is the first on the scene, with loads of mothering, particularly food. He feels it is his mission in life to feed everyone he meets. In the process he tends to eat too much himself, so he is constantly fighting the battle of the bulge.

Besides a tendency to corpulence, physically the Cancer-rising person will have a moon-shaped face and watery eyes.

People with Cancer rising give the appearance of being extremely insecure. Depending on the Sun sign, this may or may not be an accurate reflection. They seem to need a tremendous amount of emotional support from everyone in their environment. This may be a way of manipulating circumstances.

Leo

A person with a Leo Ascendant exhibits strong leadership qualities. He naturally assumes command, and other people accept his leadership as his rightful due. In any given situation, the Leo-rising person will be the center of attention. He is a natural extrovert and loves to make an entrance wherever he goes. His dramatic flair and his sense of humor help him gain access to people who will be helpful in his career.

Physically, the Leo-rising person is easy to pick out. He has thick, luxurious hair, usually of a light shade and often curly. It looks like a lion's mane. He has a very small nose, usually one that is turned up at the end. The lines around his mouth become deep as he ages so that his face takes on the appearance of a cat. He must watch the tendency to put on weight from all of his partying and indulging.

People with Leo rising have a warm, sunny disposition. Truly leonine, these people like to bask in the center of the world's attention. They have a sense of noblesse oblige, a belief that they have a responsibility to take care of the world. These people are extremely popular and attractive.

The Leo-rising person is in love with love. Life is always an adventure, like a movie, to these people. People with Leo rising are always fun to have around.

Virgo

People with Virgo rising appear to be poised and confident in all that they do. However, this is only a front, so those with Virgo rising will work twice as hard to make it a reality. They appear to be very reserved and aloof, but this is due to painful shyness and insecurity. They are unassertive but cooperative; seldom leaders, but good and loyal followers. They will always contribute to a mission. They are quiet and observant, gathering all the facts, with which they design a more efficient structure.

People with Virgo rising are easy to overlook and to take for granted. It usually isn't until after they are gone that their contribution is noted. They are good with details and have a high degree of manual dexterity. They will stick with a task until it is finished. They are often the ones who turn out the lights and lock up.

Physically they are slight in build, with delicate features and light, clear eyes. They have an air of purity and innocence.

These people are inhibited socially because of their tremendous shyness, so they are always grateful when someone else makes the first move. Once you can penetrate their reserved air, a delightful sense of humor is revealed.

Virgo Ascendants are very sensitive to the needs of others and always willing to lend a helping hand. Their willingness to serve makes it easy for them to be exploited by others. They are kind and loyal friends.

Libra

Libra on the first house cusp indicates a person who likes to surround himself with the "right people." This is a person who likes to entertain and be entertained in the finest manner. He has a very sophisticated eye, ear, and palate, so it is a delight to be in his home. He is a natural diplomat and is often called upon to mediate between the warring factions of his neighborhood, business sphere, or any other group. He can see both sides of the issue clearly and present the facts in an unbiased manner.

Physically, people with Libra rising are the best-looking people of the Zodiac. Perfectly proportioned and delicately formed, these people are the personification of grace. These qualities, together with their esthetic sense, make them elegant dressers and suave lovers.

These people appear to be the sweet light of reason in all situations, never taking a stand lest they alienate one of the participants of the discussion. They have an awesome ability to seem to agree with all the various positions when in fact they offer no opinion of their own. This ability also makes them hard to pin down when a specific answer is required. They are adept at sidestepping questions, usually by disappearing from the scene.

You will almost never see them ruffled. Their desire for harmony is so great and their abhorrence of conflict so strong that they will say anything to keep the peace. These people are most charming and will be included in everyone's circle of friends.

Scorpio

Scorpio rising indicates someone who likes to observe from the wings before he comes out on the stage. He likes to assess his environment before interacting with other people. He is not very trusting, so people tend to feel uncomfortable around him. Scorpio rising is a highly intuitive person and seems to have more information about other people than they have about him, even if they are strangers.

People with Scorpio rising are the best of friends and the worst of enemies. They are loyal and protective of their friends, always warning them of impending disasters. They can be fearsome enemies, never resting until they have wrought their revenge. They have memories like elephants, never forgetting a thing. Yet they are reluctant to reveal themselves and what they know.

Physically, the Scorpio-rising person has deep-set, dark eyes, bushy eyebrows, and a sensuous mouth. His body appears to lack muscle tension, and he must watch the tendency to overweight due to water retention.

The Scorpio-rising person has an intensity of energy that makes it difficult for him to get along with others. His mere presence can threaten his colleagues. He is, however, owing to his intensity, a tireless worker, with a fixity of purpose that sees the job through to its end.

These people like to test their own limits and in so doing usually improve the lives of those around them.

Sagittarius

Sagittarius rising indicates a person who is fun-loving and quick-witted. His keen sense of humor and natural ebullience promote the erroneous impression that he is a mental lightweight. This is not the case, as these people have a keen intellect and far-reaching perceptions. Unlike others, they have learned that intellectual depth does not preclude humor.

People with Sagittarius rising are spontaneous, love to be outrageous, and are ready to party night and day. They put a lot of energy into keeping everyone else laughing and the party going at high speed. They appear to be carefree and only concerned with the moment. This is a mask, for they never let others see what they really are. People with Sagittarius rising feel that style justifies the deed. They will wine and dine someone in a grand style, leaving others to pick up the check.

Physically, people with Sagittarius rising are often blue-eyed and rosy-cheeked, with roundish faces, small noses, eyes set close together, and a ready grin. They tend to gain weight around the hip area. Sagittarius rising gives poor muscle tone because of the lack of exercise.

People with Sagittarius rising make wonderful orators and religious leaders. They can inspire religious fervor and a social conscience in the people of their communities so that social reform is assured.

Capricorn

Capricorn rising lends a serious air to the basic personality. These people are very conservative in their approach to life and fulfill all of their responsibilities no matter how distasteful. They project an image of authority and generally attain a position of power in the community or business arena. They have a highly developed sense of duty and therefore end up shouldering more responsibility than others. They are loyal, devoted workers and fair, impartial bosses.

People with Capricorn rising tend to be very practical in their dealings with others. They are more concerned with tangible things that they can see than with abstractions. Because of their tendency to focus on practical goals, they have trouble dealing with people's emotions. They are uncomfortable in most social situations, as they do not see the purpose of such activities. If forced into a social situation, they will use the setting as an opportunity to conduct business.

Physically, people with Capricorn rising have a large and sturdy bone structure. They appear solid and square. They have long faces with a pronounced square jaw. They tend to be stiff and awkward in their movements, not so much from a lack of natural grace as from an intense self-consciousness. They have a deep-seated fear of looking ridiculous.

These people are bound to be successful in life and will take good care of anyone who travels the road with them.

Aquarius

A person with an Aquarius Ascendant appears calm, cool, and collected in all situations. This poise gets him through sticky situations and makes him feel at ease when the time and place are appropriate. Other people view this person as cold and calculating without a nerve cell in his body. Not so. He may appear cool, but he doesn't necessarily feel that way. This person is interested in people of all walks of life; social strata do not exist for him. People are attracted to him because he is so accepting of them.

The Aquarius-rising person is articulate and logical. He deals with what comes his way in a detached, low-key manner. He appears to have few problems in life. Such a person is often called upon to help others to gain perspective on their lives. This person will join groups and help them to function more efficiently than they had done before. He usually holds an office in whatever organization he joins.

Physically, people with Aquarius rising are slim, often too thin. Many have trouble keeping weight on their bodies. Many exhibit signs of nervousness such as fingernail biting, smoking, or a nervous tic in the face. Their faces are long and angular, with well-defined features. As they get older, they take on a craggy or weatherbeaten appearance. They tend to have poor circulation, so their complexion is pale.

Pisces

A person with Pisces rising appears to be warm and compassionate. Others are attracted to this person because they feel that not only will he understand what they are feeling, but he will care. This person *does* feel other people's emotions acutely but does not always know what to do about them. The Pisces-rising person is a dreamer, preferring to drift or float through life rather than to take action. He has trouble understanding other people's lack of sensitivity, since his is so highly developed. He can be shy and retiring and has learned how to make himself invisible in a group. He tends to have a pessimistic view of life and, as a result, makes things more difficult for himself than is necessary.

The Pisces-rising person is very helpful. He prefers working behind the scenes to performing in the limelight. He would rather be busy serving than stand around and be entertaining. Although he is quiet, he is an appreciative listener and has a ready and infectious laugh. He is able to create the illusion of security and success. He loves to play a role, so any five people will have five different ideas of who he is.

Physically, the Pisces-rising person is of medium build. He tends toward fleshiness because he doesn't get enough exercise. He has to watch his weight. The most outstanding feature of this person is his eyes: They are exceptionally large and deep. The compassion that shines forth from them attracts one and all.

ARIES—ASCENDANT TABLES

	MARCH 21	MARCH 22	MARCH 23	MARCH 24	MARCH 25
MIDNIGHT	SAGITTARIUS	SAGITTARIUS	SAGITTARIUS	SAGITTARIUS	SAGITTARIUS
1 A.M.	SAGITTARIUS	SAGITTARIUS	SAGITTARIUS	SAGITTARIUS	SAGITTARIUS
2 A.M.	CAPRICORN	CAPRICORN	CAPRICORN	CAPRICORN	CAPRICORN
3 A.M.	CAPRICORN	CAPRICORN	CAPRICORN	CAPRICORN	CAPRICORN
4 A.M.	AQUARIUS	AQUARIUS	AQUARIUS	AQUARIUS	AQUARIUS
5 A.M.	PISCES	PISCES	PISCES	PISCES	PISCES
6 A.M.	PISCES	PISCES	ARIES	ARIES	ARIES
7 A.M.	ARIES	ARIES	ARIES	ARIES	ARIES
8 A.M.	TAURUS	TAURUS	TAURUS	TAURUS	TAURUS
9 A.M.	GEMINI	GEMINI	GEMINI	GEMINI	GEMINI
10 A.M.	GEMINI	GEMINI	GEMINI	GEMINI	GEMINI
11 A.M.	CANCER	CANCER	CANCER	CANCER	CANCER
NOON	CANCER	CANCER	CANCER	CANCER	CANCER
1 P.M.	CANCER	CANCER	LEO	LEO	LEO
2 P.M.	LEO	LEO	LEO	LEO	LEO
3 P.M.	LEO	LEO	LEO	LEO	LEO
4 P.M.	VIRGO	VIRGO	VIRGO	VIRGO	VIRGO
5 P.M.	VIRGO	VIRGO	VIRGO	VIRGO	VIRGO
6 P.M.	VIRGO	VIRGO	VIRGO	LIBRA	LIBRA
7 P.M.	LIBRA	LIBRA	LIBRA	LIBRA	LIBRA
8 P.M.	LIBRA	LIBRA	LIBRA	LIBRA	LIBRA
9 P.M.	SCORPIO	SCORPIO	SCORPIO	SCORPIO	SCORPIO
10 P.M.	SCORPIO	SCORPIO	SCORPIO	SCORPIO	SCORPIO
11 P.M.	SAGITTARIUS	SAGITTARIUS	SAGITTARIUS	SAGITTARIUS	SAGITTARIUS

	MARCH 26	MARCH 27	MARCH 28	MARCH 29	MARCH 30
MIDNIGHT	SAGITTARIUS	SAGITTARIUS	SAGITTARIUS	SAGITTARIUS	SAGITTARIUS
1 A.M.	SAGITTARIUS	SAGITTARIUS	CAPRICORN	CAPRICORN	CAPRICORN
2 A.M.	CAPRICORN	CAPRICORN	CAPRICORN	CAPRICORN	CAPRICORN
3 A.M.	CAPRICORN	AQUARIUS	AQUARIUS	AQUARIUS	AQUARIUS
4 A.M.	AQUARIUS	AQUARIUS	AQUARIUS	AQUARIUS	AQUARIUS
5 A.M.	PISCES	PISCES	PISCES	PISCES	PISCES
6 A.M.	ARIES	ARIES	ARIES	ARIES	ARIES
7 A.M.	ARIES	TAURUS	TAURUS	TAURUS	TAURUS
8 A.M.	TAURUS	TAURUS	TAURUS	TAURUS	TAURUS
9 A.M.	GEMINI	GEMINI	GEMINI	GEMINI	GEMINI
10 A.M.	GEMINI	GEMINI	GEMINI	GEMINI	GEMINI
11 A.M.	CANCER	CANCER	CANCER	CANCER	CANCER
NOON	CANCER	CANCER	CANCER	CANCER	CANCER
1 P.M.	LEO	LEO	LEO	LEO	LEO
2 P.M.	LEO	LEO	LEO	LEO	LEO
3 P.M.	LEO	LEO	LEO	LEO	LEO
4 P.M.	VIRGO	VIRGO	VIRGO	VIRGO	VIRGO
5 P.M.	VIRGO	VIRGO	VIRGO	VIRGO	VIRGO
6 P.M.	LIBRA	LIBRA	LIBRA	LIBRA	LIBRA
7 P.M.	LIBRA	LIBRA	LIBRA	LIBRA	LIBRA
8 P.M.	LIBRA	LIBRA	LIBRA	LIBRA	LIBRA
9 P.M.	SCORPIO	SCORPIO	SCORPIO	SCORPIO	SCORPIO
10 P.M.	SCORPIO	SCORPIO	SCORPIO	SCORPIO	SCORPIO
11 P.M.	SAGITTARIUS	SAGITTARIUS	SAGITTARIUS	SAGITTARIUS	SAGITTARIUS

	MARCH 31	APRIL 1	APRIL 2	APRIL 3	APRIL 4
MIDNIGHT	SAGITTARIUS	SAGITTARIUS	SAGITTARIUS	SAGITTARIUS	SAGITTARIUS
1 A.M.	CAPRICORN	CAPRICORN	CAPRICORN	CAPRICORN	CAPRICORN
2 A.M.	CAPRICORN	CAPRICORN	CAPRICORN	CAPRICORN	CAPRICORN
3 A.M.	AQUARIUS	AQUARIUS	AQUARIUS	AQUARIUS	AQUARIUS
4 A.M.	AQUARIUS	AQUARIUS	AQUARIUS	AQUARIUS	PISCES
5 A.M.	PISCES	PISCES	PISCES	PISCES	PISCES
6 A.M.	ARIES	ARIES	ARIES	ARIES	ARIES
7 A.M.	TAURUS	TAURUS	TAURUS	TAURUS	TAURUS
8 A.M.	TAURUS	TAURUS	TAURUS	TAURUS	GEMINI
9 A.M.	GEMINI	GEMINI	GEMINI	GEMINI	GEMINI
10 A.M.	GEMINI	GEMINI	CANCER	CANCER	CANCER
11 A.M.	CANCER	CANCER	CANCER	CANCER	CANCER
NOON	CANCER	CANCER	CANCER	CANCER	CANCER
1 P.M.	LEO	LEO	LEO	LEO	LEO
2 P.M.	LEO	LEO	LEO	LEO	LEO
3 P.M.	VIRGO	VIRGO	VIRGO	VIRGO	VIRGO
4 P.M.	VIRGO	VIRGO	VIRGO	VIRGO	VIRGO
5 P.M.	VIRGO	VIRGO	VIRGO	VIRGO	VIRGO
6 P.M.	LIBRA	LIBRA	LIBRA	LIBRA	LIBRA
7 P.M.	LIBRA	LIBRA	LIBRA	LIBRA	LIBRA
8 P.M.	SCORPIO	SCORPIO	SCORPIO	SCORPIO	SCORPIO
9 P.M.	SCORPIO	SCORPIO	SCORPIO	SCORPIO	SCORPIO
10 P.M.	SCORPIO	SCORPIO	SCORPIO	SCORPIO	SCORPIO
11 P.M.	SAGITTARIUS	SAGITTARIUS	SAGITTARIUS	SAGITTARIUS	SAGITTARIUS

	APRIL 5	APRIL 6	APRIL 7	APRIL 8	APRIL 9
MIDNIGHT	SAGITTARIUS	SAGITTARIUS	SAGITTARIUS	SAGITTARIUS	SAGITTARIUS
1 A.M.	CAPRICORN	CAPRICORN	CAPRICORN	CAPRICORN	CAPRICORN
2 A.M.	CAPRICORN	CAPRICORN	CAPRICORN	CAPRICORN	CAPRICORN
3 A.M.	AQUARIUS	AQUARIUS	AQUARIUS	AQUARIUS	AQUARIUS
4 A.M.	PISCES	PISCES	PISCES	PISCES	PISCES
5 A.M.	PISCES	PISCES	ARIES	ARIES	ARIES
6 A.M.	ARIES	ARIES	ARIES	ARIES	PISCES
7 A.M.	TAURUS	TAURUS	TAURUS	TAURUS	TAURUS
8 A.M.	GEMINI	GEMINI	GEMINI	GEMINI	GEMINI
9 A.M.	GEMINI	GEMINI	GEMINI	GEMINI	GEMINI
10 A.M.	CANCER	CANCER	CANCER	CANCER	CANCER
11 A.M.	CANCER	CANCER	CANCER	CANCER	CANCER
NOON	CANCER	CANCER	CANCER	LEO	LEO
1 P.M.	LEO	LEO	LEO	LEO	LEO
2 P.M.	LEO	LEO	LEO	LEO	LEO
3 P.M.	VIRGO	VIRGO	VIRGO	VIRGO	VIRGO
4 P.M.	VIRGO	VIRGO	VIRGO	VIRGO	VIRGO
5 P.M.	VIRGO	VIRGO	LIBRA	LIBRA	LIBRA
6 P.M.	LIBRA	LIBRA	LIBRA	LIBRA	LIBRA
7 P.M.	LIBRA	LIBRA	LIBRA	LIBRA	LIBRA
8 P.M.	SCORPIO	SCORPIO	SCORPIO	SCORPIO	SCORPIO
9 P.M.	SCORPIO	SCORPIO	SCORPIO	SCORPIO	SCORPIO
10 P.M.	SCORPIO	SAGITTARIUS	SAGITTARIUS	SAGITTARIUS	SAGITTARIUS
11 P.M.	SAGITTARIUS	SAGITTARIUS	SAGITTARIUS	SAGITTARIUS	SAGITTARIUS

	APRIL 10	APRIL 11	APRIL 12	APRIL 13	APRIL 14
MIDNIGHT	SAGITTARIUS	SAGITTARIUS	CAPRICORN	CAPRICORN	CAPRICORN
1 A.M.	CAPRICORN	CAPRICORN	CAPRICORN	CAPRICORN	CAPRICORN
2 A.M.	CAPRICORN	AQUARIUS	AQUARIUS	AQUARIUS	AQUARIUS
3 A.M.	AQUARIUS	AQUARIUS	AQUARIUS	AQUARIUS	AQUARIUS
4 A.M.	PISCES	PISCES	PISCES	PISCES	PISCES
5 A.M.	ARIES	ARIES	ARIES	ARIES	ARIES
6 A.M.	PISCES	TAURUS	TAURUS	TAURUS	TAURUS
7 A.M.	TAURUS	TAURUS	TAURUS	TAURUS	TAURUS
8 A.M.	GEMINI	GEMINI	GEMINI	GEMINI	GEMINI
9 A.M.	GEMINI	GEMINI	GEMINI	GEMINI	GEMINI
10 A.M.	CANCER	CANCER	CANCER	CANCER	CANCER
11 A.M.	CANCER	CANCER	CANCER	CANCER	CANCER
NOON	LEO	LEO	LEO	LEO	LEO
1 P.M.	LEO	LEO	LEO	LEO	LEO
2 P.M.	LEO	LEO	LEO	LEO	LEO
3 P.M.	VIRGO	VIRGO	VIRGO	VIRGO	VIRGO
4 P.M.	VIRGO	VIRGO	VIRGO	VIRGO	VIRGO
5 P.M.	LIBRA	LIBRA	LIBRA	LIBRA	LIBRA
6 P.M.	LIBRA	LIBRA	LIBRA	LIBRA	LIBRA
7 P.M.	LIBRA	LIBRA	LIBRA	LIBRA	SCORPIO
8 P.M.	SCORPIO	SCORPIO	SCORPIO	SCORPIO	SCORPIO
9 P.M.	SCORPIO	SCORPIO	SCORPIO	SCORPIO	SCORPIO
10 P.M.	SAGITTARIUS	SAGITTARIUS	SAGITTARIUS	SAGITTARIUS	SAGITTARIUS
11 P.M.	SAGITTARIUS	SAGITTARIUS	SAGITTARIUS	SAGITTARIUS	SAGITTARIUS

	APRIL 15	APRIL 16	APRIL 17	APRIL 18	APRIL 19	APRIL 20
MIDNIGHT	CAPRICORN	CAPRICORN	CAPRICORN	CAPRICORN	CAPRICORN	CAPRICORN
1 A.M.	CAPRICORN	CAPRICORN	CAPRICORN	CAPRICORN	CAPRICORN	CAPRICORN
2 A.M.	AQUARIUS	AQUARIUS	AQUARIUS	AQUARIUS	AQUARIUS	AQUARIUS
3 A.M.	AQUARIUS	AQUARIUS	AQUARIUS	PISCES	PISCES	PISCES
4 A.M.	PISCES	PISCES	PISCES	PISCES	PISCES	PISCES
5 A.M.	ARIES	ARIES	ARIES	ARIES	ARIES	ARIES
6 A.M.	TAURUS	TAURUS	TAURUS	TAURUS	TAURUS	TAURUS
7 A.M.	TAURUS	TAURUS	TAURUS	GEMINI	GEMINI	GEMINI
8 A.M.	GEMINI	GEMINI	GEMINI	GEMINI	GEMINI	GEMINI
9 A.M.	GEMINI	GEMINI	CANCER	CANCER	CANCER	CANCER
10 A.M.	CANCER	CANCER	CANCER	CANCER	CANCER	CANCER
11 A.M.	CANCER	CANCER	CANCER	CANCER	CANCER	CANCER
NOON	LEO	LEO	LEO	LEO	LEO	LEO
1 P.M.	LEO	LEO	LEO	LEO	LEO	LEO
2 P.M.	VIRGO	VIRGO	VIRGO	VIRGO	VIRGO	VIRGO
3 P.M.	VIRGO	VIRGO	VIRGO	VIRGO	VIRGO	VIRGO
4 P.M.	VIRGO	VIRGO	VIRGO	VIRGO	VIRGO	VIRGO
5 P.M.	LIBRA	LIBRA	LIBRA	LIBRA	LIBRA	LIBRA
6 P.M.	LIBRA	LIBRA	LIBRA	LIBRA	LIBRA	LIBRA
7 P.M.	SCORPIO	SCORPIO	SCORPIO	SCORPIO	SCORPIO	SCORPIO
8 P.M.	SCORPIO	SCORPIO	SCORPIO	SCORPIO	SCORPIO	SCORPIO
9 P.M.	SCORPIO	SCORPIO	SCORPIO	SCORPIO	SCORPIO	SCORPIO
10 P.M.	SAGITTARIUS	SAGITTARIUS	SAGITTARIUS	SAGITTARIUS	SAGITTARIUS	SAGITTARIUS
11 P.M.	SAGITTARIUS	SAGITTARIUS	SAGITTARIUS	SAGITTARIUS	SAGITTARIUS	SAGITTARIUS

	APRIL 21	APRIL 22	APRIL 23	APRIL 24	APRIL 25
MIDNIGHT	CAPRICORN	CAPRICORN	CAPRICORN	CAPRICORN	CAPRICORN
1 A.M.	CAPRICORN	CAPRICORN	CAPRICORN	CAPRICORN	CAPRICORN
2 A.M.	AQUARIUS	AQUARIUS	AQUARIUS	AQUARIUS	AQUARIUS
3 A.M.	PISCES	PISCES	PISCES	PISCES	PISCES
4 A.M.	PISCES	ARIES	ARIES	ARIES	ARIES
5 A.M.	ARIES	ARIES	ARIES	ARIES	ARIES
6 A.M.	TAURUS	TAURUS	TAURUS	TAURUS	TAURUS
7 A.M.	GEMINI	GEMINI	GEMINI	GEMINI	GEMINI
8 A.M.	GEMINI	GEMINI	GEMINI	GEMINI	GEMINI
9 A.M.	CANCER	CANCER	CANCER	CANCER	CANCER
10 A.M.	CANCER	CANCER	CANCER	CANCER	CANCER
11 A.M.	CANCER	LEO	LEO	LEO	LEO
NOON	LEO	LEO	LEO	LEO	LEO
1 P.M.	LEO	LEO	LEO	LEO	LEO
2 P.M.	VIRGO	VIRGO	VIRGO	VIRGO	VIRGO
3 P.M.	VIRGO	VIRGO	VIRGO	VIRGO	VIRGO
4 P.M.	VIRGO	VIRGO	LIBRA	LIBRA	LIBRA
5 P.M.	LIBRA	LIBRA	LIBRA	LIBRA	LIBRA
6 P.M.	LIBRA	LIBRA	LIBRA	LIBRA	LIBRA
7 P.M.	SCORPIO	SCORPIO	SCORPIO	SCORPIO	SCORPIO
8 P.M.	SCORPIO	SCORPIO	SCORPIO	SCORPIO	SCORPIO
9 P.M.	SCORPIO	SCORPIO	SAGITTARIUS	SAGITTARIUS	SAGITTARIUS
10 P.M.	SAGITTARIUS	SAGITTARIUS	SAGITTARIUS	SAGITTARIUS	SAGITTARIUS
11 P.M.	SAGITTARIUS	SAGITTARIUS	SAGITTARIUS	SAGITTARIUS	SAGITTARIUS

	APRIL 26	APRIL 27	APRIL 28	APRIL 29	APRIL 30
MIDNIGHT	CAPRICORN	CAPRICORN	CAPRICORN	CAPRICORN	CAPRICORN
1 A.M.	AQUARIUS	AQUARIUS	AQUARIUS	AQUARIUS	AQUARIUS
2 A.M.	AQUARIUS	AQUARIUS	AQUARIUS	AQUARIUS	AQUARIUS
3 A.M.	PISCES	PISCES	PISCES	PISCES	PISCES
4 A.M.	ARIES	ARIES	ARIES	ARIES	ARIES
5 A.M.	TAURUS	TAURUS	TAURUS	TAURUS	TAURUS
6 A.M.	TAURUS	TAURUS	TAURUS	TAURUS	TAURUS
7 A.M.	GEMINI	GEMINI	GEMINI	GEMINI	GEMINI
8 A.M.	GEMINI	GEMINI	GEMINI	GEMINI	GEMINI
9 A.M.	CANCER	CANCER	CANCER	CANCER	CANCER
10 A.M.	CANCER	CANCER	CANCER	CANCER	CANCER
11 A.M.	LEO	LEO	LEO	LEO	LEO
NOON	LEO	LEO	LEO	LEO	LEO
1 P.M.	LEO	LEO	LEO	LEO	VIRGO
2 P.M.	VIRGO	VIRGO	VIRGO	VIRGO	VIRGO
3 P.M.	VIRGO	VIRGO	VIRGO	VIRGO	VIRGO
4 P.M.	LIBRA	LIBRA	LIBRA	LIBRA	LIBRA
5 P.M.	LIBRA	LIBRA	LIBRA	LIBRA	LIBRA
6 P.M.	LIBRA	LIBRA	LIBRA	SCORPIO	SCORPIO
7 P.M.	SCORPIO	SCORPIO	SCORPIO	SCORPIO	SCORPIO
8 P.M.	SCORPIO	SCORPIO	SCORPIO	SCORPIO	SCORPIO
9 P.M.	SAGITTARIUS	SAGITTARIUS	SAGITTARIUS	SAGITTARIUS	SAGITTARIUS
10 P.M.	SAGITTARIUS	SAGITTARIUS	SAGITTARIUS	SAGITTARIUS	SAGITTARIUS
11 P.M.	SAGITTARIUS	CAPRICORN	CAPRICORN	CAPRICORN	CAPRICORN

	MAY 1	MAY 2	MAY 3	MAY 4	MAY 5
MIDNIGHT	CAPRICORN	CAPRICORN	CAPRICORN	CAPRICORN	CAPRICORN
1 A.M.	AQUARIUS	AQUARIUS	AQUARIUS	AQUARIUS	AQUARIUS
2 A.M.	AQUARIUS	AQUARIUS	AQUARIUS	PISCES	PISCES
3 A.M.	PISCES	PISCES	PISCES	PISCES	PISCES
4 A.M.	ARIES	ARIES	ARIES	ARIES	ARIES
5 A.M.	TAURUS	TAURUS	TAURUS	TAURUS	TAURUS
6 A.M.	TAURUS	TAURUS	TAURUS	GEMINI	GEMINI
7 A.M.	GEMINI	GEMINI	GEMINI	GEMINI	GEMINI
8 A.M.	GEMINI	CANCER	CANCER	CANCER	CANCER
9 A.M.	CANCER	CANCER	CANCER	CANCER	CANCER
10 A.M.	CANCER	CANCER	CANCER	CANCER	CANCER
11 A.M.	LEO	LEO	LEO	LEO	LEO
NOON	LEO	LEO	LEO	LEO	LEO
1 P.M.	VIRGO	VIRGO	VIRGO	VIRGO	VIRGO
2 P.M.	VIRGO	VIRGO	VIRGO	VIRGO	VIRGO
3 P.M.	VIRGO	VIRGO	VIRGO	VIRGO	VIRGO
4 P.M.	LIBRA	LIBRA	LIBRA	LIBRA	LIBRA
5 P.M.	LIBRA	LIBRA	LIBRA	LIBRA	LIBRA
6 P.M.	SCORPIO	SCORPIO	SCORPIO	SCORPIO	SCORPIO
7 P.M.	SCORPIO	SCORPIO	SCORPIO	SCORPIO	SCORPIO
8 P.M.	SCORPIO	SCORPIO	SCORPIO	SCORPIO	SCORPIO
9 P.M.	SAGITTARIUS	SAGITTARIUS	SAGITTARIUS	SAGITTARIUS	SAGITTARIUS
10 P.M.	SAGITTARIUS	SAGITTARIUS	SAGITTARIUS	SAGITTARIUS	SAGITTARIUS
11 P.M.	CAPRICORN	CAPRICORN	CAPRICORN	CAPRICORN	CAPRICORN

	MAY 6	MAY 7	MAY 8	MAY 9	MAY 10
MIDNIGHT	CAPRICORN	CAPRICORN	CAPRICORN	CAPRICORN	CAPRICORN
1 A.M.	AQUARIUS	AQUARIUS	AQUARIUS	AQUARIUS	AQUARIUS
2 A.M.	PISCES	PISCES	PISCES	PISCES	PISCES
3 A.M.	ARIES	ARIES	ARIES	ARIES	ARIES
4 A.M.	ARIES	ARIES	ARIES	ARIES	ARIES
5 A.M.	TAURUS	TAURUS	TAURUS	TAURUS	TAURUS
6 A.M.	GEMINI	GEMINI	GEMINI	GEMINI	GEMINI
7 A.M.	GEMINI	GEMINI	GEMINI	GEMINI	GEMINI
8 A.M.	CANCER	CANCER	CANCER	CANCER	CANCER
9 A.M.	CANCER	CANCER	CANCER	CANCER	CANCER
10 A.M.	CANCER	CANCER	LEO	LEO	LEO
11 A.M.	LEO	LEO	LEO	LEO	LEO
NOON	LEO	LEO	LEO	LEO	LEO
1 P.M.	VIRGO	VIRGO	VIRGO	VIRGO	VIRGO
2 P.M.	VIRGO	VIRGO	VIRGO	VIRGO	VIRGO
3 P.M.	VIRGO	VIRGO	LIBRA	LIBRA	LIBRA
4 P.M.	LIBRA	LIBRA	LIBRA	LIBRA	LIBRA
5 P.M.	LIBRA	LIBRA	LIBRA	LIBRA	LIBRA
6 P.M.	SCORPIO	SCORPIO	SCORPIO	SCORPIO	SCORPIO
7 P.M.	SCORPIO	SCORPIO	SCORPIO	SCORPIO	SCORPIO
8 P.M.	SCORPIO	SCORPIO	SAGITTARIUS	SAGITTARIUS	SAGITTARIUS
9 P.M.	SAGITTARIUS	SAGITTARIUS	SAGITTARIUS	SAGITTARIUS	SAGITTARIUS
10 P.M.	SAGITTARIUS	SAGITTARIUS	SAGITTARIUS	SAGITTARIUS	SAGITTARIUS
11 P.M.	CAPRICORN	CAPRICORN	CAPRICORN	CAPRICORN	CAPRICORN

56

	MAY 11	MAY 12	MAY 13	MAY 14	MAY 15
MIDNIGHT	AQUARIUS	AQUARIUS	AQUARIUS	AQUARIUS	AQUARIUS
1 A.M.	AQUARIUS	AQUARIUS	AQUARIUS	AQUARIUS	AQUARIUS
2 A.M.	PISCES	PISCES	PISCES	PISCES	PISCES
3 A.M.	ARIES	ARIES	ARIES	ARIES	ARIES
4 A.M.	TAURUS	TAURUS	TAURUS	TAURUS	TAURUS
5 A.M.	TAURUS	TAURUS	TAURUS	TAURUS	TAURUS
6 A.M.	GEMINI	GEMINI	GEMINI	GEMINI	GEMINI
7 A.M.	GEMINI	GEMINI	GEMINI	GEMINI	GEMINI
8 A.M.	CANCER	CANCER	CANCER	CANCER	CANCER
9 A.M.	CANCER	CANCER	CANCER	CANCER	CANCER
10 A.M.	LEO	LEO	LEO	LEO	LEO
11 A.M.	LEO	LEO	LEO	LEO	LEO
NOON	LEO	LEO	LEO	LEO	LEO
1 P.M.	VIRGO	VIRGO	VIRGO	VIRGO	VIRGO
2 P.M.	VIRGO	VIRGO	VIRGO	VIRGO	VIRGO
3 P.M.	LIBRA	LIBRA	LIBRA	LIBRA	LIBRA
4 P.M.	LIBRA	LIBRA	LIBRA	LIBRA	LIBRA
5 P.M.	LIBRA	LIBRA	LIBRA	LIBRA	SCORPIO
6 P.M.	SCORPIO	SCORPIO	SCORPIO	SCORPIO	SCORPIO
7 P.M.	SCORPIO	SCORPIO	SCORPIO	SCORPIO	SCORPIO
8 P.M.	SAGITTARIUS	SAGITTARIUS	SAGITTARIUS	SAGITTARIUS	SAGITTARIUS
9 P.M.	SAGITTARIUS	SAGITTARIUS	SAGITTARIUS	SAGITTARIUS	SAGITTARIUS
10 P.M.	SAGITTARIUS	CAPRICORN	CAPRICORN	CAPRICORN	CAPRICORN
11 P.M.	CAPRICORN	CAPRICORN	CAPRICORN	CAPRICORN	CAPRICORN

	MAY 16	MAY 17	MAY 18	MAY 19	MAY 20
MIDNIGHT	AQUARIUS	AQUARIUS	AQUARIUS	AQUARIUS	AQUARIUS
1 A.M.	AQUARIUS	AQUARIUS	PISCES	PISCES	PISCES
2 A.M.	PISCES	PISCES	PISCES	PISCES	PISCES
3 A.M.	ARIES	ARIES	ARIES	ARIES	ARIES
4 A.M.	TAURUS	TAURUS	TAURUS	TAURUS	TAURUS
5 A.M.	TAURUS	TAURUS	TAURUS	GEMINI	GEMINI
6 A.M.	GEMINI	GEMINI	GEMINI	GEMINI	GEMINI
7 A.M.	GEMINI	GEMINI	CANCER	CANCER	CANCER
8 A.M.	CANCER	CANCER	CANCER	CANCER	CANCER
9 A.M.	CANCER	CANCER	CANCER	CANCER	CANCER
10 A.M.	LEO	LEO	LEO	LEO	LEO
11 A.M.	LEO	LEO	LEO	LEO	LEO
NOON	VIRGO	VIRGO	VIRGO	VIRGO	VIRGO
1 P.M.	VIRGO	VIRGO	VIRGO	VIRGO	VIRGO
2 P.M.	VIRGO	VIRGO	VIRGO	VIRGO	VIRGO
3 P.M.	LIBRA	LIBRA	LIBRA	LIBRA	LIBRA
4 P.M.	LIBRA	LIBRA	LIBRA	LIBRA	LIBRA
5 P.M.	SCORPIO	SCORPIO	SCORPIO	SCORPIO	SCORPIO
6 P.M.	SCORPIO	SCORPIO	SCORPIO	SCORPIO	SCORPIO
7 P.M.	SCORPIO	SCORPIO	SCORPIO	SCORPIO	SCORPIO
8 P.M.	SAGITTARIUS	SAGITTARIUS	SAGITTARIUS	SAGITTARIUS	SAGITTARIUS
9 P.M.	SAGITTARIUS	SAGITTARIUS	SAGITTARIUS	SAGITTARIUS	SAGITTARIUS
10 P.M.	CAPRICORN	CAPRICORN	CAPRICORN	CAPRICORN	CAPRICORN
11 P.M.	CAPRICORN	CAPRICORN	CAPRICORN	CAPRICORN	CAPRICORN

GEMINI—ASCENDANT TABLES

	MAY 21	MAY 22	MAY 23	MAY 24	MAY 25
MIDNIGHT	AQUARIUS	AQUARIUS	AQUARIUS	AQUARIUS	AQUARIUS
1 A.M.	PISCES	PISCES	PISCES	PISCES	PISCES
2 A.M.	PISCES	PISCES	ARIES	ARIES	ARIES
3 A.M.	ARIES	ARIES	ARIES	ARIES	ARIES
4 A.M.	TAURUS	TAURUS	TAURUS	TAURUS	TAURUS
5 A.M.	GEMINI	GEMINI	GEMINI	GEMINI	GEMINI
6 A.M.	GEMINI	GEMINI	GEMINI	GEMINI	GEMINI
7 A.M.	CANCER	CANCER	CANCER	CANCER	CANCER
8 A.M.	CANCER	CANCER	CANCER	CANCER	CANCER
9 A.M.	CANCER	CANCER	CANCER	LEO	LEO
10 A.M.	LEO	LEO	LEO	LEO	LEO
11 A.M.	LEO	LEO	LEO	LEO	LEO
NOON	VIRGO	VIRGO	VIRGO	VIRGO	VIRGO
1 P.M.	VIRGO	VIRGO	VIRGO	VIRGO	VIRGO
2 P.M.	VIRGO	VIRGO	LIBRA	LIBRA	LIBRA
3 P.M.	LIBRA	LIBRA	LIBRA	LIBRA	LIBRA
4 P.M.	LIBRA	LIBRA	LIBRA	LIBRA	LIBRA
5 P.M.	SCORPIO	SCORPIO	SCORPIO	SCORPIO	SCORPIO
6 P.M.	SCORPIO	SCORPIO	SCORPIO	SCORPIO	SCORPIO
7 P.M.	SCORPIO	SCORPIO	SAGITTARIUS	SAGITTARIUS	SAGITTARIUS
8 P.M.	SAGITTARIUS	SAGITTARIUS	SAGITTARIUS	SAGITTARIUS	SAGITTARIUS
9 P.M.	SAGITTARIUS	SAGITTARIUS	SAGITTARIUS	SAGITTARIUS	SAGITTARIUS
10 P.M.	CAPRICORN	CAPRICORN	CAPRICORN	CAPRICORN	CAPRICORN
11 P.M.	CAPRICORN	CAPRICORN	CAPRICORN	CAPRICORN	CAPRICORN

	MAY 26	MAY 27	MAY 28	MAY 29	MAY 30
MIDNIGHT	AQUARIUS	AQUARIUS	AQUARIUS	AQUARIUS	AQUARIUS
1 A.M.	PISCES	PISCES	PISCES	PISCES	PISCES
2 A.M.	ARIES	ARIES	ARIES	ARIES	ARIES
3 A.M.	TAURUS	TAURUS	TAURUS	TAURUS	TAURUS
4 A.M.	TAURUS	TAURUS	TAURUS	TAURUS	TAURUS
5 A.M.	GEMINI	GEMINI	GEMINI	GEMINI	GEMINI
6 A.M.	GEMINI	GEMINI	GEMINI	GEMINI	GEMINI
7 A.M.	CANCER	CANCER	CANCER	CANCER	CANCER
8 A.M.	CANCER	CANCER	CANCER	CANCER	CANCER
9 A.M.	LEO	LEO	LEO	LEO	LEO
10 A.M.	LEO	LEO	LEO	LEO	LEO
11 A.M.	LEO	LEO	LEO	LEO	LEO
NOON	VIRGO	VIRGO	VIRGO	VIRGO	VIRGO
1 P.M.	VIRGO	VIRGO	VIRGO	VIRGO	VIRGO
2 P.M.	LIBRA	LIBRA	LIBRA	LIBRA	LIBRA
3 P.M.	LIBRA	LIBRA	LIBRA	LIBRA	LIBRA
4 P.M.	LIBRA	LIBRA	LIBRA	LIBRA	SCORPIO
5 P.M.	SCORPIO	SCORPIO	SCORPIO	SCORPIO	SCORPIO
6 P.M.	SCORPIO	SCORPIO	SCORPIO	SCORPIO	SCORPIO
7 P.M.	SAGITTARIUS	SAGITTARIUS	SAGITTARIUS	SAGITTARIUS	SAGITTARIUS
8 P.M.	SAGITTARIUS	SAGITTARIUS	SAGITTARIUS	SAGITTARIUS	SAGITTARIUS
9 P.M.	SAGITARRIUS	SAGITTARIUS	CAPRICORN	CAPRICORN	CAPRICORN
10 P.M.	CAPRICORN	CAPRICORN	CAPRICORN	CAPRICORN	CAPRICORN
11 P.M.	AQUARIUS	AQUARIUS	AQUARIUS	AQUARIUS	AQUARIUS

	MAY 31	JUNE 1	JUNE 2	JUNE 3	JUNE 4
MIDNIGHT	AQUARIUS	AQUARIUS	AQUARIUS	PISCES	PISCES
1 A.M.	PISCES	PISCES	PISCES	PISCES	PISCES
2 A.M.	ARIES	ARIES	ARIES	ARIES	ARIES
3 A.M.	TAURUS	TAURUS	TAURUS	TAURUS	TAURUS
4 A.M.	TAURUS	TAURUS	TAURUS	GEMINI	GEMINI
5 A.M.	GEMINI	GEMINI	GEMINI	GEMINI	GEMINI
6 A.M.	GEMINI	GEMINI	CANCER	CANCER	CANCER
7 A.M.	CANCER	CANCER	CANCER	CANCER	CANCER
8 A.M.	CANCER	CANCER	CANCER	CANCER	CANCER
9 A.M.	LEO	LEO	LEO	LEO	LEO
10 A.M.	LEO	LEO	LEO	LEO	LEO
11 A.M.	VIRGO	VIRGO	VIRGO	VIRGO	VIRGO
NOON	VIRGO	VIRGO	VIRGO	VIRGO	VIRGO
1 P.M.	VIRGO	VIRGO	VIRGO	VIRGO	VIRGO
2 P.M.	LIBRA	LIBRA	LIBRA	LIBRA	LIBRA
3 P.M.	LIBRA	LIBRA	LIBRA	LIBRA	LIBRA
4 P.M.	SCORPIO	SCORPIO	SCORPIO	SCORPIO	SCORPIO
5 P.M.	SCORPIO	SCORPIO	SCORPIO	SCORPIO	SCORPIO
6 P.M.	SCORPIO	SCORPIO	SCORPIO	SCORPIO	SCORPIO
7 P.M.	SAGITTARIUS	SAGITTARIUS	SAGITTARIUS	SAGITTARIUS	SAGITTARIUS
8 P.M.	SAGITTARIUS	SAGITTARIUS	SAGITTARIUS	SAGITTARIUS	SAGITTARIUS
9 P.M.	CAPRICORN	CAPRICORN	CAPRICORN	CAPRICORN	CAPRICORN
10 P.M.	CAPRICORN	CAPRICORN	CAPRICORN	CAPRICORN	CAPRICORN
11 P.M.	AQUARIUS	AQUARIUS	AQUARIUS	AQUARIUS	AQUARIUS

	JUNE 5	JUNE 6	JUNE 7	JUNE 8	JUNE 9
MIDNIGHT	PISCES	PISCES	PISCES	PISCES	PISCES
1 A.M.	PISCES	PISCES	ARIES	ARIES	ARIES
2 A.M.	ARIES	ARIES	ARIES	ARIES	ARIES
3 A.M.	TAURUS	TAURUS	TAURUS	TAURUS	TAURUS
4 A.M.	GEMINI	GEMINI	GEMINI	GEMINI	GEMINI
5 A.M.	GEMINI	GEMINI	GEMINI	GEMINI	GEMINI
6 A.M.	CANCER	CANCER	CANCER	CANCER	CANCER
7 A.M.	CANCER	CANCER	CANCER	CANCER	CANCER
8 A.M.	CANCER	CANCER	CANCER	LEO	LEO
9 A.M.	LEO	LEO	LEO	LEO	LEO
10 A.M.	LEO	LEO	LEO	LEO	LEO
11 A.M.	VIRGO	VIRGO	VIRGO	VIRGO	VIRGO
NOON	VIRGO	VIRGO	VIRGO	VIRGO	VIRGO
1 P.M.	VIRGO	VIRGO	LIBRA	LIBRA	LIBRA
2 P.M.	LIBRA	LIBRA	LIBRA	LIBRA	LIBRA
3 P.M.	LIBRA	LIBRA	LIBRA	LIBRA	LIBRA
4 P.M.	SCORPIO	SCORPIO	SCORPIO	SCORPIO	SCORPIO
5 P.M.	SCORPIO	SCORPIO	SCORPIO	SCORPIO	SCORPIO
6 P.M.	SCORPIO	SCORPIO	SAGITTARIUS	SAGITTARIUS	SAGITTARIUS
7 P.M.	SAGITTARIUS	SAGITTARIUS	SAGITTARIUS	SAGITTARIUS	SAGITTARIUS
8 P.M.	SAGITTARIUS	SAGITTARIUS	SAGITTARIUS	SAGITTARIUS	SAGITTARIUS
9 P.M.	CAPRICORN	CAPRICORN	CAPRICORN	CAPRICORN	CAPRICORN
10 P.M.	CAPRICORN	CAPRICORN	CAPRICORN	CAPRICORN	CAPRICORN
11 P.M.	AQUARIUS	AQUARIUS	AQUARIUS	AQUARIUS	AQUARIUS

	JUNE 10	JUNE 11	JUNE 12	JUNE 13	JUNE 14
MIDNIGHT	PISCES	PISCES	PISCES	PISCES	PISCES
1 A.M.	ARIES	ARIES	ARIES	ARIES	ARIES
2 A.M.	ARIES	TAURUS	TAURUS	TAURUS	TAURUS
3 A.M.	TAURUS	TAURUS	TAURUS	TAURUS	TAURUS
4 A.M.	GEMINI	GEMINI	GEMINI	GEMINI	GEMINI
5 A.M.	GEMINI	GEMINI	GEMINI	GEMINI	GEMINI
6 A.M.	CANCER	CANCER	CANCER	CANCER	CANCER
7 A.M.	CANCER	CANCER	CANCER	CANCER	CANCER
8 A.M.	LEO	LEO	LEO	LEO	LEO
9 A.M.	LEO	LEO	LEO	LEO	LEO
10 A.M.	LEO	LEO	LEO	LEO	LEO
11 A.M.	VIRGO	VIRGO	VIRGO	VIRGO	VIRGO
NOON	VIRGO	VIRGO	VIRGO	VIRGO	VIRGO
1 P.M.	LIBRA	LIBRA	LIBRA	LIBRA	LIBRA
2 P.M.	LIBRA	LIBRA	LIBRA	LIBRA	LIBRA
3 P.M.	LIBRA	LIBRA	LIBRA	LIBRA	SCORPIO
4 P.M.	SCORPIO	SCORPIO	SCORPIO	SCORPIO	SCORPIO
5 P.M.	SCORPIO	SCORPIO	SCORPIO	SCORPIO	SCORPIO
6 P.M.	SAGITTARIUS	SAGITTARIUS	SAGITTARIUS	SAGITTARIUS	SAGITTARIUS
7 P.M.	SAGITTARIUS	SAGITTARIUS	SAGITTARIUS	SAGITTARIUS	SAGITTARIUS
8 P.M.	SAGITTARIUS	SAGITTARIUS	CAPRICORN	CAPRICORN	CAPRICORN
9 P.M.	CAPRICORN	CAPRICORN	CAPRICORN	CAPRICORN	CAPRICORN
10 P.M.	CAPRICORN	AQUARIUS	AQUARIUS	AQUARIUS	AQUARIUS
11 P.M.	AQUARIUS	AQUARIUS	AQUARIUS	AQUARIUS	AQUARIUS

	JUNE 15	JUNE 16	JUNE 17	JUNE 18	JUNE 19	JUNE 20
MIDNIGHT	PISCES	PISCES	PISCES	PISCES	PISCES	PISCES
1 A.M.	ARIES	ARIES	ARIES	ARIES	ARIES	ARIES
2 A.M.	TAURUS	TAURUS	TAURUS	TAURUS	TAURUS	TAURUS
3 A.M.	TAURUS	TAURUS	TAURUS	TAURUS	TAURUS	GEMINI
4 A.M.	GEMINI	GEMINI	GEMINI	GEMINI	GEMINI	GEMINI
5 A.M.	GEMINI	GEMINI	CANCER	CANCER	CANCER	CANCER
6 A.M.	CANCER	CANCER	CANCER	CANCER	CANCER	CANCER
7 A.M.	CANCER	CANCER	CANCER	CANCER	CANCER	CANCER
8 A.M.	LEO	LEO	LEO	LEO	LEO	LEO
9 A.M.	LEO	LEO	LEO	LEO	LEO	LEO
10 A.M.	VIRGO	VIRGO	VIRGO	VIRGO	VIRGO	VIRGO
11 A.M.	VIRGO	VIRGO	VIRGO	VIRGO	VIRGO	VIRGO
NOON	VIRGO	VIRGO	VIRGO	VIRGO	VIRGO	VIRGO
1 P.M.	LIBRA	LIBRA	LIBRA	LIBRA	LIBRA	LIBRA
2 P.M.	LIBRA	LIBRA	LIBRA	LIBRA	LIBRA	LIBRA
3 P.M.	SCORPIO	SCORPIO	SCORPIO	SCORPIO	SCORPIO	SCORPIO
4 P.M.	SCORPIO	SCORPIO	SCORPIO	SCORPIO	SCORPIO	SCORPIO
5 P.M.	SCORPIO	SCORPIO	SCORPIO	SCORPIO	SCORPIO	SCORPIO
6 P.M.	SAGITTARIUS	SAGITTARIUS	SAGITTARIUS	SAGITTARIUS	SAGITTARIUS	SAGITTARIUS
7 P.M.	SAGITTARIUS	SAGITTARIUS	SAGITTARIUS	SAGITTARIUS	SAGITTARIUS	SAGITTARIUS
8 P.M.	CAPRICORN	CAPRICORN	CAPRICORN	CAPRICORN	CAPRICORN	CAPRICORN
9 P.M.	CAPRICORN	CAPRICORN	CAPRICORN	CAPRICORN	CAPRICORN	CAPRICORN
10 P.M.	AQUARIUS	AQUARIUS	AQUARIUS	AQUARIUS	AQUARIUS	AQUARIUS
11 P.M.	AQUARIUS	AQUARIUS	AQUARIUS	PISCES	PISCES	PISCES

CANCER—ASCENDANT TABLES

	JUNE 21	JUNE 22	JUNE 23	JUNE 24	JUNE 25
MIDNIGHT	PISCES	ARIES	ARIES	ARIES	ARIES
1 A.M.	ARIES	ARIES	ARIES	ARIES	ARIES
2 A.M.	TAURUS	TAURUS	TAURUS	TAURUS	TAURUS
3 A.M.	GEMINI	GEMINI	GEMINI	GEMINI	GEMINI
4 A.M.	GEMINI	GEMINI	GEMINI	GEMINI	GEMINI
5 A.M.	CANCER	CANCER	CANCER	CANCER	CANCER
6 A.M.	CANCER	CANCER	CANCER	CANCER	CANCER
7 A.M.	CANCER	CANCER	LEO	LEO	LEO
8 A.M.	LEO	LEO	LEO	LEO	LEO
9 A.M.	LEO	LEO	LEO	LEO	LEO
10 A.M.	VIRGO	VIRGO	VIRGO	VIRGO	VIRGO
11 A.M.	VIRGO	VIRGO	VIRGO	VIRGO	VIRGO
NOON	VIRGO	VIRGO	VIRGO	LIBRA	LIBRA
1 P.M.	LIBRA	LIBRA	LIBRA	LIBRA	LIBRA
2 P.M.	LIBRA	LIBRA	LIBRA	LIBRA	LIBRA
3 P.M.	SCORPIO	SCORPIO	SCORPIO	SCORPIO	SCORPIO
4 P.M.	SCORPIO	SCORPIO	SCORPIO	SCORPIO	SCORPIO
5 P.M.	SCORPIO	SCORPIO	SAGITTARIUS	SAGITTARIUS	SAGITTARIUS
6 P.M.	SAGITTARIUS	SAGITTARIUS	SAGITTARIUS	SAGITTARIUS	SAGITTARIUS
7 P.M.	SAGITTARIUS	SAGITTARIUS	SAGITTARIUS	SAGITTARIUS	SAGITTARIUS
8 P.M.	CAPRICORN	CAPRICORN	CAPRICORN	CAPRICORN	CAPRICORN
9 P.M.	CAPRICORN	CAPRICORN	CAPRICORN	CAPRICORN	CAPRICORN
10 P.M.	AQUARIUS	AQUARIUS	AQUARIUS	AQUARIUS	AQUARIUS
11 P.M.	PISCES	PISCES	PISCES	PISCES	PISCES

	JUNE 26	JUNE 27	JUNE 28	JUNE 29	JUNE 30
MIDNIGHT	ARIES	ARIES	ARIES	ARIES	ARIES
1 A.M.	TAURUS	TAURUS	TAURUS	TAURUS	TAURUS
2 A.M.	TAURUS	TAURUS	TAURUS	TAURUS	TAURUS
3 A.M.	GEMINI	GEMINI	GEMINI	GEMINI	GEMINI
4 A.M.	GEMINI	GEMINI	GEMINI	GEMINI	GEMINI
5 A.M.	CANCER	CANCER	CANCER	CANCER	CANCER
6 A.M.	CANCER	CANCER	CANCER	CANCER	CANCER
7 A.M.	LEO	LEO	LEO	LEO	LEO
8 A.M.	LEO	LEO	LEO	LEO	LEO
9 A.M.	LEO	LEO	LEO	LEO	VIRGO
10 A.M.	VIRGO	VIRGO	VIRGO	VIRGO	VIRGO
11 A.M.	VIRGO	VIRGO	VIRGO	VIRGO	VIRGO
NOON	LIBRA	LIBRA	LIBRA	LIBRA	LIBRA
1 P.M.	LIBRA	LIBRA	LIBRA	LIBRA	LIBRA
2 P.M.	LIBRA	LIBRA	LIBRA	SCORPIO	SCORPIO
3 P.M.	SCORPIO	SCORPIO	SCORPIO	SCORPIO	SCORPIO
4 P.M.	SCORPIO	SCORPIO	SCORPIO	SCORPIO	SCORPIO
5 P.M.	SAGITTARIUS	SAGITTARIUS	SAGITTARIUS	SAGITTARIUS	SAGITTARIUS
6 P.M.	SAGITTARIUS	SAGITTARIUS	SAGITTARIUS	SAGITTARIUS	SAGITTARIUS
7 P.M.	SAGITTARIUS	CAPRICORN	CAPRICORN	CAPRICORN	CAPRICORN
8 P.M.	CAPRICORN	CAPRICORN	CAPRICORN	CAPRICORN	CAPRICORN
9 P.M.	AQUARIUS	AQUARIUS	AQUARIUS	AQUARIUS	AQUARIUS
10 P.M.	PISCES	PISCES	PISCES	PISCES	AQUARIUS
11 P.M.	ARIES	PISCES	PISCES	ARIES	PISCES

	JULY 1	JULY 2	JULY 3	JULY 4	JULY 5
MIDNIGHT	ARIES	ARIES	ARIES	ARIES	ARIES
1 A.M.	TAURUS	TAURUS	TAURUS	TAURUS	TAURUS
2 A.M.	TAURUS	TAURUS	TAURUS	GEMINI	GEMINI
3 A.M.	GEMINI	GEMINI	GEMINI	GEMINI	GEMINI
4 A.M.	GEMINI	GEMINI	CANCER	CANCER	CANCER
5 A.M.	CANCER	CANCER	CANCER	CANCER	CANCER
6 A.M.	CANCER	CANCER	CANCER	CANCER	CANCER
7 A.M.	LEO	LEO	LEO	LEO	LEO
8 A.M.	LEO	LEO	LEO	LEO	LEO
9 A.M.	VIRGO	VIRGO	VIRGO	VIRGO	VIRGO
10 A.M.	VIRGO	VIRGO	VIRGO	VIRGO	VIRGO
11 A.M.	VIRGO	VIRGO	VIRGO	VIRGO	VIRGO
NOON	LIBRA	LIBRA	LIBRA	LIBRA	LIBRA
1 P.M.	LIBRA	LIBRA	LIBRA	LIBRA	LIBRA
2 P.M.	SCORPIO	SCORPIO	SCORPIO	SCORPIO	SCORPIO
3 P.M.	SCORPIO	SCORPIO	SCORPIO	SCORPIO	SCORPIO
4 P.M.	SCORPIO	SCORPIO	SCORPIO	SCORPIO	SCORPIO
5 P.M.	SAGITTARIUS	SAGITTARIUS	SAGITTARIUS	SAGITTARIUS	SAGITTARIUS
6 P.M.	SAGITTARIUS	SAGITTARIUS	SAGITTARIUS	SAGITTARIUS	SAGITTARIUS
7 P.M.	CAPRICORN	CAPRICORN	CAPRICORN	CAPRICORN	CAPRICORN
8 P.M.	CAPRICORN	CAPRICORN	CAPRICORN	CAPRICORN	CAPRICORN
9 P.M.	AQUARIUS	AQUARIUS	AQUARIUS	AQUARIUS	AQUARIUS
10 P.M.	AQUARIUS	AQUARIUS	PISCES	PISCES	PISCES
11 P.M.	PISCES	PISCES	PISCES	PISCES	PISCES

	JULY 6	JULY 7	JULY 8	JULY 9	JULY 10
MIDNIGHT	ARIES	ARIES	ARIES	ARIES	ARIES
1 A.M.	TAURUS	TAURUS	TAURUS	TAURUS	TAURUS
2 A.M.	GEMINI	GEMINI	GEMINI	GEMINI	GEMINI
3 A.M.	GEMINI	GEMINI	GEMINI	GEMINI	GEMINI
4 A.M.	CANCER	CANCER	CANCER	CANCER	CANCER
5 A.M.	CANCER	CANCER	CANCER	CANCER	CANCER
6 A.M.	CANCER	CANCER	LEO	LEO	LEO
7 A.M.	LEO	LEO	LEO	LEO	LEO
8 A.M.	LEO	LEO	LEO	LEO	LEO
9 A.M.	VIRGO	VIRGO	VIRGO	VIRGO	VIRGO
10 A.M.	VIRGO	VIRGO	VIRGO	VIRGO	VIRGO
11 A.M.	VIRGO	VIRGO	LIBRA	LIBRA	LIBRA
NOON	LIBRA	LIBRA	LIBRA	LIBRA	LIBRA
1 P.M.	LIBRA	LIBRA	LIBRA	LIBRA	LIBRA
2 P.M.	SCORPIO	SCORPIO	SCORPIO	SCORPIO	SCORPIO
3 P.M.	SCORPIO	SCORPIO	SCORPIO	SCORPIO	SCORPIO
4 P.M.	SCORPIO	SAGITTARIUS	SAGITTARIUS	SAGITTARIUS	SAGITTARIUS
5 P.M.	SAGITTARIUS	SAGITTARIUS	SAGITTARIUS	SAGITTARIUS	SAGITTARIUS
6 P.M.	SAGITTARIUS	SAGITTARIUS	SAGITTARIUS	SAGITTARIUS	SAGITTARIUS
7 P.M.	CAPRICORN	CAPRICORN	CAPRICORN	CAPRICORN	CAPRICORN
8 P.M.	CAPRICORN	CAPRICORN	CAPRICORN	CAPRICORN	CAPRICORN
9 P.M.	AQUARIUS	AQUARIUS	AQUARIUS	AQUARIUS	AQUARIUS
10 P.M.	PISCES	PISCES	PISCES	PISCES	PISCES
11 P.M.	PISCES	ARIES	ARIES	ARIES	ARIES

	JULY 11	JULY 12	JULY 13	JULY 14	JULY 15
MIDNIGHT	TAURUS	TAURUS	TAURUS	TAURUS	TAURUS
1 A.M.	TAURUS	TAURUS	TAURUS	TAURUS	TAURUS
2 A.M.	GEMINI	GEMINI	GEMINI	GEMINI	GEMINI
3 A.M.	GEMINI	GEMINI	GEMINI	GEMINI	GEMINI
4 A.M.	CANCER	CANCER	CANCER	CANCER	CANCER
5 A.M.	CANCER	CANCER	CANCER	CANCER	CANCER
6 A.M.	LEO	LEO	LEO	LEO	LEO
7 A.M.	LEO	LEO	LEO	LEO	LEO
8 A.M.	LEO	LEO	LEO	LEO	VIRGO
9 A.M.	VIRGO	VIRGO	VIRGO	VIRGO	VIRGO
10 A.M.	VIRGO	VIRGO	VIRGO	VIRGO	VIRGO
11 A.M.	LIBRA	LIBRA	LIBRA	LIBRA	LIBRA
NOON	LIBRA	LIBRA	LIBRA	LIBRA	LIBRA
1 P.M.	LIBRA	LIBRA	LIBRA	LIBRA	SCORPIO
2 P.M.	SCORPIO	SCORPIO	SCORPIO	SCORPIO	SCORPIO
3 P.M.	SCORPIO	SCORPIO	SCORPIO	SCORPIO	SCORPIO
4 P.M.	SAGITTARIUS	SAGITTARIUS	SAGITTARIUS	SAGITTARIUS	SAGITTARIUS
5 P.M.	SAGITTARIUS	SAGITTARIUS	SAGITTARIUS	SAGITTARIUS	SAGITTARIUS
6 P.M.	SAGITTARIUS	CAPRICORN	CAPRICORN	CAPRICORN	CAPRICORN
7 P.M.	CAPRICORN	CAPRICORN	CAPRICORN	CAPRICORN	CAPRICORN
8 P.M.	AQUARIUS	AQUARIUS	AQUARIUS	AQUARIUS	AQUARIUS
9 P.M.	AQUARIUS	AQUARIUS	AQUARIUS	AQUARIUS	AQUARIUS
10 P.M.	PISCES	PISCES	PISCES	PISCES	PISCES
11 P.M.	ARIES	ARIES	ARIES	ARIES	ARIES

	JULY 16	JULY 17	JULY 18	JULY 19	JULY 20
MIDNIGHT	TAURUS	TAURUS	TAURUS	TAURUS	TAURUS
1 A.M.	TAURUS	TAURUS	TAURUS	GEMINI	GEMINI
2 A.M.	GEMINI	GEMINI	GEMINI	GEMINI	GEMINI
3 A.M.	GEMINI	GEMINI	CANCER	CANCER	CANCER
4 A.M.	CANCER	CANCER	CANCER	CANCER	CANCER
5 A.M.	CANCER	CANCER	CANCER	CANCER	CANCER
6 A.M.	LEO	LEO	LEO	LEO	LEO
7 A.M.	LEO	LEO	LEO	LEO	LEO
8 A.M.	VIRGO	VIRGO	VIRGO	VIRGO	VIRGO
9 A.M.	VIRGO	VIRGO	VIRGO	VIRGO	VIRGO
10 A.M.	VIRGO	VIRGO	VIRGO	VIRGO	VIRGO
11 A.M.	LIBRA	LIBRA	LIBRA	LIBRA	LIBRA
NOON	LIBRA	LIBRA	LIBRA	LIBRA	LIBRA
1 P.M.	SCORPIO	SCORPIO	SCORPIO	SCORPIO	SCORPIO
2 P.M.	SCORPIO	SCORPIO	SCORPIO	SCORPIO	SCORPIO
3 P.M.	SCORPIO	SCORPIO	SCORPIO	SCORPIO	SCORPIO
4 P.M.	SAGITTARIUS	SAGITTARIUS	SAGITTARIUS	SAGITTARIUS	SAGITTARIUS
5 P.M.	SAGITTARIUS	SAGITTARIUS	SAGITTARIUS	SAGITTARIUS	SAGITTARIUS
6 P.M.	CAPRICORN	CAPRICORN	CAPRICORN	CAPRICORN	CAPRICORN
7 P.M.	CAPRICORN	CAPRICORN	CAPRICORN	CAPRICORN	CAPRICORN
8 P.M.	AQUARIUS	AQUARIUS	AQUARIUS	AQUARIUS	AQUARIUS
9 P.M.	AQUARIUS	AQUARIUS	PISCES	PISCES	PISCES
10 P.M.	PISCES	PISCES	PISCES	PISCES	PISCES
11 P.M.	ARIES	ARIES	ARIES	ARIES	ARIES

LEO—ASCENDANT TABLES

	JULY 21	JULY 22	JULY 23	JULY 24	JULY 25
MIDNIGHT	TAURUS	TAURUS	TAURUS	TAURUS	TAURUS
1 A.M.	GEMINI	GEMINI	GEMINI	GEMINI	GEMINI
2 A.M.	GEMINI	GEMINI	GEMINI	GEMINI	GEMINI
3 A.M.	CANCER	CANCER	CANCER	CANCER	CANCER
4 A.M.	CANCER	CANCER	CANCER	CANCER	CANCER
5 A.M.	CANCER	CANCER	LEO	LEO	LEO
6 A.M.	LEO	LEO	LEO	LEO	LEO
7 A.M.	LEO	LEO	LEO	LEO	LEO
8 A.M.	VIRGO	VIRGO	VIRGO	VIRGO	VIRGO
9 A.M.	VIRGO	VIRGO	VIRGO	VIRGO	VIRGO
10 A.M.	VIRGO	VIRGO	LIBRA	LIBRA	LIBRA
11 A.M.	LIBRA	LIBRA	LIBRA	LIBRA	LIBRA
NOON	LIBRA	LIBRA	LIBRA	LIBRA	LIBRA
1 P.M.	SCORPIO	SCORPIO	SCORPIO	SCORPIO	SCORPIO
2 P.M.	SCORPIO	SCORPIO	SCORPIO	SCORPIO	SCORPIO
3 P.M.	SCORPIO	SCORPIO	SAGITTARIUS	SAGITTARIUS	SAGITTARIUS
4 P.M.	SAGITTARIUS	SAGITTARIUS	SAGITTARIUS	SAGITTARIUS	SAGITTARIUS
5 P.M.	SAGITTARIUS	SAGITTARIUS	SAGITTARIUS	SAGITTARIUS	SAGITTARIUS
6 P.M.	CAPRICORN	CAPRICORN	CAPRICORN	CAPRICORN	CAPRICORN
7 P.M.	CAPRICORN	CAPRICORN	CAPRICORN	CAPRICORN	CAPRICORN
8 P.M.	AQUARIUS	AQUARIUS	AQUARIUS	AQUARIUS	AQUARIUS
9 P.M.	PISCES	PISCES	PISCES	PISCES	PISCES
10 P.M.	PISCES	ARIES	ARIES	ARIES	ARIES
11 P.M.	ARIES	ARIES	ARIES	ARIES	ARIES

	JULY 26	JULY 27	JULY 28	JULY 29	JULY 30
MIDNIGHT	TAURUS	TAURUS	TAURUS	TAURUS	TAURUS
1 A.M.	GEMINI	GEMINI	GEMINI	GEMINI	GEMINI
2 A.M.	GEMINI	GEMINI	GEMINI	GEMINI	GEMINI
3 A.M.	CANCER	CANCER	CANCER	CANCER	CANCER
4 A.M.	CANCER	CANCER	CANCER	CANCER	CANCER
5 A.M.	LEO	LEO	LEO	LEO	LEO
6 A.M.	LEO	LEO	LEO	LEO	LEO
7 A.M.	LEO	LEO	LEO	LEO	LEO
8 A.M.	VIRGO	VIRGO	VIRGO	VIRGO	VIRGO
9 A.M.	VIRGO	VIRGO	VIRGO	VIRGO	VIRGO
10 A.M.	LIBRA	LIBRA	LIBRA	LIBRA	LIBRA
11 A.M.	LIBRA	LIBRA	LIBRA	LIBRA	LIBRA
NOON	LIBRA	LIBRA	LIBRA	LIBRA	SCORPIO
1 P.M.	SCORPIO	SCORPIO	SCORPIO	SCORPIO	SCORPIO
2 P.M.	SCORPIO	SCORPIO	SCORPIO	SCORPIO	SCORPIO
3 P.M.	SAGITTARIUS	SAGITTARIUS	SAGITTARIUS	SAGITTARIUS	SAGITTARIUS
4 P.M.	SAGITTARIUS	SAGITTARIUS	SAGITTARIUS	SAGITTARIUS	SAGITTARIUS
5 P.M.	SAGITTARIUS	CAPRICORN	CAPRICORN	CAPRICORN	CAPRICORN
6 P.M.	CAPRICORN	CAPRICORN	CAPRICORN	CAPRICORN	CAPRICORN
7 P.M.	AQUARIUS	AQUARIUS	AQUARIUS	AQUARIUS	AQUARIUS
8 P.M.	AQUARIUS	AQUARIUS	AQUARIUS	AQUARIUS	AQUARIUS
9 P.M.	PISCES	PISCES	PISCES	PISCES	PISCES
10 P.M.	ARIES	ARIES	ARIES	ARIES	ARIES
11 P.M.	TAURUS	TAURUS	TAURUS	TAURUS	TAURUS

	JULY 31	AUGUST 1	AUGUST 2	AUGUST 3	AUGUST 4
MIDNIGHT	TAURUS	TAURUS	GEMINI	GEMINI	GEMINI
1 A.M.	GEMINI	GEMINI	GEMINI	GEMINI	GEMINI
2 A.M.	GEMINI	GEMINI	CANCER	CANCER	CANCER
3 A.M.	CANCER	CANCER	CANCER	CANCER	CANCER
4 A.M.	CANCER	CANCER	CANCER	CANCER	CANCER
5 A.M.	LEO	LEO	LEO	LEO	LEO
6 A.M.	LEO	LEO	LEO	LEO	LEO
7 A.M.	LEO	VIRGO	VIRGO	VIRGO	VIRGO
8 A.M.	VIRGO	VIRGO	VIRGO	VIRGO	VIRGO
9 A.M.	VIRGO	VIRGO	VIRGO	VIRGO	VIRGO
10 A.M.	LIBRA	LIBRA	LIBRA	LIBRA	LIBRA
11 A.M.	LIBRA	LIBRA	LIBRA	LIBRA	LIBRA
NOON	SCORPIO	SCORPIO	SCORPIO	SCORPIO	SCORPIO
1 P.M.	SCORPIO	SCORPIO	SCORPIO	SCORPIO	SCORPIO
2 P.M.	SCORPIO	SCORPIO	SCORPIO	SCORPIO	SCORPIO
3 P.M.	SAGITTARIUS	SAGITTARIUS	SAGITTARIUS	SAGITTARIUS	SAGITTARIUS
4 P.M.	SAGITTARIUS	SAGITTARIUS	SAGITTARIUS	SAGITTARIUS	SAGITTARIUS
5 P.M.	CAPRICORN	CAPRICORN	CAPRICORN	CAPRICORN	CAPRICORN
6 P.M.	CAPRICORN	CAPRICORN	CAPRICORN	CAPRICORN	CAPRICORN
7 P.M.	AQUARIUS	AQUARIUS	AQUARIUS	AQUARIUS	AQUARIUS
8 P.M.	AQUARIUS	AQUARIUS	AQUARIUS	PISCES	PISCES
9 P.M.	PISCES	PISCES	PISCES	PISCES	PISCES
10 P.M.	ARIES	ARIES	ARIES	ARIES	ARIES
11 P.M.	TAURUS	TAURUS	TAURUS	TAURUS	TAURUS

	AUGUST 5	AUGUST 6	AUGUST 7	AUGUST 8	AUGUST 9
MIDNIGHT	GEMINI	GEMINI	GEMINI	GEMINI	GEMINI
1 A.M.	GEMINI	GEMINI	GEMINI	GEMINI	GEMINI
2 A.M.	CANCER	CANCER	CANCER	CANCER	CANCER
3 A.M.	CANCER	CANCER	CANCER	CANCER	CANCER
4 A.M.	CANCER	CANCER	LEO	LEO	LEO
5 A.M.	LEO	LEO	LEO	LEO	LEO
6 A.M.	LEO	LEO	LEO	LEO	LEO
7 A.M.	VIRGO	VIRGO	VIRGO	VIRGO	VIRGO
8 A.M.	VIRGO	VIRGO	VIRGO	VIRGO	VIRGO
9 A.M.	VIRGO	VIRGO	LIBRA	LIBRA	LIBRA
10 A.M.	LIBRA	LIBRA	LIBRA	LIBRA	LIBRA
11 A.M.	LIBRA	LIBRA	LIBRA	LIBRA	LIBRA
NOON	SCORPIO	SCORPIO	SCORPIO	SCORPIO	SCORPIO
1 P.M.	SCORPIO	SCORPIO	SCORPIO	SCORPIO	SCORPIO
2 P.M.	SCORPIO	SCORPIO	SAGITTARIUS	SAGITTARIUS	SAGITTARIUS
3 P.M.	SAGITTARIUS	SAGITTARIUS	SAGITTARIUS	SAGITTARIUS	SAGITTARIUS
4 P.M.	SAGITTARIUS	SAGITTARIUS	SAGITTARIUS	SAGITTARIUS	SAGITTARIUS
5 P.M.	CAPRICORN	CAPRICORN	CAPRICORN	CAPRICORN	CAPRICORN
6 P.M.	CAPRICORN	CAPRICORN	CAPRICORN	CAPRICORN	CAPRICORN
7 P.M.	AQUARIUS	AQUARIUS	AQUARIUS	AQUARIUS	AQUARIUS
8 P.M.	PISCES	PISCES	PISCES	PISCES	PISCES
9 P.M.	PISCES	PISCES	PISCES	ARIES	ARIES
10 P.M.	ARIES	ARIES	ARIES	ARIES	ARIES
11 P.M.	TAURUS	TAURUS	TAURUS	TAURUS	TAURUS

	AUGUST 10	AUGUST 11	AUGUST 12	AUGUST 13	AUGUST 14	AUGUST 15
MIDNIGHT	GEMINI	GEMINI	GEMINI	GEMINI	GEMINI	GEMINI
1 A.M.	GEMINI	GEMINI	GEMINI	GEMINI	GEMINI	GEMINI
2 A.M.	CANCER	CANCER	CANCER	CANCER	CANCER	CANCER
3 A.M.	CANCER	CANCER	CANCER	CANCER	CANCER	CANCER
4 A.M.	LEO	LEO	LEO	LEO	LEO	LEO
5 A.M.	LEO	LEO	LEO	LEO	LEO	LEO
6 A.M.	LEO	LEO	LEO	LEO	LEO	LEO
7 A.M.	VIRGO	VIRGO	VIRGO	VIRGO	VIRGO	VIRGO
8 A.M.	VIRGO	VIRGO	VIRGO	VIRGO	VIRGO	VIRGO
9 A.M.	LIBRA	LIBRA	LIBRA	LIBRA	LIBRA	LIBRA
10 A.M.	LIBRA	LIBRA	LIBRA	LIBRA	LIBRA	LIBRA
11 A.M.	LIBRA	LIBRA	LIBRA	LIBRA	SCORPIO	SCORPIO
NOON	SCORPIO	SCORPIO	SCORPIO	SCORPIO	SCORPIO	SCORPIO
1 P.M.	SCORPIO	SCORPIO	SCORPIO	SCORPIO	SCORPIO	SAGITTARIUS
2 P.M.	SAGITTARIUS	SAGITTARIUS	SAGITTARIUS	SAGITTARIUS	SAGITTARIUS	SAGITTARIUS
3 P.M.	SAGITTARIUS	SAGITTARIUS	SAGITTARIUS	SAGITTARIUS	SAGITTARIUS	SAGITTARIUS
4 P.M.	SAGITTARIUS	SAGITTARIUS	CAPRICORN	CAPRICORN	CAPRICORN	CAPRICORN
5 P.M.	CAPRICORN	CAPRICORN	CAPRICORN	CAPRICORN	CAPRICORN	CAPRICORN
6 P.M.	CAPRICORN	AQUARIUS	AQUARIUS	AQUARIUS	AQUARIUS	AQUARIUS
7 P.M.	AQUARIUS	AQUARIUS	AQUARIUS	AQUARIUS	AQUARIUS	AQUARIUS
8 P.M.	PISCES	PISCES	PISCES	PISCES	PISCES	PISCES
9 P.M.	ARIES	ARIES	ARIES	ARIES	ARIES	ARIES
10 P.M.	ARIES	TAURUS	TAURUS	TAURUS	TAURUS	TAURUS
11 P.M.	TAURUS	TAURUS	TAURUS	TAURUS	TAURUS	TAURUS

| --- | --- | --- | --- | --- | --- | --- |
MIDNIGHT	GEMINI	GEMINI	GEMINI	GEMINI	GEMINI	GEMINI
1 A.M.	GEMINI	GEMINI	CANCER	CANCER	CANCER	CANCER
2 A.M.	CANCER	CANCER	CANCER	CANCER	CANCER	CANCER
3 A.M.	CANCER	CANCER	CANCER	CANCER	CANCER	CANCER
4 A.M.	LEO	LEO	LEO	LEO	LEO	LEO
5 A.M.	LEO	LEO	LEO	LEO	LEO	LEO
6 A.M.	VIRGO	VIRGO	VIRGO	VIRGO	VIRGO	VIRGO
7 A.M.	VIRGO	VIRGO	VIRGO	VIRGO	VIRGO	VIRGO
8 A.M.	VIRGO	VIRGO	VIRGO	VIRGO	VIRGO	LIBRA
9 A.M.	LIBRA	LIBRA	LIBRA	LIBRA	LIBRA	LIBRA
10 A.M.	LIBRA	LIBRA	LIBRA	LIBRA	LIBRA	LIBRA
11 A.M.	SCORPIO	SCORPIO	SCORPIO	SCORPIO	SCORPIO	SCORPIO
NOON	SCORPIO	SCORPIO	SCORPIO	SCORPIO	SCORPIO	SCORPIO
1 P.M.	SCORPIO	SCORPIO	SCORPIO	SCORPIO	SCORPIO	SCORPIO
2 P.M.	SAGITTARIUS	SAGITTARIUS	SAGITTARIUS	SAGITTARIUS	SAGITTARIUS	SAGITTARIUS
3 P.M.	SAGITTARIUS	SAGITTARIUS	SAGITTARIUS	SAGITTARIUS	SAGITTARIUS	SAGITTARIUS
4 P.M.	CAPRICORN	CAPRICORN	CAPRICORN	CAPRICORN	CAPRICORN	CAPRICORN
5 P.M.	CAPRICORN	CAPRICORN	CAPRICORN	CAPRICORN	CAPRICORN	CAPRICORN
6 P.M.	AQUARIUS	AQUARIUS	AQUARIUS	AQUARIUS	AQUARIUS	AQUARIUS
7 P.M.	AQUARIUS	AQUARIUS	PISCES	PISCES	PISCES	PISCES
8 P.M.	PISCES	PISCES	PISCES	PISCES	PISCES	ARIES
9 P.M.	ARIES	ARIES	ARIES	ARIES	ARIES	ARIES
10 P.M.	TAURUS	TAURUS	TAURUS	TAURUS	TAURUS	TAURUS
11 P.M.	TAURUS	TAURUS	GEMINI	GEMINI	GEMINI	GEMINI

VIRGO—ASCENDANT TABLES

	AUGUST 22	AUGUST 23	AUGUST 24	AUGUST 25	AUGUST 26
MIDNIGHT	GEMINI	GEMINI	GEMINI	GEMINI	GEMINI
1 A.M.	CANCER	CANCER	CANCER	CANCER	CANCER
2 A.M.	CANCER	CANCER	CANCER	CANCER	CANCER
3 A.M.	LEO	LEO	LEO	LEO	LEO
4 A.M.	LEO	LEO	LEO	LEO	LEO
5 A.M.	LEO	LEO	LEO	LEO	LEO
6 A.M.	VIRGO	VIRGO	VIRGO	VIRGO	VIRGO
7 A.M.	VIRGO	VIRGO	VIRGO	VIRGO	VIRGO
8 A.M.	LIBRA	LIBRA	LIBRA	LIBRA	LIBRA
9 A.M.	LIBRA	LIBRA	LIBRA	LIBRA	LIBRA
10 A.M.	LIBRA	LIBRA	LIBRA	LIBRA	LIBRA
11 A.M.	SCORPIO	SCORPIO	SCORPIO	SCORPIO	SCORPIO
NOON	SCORPIO	SCORPIO	SCORPIO	SCORPIO	SCORPIO
1 P.M.	SAGITTARIUS	SAGITTARIUS	SAGITTARIUS	SAGITTARIUS	SAGITTARIUS
2 P.M.	SAGITTARIUS	SAGITTARIUS	SAGITTARIUS	SAGITTARIUS	SAGITTARIUS
3 P.M.	SAGITTARIUS	SAGITTARIUS	SAGITTARIUS	SAGITTARIUS	SAGITTARIUS
4 P.M.	CAPRICORN	CAPRICORN	CAPRICORN	CAPRICORN	CAPRICORN
5 P.M.	CAPRICORN	CAPRICORN	CAPRICORN	CAPRICORN	AQUARIUS
6 P.M.	AQUARIUS	AQUARIUS	AQUARIUS	AQUARIUS	AQUARIUS
7 P.M.	PISCES	PISCES	PISCES	PISCES	PISCES
8 P.M.	ARIES	ARIES	ARIES	ARIES	ARIES
9 P.M.	ARIES	ARIES	ARIES	ARIES	TAURUS
10 P.M.	TAURUS	TAURUS	TAURUS	TAURUS	TAURUS
11 P.M.	GEMINI	GEMINI	GEMINI	GEMINI	GEMINI

	AUGUST 27	AUGUST 28	AUGUST 29	AUGUST 30	AUGUST 31
MIDNIGHT	GEMINI	GEMINI	GEMINI	GEMINI	GEMINI
1 A.M.	CANCER	CANCER	CANCER	CANCER	CANCER
2 A.M.	CANCER	CANCER	CANCER	CANCER	CANCER
3 A.M.	LEO	LEO	LEO	LEO	LEO
4 A.M.	LEO	LEO	LEO	LEO	LEO
5 A.M.	LEO	LEO	LEO	LEO	VIRGO
6 A.M.	VIRGO	VIRGO	VIRGO	VIRGO	VIRGO
7 A.M.	VIRGO	VIRGO	VIRGO	VIRGO	VIRGO
8 A.M.	LIBRA	LIBRA	LIBRA	LIBRA	LIBRA
9 A.M.	LIBRA	LIBRA	LIBRA	LIBRA	LIBRA
10 A.M.	LIBRA	LIBRA	SCORPIO	SCORPIO	SCORPIO
11 A.M.	SCORPIO	SCORPIO	SCORPIO	SCORPIO	SCORPIO
NOON	SCORPIO	SCORPIO	SCORPIO	SCORPIO	SCORPIO
1 P.M.	SAGITTARIUS	SAGITTARIUS	SAGITTARIUS	SAGITTARIUS	SAGITTARIUS
2 P.M.	SAGITTARIUS	SAGITTARIUS	SAGITTARIUS	SAGITTARIUS	SAGITTARIUS
3 P.M.	CAPRICORN	CAPRICORN	CAPRICORN	CAPRICORN	CAPRICORN
4 P.M.	CAPRICORN	CAPRICORN	CAPRICORN	CAPRICORN	CAPRICORN
5 P.M.	AQUARIUS	AQUARIUS	AQUARIUS	AQUARIUS	AQUARIUS
6 P.M.	AQUARIUS	AQUARIUS	AQUARIUS	AQUARIUS	AQUARIUS
7 P.M.	PISCES	PISCES	PISCES	PISCES	PISCES
8 P.M.	ARIES	ARIES	ARIES	ARIES	ARIES
9 P.M.	TAURUS	TAURUS	TAURUS	TAURUS	TAURUS
10 P.M.	TAURUS	TAURUS	TAURUS	TAURUS	TAURUS
11 P.M.	GEMINI	GEMINI	GEMINI	GEMINI	GEMINI

	SEPTEMBER 1	SEPTEMBER 2	SEPTEMBER 3	SEPTEMBER 4	SEPTEMBER 5
MIDNIGHT	CANCER	CANCER	CANCER	CANCER	CANCER
1 A.M.	CANCER	CANCER	CANCER	CANCER	CANCER
2 A.M.	CANCER	CANCER	CANCER	CANCER	CANCER
3 A.M.	LEO	LEO	LEO	LEO	LEO
4 A.M.	LEO	LEO	LEO	LEO	LEO
5 A.M.	VIRGO	VIRGO	VIRGO	VIRGO	VIRGO
6 A.M.	VIRGO	VIRGO	VIRGO	VIRGO	VIRGO
7 A.M.	VIRGO	VIRGO	VIRGO	VIRGO	VIRGO
8 A.M.	LIBRA	LIBRA	LIBRA	LIBRA	LIBRA
9 A.M.	LIBRA	LIBRA	LIBRA	LIBRA	LIBRA
10 A.M.	SCORPIO	SCORPIO	SCORPIO	SCORPIO	SCORPIO
11 A.M.	SCORPIO	SCORPIO	SCORPIO	SCORPIO	SCORPIO
NOON	SCORPIO	SCORPIO	SCORPIO	SCORPIO	SCORPIO
1 P.M.	SAGITTARIUS	SAGITTARIUS	SAGITTARIUS	SAGITTARIUS	SAGITTARIUS
2 P.M.	SAGITTARIUS	SAGITTARIUS	SAGITTARIUS	SAGITTARIUS	SAGITTARIUS
3 P.M.	CAPRICORN	CAPRICORN	CAPRICORN	CAPRICORN	CAPRICORN
4 P.M.	CAPRICORN	CAPRICORN	CAPRICORN	CAPRICORN	CAPRICORN
5 P.M.	AQUARIUS	AQUARIUS	AQUARIUS	AQUARIUS	AQUARIUS
6 P.M.	AQUARIUS	AQUARIUS	PISCES	PISCES	PISCES
7 P.M.	PISCES	PISCES	PISCES	PISCES	PISCES
8 P.M.	ARIES	ARIES	ARIES	ARIES	ARIES
9 P.M.	TAURUS	TAURUS	TAURUS	TAURUS	TAURUS
10 P.M.	TAURUS	TAURUS	GEMINI	GEMINI	GEMINI
11 P.M.	GEMINI	GEMINI	GEMINI	GEMINI	GEMINI

	SEPTEMBER 6	SEPTEMBER 7	SEPTEMBER 8	SEPTEMBER 9	SEPTEMBER 10
MIDNIGHT	CANCER	CANCER	CANCER	CANCER	CANCER
1 A.M.	CANCER	CANCER	CANCER	CANCER	CANCER
2 A.M.	CANCER	LEO	LEO	LEO	LEO
3 A.M.	LEO	LEO	LEO	LEO	LEO
4 A.M.	LEO	LEO	LEO	LEO	LEO
5 A.M.	VIRGO	VIRGO	VIRGO	VIRGO	VIRGO
6 A.M.	VIRGO	VIRGO	VIRGO	VIRGO	VIRGO
7 A.M.	VIRGO	LIBRA	LIBRA	LIBRA	LIBRA
8 A.M.	LIBRA	LIBRA	LIBRA	LIBRA	LIBRA
9 A.M.	LIBRA	LIBRA	LIBRA	LIBRA	LIBRA
10 A.M.	SCORPIO	SCORPIO	SCORPIO	SCORPIO	SCORPIO
11 A.M.	SCORPIO	SCORPIO	SCORPIO	SCORPIO	SCORPIO
NOON	SAGITTARIUS	SAGITTARIUS	SAGITTARIUS	SAGITTARIUS	SAGITTARIUS
1 P.M.	SAGITTARIUS	SAGITTARIUS	SAGITTARIUS	SAGITTARIUS	SAGITTARIUS
2 P.M.	SAGITTARIUS	SAGITTARIUS	SAGITTARIUS	SAGITTARIUS	SAGITTARIUS
3 P.M.	CAPRICORN	CAPRICORN	CAPRICORN	CAPRICORN	CAPRICORN
4 P.M.	CAPRICORN	CAPRICORN	CAPRICORN	CAPRICORN	AQUARIUS
5 P.M.	AQUARIUS	AQUARIUS	AQUARIUS	AQUARIUS	AQUARIUS
6 P.M.	PISCES	PISCES	PISCES	PISCES	PISCES
7 P.M.	ARIES	ARIES	ARIES	ARIES	ARIES
8 P.M.	ARIES	ARIES	ARIES	ARIES	TAURUS
9 P.M.	TAURUS	TAURUS	TAURUS	TAURUS	TAURUS
10 P.M.	GEMINI	GEMINI	GEMINI	GEMINI	GEMINI
11 P.M.	GEMINI	GEMINI	GEMINI	GEMINI	GEMINI

	SEPTEMBER 11	SEPTEMBER 12	SEPTEMBER 13	SEPTEMBER 14	SEPTEMBER 15
MIDNIGHT	CANCER	CANCER	CANCER	CANCER	CANCER
1 A.M.	CANCER	CANCER	CANCER	CANCER	CANCER
2 A.M.	LEO	LEO	LEO	LEO	LEO
3 A.M.	LEO	LEO	LEO	LEO	LEO
4 A.M.	LEO	LEO	LEO	VIRGO	VIRGO
5 A.M.	VIRGO	VIRGO	VIRGO	VIRGO	VIRGO
6 A.M.	VIRGO	VIRGO	VIRGO	VIRGO	VIRGO
7 A.M.	LIBRA	LIBRA	LIBRA	LIBRA	LIBRA
8 A.M.	LIBRA	LIBRA	LIBRA	LIBRA	LIBRA
9 A.M.	LIBRA	LIBRA	SCORPIO	SCORPIO	SCORPIO
10 A.M.	SCORPIO	SCORPIO	SCORPIO	SCORPIO	SCORPIO
11 A.M.	SCORPIO	SCORPIO	SCORPIO	SCORPIO	SCORPIO
NOON	SAGITTARIUS	SAGITTARIUS	SAGITTARIUS	SAGITTARIUS	SAGITTARIUS
1 P.M.	SAGITTARIUS	SAGITTARIUS	SAGITTARIUS	SAGITTARIUS	SAGITTARIUS
2 P.M.	CAPRICORN	CAPRICORN	CAPRICORN	CAPRICORN	CAPRICORN
3 P.M.	CAPRICORN	CAPRICORN	CAPRICORN	CAPRICORN	CAPRICORN
4 P.M.	AQUARIUS	AQUARIUS	AQUARIUS	AQUARIUS	AQUARIUS
5 P.M.	AQUARIUS	AQUARIUS	AQUARIUS	AQUARIUS	AQUARIUS
6 P.M.	PISCES	PISCES	PISCES	PISCES	PISCES
7 P.M.	ARIES	ARIES	ARIES	ARIES	ARIES
8 P.M.	TAURUS	TAURUS	TAURUS	TAURUS	TAURUS
9 P.M.	TAURUS	TAURUS	TAURUS	TAURUS	TAURUS
10 P.M.	GEMINI	GEMINI	GEMINI	GEMINI	GEMINI
11 P.M.	GEMINI	GEMINI	GEMINI	GEMINI	GEMINI

	SEPTEMBER 16	SEPTEMBER 17	SEPTEMBER 18	SEPTEMBER 19	SEPTEMBER 20	SEPTEMBER 21
MIDNIGHT	CANCER	CANCER	CANCER	CANCER	CANCER	CANCER
1 A.M.	CANCER	CANCER	CANCER	CANCER	CANCER	LEO
2 A.M.	LEO	LEO	LEO	LEO	LEO	LEO
3 A.M.	LEO	LEO	LEO	LEO	LEO	LEO
4 A.M.	VIRGO	VIRGO	VIRGO	VIRGO	VIRGO	VIRGO
5 A.M.	VIRGO	VIRGO	VIRGO	VIRGO	VIRGO	VIRGO
6 A.M.	VIRGO	VIRGO	VIRGO	VIRGO	VIRGO	LIBRA
7 A.M.	LIBRA	LIBRA	LIBRA	LIBRA	LIBRA	LIBRA
8 A.M.	LIBRA	LIBRA	LIBRA	LIBRA	LIBRA	LIBRA
9 A.M.	SCORPIO	SCORPIO	SCORPIO	SCORPIO	SCORPIO	SCORPIO
10 A.M.	SCORPIO	SCORPIO	SCORPIO	SCORPIO	SCORPIO	SCORPIO
11 A.M.	SCORPIO	SCORPIO	SCORPIO	SCORPIO	SCORPIO	SAGITTARIUS
NOON	SAGITTARIUS	SAGITTARIUS	SAGITTARIUS	SAGITTARIUS	SAGITTARIUS	SAGITTARIUS
1 P.M.	SAGITTARIUS	SAGITTARIUS	SAGITTARIUS	SAGITTARIUS	SAGITTARIUS	SAGITTARIUS
2 P.M.	CAPRICORN	CAPRICORN	CAPRICORN	CAPRICORN	CAPRICORN	CAPRICORN
3 P.M.	CAPRICORN	CAPRICORN	CAPRICORN	CAPRICORN	CAPRICORN	CAPRICORN
4 P.M.	AQUARIUS	AQUARIUS	AQUARIUS	AQUARIUS	AQUARIUS	AQUARIUS
5 P.M.	PISCES	PISCES	PISCES	PISCES	PISCES	PISCES
6 P.M.	PISCES	PISCES	PISCES	PISCES	PISCES	ARIES
7 P.M.	ARIES	ARIES	ARIES	ARIES	ARIES	ARIES
8 P.M.	TAURUS	TAURUS	TAURUS	TAURUS	TAURUS	TAURUS
9 P.M.	TAURUS	GEMINI	GEMINI	GEMINI	GEMINI	GEMINI
10 P.M.	GEMINI	GEMINI	GEMINI	GEMINI	GEMINI	GEMINI
11 P.M.	CANCER	CANCER	CANCER	CANCER	CANCER	CANCER

LIBRA—ASCENDANT TABLES

	SEPTEMBER 22	SEPTEMBER 23	SEPTEMBER 24	SEPTEMBER 25	SEPTEMBER 26
MIDNIGHT	CANCER	CANCER	CANCER	CANCER	CANCER
1 A.M.	LEO	LEO	LEO	LEO	LEO
2 A.M.	LEO	LEO	LEO	LEO	LEO
3 A.M.	LEO	LEO	LEO	LEO	LEO
4 A.M.	VIRGO	VIRGO	VIRGO	VIRGO	VIRGO
5 A.M.	VIRGO	VIRGO	VIRGO	VIRGO	VIRGO
6 A.M.	LIBRA	LIBRA	LIBRA	LIBRA	LIBRA
7 A.M.	LIBRA	LIBRA	LIBRA	LIBRA	LIBRA
8 A.M.	LIBRA	LIBRA	LIBRA	LIBRA	LIBRA
9 A.M.	SCORPIO	SCORPIO	SCORPIO	SCORPIO	SCORPIO
10 A.M.	SCORPIO	SCORPIO	SCORPIO	SCORPIO	SCORPIO
11 A.M.	SAGITTARIUS	SAGITTARIUS	SAGITTARIUS	SAGITTARIUS	SAGITTARIUS
NOON	SAGITTARIUS	SAGITTARIUS	SAGITTARIUS	SAGITTARIUS	SAGITTARIUS
1 P.M.	SAGITTARIUS	SAGITTARIUS	SAGITTARIUS	SAGITTARIUS	SAGITTARIUS
2 P.M.	CAPRICORN	CAPRICORN	CAPRICORN	CAPRICORN	CAPRICORN
3 P.M.	CAPRICORN	CAPRICORN	CAPRICORN	CAPRICORN	AQUARIUS
4 P.M.	AQUARIUS	AQUARIUS	AQUARIUS	AQUARIUS	AQUARIUS
5 P.M.	PISCES	PISCES	PISCES	PISCES	PISCES
6 P.M.	ARIES	ARIES	ARIES	ARIES	ARIES
7 P.M.	ARIES	TAURUS	TAURUS	TAURUS	TAURUS
8 P.M.	TAURUS	TAURUS	TAURUS	TAURUS	TAURUS
9 P.M.	GEMINI	GEMINI	GEMINI	GEMINI	GEMINI
10 P.M.	GEMINI	GEMINI	GEMINI	GEMINI	GEMINI
11 P.M.	CANCER	CANCER	CANCER	CANCER	CANCER

	SEPTEMBER 27	SEPTEMBER 28	SEPTEMBER 29	SEPTEMBER 30	OCTOBER 1
MIDNIGHT	CANCER	CANCER	CANCER	CANCER	CANCER
1 A.M.	LEO	LEO	LEO	LEO	LEO
2 A.M.	LEO	LEO	LEO	LEO	LEO
3 A.M.	LEO	LEO	LEO	LEO	VIRGO
4 A.M.	VIRGO	VIRGO	VIRGO	VIRGO	VIRGO
5 A.M.	VIRGO	VIRGO	VIRGO	VIRGO	VIRGO
6 A.M.	LIBRA	LIBRA	LIBRA	LIBRA	LIBRA
7 A.M.	LIBRA	LIBRA	LIBRA	LIBRA	LIBRA
8 A.M.	LIBRA	SCORPIO	SCORPIO	SCORPIO	SCORPIO
9 A.M.	SCORPIO	SCORPIO	SCORPIO	SCORPIO	SCORPIO
10 A.M.	SCORPIO	SCORPIO	SCORPIO	SCORPIO	SCORPIO
11 A.M.	SAGITTARIUS	SAGITTARIUS	SAGITTARIUS	SAGITTARIUS	SAGITTARIUS
NOON	SAGITTARIUS	SAGITTARIUS	SAGITTARIUS	SAGITTARIUS	SAGITTARIUS
1 P.M.	SAGITTARIUS	CAPRICORN	CAPRICORN	CAPRICORN	CAPRICORN
2 P.M.	CAPRICORN	CAPRICORN	CAPRICORN	CAPRICORN	CAPRICORN
3 P.M.	AQUARIUS	AQUARIUS	AQUARIUS	AQUARIUS	AQUARIUS
4 P.M.	AQUARIUS	AQUARIUS	AQUARIUS	AQUARIUS	AQUARIUS
5 P.M.	PISCES	PISCES	PISCES	PISCES	PISCES
6 P.M.	ARIES	ARIES	ARIES	ARIES	ARIES
7 P.M.	TAURUS	TAURUS	TAURUS	TAURUS	TAURUS
8 P.M.	TAURUS	TAURUS	TAURUS	TAURUS	GEMINI
9 P.M.	GEMINI	GEMINI	GEMINI	GEMINI	GEMINI
10 P.M.	GEMINI	GEMINI	GEMINI	GEMINI	CANCER
11 P.M.	CANCER	CANCER	CANCER	CANCER	CANCER

	OCTOBER 2	OCTOBER 3	OCTOBER 4	OCTOBER 5	OCTOBER 6
MIDNIGHT	CANCER	CANCER	CANCER	CANCER	CANCER
1 A.M.	LEO	LEO	LEO	LEO	LEO
2 A.M.	LEO	LEO	LEO	LEO	LEO
3 A.M.	VIRGO	VIRGO	VIRGO	VIRGO	VIRGO
4 A.M.	VIRGO	VIRGO	VIRGO	VIRGO	VIRGO
5 A.M.	VIRGO	VIRGO	VIRGO	VIRGO	VIRGO
6 A.M.	LIBRA	LIBRA	LIBRA	LIBRA	LIBRA
7 A.M.	LIBRA	LIBRA	LIBRA	LIBRA	LIBRA
8 A.M.	SCORPIO	SCORPIO	SCORPIO	SCORPIO	SCORPIO
9 A.M.	SCORPIO	SCORPIO	SCORPIO	SCORPIO	SCORPIO
10 A.M.	SCORPIO	SCORPIO	SCORPIO	SAGITTARIUS	SAGITTARIUS
11 A.M.	SAGITTARIUS	SAGITTARIUS	SAGITTARIUS	SAGITTARIUS	SAGITTARIUS
NOON	SAGITTARIUS	SAGITTARIUS	SAGITTARIUS	SAGITTARIUS	SAGITTARIUS
1 P.M.	CAPRICORN	CAPRICORN	CAPRICORN	CAPRICORN	CAPRICORN
2 P.M.	CAPRICORN	CAPRICORN	CAPRICORN	CAPRICORN	CAPRICORN
3 P.M.	AQUARIUS	AQUARIUS	AQUARIUS	AQUARIUS	AQUARIUS
4 P.M.	AQUARIUS	PISCES	PISCES	PISCES	PISCES
5 P.M.	PISCES	PISCES	PISCES	PISCES	ARIES
6 P.M.	ARIES	ARIES	ARIES	ARIES	ARIES
7 P.M.	TAURUS	TAURUS	TAURUS	TAURUS	TAURUS
8 P.M.	GEMINI	GEMINI	GEMINI	GEMINI	GEMINI
9 P.M.	GEMINI	GEMINI	GEMINI	GEMINI	GEMINI
10 P.M.	CANCER	CANCER	CANCER	CANCER	CANCER
11 P.M.	CANCER	CANCER	CANCER	CANCER	CANCER

	OCTOBER 7	OCTOBER 8	OCTOBER 9	OCTOBER 10	OCTOBER 11
MIDNIGHT	LEO	LEO	LEO	LEO	LEO
1 A.M.	LEO	LEO	LEO	LEO	LEO
2 A.M.	LEO	LEO	LEO	LEO	LEO
3 A.M.	VIRGO	VIRGO	VIRGO	VIRGO	VIRGO
4 A.M.	VIRGO	VIRGO	VIRGO	VIRGO	VIRGO
5 A.M.	LIBRA	LIBRA	LIBRA	LIBRA	LIBRA
6 A.M.	LIBRA	LIBRA	LIBRA	LIBRA	LIBRA
7 A.M.	LIBRA	LIBRA	LIBRA	LIBRA	LIBRA
8 A.M.	SCORPIO	SCORPIO	SCORPIO	SCORPIO	SCORPIO
9 A.M.	SCORPIO	SCORPIO	SCORPIO	SCORPIO	SCORPIO
10 A.M.	SAGITTARIUS	SAGITTARIUS	SAGITTARIUS	SAGITTARIUS	SAGITTARIUS
11 A.M.	SAGITTARIUS	SAGITTARIUS	SAGITTARIUS	SAGITTARIUS	SAGITTARIUS
NOON	SAGITTARIUS	SAGITTARIUS	SAGITTARIUS	SAGITTARIUS	CAPRICORN
1 P.M.	CAPRICORN	CAPRICORN	CAPRICORN	CAPRICORN	CAPRICORN
2 P.M.	CAPRICORN	CAPRICORN	CAPRICORN	CAPRICORN	AQUARIUS
3 P.M.	AQUARIUS	AQUARIUS	AQUARIUS	AQUARIUS	AQUARIUS
4 P.M.	PISCES	PISCES	PISCES	PISCES	PISCES
5 P.M.	ARIES	ARIES	ARIES	ARIES	ARIES
6 P.M.	ARIES	ARIES	ARIES	TAURUS	TAURUS
7 P.M.	TAURUS	TAURUS	TAURUS	TAURUS	TAURUS
8 P.M.	GEMINI	GEMINI	GEMINI	GEMINI	GEMINI
9 P.M.	GEMINI	GEMINI	GEMINI	GEMINI	GEMINI
10 P.M.	CANCER	CANCER	CANCER	CANCER	CANCER
11 P.M.	CANCER	CANCER	CANCER	CANCER	CANCER

	OCTOBER 12	OCTOBER 13	OCTOBER 14	OCTOBER 15	OCTOBER 16	OCTOBER 17
MIDNIGHT	LEO	LEO	LEO	LEO	LEO	LEO
1 A.M.	LEO	LEO	LEO	LEO	LEO	LEO
2 A.M.	LEO	LEO	LEO	VIRGO	VIRGO	VIRGO
3 A.M.	VIRGO	VIRGO	VIRGO	VIRGO	VIRGO	VIRGO
4 A.M.	VIRGO	VIRGO	VIRGO	VIRGO	VIRGO	VIRGO
5 A.M.	LIBRA	LIBRA	LIBRA	LIBRA	LIBRA	LIBRA
6 A.M.	LIBRA	LIBRA	LIBRA	LIBRA	LIBRA	LIBRA
7 A.M.	LIBRA	LIBRA	LIBRA	SCORPIO	SCORPIO	SCORPIO
8 A.M.	SCORPIO	SCORPIO	SCORPIO	SCORPIO	SCORPIO	SCORPIO
9 A.M.	SCORPIO	SCORPIO	SCORPIO	SCORPIO	SCORPIO	SCORPIO
10 A.M.	SAGITTARIUS	SAGITTARIUS	SAGITTARIUS	SAGITTARIUS	SAGITTARIUS	SAGITTARIUS
11 A.M.	SAGITTARIUS	SAGITTARIUS	SAGITTARIUS	SAGITTARIUS	SAGITTARIUS	SAGITTARIUS
NOON	CAPRICORN	CAPRICORN	CAPRICORN	CAPRICORN	CAPRICORN	CAPRICORN
1 P.M.	CAPRICORN	CAPRICORN	CAPRICORN	CAPRICORN	CAPRICORN	CAPRICORN
2 P.M.	AQUARIUS	AQUARIUS	AQUARIUS	AQUARIUS	AQUARIUS	AQUARIUS
3 P.M.	AQUARIUS	AQUARIUS	AQUARIUS	AQUARIUS	AQUARIUS	PISCES
4 P.M.	PISCES	PISCES	PISCES	PISCES	PISCES	PISCES
5 P.M.	ARIES	ARIES	ARIES	ARIES	ARIES	ARIES
6 P.M.	TAURUS	TAURUS	TAURUS	TAURUS	TAURUS	TAURUS
7 P.M.	TAURUS	TAURUS	TAURUS	TAURUS	TAURUS	TAURUS
8 P.M.	GEMINI	GEMINI	GEMINI	GEMINI	GEMINI	GEMINI
9 P.M.	GEMINI	GEMINI	GEMINI	GEMINI	CANCER	CANCER
10 P.M.	CANCER	CANCER	CANCER	CANCER	CANCER	CANCER
11 P.M.	CANCER	CANCER	CANCER	CANCER	CANCER	CANCER

	OCTOBER 18	OCTOBER 19	OCTOBER 20	OCTOBER 21	OCTOBER 22
MIDNIGHT	LEO	LEO	LEO	LEO	LEO
1 A.M.	LEO	LEO	LEO	LEO	LEO
2 A.M.	VIGRO	VIRGO	VIRGO	VIRGO	VIRGO
3 A.M.	VIRGO	VIRGO	VIRGO	VIRGO	VIRGO
4 A.M.	VIRGO	VIRGO	VIRGO	VIRGO	LIBRA
5 A.M.	LIBRA	LIBRA	LIBRA	LIBRA	LIBRA
6 A.M.	LIBRA	LIBRA	LIBRA	LIBRA	LIBRA
7 A.M.	SCORPIO	SCORPIO	SCORPIO	SCORPIO	SCORPIO
8 A.M.	SCORPIO	SCORPIO	SCORPIO	SCORPIO	SCORPIO
9 A.M.	SCORPIO	SCORPIO	SCORPIO	SCORPIO	SAGITTARIUS
10 A.M.	SAGITTARIUS	SAGITTARIUS	SAGITTARIUS	SAGITTARIUS	SAGITTARIUS
11 A.M.	SAGITTARIUS	SAGITTARIUS	SAGITTARIUS	SAGITTARIUS	SAGITTARIUS
NOON	CAPRICORN	CAPRICORN	CAPRICORN	CAPRICORN	CAPRICORN
1 P.M.	CAPRICORN	CAPRICORN	CAPRICORN	CAPRICORN	CAPRICORN
2 P.M.	AQUARIUS	AQUARIUS	AQUARIUS	AQUARIUS	AQUARIUS
3 P.M.	PISCES	PISCES	PISCES	PISCES	PISCES
4 P.M.	PISCES	PISCES	PISCES	ARIES	ARIES
5 P.M.	ARIES	ARIES	ARIES	ARIES	ARIES
6 P.M.	TAURUS	TAURUS	TAURUS	TAURUS	TAURUS
7 P.M.	GEMINI	GEMINI	GEMINI	GEMINI	GEMINI
8 P.M.	GEMINI	GEMINI	GEMINI	GEMINI	GEMINI
9 P.M.	CANCER	CANCER	CANCER	CANCER	CANCER
10 P.M.	CANCER	CANCER	CANCER	CANCER	CANCER
11 P.M.	CANCER	CANCER	CANCER	CANCER	LEO

SCORPIO—ASCENDANT TABLES

	OCTOBER 23	OCTOBER 24	OCTOBER 25	OCTOBER 26	OCTOBER 27
MIDNIGHT	LEO	LEO	LEO	LEO	LEO
1 A.M.	LEO	LEO	LEO	LEO	LEO
2 A.M.	VIRGO	VIRGO	VIRGO	VIRGO	VIRGO
3 A.M.	VIRGO	VIRGO	VIRGO	VIRGO	VIRGO
4 A.M.	LIBRA	LIBRA	LIBRA	LIBRA	LIBRA
5 A.M.	LIBRA	LIBRA	LIBRA	LIBRA	LIBRA
6 A.M.	LIBRA	LIBRA	LIBRA	LIBRA	LIBRA
7 A.M.	SCORPIO	SCORPIO	SCORPIO	SCORPIO	SCORPIO
8 A.M.	SCORPIO	SCORPIO	SCORPIO	SCORPIO	SCORPIO
9 A.M.	SAGITTARIUS	SAGITTARIUS	SAGITTARIUS	SAGITTARIUS	SAGITTARIUS
10 A.M.	SAGITTARIUS	SAGITTARIUS	SAGITTARIUS	SAGITTARIUS	SAGITTARIUS
11 A.M.	SAGITTARIUS	SAGITTARIUS	SAGITTARIUS	SAGITTARIUS	CAPRICORN
NOON	CAPRICORN	CAPRICORN	CAPRICORN	CAPRICORN	CAPRICORN
1 P.M.	CAPRICORN	CAPRICORN	CAPRICORN	AQUARIUS	AQUARIUS
2 P.M.	AQUARIUS	AQUARIUS	AQUARIUS	AQUARIUS	AQUARIUS
3 P.M.	PISCES	PISCES	PISCES	PISCES	PISCES
4 P.M.	ARIES	ARIES	ARIES	ARIES	ARIES
5 P.M.	ARIES	ARIES	ARIES	TAURUS	TAURUS
6 P.M.	TAURUS	TAURUS	TAURUS	TAURUS	TAURUS
7 P.M.	GEMINI	GEMINI	GEMINI	GEMINI	GEMINI
8 P.M.	GEMINI	GEMINI	GEMINI	GEMINI	GEMINI
9 P.M.	CANCER	CANCER	CANCER	CANCER	CANCER
10 P.M.	CANCER	CANCER	CANCER	CANCER	CANCER
11 P.M.	LEO	LEO	LEO	LEO	LEO

	OCTOBER 28	OCTOBER 29	OCTOBER 30	OCTOBER 31	NOVEMBER 1
MIDNIGHT	LEO	LEO	LEO	LEO	LEO
1 A.M.	LEO	LEO	VIRGO	VIRGO	VIRGO
2 A.M.	VIRGO	VIRGO	VIRGO	VIRGO	VIRGO
3 A.M.	VIRGO	VIRGO	VIRGO	VIRGO	VIRGO
4 A.M.	LIBRA	LIBRA	LIBRA	LIBRA	LIBRA
5 A.M.	LIBRA	LIBRA	LIBRA	LIBRA	LIBRA
6 A.M.	LIBRA	LIBRA	SCORPIO	SCORPIO	SCORPIO
7 A.M.	SCORPIO	SCORPIO	SCORPIO	SCORPIO	SCORPIO
8 A.M.	SCORPIO	SCORPIO	SCORPIO	SCORPIO	SCORPIO
9 A.M.	SAGITTARIUS	SAGITTARIUS	SAGITTARIUS	SAGITTARIUS	SAGITTARIUS
10 A.M.	SAGITTARIUS	SAGITTARIUS	SAGITTARIUS	SAGITTARIUS	SAGITTARIUS
11 A.M.	CAPRICORN	CAPRICORN	CAPRICORN	CAPRICORN	CAPRICORN
NOON	CAPRICORN	CAPRICORN	CAPRICORN	CAPRICORN	CAPRICORN
1 P.M.	AQUARIUS	AQUARIUS	AQUARIUS	AQUARIUS	AQUARIUS
2 P.M.	AQUARIUS	AQUARIUS	AQUARIUS	AQUARIUS	AQUARIUS
3 P.M.	PISCES	PISCES	PISCES	PISCES	PISCES
4 P.M.	ARIES	ARIES	ARIES	ARIES	ARIES
5 P.M.	TAURUS	TAURUS	TAURUS	TAURUS	TAURUS
6 P.M.	TAURUS	TAURUS	TAURUS	TAURUS	TAURUS
7 P.M.	GEMINI	GEMINI	GEMINI	GEMINI	GEMINI
8 P.M.	GEMINI	GEMINI	GEMINI	GEMINI	CANCER
9 P.M.	CANCER	CANCER	CANCER	CANCER	CANCER
10 P.M.	CANCER	CANCER	CANCER	CANCER	CANCER
11 P.M.	LEO	LEO	LEO	LEO	LEO

	NOVEMBER 2	NOVEMBER 3	NOVEMBER 4	NOVEMBER 5	NOVEMBER 6
MIDNIGHT	LEO	LEO	LEO	LEO	LEO
1 A.M.	VIRGO	VIRGO	VIRGO	VIRGO	VIRGO
2 A.M.	VIRGO	VIRGO	VIRGO	VIRGO	VIRGO
3 A.M.	VIRGO	VIRGO	VIRGO	VIRGO	LIBRA
4 A.M.	LIBRA	LIBRA	LIBRA	LIBRA	LIBRA
5 A.M.	LIBRA	LIBRA	LIBRA	LIBRA	LIBRA
6 A.M.	SCORPIO	SCORPIO	SCORPIO	SCORPIO	SCORPIO
7 A.M.	SCORPIO	SCORPIO	SCORPIO	SCORPIO	SCORPIO
8 A.M.	SCORPIO	SCORPIO	SCORPIO	SCORPIO	SAGITTARIUS
9 A.M.	SAGITTARIUS	SAGITTARIUS	SAGITTARIUS	SAGITTARIUS	SAGITTARIUS
10 A.M.	SAGITTARIUS	SAGITTARIUS	SAGITTARIUS	SAGITTARIUS	SAGITTARIUS
11 A.M.	CAPRICORN	CAPRICORN	CAPRICORN	CAPRICORN	CAPRICORN
NOON	CAPRICORN	CAPRICORN	CAPRICORN	CAPRICORN	CAPRICORN
1 P.M.	AQUARIUS	AQUARIUS	AQUARIUS	AQUARIUS	AQUARIUS
2 P.M.	PISCES	PISCES	PISCES	PISCES	PISCES
3 P.M.	PISCES	PISCES	PISCES	ARIES	ARIES
4 P.M.	ARIES	ARIES	ARIES	ARIES	ARIES
5 P.M.	TAURUS	TAURUS	TAURUS	TAURUS	TAURUS
6 P.M.	GEMINI	GEMINI	GEMINI	GEMINI	GEMINI
7 P.M.	GEMINI	GEMINI	GEMINI	GEMINI	GEMINI
8 P.M.	CANCER	CANCER	CANCER	CANCER	CANCER
9 P.M.	CANCER	CANCER	CANCER	CANCER	CANCER
10 P.M.	CANCER	CANCER	CANCER	CANCER	CANCER
11 P.M.	LEO	LEO	LEO	LEO	LEO

	NOVEMBER 7	NOVEMBER 8	NOVEMBER 9	NOVEMBER 10	NOVEMBER 11
MIDNIGHT	LEO	LEO	LEO	LEO	LEO
1 A.M.	VIRGO	VIRGO	VIRGO	VIRGO	VIRGO
2 A.M.	VIRGO	VIRGO	VIRGO	VIRGO	VIRGO
3 A.M.	LIBRA	LIBRA	LIBRA	LIBRA	LIBRA
4 A.M.	LIBRA	LIBRA	LIBRA	LIBRA	LIBRA
5 A.M.	LIBRA	LIBRA	LIBRA	LIBRA	LIBRA
6 A.M.	SCORPIO	SCORPIO	SCORPIO	SCORPIO	SCORPIO
7 A.M.	SCORPIO	SCORPIO	SCORPIO	SCORPIO	SCORPIO
8 A.M.	SAGITTARIUS	SAGITTARIUS	SAGITTARIUS	SAGITTARIUS	SAGITTARIUS
9 A.M.	SAGITTARIUS	SAGITTARIUS	SAGITTARIUS	SAGITTARIUS	SAGITTARIUS
10 A.M.	SAGITTARIUS	SAGITTARIUS	SAGITTARIUS	SAGITTARIUS	CAPRICORN
11 A.M.	CAPRICORN	CAPRICORN	CAPRICORN	CAPRICORN	CAPRICORN
NOON	CAPRICORN	CAPRICORN	CAPRICORN	AQUARIUS	AQUARIUS
1 P.M.	AQUARIUS	AQUARIUS	AQUARIUS	AQUARIUS	AQUARIUS
2 P.M.	PISCES	PISCES	PISCES	PISCES	PISCES
3 P.M.	ARIES	ARIES	ARIES	ARIES	ARIES
4 P.M.	ARIES	ARIES	ARIES	ARIES	TAURUS
5 P.M.	TAURUS	TAURUS	TAURUS	TAURUS	TAURUS
6 P.M.	GEMINI	GEMINI	GEMINI	GEMINI	GEMINI
7 P.M.	GEMINI	GEMINI	GEMINI	GEMINI	GEMINI
8 P.M.	CANCER	CANCER	CANCER	CANCER	CANCER
9 P.M.	CANCER	CANCER	CANCER	CANCER	CANCER
10 P.M.	LEO	LEO	LEO	LEO	LEO
11 P.M.	LEO	LEO	LEO	LEO	LEO

	NOVEMBER 12	NOVEMBER 13	NOVEMBER 14	NOVEMBER 15	NOVEMBER 16
MIDNIGHT	LEO	LEO	LEO	VIRGO	VIRGO
1 A.M.	VIRGO	VIRGO	VIRGO	VIRGO	VIRGO
2 A.M.	VIRGO	VIRGO	VIRGO	VIRGO	VIRGO
3 A.M.	LIBRA	LIBRA	LIBRA	LIBRA	LIBRA
4 A.M.	LIBRA	LIBRA	LIBRA	LIBRA	LIBRA
5 A.M.	LIBRA	LIBRA	SCORPIO	SCORPIO	SCORPIO
6 A.M.	SCORPIO	SCORPIO	SCORPIO	SCORPIO	SCORPIO
7 A.M.	SCORPIO	SCORPIO	SCORPIO	SCORPIO	SCORPIO
8 A.M.	SAGITTARIUS	SAGITTARIUS	SAGITTARIUS	SAGITTARIUS	SAGITTARIUS
9 A.M.	SAGITTARIUS	SAGITTARIUS	SAGITTARIUS	SAGITTARIUS	SAGITTARIUS
10 A.M.	CAPRICORN	CAPRICORN	CAPRICORN	CAPRICORN	CAPRICORN
11 A.M.	CAPRICORN	CAPRICORN	CAPRICORN	CAPRICORN	CAPRICORN
NOON	AQUARIUS	AQUARIUS	AQUARIUS	AQUARIUS	AQUARIUS
1 P.M.	AQUARIUS	AQUARIUS	AQUARIUS	AQUARIUS	AQUARIUS
2 P.M.	PISCES	PISCES	PISCES	PISCES	PISCES
3 P.M.	ARIES	ARIES	ARIES	ARIES	ARIES
4 P.M.	TAURUS	TAURUS	TAURUS	TAURUS	TAURUS
5 P.M.	TAURUS	TAURUS	TAURUS	TAURUS	TAURUS
6 P.M.	GEMINI	GEMINI	GEMINI	GEMINI	GEMINI
7 P.M.	GEMINI	GEMINI	GEMINI	GEMINI	CANCER
8 P.M.	CANCER	CANCER	CANCER	CANCER	CANCER
9 P.M.	CANCER	CANCER	CANCER	CANCER	CANCER
10 P.M.	LEO	LEO	LEO	LEO	LEO
11 P.M.	LEO	LEO	LEO	LEO	LEO

	NOVEMBER 17	NOVEMBER 18	NOVEMBER 19	NOVEMBER 20	NOVEMBER 21	NOVEMBER 22
MIDNIGHT	VIRGO	VIRGO	VIRGO	VIRGO	VIRGO	VIRGO
1 A.M.	VIRGO	VIRGO	VIRGO	VIRGO	VIRGO	VIRGO
2 A.M.	VIRGO	VIRGO	VIRGO	VIRGO	LIBRA	LIBRA
3 A.M.	LIBRA	LIBRA	LIBRA	LIBRA	LIBRA	LIBRA
4 A.M.	LIBRA	LIBRA	LIBRA	LIBRA	LIBRA	LIBRA
5 A.M.	SCORPIO	SCORPIO	SCORPIO	SCORPIO	SCORPIO	SCORPIO
6 A.M.	SCORPIO	SCORPIO	SCORPIO	SCORPIO	SCORPIO	SCORPIO
7 A.M.	SCORPIO	SCORPIO	SCORPIO	SCORPIO	SAGITTARIUS	SAGITTARIUS
8 A.M.	SAGITTARIUS	SAGITTARIUS	SAGITTARIUS	SAGITTARIUS	SAGITTARIUS	SAGITTARIUS
9 A.M.	SAGITTARIUS	SAGITTARIUS	SAGITTARIUS	SAGITTARIUS	SAGITTARIUS	SAGITTARIUS
10 A.M.	CAPRICORN	CAPRICORN	CAPRICORN	CAPRICORN	CAPRICORN	CAPRICORN
11 A.M.	CAPRICORN	CAPRICORN	CAPRICORN	CAPRICORN	CAPRICORN	CAPRICORN
NOON	AQUARIUS	AQUARIUS	AQUARIUS	AQUARIUS	AQUARIUS	AQUARIUS
1 P.M.	PISCES	PISCES	PISCES	PISCES	PISCES	PISCES
2 P.M.	PISCES	PISCES	PISCES	ARIES	ARIES	ARIES
3 P.M.	ARIES	ARIES	ARIES	ARIES	ARIES	ARIES
4 P.M.	TAURUS	TAURUS	TAURUS	TAURUS	TAURUS	TAURUS
5 P.M.	GEMINI	GEMINI	GEMINI	GEMINI	GEMINI	GEMINI
6 P.M.	GEMINI	GEMINI	GEMINI	GEMINI	GEMINI	GEMINI
7 P.M.	CANCER	CANCER	CANCER	CANCER	CANCER	CANCER
8 P.M.	CANCER	CANCER	CANCER	CANCER	CANCER	CANCER
9 P.M.	CANCER	CANCER	CANCER	CANCER	CANCER	LEO
10 P.M.	LEO	LEO	LEO	LEO	LEO	LEO
11 P.M.	LEO	LEO	LEO	LEO	LEO	LEO

SAGITTARIUS—ASCENDANT TABLES

	NOVEMBER 23	NOVEMBER 24	NOVEMBER 25	NOVEMBER 26
MIDNIGHT	VIRGO	VIRGO	VIRGO	VIRGO
1 A.M.	VIRGO	VIRGO	VIRGO	VIRGO
2 A.M.	LIBRA	LIBRA	LIBRA	LIBRA
3 A.M.	LIBRA	LIBRA	LIBRA	LIBRA
4 A.M.	LIBRA	LIBRA	LIBRA	LIBRA
5 A.M.	SCORPIO	SCORPIO	SCORPIO	SCORPIO
6 A.M.	SCORPIO	SCORPIO	SCORPIO	SCORPIO
7 A.M.	SAGITTARIUS	SAGITTARIUS	SAGITTARIUS	SAGITTARIUS
8 A.M.	SAGITTARIUS	SAGITTARIUS	SAGITTARIUS	SAGITTARIUS
9 A.M.	SAGITTARIUS	SAGITTARIUS	SAGITTARIUS	CAPRICORN
10 A.M.	CAPRICORN	CAPRICORN	CAPRICORN	CAPRICORN
11 A.M.	CAPRICORN	CAPRICORN	AQUARIUS	AQUARIUS
NOON	AQUARIUS	AQUARIUS	AQUARIUS	AQUARIUS
1 P.M.	PISCES	PISCES	PISCES	PISCES
2 P.M.	ARIES	ARIES	ARIES	ARIES
3 P.M.	ARIES	ARIES	ARIES	TAURUS
4 P.M.	TAURUS	TAURUS	TAURUS	TAURUS
5 P.M.	GEMINI	GEMINI	GEMINI	GEMINI
6 P.M.	GEMINI	GEMINI	GEMINI	GEMINI
7 P.M.	CANCER	CANCER	CANCER	CANCER
8 P.M.	CANCER	CANCER	CANCER	CANCER
9 P.M.	LEO	LEO	LEO	LEO
10 P.M.	LEO	LEO	LEO	LEO
11 P.M.	LEO	LEO	LEO	LEO

	NOVEMBER 27	NOVEMBER 28	NOVEMBER 29	NOVEMBER 30	DECEMBER 1
MIDNIGHT	VIRGO	VIRGO	VIRGO	VIRGO	VIRGO
1 A.M.	VIRGO	VIRGO	VIRGO	VIRGO	VIRGO
2 A.M.	LIBRA	LIBRA	LIBRA	LIBRA	LIBRA
3 A.M.	LIBRA	LIBRA	LIBRA	LIBRA	LIBRA
4 A.M.	LIBRA	LIBRA	LIBRA	LIBRA	LIBRA
5 A.M.	SCORPIO	SCORPIO	SCORPIO	SCORPIO	SCORPIO
6 A.M.	SCORPIO	SCORPIO	SCORPIO	SCORPIO	SCORPIO
7 A.M.	SAGITTARIUS	SAGITTARIUS	SAGITTARIUS	SAGITTARIUS	SCORPIO
8 A.M.	SAGITTARIUS	SAGITTARIUS	SAGITTARIUS	SAGITTARIUS	SAGITTARIUS
9 A.M.	CAPRICORN	CAPRICORN	CAPRICORN	CAPRICORN	SAGITTARIUS
10 A.M.	CAPRICORN	CAPRICORN	CAPRICORN	CAPRICORN	CAPRICORN
11 A.M.	AQUARIUS	AQUARIUS	AQUARIUS	AQUARIUS	CAPRICORN
NOON	AQUARIUS	AQUARIUS	AQUARIUS	AQUARIUS	AQUARIUS
1 P.M.	PISCES	PISCES	PISCES	PISCES	PISCES
2 P.M.	ARIES	ARIES	ARIES	ARIES	ARIES
3 P.M.	TAURUS	TAURUS	TAURUS	TAURUS	TAURUS
4 P.M.	TAURUS	TAURUS	TAURUS	TAURUS	TAURUS
5 P.M.	GEMINI	GEMINI	GEMINI	GEMINI	GEMINI
6 P.M.	GEMINI	GEMINI	GEMINI	GEMINI	GEMINI
7 P.M.	CANCER	CANCER	CANCER	CANCER	CANCER
8 P.M.	CANCER	CANCER	CANCER	CANCER	CANCER
9 P.M.	LEO	LEO	LEO	LEO	LEO
10 P.M.	LEO	LEO	LEO	LEO	LEO
11 P.M.	LEO	LEO	LEO	LEO	VIRGO

	DECEMBER 2	DECEMBER 3	DECEMBER 4	DECEMBER 5	DECEMBER 6
MIDNIGHT	VIRGO	VIRGO	VIRGO	VIRGO	VIRGO
1 A.M.	VIRGO	VIRGO	VIRGO	VIRGO	VIRGO
2 A.M.	LIBRA	LIBRA	LIBRA	LIBRA	LIBRA
3 A.M.	LIBRA	LIBRA	LIBRA	LIBRA	LIBRA
4 A.M.	SCORPIO	SCORPIO	SCORPIO	SCORPIO	SCORPIO
5 A.M.	SCORPIO	SCORPIO	SCORPIO	SCORPIO	SCORPIO
6 A.M.	SCORPIO	SCORPIO	SCORPIO	SCORPIO	SAGITTARIUS
7 A.M.	SAGITTARIUS	SAGITTARIUS	SAGITTARIUS	SAGITTARIUS	SAGITTARIUS
8 A.M.	SAGITTARIUS	SAGITTARIUS	SAGITTARIUS	SAGITTARIUS	SAGITTARIUS
9 A.M.	CAPRICORN	CAPRICORN	CAPRICORN	CAPRICORN	CAPRICORN
10 A.M.	CAPRICORN	CAPRICORN	CAPRICORN	CAPRICORN	CAPRICORN
11 A.M.	AQUARIUS	AQUARIUS	AQUARIUS	AQUARIUS	AQUARIUS
NOON	AQUARIUS	PISCES	PISCES	PISCES	PISCES
1 P.M.	PISCES	PISCES	PISCES	PISCES	ARIES
2 P.M.	ARIES	ARIES	ARIES	ARIES	ARIES
3 P.M.	TAURUS	TAURUS	TAURUS	TAURUS	TAURUS
4 P.M.	GEMINI	GEMINI	GEMINI	GEMINI	GEMINI
5 P.M.	GEMINI	GEMINI	GEMINI	GEMINI	GEMINI
6 P.M.	CANCER	CANCER	CANCER	CANCER	CANCER
7 P.M.	CANCER	CANCER	CANCER	CANCER	CANCER
8 P.M.	CANCER	CANCER	CANCER	CANCER	CANCER
9 P.M.	LEO	LEO	LEO	LEO	LEO
10 P.M.	LEO	LEO	LEO	LEO	LEO
11 P.M.	VIRGO	VIRGO	VIRGO	VIRGO	VIRGO

	DECEMBER 7	DECEMBER 8	DECEMBER 9	DECEMBER 10	DECEMBER 11
MIDNIGHT	VIRGO	VIRGO	VIRGO	VIRGO	VIRGO
1 A.M.	LIBRA	LIBRA	LIBRA	LIBRA	LIBRA
2 A.M.	LIBRA	LIBRA	LIBRA	LIBRA	LIBRA
3 A.M.	LIBRA	LIBRA	LIBRA	LIBRA	LIBRA
4 A.M.	SCORPIO	SCORPIO	SCORPIO	SCORPIO	SCORPIO
5 A.M.	SCORPIO	SCORPIO	SCORPIO	SCORPIO	SCORPIO
6 A.M.	SAGITTARIUS	SAGITTARIUS	SAGITTARIUS	SAGITTARIUS	SAGITTARIUS
7 A.M.	SAGITTARIUS	SAGITTARIUS	SAGITTARIUS	SAGITTARIUS	SAGITTARIUS
8 A.M.	SAGITTARIUS	SAGITTARIUS	SAGITTARIUS	SAGITTARIUS	CAPRICORN
9 A.M.	CAPRICORN	CAPRICORN	CAPRICORN	CAPRICORN	CAPRICORN
10 A.M.	CAPRICORN	CAPRICORN	CAPRICORN	AQUARIUS	AQUARIUS
11 A.M.	AQUARIUS	AQUARIUS	AQUARIUS	AQUARIUS	AQUARIUS
NOON	PISCES	PISCES	PISCES	PISCES	PISCES
1 P.M.	ARIES	ARIES	ARIES	ARIES	ARIES
2 P.M.	ARIES	ARIES	ARIES	ARIES	TAURUS
3 P.M.	TAURUS	TAURUS	TAURUS	TAURUS	TAURUS
4 P.M.	GEMINI	GEMINI	GEMINI	GEMINI	GEMINI
5 P.M.	GEMINI	GEMINI	GEMINI	GEMINI	GEMINI
6 P.M.	CANCER	CANCER	CANCER	CANCER	CANCER
7 P.M.	CANCER	CANCER	CANCER	CANCER	CANCER
8 P.M.	LEO	LEO	LEO	LEO	LEO
9 P.M.	LEO	LEO	LEO	LEO	LEO
10 P.M.	LEO	LEO	LEO	LEO	LEO
11 P.M.	VIRGO	VIRGO	VIRGO	VIRGO	VIRGO

	DECEMBER 12	DECEMBER 13	DECEMBER 14	DECEMBER 15	DECEMBER 16
MIDNIGHT	VIRGO	VIRGO	VIRGO	VIRGO	VIRGO
1 A.M.	LIBRA	LIBRA	LIBRA	LIBRA	LIBRA
2 A.M.	LIBRA	LIBRA	LIBRA	LIBRA	LIBRA
3 A.M.	LIBRA	LIBRA	SCORPIO	SCORPIO	SCORPIO
4 A.M.	SCORPIO	SCORPIO	SCORPIO	SCORPIO	SCORPIO
5 A.M.	SCORPIO	SCORPIO	SCORPIO	SCORPIO	SCORPIO
6 A.M.	SAGITTARIUS	SAGITTARIUS	SAGITTARIUS	SAGITTARIUS	SAGITTARIUS
7 A.M.	SATITTARIUS	SAGITTARIUS	SAGITTARIUS	SAGITTARIUS	SAGITTARIUS
8 A.M.	CAPRICORN	CAPRICORN	CAPRICORN	CAPRICORN	CAPRICORN
9 A.M.	CAPRICORN	CAPRICORN	CAPRICORN	CAPRICORN	CAPRICORN
10 A.M.	AQUARIUS	AQUARIUS	AQUARIUS	AQUARIUS	AQUARIUS
11 A.M.	AQUARIUS	AQUARIUS	AQUARIUS	AQUARIUS	AQUARIUS
NOON	PISCES	PISCES	PISCES	PISCES	PISCES
1 P.M.	ARIES	ARIES	ARIES	ARIES	ARIES
2 P.M.	TAURUS	TAURUS	TAURUS	TAURUS	TAURUS
3 P.M.	TAURUS	TAURUS	TAURUS	TAURUS	TAURUS
4 P.M.	GEMINI	GEMINI	GEMINI	GEMINI	GEMINI
5 P.M.	GEMINI	GEMINI	GEMINI	GEMINI	GEMINI
6 P.M.	CANCER	CANCER	CANCER	CANCER	CANCER
7 P.M.	CANCER	CANCER	CANCER	CANCER	CANCER
8 P.M.	LEO	LEO	LEO	LEO	LEO
9 P.M.	LEO	LEO	LEO	LEO	LEO
10 P.M.	LEO	LEO	LEO	VIRGO	VIRGO
11 P.M.	VIRGO	VIRGO	VIRGO	VIRGO	VIRGO

	DECEMBER 17	DECEMBER 18	DECEMBER 19	DECEMBER 20
MIDNIGHT	VIRGO	VIRGO	VIRGO	VIRGO
1 A.M.	LIBRA	LIBRA	LIBRA	LIBRA
2 A.M.	LIBRA	LIBRA	LIBRA	LIBRA
3 A.M.	SCORPIO	SCORPIO	SCORPIO	SCORPIO
4 A.M.	SCORPIO	SCORPIO	SCORPIO	SCORPIO
5 A.M.	SCORPIO	SCORPIO	SCORPIO	SCORPIO
6 A.M.	SAGITTARIUS	SAGITTARIUS	SAGITTARIUS	SAGITTARIUS
7 A.M.	SAGITTARIUS	SAGITTARIUS	SAGITTARIUS	SAGITTARIUS
8 A.M.	CAPRICORN	CAPRICORN	CAPRICORN	CAPRICORN
9 A.M.	CAPRICORN	CAPRICORN	CAPRICORN	CAPRICORN
10 A.M.	AQUARIUS	AQUARIUS	AQUARIUS	AQUARIUS
11 A.M.	AQUARIUS	PISCES	PISCES	PISCES
NOON	PISCES	PISCES	PISCES	PISCES
1 P.M.	ARIES	ARIES	ARIES	ARIES
2 P.M.	TAURUS	TAURUS	TAURUS	TAURUS
3 P.M.	TAURUS	TAURUS	GEMINI	GEMINI
4 P.M.	GEMINI	GEMINI	GEMINI	GEMINI
5 P.M.	CANCER	CANCER	CANCER	CANCER
6 P.M.	CANCER	CANCER	CANCER	CANCER
7 P.M.	CANCER	CANCER	CANCER	CANCER
8 P.M.	LEO	LEO	LEO	LEO
9 P.M.	LEO	LEO	LEO	LEO
10 P.M.	VIRGO	VIRGO	VIRGO	VIRGO
11 P.M.	VIRGO	VIRGO	VIRGO	VIRGO

CAPRICORN—ASCENDANT TABLES

	DECEMBER 21	DECEMBER 22	DECEMBER 23	DECEMBER 24	DECEMBER 25
MIDNIGHT	VIRGO	LIBRA	LIBRA	LIBRA	LIBRA
1 A.M.	LIBRA	LIBRA	LIBRA	LIBRA	LIBRA
2 A.M.	LIBRA	LIBRA	LIBRA	LIBRA	LIBRA
3 A.M.	SCORPIO	SCORPIO	SCORPIO	SCORPIO	SCORPIO
4 A.M.	SCORPIO	SCORPIO	SCORPIO	SCORPIO	SCORPIO
5 A.M.	SAGITTARIUS	SAGITTARIUS	SAGITTARIUS	SAGITTARIUS	SAGITTARIUS
6 A.M.	SAGITTARIUS	SAGITTARIUS	SAGITTARIUS	SAGITTARIUS	SAGITTARIUS
7 A.M.	SAGITTARIUS	SAGITTARIUS	SAGITTARIUS	SAGITTARIUS	SAGITTARIUS
8 A.M.	CAPRICORN	CAPRICORN	CAPRICORN	CAPRICORN	CAPRICORN
9 A.M.	CAPRICORN	CAPRICORN	CAPRICORN	CAPRICORN	CAPRICORN
10 A.M.	AQUARIUS	AQUARIUS	AQUARIUS	AQUARIUS	AQUARIUS
11 A.M.	PISCES	PISCES	PISCES	PISCES	PISCES
NOON	PISCES	ARIES	ARIES	ARIES	ARIES
1 P.M.	ARIES	ARIES	ARIES	ARIES	ARIES
2 P.M.	TAURUS	TAURUS	TAURUS	TAURUS	TAURUS
3 P.M.	GEMINI	GEMINI	GEMINI	GEMINI	GEMINI
4 P.M.	GEMINI	GEMINI	GEMINI	GEMINI	GEMINI
5 P.M.	CANCER	CANCER	CANCER	CANCER	CANCER
6 P.M.	CANCER	CANCER	CANCER	CANCER	CANCER
7 P.M.	CANCER	LEO	LEO	LEO	LEO
8 P.M.	LEO	LEO	LEO	LEO	LEO
9 P.M.	LEO	LEO	LEO	LEO	LEO
10 P.M.	VIRGO	VIRGO	VIRGO	VIRGO	VIRGO
11 P.M.	VIRGO	VIRGO	VIRGO	VIRGO	VIRGO

	DECEMBER 26	DECEMBER 27	DECEMBER 28	DECEMBER 29	DECEMBER 30
MIDNIGHT	LIBRA	LIBRA	LIBRA	LIBRA	LIBRA
1 A.M.	LIBRA	LIBRA	LIBRA	LIBRA	LIBRA
2 A.M.	LIBRA	LIBRA	LIBRA	SCORPIO	SCORPIO
3 A.M.	SCORPIO	SCORPIO	SCORPIO	SCORPIO	SCORPIO
4 A.M.	SCORPIO	SCORPIO	SCORPIO	SCORPIO	SCORPIO
5 A.M.	SAGITTARIUS	SAGITTARIUS	SAGITTARIUS	SAGITTARIUS	SAGITTARIUS
6 A.M.	SAGITTARIUS	SAGITTARIUS	SAGITTARIUS	SAGITTARIUS	SAGITTARIUS
7 A.M.	SAGITTARIUS	CAPRICORN	CAPRICORN	CAPRICORN	CAPRICORN
8 A.M.	CAPRICORN	CAPRICORN	CAPRICORN	CAPRICORN	CAPRICORN
9 A.M.	AQUARIUS	AQUARIUS	AQUARIUS	AQUARIUS	AQUARIUS
10 A.M.	AQUARIUS	AQUARIUS	AQUARIUS	AQUARIUS	AQUARIUS
11 A.M.	PISCES	PISCES	PISCES	PISCES	PISCES
NOON	ARIES	ARIES	ARIES	ARIES	ARIES
1 P.M.	TAURUS	TAURUS	TAURUS	TAURUS	TAURUS
2 P.M.	TAURUS	TAURUS	TAURUS	TAURUS	TAURUS
3 P.M.	GEMINI	GEMINI	GEMINI	GEMINI	GEMINI
4 P.M.	GEMINI	GEMINI	GEMINI	GEMINI	GEMINI
5 P.M.	CANCER	CANCER	CANCER	CANCER	CANCER
6 P.M.	CANCER	CANCER	CANCER	CANCER	CANCER
7 P.M.	LEO	LEO	LEO	LEO	LEO
8 P.M.	LEO	LEO	LEO	LEO	LEO
9 P.M.	LEO	LEO	LEO	LEO	VIRGO
10 P.M.	VIRGO	VIRGO	VIRGO	VIRGO	VIRGO
11 P.M.	VIRGO	VIRGO	VIRGO	VIRGO	VIRGO

	DECEMBER 31	JANUARY 1	JANUARY 2	JANUARY 3	JANUARY 4
MIDNIGHT	LIBRA	LIBRA	LIBRA	LIBRA	LIBRA
1 A.M.	LIBRA	LIBRA	LIBRA	LIBRA	LIBRA
2 A.M.	SCORPIO	SCORPIO	SCORPIO	SCORPIO	SCORPIO
3 A.M.	SCORPIO	SCORPIO	SCORPIO	SCORPIO	SCORPIO
4 A.M.	SCORPIO	SCORPIO	SCORPIO	SCORPIO	SCORPIO
5 A.M.	SAGITTARIUS	SAGITTARIUS	SAGITTARIUS	SAGITTARIUS	SAGITTARIUS
6 A.M.	SAGITTARIUS	SAGITTARIUS	SAGITTARIUS	SAGITTARIUS	SAGITTARIUS
7 A.M.	CAPRICORN	CAPRICORN	CAPRICORN	CAPRICORN	CAPRICORN
8 A.M.	CAPRICORN	CAPRICORN	CAPRICORN	CAPRICORN	CAPRICORN
9 A.M.	AQUARIUS	AQUARIUS	AQUARIUS	AQUARIUS	AQUARIUS
10 A.M.	AQUARIUS	AQUARIUS	PISCES	PISCES	PISCES
11 A.M.	PISCES	PISCES	PISCES	PISCES	PISCES
NOON	ARIES	ARIES	ARIES	ARIES	ARIES
1 P.M.	TAURUS	TAURUS	TAURUS	TAURUS	TAURUS
2 P.M.	TAURUS	GEMINI	GEMINI	GEMINI	GEMINI
3 P.M.	GEMINI	GEMINI	GEMINI	GEMINI	GEMINI
4 P.M.	GEMINI	CANCER	CANCER	CANCER	CANCER
5 P.M.	CANCER	CANCER	CANCER	CANCER	CANCER
6 P.M.	CANCER	CANCER	CANCER	CANCER	CANCER
7 P.M.	LEO	LEO	LEO	LEO	LEO
8 P.M.	LEO	LEO	LEO	LEO	LEO
9 P.M.	VIRGO	VIRGO	VIRGO	VIRGO	VIRGO
10 P.M.	VIRGO	VIRGO	VIRGO	VIRGO	VIRGO
11 P.M.	VIRGO	VIRGO	VIRGO	VIRGO	VIRGO

	JANUARY 5	JANUARY 6	JANUARY 7	JANUARY 8	JANUARY 9
MIDNIGHT	LIBRA	LIBRA	LIBRA	LIBRA	LIBRA
1 A.M.	LIBRA	LIBRA	LIBRA	LIBRA	LIBRA
2 A.M.	SCORPIO	SCORPIO	SCORPIO	SCORPIO	SCORPIO
3 A.M.	SCORPIO	SCORPIO	SCORPIO	SCORPIO	SCORPIO
4 A.M.	SAGITTARIUS	SAGITTARIUS	SAGITTARIUS	SAGITTARIUS	SAGITTARIUS
5 A.M.	SAGITTARIUS	SAGITTARIUS	SAGITTARIUS	SAGITTARIUS	SAGITTARIUS
6 A.M.	SAGITTARIUS	SAGITTARIUS	CAPRICORN	CAPRICORN	CAPRICORN
7 A.M.	CAPRICORN	CAPRICORN	CAPRICORN	CAPRICORN	CAPRICORN
8 A.M.	CAPRICORN	CAPRICORN	AQUARIUS	AQUARIUS	AQUARIUS
9 A.M.	AQUARIUS	AQUARIUS	AQUARIUS	AQUARIUS	AQUARIUS
10 A.M.	PISCES	PISCES	PISCES	PISCES	PISCES
11 A.M.	PISCES	ARIES	ARIES	ARIES	ARIES
NOON	ARIES	ARIES	ARIES	ARIES	ARIES
1 P.M.	TAURUS	TAURUS	TAURUS	TAURUS	TAURUS
2 P.M.	GEMINI	GEMINI	GEMINI	GEMINI	GEMINI
3 P.M.	GEMINI	GEMINI	GEMINI	GEMINI	GEMINI
4 P.M.	CANCER	CANCER	CANCER	CANCER	CANCER
5 P.M.	CANCER	CANCER	CANCER	CANCER	CANCER
6 P.M.	CANCER	LEO	LEO	LEO	LEO
7 P.M.	LEO	LEO	LEO	LEO	LEO
8 P.M.	LEO	LEO	LEO	LEO	LEO
9 P.M.	VIRGO	VIRGO	VIRGO	VIRGO	VIRGO
10 P.M.	VIRGO	VIRGO	VIRGO	VIRGO	VIRGO
11 P.M.	VIRGO	LIBRA	LIBRA	LIBRA	LIBRA

	JANUARY 10	JANUARY 11	JANUARY 12	JANUARY 13	JANUARY 14
MIDNIGHT	LIBRA	LIBRA	LIBRA	LIBRA	LIBRA
1 A.M.	LIBRA	LIBRA	LIBRA	SCORPIO	SCORPIO
2 A.M.	SCORPIO	SCORPIO	SCORPIO	SCORPIO	SCORPIO
3 A.M.	SCORPIO	SCORPIO	SCORPIO	SCORPIO	SCORPIO
4 A.M.	SAGITTARIUS	SAGITTARIUS	SAGITTARIUS	SAGITTARIUS	SAGITTARIUS
5 A.M.	SAGITTARIUS	SAGITTARIUS	SAGITTARIUS	SAGITTARIUS	SAGITTARIUS
6 A.M.	CAPRICORN	CAPRICORN	CAPRICORN	CAPRICORN	CAPRICORN
7 A.M.	CAPRICORN	CAPRICORN	CAPRICORN	CAPRICORN	CAPRICORN
8 A.M.	AQUARIUS	AQUARIUS	AQUARIUS	AQUARIUS	AQUARIUS
9 A.M.	AQUARIUS	AQUARIUS	AQUARIUS	AQUARIUS	AQUARIUS
10 A.M.	PISCES	PISCES	PISCES	PISCES	PISCES
11 A.M.	ARIES	ARIES	ARIES	ARIES	ARIES
NOON	TAURUS	TAURUS	TAURUS	TAURUS	TAURUS
1 P.M.	TAURUS	TAURUS	TAURUS	TAURUS	TAURUS
2 P.M.	GEMINI	GEMINI	GEMINI	GEMINI	GEMINI
3 P.M.	GEMINI	GEMINI	GEMINI	GEMINI	GEMINI
4 P.M.	CANCER	CANCER	CANCER	CANCER	CANCER
5 P.M.	CANCER	CANCER	CANCER	CANCER	CANCER
6 P.M.	LEO	LEO	LEO	LEO	LEO
7 P.M.	LEO	LEO	LEO	LEO	LEO
8 P.M.	LEO	LEO	LEO	LEO	VIRGO
9 P.M.	VIRGO	VIRGO	VIRGO	VIRGO	VIRGO
10 P.M.	VIRGO	VIRGO	VIRGO	VIRGO	VIRGO
11 P.M.	LIBRA	LIBRA	LIBRA	LIBRA	LIBRA

	JANUARY 15	JANUARY 16	JANUARY 17	JANUARY 18	JANUARY 19
MIDNIGHT	LIBRA	LIBRA	LIBRA	LIBRA	LIBRA
1 A.M.	SCORPIO	SCORPIO	SCORPIO	SCORPIO	SCORPIO
2 A.M.	SCORPIO	SCORPIO	SCORPIO	SCORPIO	SCORPIO
3 A.M.	SCORPIO	SCORPIO	SCORPIO	SCORPIO	SCORPIO
4 A.M.	SAGITTARIUS	SAGITTARIUS	SAGITTARIUS	SAGITTARIUS	SAGITTARIUS
5 A.M.	SAGITTARIUS	SAGITTARIUS	SAGITTARIUS	SAGITTARIUS	SAGITTARIUS
6 A.M.	CAPRICORN	CAPRICORN	CAPRICORN	CAPRICORN	CAPRICORN
7 A.M.	CAPRICORN	CAPRICORN	CAPRICORN	CAPRICORN	CAPRICORN
8 A.M.	AQUARIUS	AQUARIUS	AQUARIUS	AQUARIUS	AQUARIUS
9 A.M.	AQUARIUS	AQUARIUS	PISCES	PISCES	PISCES
10 A.M.	PISCES	PISCES	PISCES	PISCES	PISCES
11 A.M.	ARIES	ARIES	ARIES	ARIES	ARIES
NOON	TAURUS	TAURUS	TAURUS	TAURUS	TAURUS
1 P.M.	GEMINI	GEMINI	GEMINI	GEMINI	GEMINI
2 P.M.	GEMINI	GEMINI	GEMINI	GEMINI	GEMINI
3 P.M.	CANCER	CANCER	CANCER	CANCER	CANCER
4 P.M.	CANCER	CANCER	CANCER	CANCER	CANCER
5 P.M.	CANCER	CANCER	CANCER	CANCER	CANCER
6 P.M.	LEO	LEO	LEO	LEO	LEO
7 P.M.	LEO	LEO	LEO	LEO	LEO
8 P.M.	VIRGO	VIRGO	VIRGO	VIRGO	VIRGO
9 P.M.	VIRGO	VIRGO	VIRGO	VIRGO	VIRGO
10 P.M.	VIRGO	VIRGO	VIRGO	VIRGO	VIRGO
11 P.M.	LIBRA	LIBRA	LIBRA	LIBRA	LIBRA

AQUARIUS—ASCENDANT TABLES

	JANUARY 20	JANUARY 21	JANUARY 22	JANUARY 23	JANUARY 24
MIDNIGHT	LIBRA	LIBRA	LIBRA	LIBRA	LIBRA
1 A.M.	SCORPIO	SCORPIO	SCORPIO	SCORPIO	SCORPIO
2 A.M.	SCORPIO	SCORPIO	SCORPIO	SCORPIO	SCORPIO
3 A.M.	SCORPIO	SAGITTARIUS	SAGITTARIUS	SAGITTARIUS	SAGITTARIUS
4 A.M.	SAGITTARIUS	SAGITTARIUS	SAGITTARIUS	SAGITTARIUS	SAGITTARIUS
5 A.M.	SAGITTARIUS	SAGITTARIUS	SAGITTARIUS	SAGITTARIUS	SAGITTARIUS
6 A.M.	CAPRICORN	CAPRICORN	CAPRICORN	CAPRICORN	CAPRICORN
7 A.M.	CAPRICORN	CAPRICORN	CAPRICORN	CAPRICORN	CAPRICORN
8 A.M.	AQUARIUS	AQUARIUS	AQUARIUS	AQUARIUS	AQUARIUS
9 A.M.	PISCES	PISCES	PISCES	PISCES	PISCES
10 A.M.	PISCES	ARIES	ARIES	ARIES	ARIES
11 A.M.	ARIES	ARIES	ARIES	ARIES	ARIES
NOON	TAURUS	TAURUS	TAURUS	TAURUS	TAURUS
1 P.M.	GEMINI	GEMINI	GEMINI	GEMINI	GEMINI
2 P.M.	GEMINI	GEMINI	GEMINI	GEMINI	GEMINI
3 P.M.	CANCER	CANCER	CANCER	CANCER	CANCER
4 P.M.	CANCER	CANCER	CANCER	CANCER	CANCER
5 P.M.	CANCER	LEO	LEO	LEO	LEO
6 P.M.	LEO	LEO	LEO	LEO	LEO
7 P.M.	LEO	LEO	LEO	LEO	LEO
8 P.M.	VIRGO	VIRGO	VIRGO	VIRGO	VIRGO
9 P.M.	VIRGO	VIRGO	VIRGO	VIRGO	VIRGO
10 P.M.	VIRGO	LIBRA	LIBRA	LIBRA	LIBRA
11 P.M.	LIBRA	LIBRA	LIBRA	LIBRA	LIBRA

	JANUARY 25	JANUARY 26	JANUARY 27	JANUARY 28	JANUARY 29
MIDNIGHT	LIBRA	LIBRA	LIBRA	LIBRA	SCORPIO
1 A.M.	SCORPIO	SCORPIO	SCORPIO	SCORPIO	SCORPIO
2 A.M.	SCORPIO	SCORPIO	SCORPIO	SCORPIO	SCORPIO
3 A.M.	SAGITTARIUS	SAGITTARIUS	SAGITTARIUS	SAGITTARIUS	SAGITTARIUS
4 A.M.	SAGITTARIUS	SAGITTARIUS	SAGITTARIUS	SAGITTARIUS	SAGITTARIUS
5 A.M.	SAGITTARIUS	CAPRICORN	CAPRICORN	CAPRICORN	CAPRICORN
6 A.M.	CAPRICORN	CAPRICORN	CAPRICORN	CAPRICORN	CAPRICORN
7 A.M.	AQUARIUS	AQUARIUS	AQUARIUS	AQUARIUS	AQUARIUS
8 A.M.	AQUARIUS	AQUARIUS	AQUARIUS	AQUARIUS	AQUARIUS
9 A.M.	PISCES	PISCES	PISCES	PISCES	PISCES
10 A.M.	ARIES	ARIES	ARIES	ARIES	ARIES
11 A.M.	TAURUS	TAURUS	TAURUS	TAURUS	TAURUS
NOON	TAURUS	TAURUS	TAURUS	TAURUS	TAURUS
1 P.M.	GEMINI	GEMINI	GEMINI	GEMINI	GEMINI
2 P.M.	GEMINI	GEMINI	GEMINI	GEMINI	GEMINI
3 P.M.	CANCER	CANCER	CANCER	CANCER	CANCER
4 P.M.	CANCER	CANCER	CANCER	CANCER	CANCER
5 P.M.	LEO	LEO	LEO	LEO	LEO
6 P.M.	LEO	LEO	LEO	LEO	LEO
7 P.M.	LEO	LEO	LEO	LEO	VIRGO
8 P.M.	VIRGO	VIRGO	VIRGO	VIRGO	VIRGO
9 P.M.	VIRGO	VIRGO	VIRGO	VIRGO	VIRGO
10 P.M.	LIBRA	LIBRA	LIBRA	LIBRA	LIBRA
11 P.M.	LIBRA	LIBRA	LIBRA	LIBRA	LIBRA

	JANUARY 30	JANUARY 31	FEBRUARY 1	FEBRUARY 2	FEBRUARY 3
MIDNIGHT	SCORPIO	SCORPIO	SCORPIO	SCORPIO	SCORPIO
1 A.M.	SCORPIO	SCORPIO	SCORPIO	SCORPIO	SCORPIO
2 A.M.	SCORPIO	SCORPIO	SCORPIO	SCORPIO	SCORPIO
3 A.M.	SAGITTARIUS	SAGITTARIUS	SAGITTARIUS	SAGITTARIUS	SAGITTARIUS
4 A.M.	SAGITTARIUS	SAGITTARIUS	SAGITTARIUS	SAGITTARIUS	SAGITTARIUS
5 A.M.	CAPRICORN	CAPRICORN	CAPRICORN	CAPRICORN	CAPRICORN
6 A.M.	CAPRICORN	CAPRICORN	CAPRICORN	CAPRICORN	CAPRICORN
7 A.M.	AQUARIUS	AQUARIUS	AQUARIUS	AQUARIUS	AQUARIUS
8 A.M.	AQUARIUS	AQUARIUS	PISCES	PISCES	PISCES
9 A.M.	PISCES	PISCES	PISCES	PISCES	PISCES
10 A.M.	ARIES	ARIES	ARIES	ARIES	ARIES
11 A.M.	TAURUS	TAURUS	TAURUS	TAURUS	TAURUS
NOON	TAURUS	TAURUS	GEMINI	GEMINI	GEMINI
1 P.M.	GEMINI	GEMINI	GEMINI	GEMINI	GEMINI
2 P.M.	GEMINI	CANCER	CANCER	CANCER	CANCER
3 P.M.	CANCER	CANCER	CANCER	CANCER	CANCER
4 P.M.	CANCER	CANCER	CANCER	CANCER	CANCER
5 P.M.	LEO	LEO	LEO	LEO	LEO
6 P.M.	LEO	LEO	LEO	LEO	LEO
7 P.M.	VIRGO	VIRGO	VIRGO	VIRGO	VIRGO
8 P.M.	VIRGO	VIRGO	VIRGO	VIRGO	VIRGO
9 P.M.	VIRGO	VIRGO	VIRGO	VIRGO	VIRGO
10 P.M.	LIBRA	LIBRA	LIBRA	LIBRA	LIBRA
11 P.M.	LIBRA	LIBRA	LIBRA	LIBRA	LIBRA

	FEBRUARY 4	FEBRUARY 5	FEBRUARY 6	FEBRUARY 7	FEBRUARY 8
MIDNIGHT	SCORPIO	SCORPIO	SCORPIO	SCORPIO	SCORPIO
1 A.M.	SCORPIO	SCORPIO	SCORPIO	SCORPIO	SCORPIO
2 A.M.	SCORPIO	SAGITTARIUS	SAGITTARIUS	SAGITTARIUS	SAGITTARIUS
3 A.M.	SAGITTARIUS	SAGITTARIUS	SAGITTARIUS	SAGITTARIUS	SAGITTARIUS
4 A.M.	SAGITTARIUS	SAGITTARIUS	SAGITTARIUS	SAGITTARIUS	SAGITTARIUS
5 A.M.	CAPRICORN	CAPRICORN	CAPRICORN	CAPRICORN	CAPRICORN
6 A.M.	CAPRICORN	CAPRICORN	CAPRICORN	CAPRICORN	CAPRICORN
7 A.M.	AQUARIUS	AQUARIUS	AQUARIUS	AQUARIUS	AQUARIUS
8 A.M.	PISCES	PISCES	PISCES	PISCES	PISCES
9 A.M.	PISCES	ARIES	ARIES	ARIES	ARIES
10 A.M.	ARIES	ARIES	ARIES	ARIES	ARIES
11 A.M.	TAURUS	TAURUS	TAURUS	TAURUS	TAURUS
NOON	GEMINI	GEMINI	GEMINI	GEMINI	GEMINI
1 P.M.	GEMINI	GEMINI	GEMINI	GEMINI	GEMINI
2 P.M.	CANCER	CANCER	CANCER	CANCER	CANCER
3 P.M.	CANCER	CANCER	CANCER	CANCER	CANCER
4 P.M.	CANCER	CANCER	CANCER	LEO	LEO
5 P.M.	LEO	LEO	LEO	LEO	LEO
6 P.M.	LEO	LEO	LEO	LEO	LEO
7 P.M.	VIRGO	VIRGO	VIRGO	VIRGO	VIRGO
8 P.M.	VIRGO	VIRGO	VIRGO	VIRGO	VIRGO
9 P.M.	VIRGO	LIBRA	LIBRA	LIBRA	LIBRA
10 P.M.	LIBRA	LIBRA	LIBRA	LIBRA	LIBRA
11 P.M.	LIBRA	LIBRA	LIBRA	LIBRA	LIBRA

	FEBRUARY 9	FEBRUARY 10	FEBRUARY 11	FEBRUARY 12	FEBRUARY 13
MIDNIGHT	SCORPIO	SCORPIO	SCORPIO	SCORPIO	SCORPIO
1 A.M.	SCORPIO	SCORPIO	SCORPIO	SCORPIO	SCORPIO
2 A.M.	SAGITTARIUS	SAGITTARIUS	SAGITTARIUS	SAGITTARIUS	SAGITTARIUS
3 A.M.	SAGITTARIUS	SAGITTARIUS	SAGITTARIUS	SAGITTARIUS	SAGITTARIUS
4 A.M.	SAGITTARIUS	CAPRICORN	CAPRICORN	CAPRICORN	CAPRICORN
5 A.M.	CAPRICORN	CAPRICORN	CAPRICORN	CAPRICORN	CAPRICORN
6 A.M.	CAPRICORN	AQUARIUS	AQUARIUS	AQUARIUS	AQUARIUS
7 A.M.	AQUARIUS	AQUARIUS	AQUARIUS	AQUARIUS	AQUARIUS
8 A.M.	PISCES	PISCES	PISCES	PISCES	PISCES
9 A.M.	ARIES	ARIES	ARIES	ARIES	ARIES
10 A.M.	TAURUS	TAURUS	TAURUS	TAURUS	TAURUS
11 A.M.	TAURUS	TAURUS	TAURUS	TAURUS	TAURUS
NOON	GEMINI	GEMINI	GEMINI	GEMINI	GEMINI
1 P.M.	GEMINI	GEMINI	GEMINI	GEMINI	GEMINI
2 P.M.	CANCER	CANCER	CANCER	CANCER	CANCER
3 P.M.	CANCER	CANCER	CANCER	CANCER	CANCER
4 P.M.	LEO	LEO	LEO	LEO	LEO
5 P.M.	LEO	LEO	LEO	LEO	LEO
6 P.M.	LEO	LEO	LEO	LEO	VIRGO
7 P.M.	VIRGO	VIRGO	VIRGO	VIRGO	VIRGO
8 P.M.	VIRGO	VIRGO	VIRGO	VIRGO	VIRGO
9 P.M.	LIBRA	LIBRA	LIBRA	LIBRA	LIBRA
10 P.M.	LIBRA	LIBRA	LIBRA	LIBRA	LIBRA
11 P.M.	LIBRA	LIBRA	LIBRA	LIBRA	SCORPIO

	FEBRUARY 14	FEBRUARY 15	FEBRUARY 16	FEBRUARY 17	FEBRUARY 18
MIDNIGHT	SCORPIO	SCORPIO	SCORPIO	SCORPIO	SCORPIO
1 A.M.	SCORPIO	SCORPIO	SCORPIO	SCORPIO	SCORPIO
2 A.M.	SAGITTARIUS	SAGITTARIUS	SAGITTARIUS	SAGITTARIUS	SAGITTARIUS
3 A.M.	SAGITTARIUS	SAGITTARIUS	SAGITTARIUS	SAGITTARIUS	SAGITTARIUS
4 A.M.	CAPRICORN	CAPRICORN	CAPRICORN	CAPRICORN	CAPRICORN
5 A.M.	CAPRICORN	CAPRICORN	CAPRICORN	CAPRICORN	CAPRICORN
6 A.M.	AQUARIUS	AQUARIUS	AQUARIUS	AQUARIUS	AQUARIUS
7 A.M.	AQUARIUS	AQUARIUS	AQUARIUS	AQUARIUS	AQUARIUS
8 A.M.	PISCES	PISCES	PISCES	PISCES	PISCES
9 A.M.	ARIES	ARIES	ARIES	ARIES	PISCES
10 A.M.	TAURUS	TAURUS	TAURUS	TAURUS	ARIES
11 A.M.	TAURUS	TAURUS	GEMINI	GEMINI	TAURUS
NOON	GEMINI	GEMINI	GEMINI	GEMINI	GEMINI
1 P.M.	GEMINI	CANCER	CANCER	CANCER	CANCER
2 P.M.	CANCER	CANCER	CANCER	CANCER	CANCER
3 P.M.	CANCER	CANCER	CANCER	CANCER	CANCER
4 P.M.	LEO	LEO	LEO	LEO	LEO
5 P.M.	LEO	LEO	LEO	LEO	LEO
6 P.M.	VIRGO	VIRGO	VIRGO	VIRGO	VIRGO
7 P.M.	VIRGO	VIRGO	VIRGO	VIRGO	VIRGO
8 P.M.	VIRGO	VIRGO	VIRGO	VIRGO	VIRGO
9 P.M.	LIBRA	LIBRA	LIBRA	LIBRA	LIBRA
10 P.M.	LIBRA	LIBRA	LIBRA	LIBRA	LIBRA
11 P.M.	SCORPIO	SCORPIO	SCORPIO	SCORPIO	SCORPIO

PISCES—ASCENDANT TABLES

	FEBRUARY 19	FEBRUARY 20	FEBRUARY 21	FEBRUARY 22	FEBRUARY 23
MIDNIGHT	SCORPIO	SCORPIO	SCORPIO	SCORPIO	SCORPIO
1 A.M.	SCORPIO	SAGITTARIUS	SAGITTARIUS	SAGITTARIUS	SAGITTARIUS
2 A.M.	SAGITTARIUS	SAGITTARIUS	SAGITTARIUS	SAGITTARIUS	SAGITTARIUS
3 A.M.	SAGITTARIUS	SAGITTARIUS	SAGITTARIUS	SAGITTARIUS	SAGITTARIUS
4 A.M.	CAPRICORN	CAPRICORN	CAPRICORN	CAPRICORN	CAPRICORN
5 A.M.	CAPRICORN	CAPRICORN	CAPRICORN	CAPRICORN	CAPRICORN
6 A.M.	AQUARIUS	AQUARIUS	AQUARIUS	AQUARIUS	AQUARIUS
7 A.M.	PISCES	PISCES	PISCES	PISCES	PISCES
8 A.M.	PISCES	ARIES	ARIES	ARIES	ARIES
9 A.M.	ARIES	ARIES	ARIES	ARIES	ARIES
10 A.M.	TAURUS	TAURUS	TAURUS	TAURUS	TAURUS
11 A.M.	GEMINI	GEMINI	GEMINI	GEMINI	GEMINI
NOON	GEMINI	GEMINI	GEMINI	GEMINI	GEMINI
1 P.M.	CANCER	CANCER	CANCER	CANCER	CANCER
2 P.M.	CANCER	CANCER	CANCER	CANCER	CANCER
3 P.M.	CANCER	CANCER	CANCER	LEO	LEO
4 P.M.	LEO	LEO	LEO	LEO	LEO
5 P.M.	LEO	LEO	LEO	LEO	LEO
6 P.M.	VIRGO	VIRGO	VIRGO	VIRGO	VIRGO
7 P.M.	VIRGO	VIRGO	VIRGO	VIRGO	VIRGO
8 P.M.	VIRGO	LIBRA	LIBRA	LIBRA	LIBRA
9 P.M.	LIBRA	LIBRA	LIBRA	LIBRA	LIBRA
10 P.M.	SCORPIO	SCORPIO	SCORPIO	SCORPIO	LIBRA
11 P.M.	SCORPIO	SCORPIO	SCORPIO	SCORPIO	SCORPIO

	FEBRUARY 24	FEBRUARY 25	FEBRUARY 26	FEBRUARY 27	FEBRUARY 28
MIDNIGHT	SCORPIO	SCORPIO	SCORPIO	SCORPIO	SCORPIO
1 A.M.	SAGITTARIUS	SAGITTARIUS	SAGITTARIUS	SAGITTARIUS	SAGITTARIUS
2 A.M.	SAGITTARIUS	SAGITTARIUS	SAGITTARIUS	SAGITTARIUS	SAGITTARIUS
3 A.M.	SAGITTARIUS	SAGITTARIUS	SAGITTARIUS	SAGITTARIUS	CAPRICORN
4 A.M.	CAPRICORN	CAPRICORN	CAPRICORN	CAPRICORN	CAPRICORN
5 A.M.	AQUARIUS	AQUARIUS	AQUARIUS	AQUARIUS	AQUARIUS
6 A.M.	AQUARIUS	AQUARIUS	AQUARIUS	AQUARIUS	AQUARIUS
7 A.M.	PISCES	PISCES	PISCES	PISCES	PISCES
8 A.M.	ARIES	ARIES	ARIES	ARIES	ARIES
9 A.M.	TAURUS	TAURUS	TAURUS	TAURUS	TAURUS
10 A.M.	TAURUS	TAURUS	TAURUS	TAURUS	TAURUS
11 A.M.	GEMINI	GEMINI	GEMINI	GEMINI	GEMINI
NOON	GEMINI	GEMINI	GEMINI	GEMINI	GEMINI
1 P.M.	CANCER	CANCER	CANCER	CANCER	CANCER
2 P.M.	CANCER	CANCER	CANCER	CANCER	CANCER
3 P.M.	LEO	LEO	LEO	LEO	LEO
4 P.M.	LEO	LEO	LEO	LEO	LEO
5 P.M.	LEO	LEO	LEO	LEO	LEO
6 P.M.	VIRGO	VIRGO	VIRGO	VIRGO	VIRGO
7 P.M.	VIRGO	VIRGO	VIRGO	VIRGO	VIRGO
8 P.M.	LIBRA	LIBRA	LIBRA	LIBRA	LIBRA
9 P.M.	LIBRA	LIBRA	LIBRA	LIBRA	LIBRA
10 P.M.	LIBRA	LIBRA	SCORPIO	SCORPIO	SCORPIO
11 P.M.	SCORPIO	SCORPIO	SCORPIO	SCORPIO	SCORPIO

	FEBRUARY 29	MARCH 1	MARCH 2	MARCH 3	MARCH 4
MIDNIGHT	SCORPIO	SCORPIO	SCORPIO	SCORPIO	SCORPIO
1 A.M.	SAGITTARIUS	SAGITTARIUS	SAGITTARIUS	SAGITTARIUS	SAGITTARIUS
2 A.M.	SAGITTARIUS	SAGITTARIUS	SAGITTARIUS	SAGITTARIUS	SAGITTARIUS
3 A.M.	CAPRICORN	CAPRICORN	CAPRICORN	CAPRICORN	CAPRICORN
4 A.M.	CAPRICORN	CAPRICORN	CAPRICORN	CAPRICORN	CAPRICORN
5 A.M.	AQUARIUS	AQUARIUS	AQUARIUS	AQUARIUS	AQUARIUS
6 A.M.	AQUARIUS	AQUARIUS	AQUARIUS	AQUARIUS	PISCES
7 A.M.	PISCES	PISCES	PISCES	PISCES	PISCES
8 A.M.	ARIES	ARIES	ARIES	ARIES	ARIES
9 A.M.	TAURUS	TAURUS	TAURUS	TAURUS	TAURUS
10 A.M.	TAURUS	TAURUS	GEMINI	GEMINI	GEMINI
11 A.M.	GEMINI	GEMINI	GEMINI	GEMINI	GEMINI
NOON	GEMINI	GEMINI	CANCER	CANCER	CANCER
1 P.M.	CANCER	CANCER	CANCER	CANCER	CANCER
2 P.M.	CANCER	CANCER	CANCER	CANCER	CANCER
3 P.M.	LEO	LEO	LEO	LEO	LEO
4 P.M.	LEO	LEO	LEO	LEO	LEO
5 P.M.	VIRGO	VIRGO	VIRGO	VIRGO	VIRGO
6 P.M.	VIRGO	VIRGO	VIRGO	VIRGO	VIRGO
7 P.M.	VIRGO	VIRGO	VIRGO	VIRGO	VIRGO
8 P.M.	LIBRA	LIBRA	LIBRA	LIBRA	LIBRA
9 P.M.	LIBRA	LIBRA	LIBRA	LIBRA	LIBRA
10 P.M.	SCORPIO	SCORPIO	SCORPIO	SCORPIO	SCORPIO
11 P.M.	SCORPIO	SCORPIO	SCORPIO	SCORPIO	SCORPIO

	MARCH 5	MARCH 6	MARCH 7	MARCH 8	MARCH 9
MIDNIGHT	SCORPIO	SCORPIO	SAGITTARIUS	SAGITTARIUS	SAGITTARIUS
1 A.M.	SAGITTARIUS	SAGITTARIUS	SAGITTARIUS	SAGITTARIUS	SAGITTARIUS
2 A.M.	SAGITTARIUS	SAGITTARIUS	SAGITTARIUS	SAGITTARIUS	SAGITTARIUS
3 A.M.	CAPRICORN	CAPRICORN	CAPRICORN	CAPRICORN	CAPRICORN
4 A.M.	CAPRICORN	CAPRICORN	CAPRICORN	CAPRICORN	CAPRICORN
5 A.M.	AQUARIUS	AQUARIUS	AQUARIUS	AQUARIUS	AQUARIUS
6 A.M.	PISCES	PISCES	PISCES	PISCES	PISCES
7 A.M.	PISCES	PISCES	ARIES	ARIES	ARIES
8 A.M.	ARIES	ARIES	ARIES	ARIES	ARIES
9 A.M.	TAURUS	TAURUS	TAURUS	TAURUS	TAURUS
10 A.M.	GEMINI	GEMINI	GEMINI	GEMINI	GEMINI
11 A.M.	GEMINI	GEMINI	GEMINI	GEMINI	GEMINI
NOON	CANCER	CANCER	CANCER	CANCER	CANCER
1 P.M.	CANCER	CANCER	CANCER	CANCER	CANCER
2 P.M.	CANCER	CANCER	CANCER	LEO	LEO
3 P.M.	LEO	LEO	LEO	LEO	LEO
4 P.M.	LEO	LEO	LEO	LEO	LEO
5 P.M.	VIRGO	VIRGO	VIRGO	VIRGO	VIRGO
6 P.M.	VIRGO	VIRGO	VIRGO	VIRGO	VIRGO
7 P.M.	VIRGO	VIRGO	LIBRA	LIBRA	LIBRA
8 P.M.	LIBRA	LIBRA	LIBRA	LIBRA	LIBRA
9 P.M.	LIBRA	LIBRA	LIBRA	LIBRA	LIBRA
10 P.M.	SCORPIO	SCORPIO	SCORPIO	SCORPIO	SCORPIO
11 P.M.	SCORPIO	SCORPIO	SCORPIO	SCORPIO	SCORPIO

	MARCH 10	MARCH 11	MARCH 12	MARCH 13	MARCH 14	MARCH 15
MIDNIGHT	SAGITTARIUS	SAGITTARIUS	SAGITTARIUS	SAGITTARIUS	SAGITTARIUS	SAGITTARIUS
1 A.M.	SAGITTARIUS	SAGITTARIUS	SAGITTARIUS	SAGITTARIUS	SAGITTARIUS	SAGITTARIUS
2 A.M.	CAPRICORN	CAPRICORN	CAPRICORN	CAPRICORN	CAPRICORN	CAPRICORN
3 A.M.	CAPRICORN	CAPRICORN	CAPRICORN	CAPRICORN	CAPRICORN	CAPRICORN
4 A.M.	CAPRICORN	AQUARIUS	AQUARIUS	AQUARIUS	AQUARIUS	AQUARIUS
5 A.M.	AQUARIUS	AQUARIUS	AQUARIUS	AQUARIUS	AQUARIUS	AQUARIUS
6 A.M.	PISCES	PISCES	PISCES	PISCES	PISCES	PISCES
7 A.M.	PISCES	ARIES	ARIES	ARIES	ARIES	ARIES
8 A.M.	ARIES	ARIES	ARIES	ARIES	TAURUS	TAURUS
9 A.M.	TAURUS	TAURUS	TAURUS	TAURUS	TAURUS	TAURUS
10 A.M.	GEMINI	GEMINI	GEMINI	GEMINI	GEMINI	GEMINI
11 A.M.	GEMINI	GEMINI	GEMINI	GEMINI	GEMINI	GEMINI
NOON	CANCER	CANCER	CANCER	CANCER	CANCER	CANCER
1 P.M.	CANCER	CANCER	CANCER	CANCER	CANCER	CANCER
2 P.M.	CANCER	CANCER	LEO	LEO	LEO	LEO
3 P.M.	LEO	LEO	LEO	LEO	LEO	LEO
4 P.M.	LEO	LEO	LEO	LEO	LEO	LEO
5 P.M.	VIRGO	VIRGO	VIRGO	VIRGO	VIRGO	VIRGO
6 P.M.	VIRGO	VIRGO	VIRGO	VIRGO	VIRGO	VIRGO
7 P.M.	VIRGO	LIBRA	LIBRA	LIBRA	LIBRA	LIBRA
8 P.M.	LIBRA	LIBRA	LIBRA	LIBRA	LIBRA	LIBRA
9 P.M.	LIBRA	LIBRA	LIBRA	LIBRA	LIBRA	SCORPIO
10 P.M.	SCORPIO	SCORPIO	SCORPIO	SCORPIO	SCORPIO	SCORPIO
11 P.M.	SCORPIO	SCORPIO	SCORPIO	SCORPIO	SCORPIO	SCORPIO

	MARCH 16	MARCH 17	MARCH 18	MARCH 19	MARCH 20
MIDNIGHT	SAGITTARIUS	SAGITTARIUS	SAGITTARIUS	SAGITTARIUS	SAGITTARIUS
1 A.M.	SAGITTARIUS	SAGITTARIUS	SAGITTARIUS	SAGITTARIUS	SAGITTARIUS
2 A.M.	CAPRICORN	CAPRICORN	CAPRICORN	CAPRICORN	CAPRICORN
3 A.M.	CAPRICORN	CAPRICORN	CAPRICORN	CAPRICORN	CAPRICORN
4 A.M.	AQUARIUS	AQUARIUS	AQUARIUS	AQUARIUS	AQUARIUS
5 A.M.	AQUARIUS	AQUARIUS	AQUARIUS	AQUARIUS	AQUARIUS
6 A.M.	PISCES	PISCES	PISCES	PISCES	PISCES
7 A.M.	ARIES	ARIES	ARIES	ARIES	ARIES
8 A.M.	TAURUS	TAURUS	TAURUS	TAURUS	TAURUS
9 A.M.	TAURUS	TAURUS	TAURUS	GEMINI	GEMINI
10 A.M.	GEMINI	GEMINI	GEMINI	GEMINI	GEMINI
11 A.M.	GEMINI	GEMINI	CANCER	CANCER	CANCER
NOON	CANCER	CANCER	CANCER	CANCER	CANCER
1 P.M.	CANCER	CANCER	CANCER	CANCER	CANCER
2 P.M.	LEO	LEO	LEO	LEO	LEO
3 P.M.	LEO	LEO	LEO	LEO	LEO
4 P.M.	VIRGO	VIRGO	VIRGO	VIRGO	VIRGO
5 P.M.	VIRGO	VIRGO	VIRGO	VIRGO	VIRGO
6 P.M.	VIRGO	VIRGO	VIRGO	VIRGO	VIRGO
7 P.M.	LIBRA	LIBRA	LIBRA	LIBRA	LIBRA
8 P.M.	LIBRA	LIBRA	LIBRA	LIBRA	LIBRA
9 P.M.	SCORPIO	SCORPIO	SCORPIO	SCORPIO	SCORPIO
10 P.M.	SCORPIO	SCORPIO	SCORPIO	SCORPIO	SCORPIO
11 P.M.	SCORPIO	SCORPIO	SCORPIO	SCORPIO	SCORPIO

(IV)
Analysis of Character

Aries

As this is the first sign of the Zodiac and the sign of the spring season, it is easy to understand the desire of Aries people to be first in all that they do. They want to excel in everything they undertake and usually manage to do so. They are self-starters and tend to rush into enterprises with enthusiasm and daring. They are extremely ambitious and quite daring but usually in a practical way. They are fine at quick decisions and speedy action but often seem to lack the endurance needed to complete their plans against strong opposition. They may turn to new objectives. Their pioneering nature makes them valuable for starting projects and then allowing others to complete them. Their ability for leadership makes this possible, as they can inspire others.

Aries people tend to resent authority, so they more easily have trouble with their superiors. Although they dislike taking orders, once they have done so, they will carry them out completely and expeditiously. They can be a bit headstrong and have to guard against impatience and hasty speech. They often succeed against great odds through their disregard of the strength of the people or forces against them. But they sometimes fail because of that same carelessness.

Arians are very honest and fair in their financial affairs. Although they are extremely generous and will spend very freely, they like to feel that they are getting full value for their money. They are not the sort to make much of an effort to build up a reserve for a rainy day, as the present moment is too important to them. They enjoy spending money to impress their friends and associates and for the good of their loved ones. Aries women are inclined to spend more on hats than women born under the other signs.

Although their constitution seems quite powerful, they are inclined to short, sharp attacks of illness, especially fevers, indigestion, or headaches. But their recovery is usually quicker than that of other people. They have a tendency to overwork themselves both mentally and physically. Aries people can become very trying when they are sick, as they become irritable and impatient. This is probably because they have a fear of death until they have acquired a belief in the immortality of the soul. Because of their daring and somewhat reckless nature, they have to guard against accidents. They tend to drive too fast and to be impatient with other drivers.

Letter writing is not a strong point with Arians, so their letters are likely to be abrupt and may sound dictatorial. This can anger or confuse the recipient. They are much better at using the telephone and in direct conversation. They are noted for their snap judgments and may become impatient with slower thinkers. But they are fine diplomats when an emergency arises or when some advantage can be gained by sudden diplomatic action. Otherwise they tend to say what they feel even if it produces a quarrel. Aries husbands and wives are not averse to quarreling in public.

Their dislike of authority often leads Aries people to leave home quite early in life. They want to escape the advice and supervision of their parents. But, when in later years they have established a home of their own, they make every effort to see that it is comfortable and that their loved ones are happy in it. They like a home that they can show off to their friends and associates. The Aries man may have a wandering eye for a pretty face or an enticing figure, but he is too conventional to cause domestic rifts through any serious affairs.

As a lover, the Aries man is also quite conventional but extremely passionate and inclined to be a bit selfish. Once he has chosen the woman he wants, he will devote all his time and attention to winning her. And he is a difficult man to compete with. He is not the sort to accept advice or to believe that anyone else knows the tactics of love better than he does.

Aries women are very romantic and are inclined to let the man of their choice know exactly how they feel about him. Being idealistic, they are quite often hurt, but they are too independent to cry on the shoulders of their sympathizers. They are not likely to allow gossip or the opinions of others to interfere with their love life. Quite often the Arian woman's independent and proud manner scares away the men who would be best for her. As with most of their activities, Aries people tend to marry in haste and repent at leisure.

There are few people as capable of handling the routine affairs of business as are Aries people. Their ability to make quick decisions, to show their authority, and to be especially firm is particularly valuable to business activities. But they may run into trouble when they are forced to contend with unexpected events outside the normal business plans. New problems can be especially frustrating. They are especially generous with their employees but may lack the sympathy necessary to obtain the full cooperation of their workers.

Aries people are good talkers and have the ability to sway an audience with their enthusiasm and eloquence. They usually go straight to the point and are clear and precise. However, in friendship they tend to talk about themselves too much. Their conservation, even then, may be interesting. At times, they are too critical or too outspoken.

Some qualities that Aries people have to guard against are impatience, quick anger, and a dictatorial manner. They must not allow their ambition to make them inconsiderate of others. A tendency to brag should be avoided. They also have to guard against becoming discouraged too quickly when circumstances deny them immediate success. They have to cultivate a staying power.

The good qualities of Aries people are abundant. They make fine leaders with an ability to gather loyal followers. They are sincere in friendship and generous to a fault. Their daring and enterprise lead them into successful accomplishments. Their pioneering nature is much needed by humanity. They are always interesting and fun to be with. Home and family, friends, and acquaintances are important to them and are never disregarded. Their mental energy makes them practical and fine business people. People who need help and assurance can always rely on the energy and knowledge of Aries people.

People born with the Sun in the sign of Gemini, Leo, Sagittarius or Aquarius are the most compatible with Aries people.

People born under Cancer, Libra, or Capricorn can be a bit difficult for Arians.

Taurus

People born under the sign of Taurus are the good, solid types who keep things going and help to stabilize what others have put together. Their physical build is usually quite strong, solid, and somewhat stocky. They are quite muscular and have good equilibrium, which makes them good acrobats or ballet dancers, though many follow a business or financial career. Many Taureans are good singers, since their sign rules the throat.

The throat is in fact the most sensitive part of the Taurean's body. The sign of Taurus is also related to the heart and reproductive organs, so these parts also should be protected. The constitution is usually strong, and with their great power of endurance Taureans can resist illness longer than most of the other signs. Their illnesses are usually slower to start, and they take longer to reach a final recovery. They should follow diets low in fats and foods that heat the blood. Moderation in food and drink is required.

Taurus people are a bit slow to get started, for they like to be sure that their plans are complete. They do not have a great deal of initiative, but once they take over something already begun, they are sure to complete it. They are the most determined and obstinate of the signs. Once they make up their minds, there is little to deny them success. They may resist change, but once changes are forced upon them, they will take them in stride.

Taureans are very honest and trustworthy in financial affairs. As Taurus is the money sign of the Zodiac, these people have an instinctive ability to handle money. They are not likely to spend foolishly, but are not stingy either. They like to have financial reserves and may have money put aside that other people do not know about.

The Taurean's honesty and integrity tend to produce good results in business affairs. The quiet reserve and calm assurance of Taurus people make others feel that they can be trusted. They seldom involve themselves in office politics or any sort of double-dealing. It is a bit difficult for Taureans to express themselves, either in writing or speech. But they do have some ability for self-expression through beauty and the arts.

Taurus people are very fond of their homes and family life. They make good parents, as they give both pleasure and necessities to their offspring. Their conventional and easygoing nature make them the best of marriage partners. They are not the sort to risk disturbing a marital relationship by dabbling in romantic affairs. They lead a conventional sex life, as a matter of course.

Friendship is important to Taurus people, and they are very warmhearted and loyal to their friends. Their patience and tolerance keep them from being critical or finding fault. Their self-control is great, but when they are pushed too far, their temper can be very frightening.

The solid strength of Taurus people tends to show up in all that they do. Everything has to be started on a sound foundation, so they plan accordingly. They are interested in stability and lasting qualities, so they take a long time to reach decisions. To more rapid thinkers, they can quite often be very trying. Their sense of beauty is strong, and has a practical and enduring quality about it. They are not likely to gamble, for they have the patience to work and wait for success. Even when they fail at a project, they will gather up the pieces and continue trying until they are successful.

Although Taureans are noted for hard work and steady effort, there are times when they will let everything go and do nothing but loaf. When Taurus homemakers have such spells, their housekeeping will be sadly neglected. Taurus husbands are not especially interested in going out in the evening, and their tendency to avoid conversation may be trying to some wives.

Taurus people are inclined to remain in their place of birth and in the same occupation and place of work for a long time. They enjoy being in a rut and have to be forced out of it by drastic circumstances. They do not like to have their routine interrupted or their schedule changed.

Of the few negative qualities that Taureans have, perhaps the greatest is stubbornness. Taurus is the most obstinate sign of the Zodiac; being an earth sign it is hard to move. Once Taurus people have made up their minds, little can be done to change them. Opposition seems to increase their determination. They have to guard against a tendency to be lazy, and, since their appetites are quite large, they must beware of overindulging in food or drink. They seem to be more interested in quantity than in quality.

The Taurus good qualities are numerous. Their steadfast ability to build up what others have started and their good nature make them very necessary to humanity. They mold and hold things together. They are good financiers, bankers, and the solid citizens of their community. They are trusted and looked up to, as their ideas are sound, logical, and free from snap judgments. They attract confidence. Seldom do they indulge in anything underhanded. They are not the sort to attract gossip.

Taurus people get along best and are happiest when associating with people born under the Sun signs of Cancer, Virgo, Capricorn, and Pisces.

People with the Sun in Leo, Scorpio, or Aquarius are not likely to be compatible with the Taurus nature.

Gemini

Versatility and duality are two words that go a long way in describing people born under the sign of Gemini. They tend to have two or more things in the fire at the same time. They are also collectors of ideas and information, which they store away and bring out to enliven their conversation on almost any subject. They are restless in mind and body and have to be active, in some way, most of the time.

These people tend to be nervous and seem to rely on their nerves for their good health. They can easily exhaust this nervous strength. However, their health is usually good, although they are not physically robust and may have quite a few minor complaints. They can stand a good deal of strain, and disease does not seem to affect them as much as it does the other signs. Their lungs are the part of the body that should be given the most care. The feet and the digestive system can also be easily affected. Their mental outlook is important to their health, as they can think themselves into ill health.

The minds of Gemini people act so quickly and so logically that they appear quite brilliant, although they are not noted for their originality. They are deep thinkers and have the ability to connect ideas and to reach reasonable conclusions. They quite often appear cold and unfeeling because they lack strong emotions and appeal to reason rather than to the feelings; thus they may hurt people's feelings without realizing it.

Gemini people do not especially like physical work; they are more inclined to live by their wits. They are financial schemers who seek ways to make money without the boredom of a monotonous job. They make good writers, especially of short stories. They make good reporters, for their perceptions are very strong. Their financial sense may be affected by their emotions, so money slips from their hands very easily.

Gemini people speak and write logically and interestingly. They have no trouble making people understand them. Sometimes, in speech, they will wander away from their subject or may repeat themselves. But for short, sharp, clever remarks, the Gemini has no equal. Geminis are not physically aggressive but are good fighters with words.

Gemini people take other people as a matter of course and seldom become very affectionate or deeply involved. Although family life does not hold a great deal of interest for them, they accept it without argument. Domesticity does not worry them or especially interest them. Gemini people do not make a very great effort to leave their home and parents, but usually do so. They adapt themselves to their surroundings and can be at home wherever they hang their hats.

Love is not an especially strong trait of Gemini people. They tend to be dabblers in romance and seek variety and mental rather than physical compatibility. They are inclined to be a bit shallow in love. It is difficult for them to show any real feeling. Geminis have a greater attraction to entering religious life than do people born under the other signs.

In marriage, Gemini people are not the sort to be disagreeable or cause any disturbing conditions. Minor irritations are likely, but real problems are often avoided. Warm-blooded people married to Geminis can be quite unhappy because of the lack of warmth they receive. Gemini people have trouble giving themselves completely to anyone. They tend to flirt a great deal.

Business affairs are likely to be a bit difficult for these people. They are good promoters and agents. Anything that brings information to others, such as newspapers, appeals to them. They make good teachers and lecturers, for they can easily pass on their knowledge. But they have to be cautious in the business world, as there is a danger of self-deception and of becoming involved in far-fetched schemes. They are not the sort to stay at one endeavor very long. Their desire for novelty and diversity leads them to jump from one job to another. They easily become jacks of all trades.

As employers they are likely to seem cold and unfeeling with their workers because they lack sympathy. They expect good work and are willing to pay for it, but their approach to work relationships is strictly businesslike.

Geminis can be especially good in public affairs, but when upsets occur, they have difficulty understanding their source. They are good at arguing and smoothing over hurt feelings but may never reach the cause of the trouble.

The desire for change and novelty is one of their biggest negative qualities. It leads them into too many different activities at the same time, so that they scatter their forces. Their lack of feeling is also detrimental to their efforts for success. Their sometimes thoughtless speech can endanger their friendships. They need to cultivate a determination to stay with a subject until they have mastered it.

Their good qualitites are many and varied. They are easy to get along with and always interesting. They seem to enjoy anything for a time, until it becomes boring. Their wealth of knowledge makes them versatile, and their unpredictability adds a dash of spice to their nature. They are trying to slow thinkers but can be especially helpful to them as teachers. Their senses are acute, so they make good music critics. All exchanges, of goods or ideas, appeal to them. They like to know what people are doing and why they are doing it. They are usually fun to be with.

Gemini people are happiest when associating with people born under the sign of Aries, Leo, Libra, or Aquarius.

They are not so happy with people born under the sign of Virgo, Sagittarius, or Pisces.

Cancer

As Cancer is the home-loving sign of the Zodiac, people born under this sign are bound up with their home and family. Their interests tend to center on the activities related to their way of living and the people they have to care for. They are not the sort to leave home early in life, and they respect their parents. Even the men of this sign usually have a strong maternal instinct. They like children and may have a large family whom they enjoy doing for. But they tend to be overindulgent with their loved ones. They like to entertain, and their interest in good food makes them good chefs. They need to use moderation in their eating, as they enjoy hot and highly seasoned foods. They are usually very patriotic.

The health of Cancer people is especially connected with the digestive system. The stomach is the sensitive part of the body for them. Also, the head and knees are easily affected. They tend to be quite delicate children, and should be protected, especially during the first four years, which may be critical. Moderation in food and drink is especially necessary because they tend to put on weight as they grow older. A good diet is important since most of their health problems involve the digestive system. They are not especially easy patients to care for, as they have a tendency to exaggerate their symptoms and their suffering.

Cancer is an emotional sign, and these people usually react to circumstances through their feelings and emotions rather than their thinking ability. Although they are quite reserved, they can be sensational. Their depth of feeling and romantic nature make them fine husbands and wives. They are happy in their homes and are not the sort to seek novelty through outside affairs.

Cancerians are tenacious and usually hang on to whatever they obtain. Being interested in the past and in history, they often collect antiques. But they also are interested in what is new and out of the ordinary. This makes them somewhat changeable. A Cancerian may allow her closets to fill up with clothes that are out of date and that she may never use again.

In their search for success, Cancer people have the patience to work silently toward their goals without expecting immediate success. They gradually wear away opposition or obstacles and are not deterred by rebuffs. But their feelings are usually hurt by criticism or imagined insults to their dignity. Sometimes, Cancerians are too sure of their own ability and their correct vision of the future. They may be quite unrealistic. And their habit of taking things personally can make them inconsiderate of others.

These people have an ability to make good in the business world through their tenacity of purpose and their willingness to move slowly. Like the sea, they steadily beat against the rocks of adversity, and they eventually come out ahead of people whose actions are more spectacular. They are shrewd and thrifty and quite conventional, so they seldom take any financial risks. They are often thrust into public acclaim without seeking it. They enjoy doing for others, which makes them fine for handling welfare work such as feeding the needy. Food and drink are lines which may be of business interest to them. They make good storekeepers. Real estate, especially homes and farms, can become a good business pursuit. They also tend to be interested in the sea and its products.

Because of their emotional and feeling capacity, Cancer people usually have some ability for music, poetry, or painting. Their creative projects usually have an emotional appeal. But they often lack a desire strong enough to keep them doing the work that artistic pursuits demand. Cancer people can be lax and not very energetic. They have to have a strong interest to make them really exert themselves. That is where their interests in their home are invaluable; nothing is too tedious or difficult where their home and family are involved.

They are especially honest in their financial dealings and expect others to be just as honest. They are usually careful with their money and not inclined to spend on themselves, though they can be extravagant and overindulgent in spending on their loved ones. As there is a strong tendency to worry over money, their health is better when they are earning enough to allay any worry.

In spite of their reserved and dignified manner, Cancer people have a good many friends. Their warmth and sincerity attract people and lead to enjoyable friendships. They make dependable and sympathetic friends. But they are extremely sensitive, and any fancied slight will make the association very delicate. They often surprise people by their reactions to petty remarks; they withdraw into a shell of silence. They tend to believe that people are gossiping about them.

This sensitivity is one of their negative qualities and should be guarded against. It can alienate people whose support is needed. It may even endanger a marriage. Cancerians are inclined to be timid, or may appear so through their desire not to create a disturbance. They have to guard against allowing their surroundings and their associates to influence them.

The positive qualities of Cancer people stem from their warmth of feeling and their desire to help others. They do not brag about their good deeds but enjoy giving their time and energies to helping people. They are very patient and seldom lose their temper or become aggressive. But they can be very forceful. They are loyal to their employers, friends, family, and country. Opposition does not seem to anger them or deter their eventual success. Both men and women of this sign are especially romantic and affectionate, which attracts friendship and love.

Cancer people are happiest when associating with people born under the signs of Taurus, Virgo, Scorpio, and Pisces. These people are the most compatible with the Cancer warmth.

People born under the signs of Aries, Libra, and Capricorn are likely to create problems for Cancer people.

Leo

Leo is called the royal sign of the Zodiac, for the Sun has the most strength in it. People born under this sign have an ability to lead others and to become important in whatever endeavor captures their interest. Their nature easily attracts influential people so they receive favors and much good will. Often, they are quite lucky. They are not especially fond of work, so they avoid menial tasks and physical effort whenever possible. But when they have to show others how to do things, they will undertake any sort of activity. They do their best in positions where they have some authority over others and where they can exercise their initiative. Being straightforward and above duplicity, they can be rather easily deceived by people who have fewer scruples. But when they discover that they have been betrayed, they are likely to forgive and forget, as they are not the vengeful sort. Their anger is quick, especially when their dignity has been offended, but it is soon over and leaves no grudges. Sometimes they are a bit dictatorial and demanding and can be quite irritating when expecting people to cater to their whims.

Leo people are extremely generous with their money and expect others to be that way also. They like money for what it can buy and for the power it creates. But they do not hoard money, so they have trouble building up a reserve. Their ideas regarding money tend to be large and expansive but not always very practical. Being somewhat trusting, they are easily defrauded. They can be rather easily influenced but can never be forced into anything.

The sign of Leo rules the heart and lower back, so those are the most sensitive parts of the body for Leo people. Also, the throat, circulatory system, and reproductive organs should be given protection. The Leo constitution is usually strong and the organs are not easily affected. Some Leos are easily disturbed by illness, but once their confidence returns, their fighting ability brings a ready response to treatment. They have so much vitality that they may put too much of a strain on it. They should never allow their enthusiasm to lead them into neglecting their rest. But, like their namesake, the lion, they have an ability to relax completely.

Leo people are not especially interested in leaving home, but they expect family affairs to revolve around them. They seem to take it for granted that they deserve the attention they receive. When they are unsuccessful in earning the acclaim of the public, they may become quite dominating in their homes.

In marriage, Leo people are very loyal and take their marriage vows very seriously; their promise is very important to them. They often remain married under very difficult circumstances and resort to divorce only when there is no other remedy. As Leo is the sign of children, Leo parents are very fond of their offspring. They seem to know how to get along with them and how to make them happy. But they can at times be a bit too severe in disciplining their children.

In speech and writing, Leo people are eloquent, frank, and direct. They know how to appeal to the emotions, as their feelings are very strong. They may be a little boastful or may exaggerate. They generate enthusiasm and optimism.

Although Leo people tend to be conventional in love, they can be very romantic, though somewhat oversentimental. They are very steadfast once their heart is given. They tend to spoil their loved ones and shower them with the best of everything. They expect a good deal from their loved ones because they give so much of themselves.

Leo people are artistic and dramatic, so the theater and entertaining are strong attractions for them. Some Leos look for careers in the theater just for pleasure and to feel important; they enjoy applause. They do well in the business world once they have risen to executive positions. As employees they are loyal and will work for their employers without holding back. They like to feel appreciated, so employers will receive the best from them by acknowledging their ability. Their pride is quite often the incentive that carries them into high positions where they are looked up to. Honor and recognition seem more important to them than the money involved. Their determination and their ability to concentrate on one objective at a time lead to success.

Leo people are able to get along with people in all walks of life, so they make many friends. They are socially active and enjoy entertaining, either at home or in the finest of restaurants. Nothing is too good for their guests. They are the sort who can combine business with pleasure. As with all their relationships, they are loyal to their friends and always ready to lend a helping hand. Their dignity gives them an appearance of aloofness, which keeps them from becoming especially intimate with anyone.

The positive qualities of Leo people make them important to humanity as a stabilizing force. They are dependable and responsible and can lead people into better times as well as into war. But Leo people are not the sort to like physical violence. They appear so ready to fight that they seldom have to. They can show people how to live together in love and harmony, as their depth of feeling is inspiring to others. Their executive ability is used for good as they shun anything that can be of harm to others. They attempt to shine on all that surrounds them.

Their negative qualities tend to be exaggerations of their good qualities. Their ability for leadership can become dominating and lead to tyranny. They can be selfish and self-centered with no regard for others. They may concentrate on obtaining the good will of important persons but can be quite condescending to people they feel are inferior. Fortunately, it is very seldom that the negative qualities are strong, for a truly negative Leo is one of the most disagreeable persons.

Leos get along best with people who have the Sun in the sign of Aries, Gemini, Libra, or Sagittarius.

They are not happy with people born under the sign of Taurus, Scorpio, or Aquarius.

Virgo

People born under the sign of Virgo are critics and analysts. They enjoy work for its own sake and believe that it is necessary for success. They tend to remain in one job for a long time and depend upon their good work and diligence to bring them promotion and more pay. They find it difficult to boost themselves, so they are willing to let their work speak for them. They are fine workers, as they are careful with details and seldom make mistakes. But they can become a bit fussy with minor matters and can become bound by rules and regulations. It is rather difficult for them to be expansive and to grasp the broader picture or concept of a project. Success comes later in life to these people and is always well earned.

Virgos are especially good in the business world, as they are good at finding bargains and weeding out what is not useful. Their perceptiveness and analytical ability become very useful to themselves or to their employers. They can find loopholes and discover ways and means to get around the opposition of others. They will take great pains, for they highly enjoy winning a business advantage or obtaining a bargain.

Financial affairs are handled carefully and kept free from waste and reckless spending. Virgo people are careful with their pennies and build up their fortunes slowly. They do not take financial risks. Other people often think they are stingy, but it is only their sensible attitude toward money. When their financial assistance is needed, it is given willingly and with no strings attached. They enjoy doing for others.

The sign Virgo rules the bowels and solar plexus, and these parts of the body are most easily affected by disease among Virgos. The nervous system, feet, and lungs should also be protected. The strong interest in health and hygiene that Virgo people usually have gives them an ability to ward off many of the health problems that come to others. They tend to be moderate and to live quiet lives free from physical strain or overexertion. They are not self-indulgent. After they have passed their infant years, they are about the longest-lived people of the twelve signs. They usually maintain a slender figure, which gives them a youthful appearance for most of their lives. Sometimes their interest in diet and health makes them quite tiresome to their companions. But they seem instinctively to know what is best for them, and their advice is helpful to others.

They are not especially interesting talkers or letter writers because they concentrate on details, which can be tedious to read or listen to. But people desiring knowledge should heed their words.

Virgo is an earthy and intellectual sign, and so these people seem to lack the warmth and depth of feeling that bring romance. They can be a bit self-centered in their love affairs and find it difficult to give completely of themselves. They are seldom passionate or really affectionate. But this indifference easily attracts the sort of people who do not want serious relationships, so that they are quite often very popular with the opposite sex. Women tend to feel safer with Virgo men because they feel that nothing serious will result from the association.

Virgo people make good partners, either in business or marriage. They are quite content in their domestic lives and are not the sort to do anything to disturb a tranquil atmosphere. They are not easily angered or made impatient but can be a bit fussy about small details in the home. They may be critical but not unpleasantly so, as they are only interested in what is best for their associates.

They make some of the finest parents of any of the signs because they are constantly thinking of whatever is best for their children. They do not mind taking infinite pains for the good of their offspring. Their children are usually brought up in a quiet routine. Since Virgos believe in the value of knowledge, they provide their children with a good education.

Virgo people are the sympathetic sort. They treat their employees fairly and are not domineering or arrogant. They expect much care with details and may be irritated with mistakes. Their employees are usually contented.

Virgo people usually prefer a business career rather than a profession. But, they make fine lawyers in special fields. Their attention to detail make them good financial advisers, especially for people who seek safety for their funds. They do well in partnership, especially with people who have large, expansive plans and need someone to handle the details. Their diligence and trustworthiness make them good in public affairs. They can find ways and means for improving conditions. In science, they are fine for research work.

Their friendships are usually with people who have the same interests and the same education. Mental compatibility is important. They are good friends, especially when money, time, or effort is needed. They are always willing to be of service.

Their good qualities are many and of much use to the world. Their work and service do much to make life more pleasant and easier for all of us. They use their intelligence in all that they do and make good teachers. Their ability to analyze people and situations makes them especially valuable to people who lack perception. They are good critics. They make fine advisers in regard to diet and hygiene. They are careful business people who do their best for their associates in business, as they will for themselves.

Their few negative qualities tend to make their lives monotonous and uneventful. Their tendency to work and wait delays their success. They should learn to "blow their own horn." Their interest in small details can cause them to miss big opportunities. They should learn to put more feeling and warmth into their relationships.

Virgo people are happiest when associating with people whose Sun is in the sign of Taurus, Cancer, or Scorpio.

People born with the Sun in Gemini, Sagittarius, or Pisces can create problems for them.

Libra

With the scales as the symbol of Libra, people born under this sign are especially interested in balance and equilibrium. They like to know both sides of a question so that they can weigh the pros and cons and arrive at a correct judgment. Because of their tendency not to make hasty decisions, they may seem undecided, but their final decisions will be fair to all concerned. With balance and symmetry so important to them, they make good architects and artists. Beauty in all things is important to them. They know how to dress attractively, have a good color sense, and are very fastidious. They do not like vulgarity nor do they want to get their hands dirty. They are easy to get along with, for they go out of their way to be pleasant. They avoid arguments and try to settle differences reasonably. But they make excellent fighters when there is a strong necessity for quick and drastic action.

Librans live on their nerves to a great extent, so their health is easily disturbed through their surroundings and from associating with uncongenial people. But they respond to treatment very readily. The loins, kidneys, and spinal cord are the sensitive parts of the body. Also, the head, stomach, knees, and ovaries are more easily affected. When these people are thrown off balance, the nerves can easily create digestive trouble. However, the spine and kidneys are the most vulnerable parts. Libra people are naturally moderate in all their activities. They are not likely to eat or drink too much. They have a great deal of vitality but have to learn to use it wisely so that they do not pass certain limits. They usually take everything as easily as possible and avoid strain of all kinds. Their natural good sense gives them a long life.

Libra people have a rather careless attitude toward money,

which is not especially important to them. They quite often dabble in artistic work or take on projects that give them pleasure but that may not be very lucrative. They are fine mathematicians, however, and do most anything with figures. They are not too fond of work, but once money becomes especially important to them, they can become very successful.

These people have a great deal of charm both in writing and speaking. They have an ability to get what they want from people by presenting logical arguments and by appealing to a sense of justice. Their minds are intriguing and they make dangerous opponents in debate. They can often obtain the sympathy of the people who are against them. They may even get what they want by arousing the anger of others.

Librans are not especially domestic, but their charm and pleasant manners make their home life fairly free from strife. They are not likely to show any deep affection for their home, but they seldom separate from their family.

Librans seem to know the feminine mind as well as the masculine, which makes them experts in love. Their wide range of understanding gives them an ability to attract others and to create happy relationships. They easily adapt themselves to the plans and desires of others. They enjoy this ability for conquest because they like playing a part. They can become dabblers in love and may leave a string of broken hearts behind them. They do not seem to have an ability for deep affection, so a long life of happiness with the same person may be denied them. Sometimes they are not happy with the responsibility of marriage, although they know all the ways of pleasing their mates. They are especially tactful, and when serious problems arise, they can avert real trouble through their cleverness.

Libra people are especially interested in and fond of their children. They give them respect and treat them as equals. They have an ability to choose what is best for their offspring. But they do not leave much room for the children to make their own decisions, especially about their careers. This can be detrimental to the children, who may be overly dominated.

As Libra is the sign of marriage and partnership, Librans make good business partners rather than marriage partners. They get along well in business relationships because they are persuasive and will settle differences through friendly discussion rather than force or drastic action. They like to smooth out whatever problems develop without rocking the boat. They have an ability to keep conditions on an even keel. Because of their sense of justice, they make good employers. But sometimes they are too easygoing and their employees take advantage of them.

They are not against new ideas or new methods but are not especially enterprising and can run into difficulties when confronted by strong competition. Money does not seem important enough for the concentrated effort to earn it. Financial or professional pursuits appeal to them more than commercial pursuits. They are fine at work connected with religion, science, or philosophy.

Librans have a great many good qualities, the desire for justice and fair play being the greatest. They stand between the extremes of human character and do much to unite the two under moderate and conservative conditions. They are artistic, interesting, and charming and can soothe hurt feelings and appease anger. Keeping people and conditions in equilibrium does a great deal to avert conflict and unhappiness. They are especially interested in freedom and can become fierce fighters for the rights of the oppressed; restraint is abhorrent to them.

Once of their greatest negative qualities is the tendency to delay decisions or to avoid the responsibility for them. They can also become quite cold and unfeeling, especially in matters of love. And they have to guard against becoming too clever and too sly. The right parental guidance early in life can protect them against such negative qualities.

Libra people are happiest when in association with people who were born under the sign of Gemini, Leo, Sagittarius, or Aquarius.

They do not get along well with people born under the sign of Aries, Cancer, or Capricorn.

Scorpio

People born under the sign of Scorpio are the most determined, reserved, and secretive of all the personalities of the Zodiac. They have very strong characteristics. Once they have formulated a plan of action, they will allow no one and nothing to interfere with their progress. They are inclined to be skeptical and suspicious but are very enterprising and daring. They are very energetic and have a strong reserve force. They like to travel, especially by water. They tend to be blunt and always go right to the point. They are never afraid to call a spade a spade. They tend to be tactless, always speaking their mind even when it can alienate people whose good will they need. They are original, scientific, and creative. Their success often comes through their daring. They are good contractors, chemists, engineers, surgeons, and detectives.

The great vitality of people born under Scorpio usually gives them an especially long life. However, as this sign is related to the reproductive organs of the body, these parts have to be protected against disease. Also, the heart, back, and throat should be guarded. The chemistry of the body can be thrown out of balance especially through overindulgence, bringing on digestive complaints. The various liquid systems of the body should not be neglected.

When Scorpio people are taken sick, they at once concentrate on the cure. They usually go to bed and resort to the strongest treatment possible. They dislike the time wasted in sickness and respond readily to treatment. Whenever possible they will resort to surgery. They never neglect the necessary attention to health.

Scorpio people quite often build up large fortunes through their determination and ability to concentrate on the details of making money. They have an ability to turn everything to their advantage.

They often use their fortunes for the good of humanity, but it has to be used along lines of their choosing.

Of all the signs, Scorpio people are the most passionate in their love life. Their magnetism makes it possible to attract anyone who interests them. They can be a bit selfish and may think more of themselves than of their loved ones. The Scorpio woman will give up everything and everyone for the man she loves.

Scorpio people can have disappointment and problems in marriage when their spouse is also of a strong character. Trouble and divorce are certain to follow. They need mates who are docile and easily ruled to make their marriages successful. Scorpio people like large families and usually have quite a few children. But they do not make especially good parents because they seem to forget that the children have temperaments and characteristics different from their own. They may be strongly devoted to their children, but they expect the children to do just as they wish. They tend to dominate their household and expect to have their desires and plans fulfilled. Children of Scorpio parents often leave home early in life.

Much as in marriage, Scorpio people can have difficulties in business partnerships. They expect and are determined to be the boss of the partnership. People with less strong natures are their best partners, as they are willing to leave the responsibilities to their partners and to attend to the routine affairs.

The foresight of Scorpio people is great, so they can protect themselves against future dangers in business affairs. Their fixity of purpose and energetic determination usually assure them of success in business. But problems often arise through their lack of ability to adapt to circumstances and their refusal to change their mind or decisions. They can lose everything through their stubbornness and their desire to continue along the line they have started.

Scorpio people often have problems in public affairs. They find it difficult to be diplomatic and tactful. They can be too blunt and abrupt to obtain the support and good will of influential people or the public. They tend to take opposition personally and are easily angered. It is difficult for them to see the other person's point of view.

These people make fine research chemists and scientific investigators because of their wide range of knowledge and their ability to concentrate on the important facts involved. They have the patience for experimenting. They usually make better surgeons than doctors because they lack a good bedside manner. They usually know where and how to operate and have the assurance to do so successfully. But they lack a certain amount of sympathy for their patients because of their own disregard for pain.

Scorpio children are usually strong and have a fine constitution. They have much energy and need to be given things to do as an outlet for it. They should be taught to share their possessions so that they do not become selfish. They need a wide education so that they can use their abilities to the greatest extent.

Scorpio people get along well with friends if the relationship is kept on an impersonal level. Close friendships can contain the same problems as marriage or partnership. They are willing to put themselves out for their friends and are always ready to help. But they expect their friends to abide by their advice and plans.

The positive qualities of Scorpio people are their determination, their ability to concentrate, and their energy in carrying things out. Their research ability can do much for humanity, especially in the field of chemistry. Their minds are observant and constructive. Their will power and ability to work long hours lead them to success. Nothing is too much for them once they have set out to reach a goal. They are courageous and daring and always ready to accept a challenge.

The negative Scorpio qualities can make their lives very difficult. They have to learn sympathy for others and have to guard against selfishness. They also have to control their temper, which can be violent.

Scorpio people get along best with people who have the Sun in the sign of Cancer, Virgo, Capricorn, or Pisces.

They are not happy when in close association with people whose Sun is in Taurus, Leo, or Aquarius.

Sagittarius

People born under the sign of Sagittarius are noted for their honesty, candor, and clear vision. They are direct and have little use for people who use subterfuge. Sometimes their habit of telling the truth can hurt the feelings of more sensitive people. They also have a rather rough sense of humor, which creates problems for them.

These people are restless and need much activity, so they often go in for sports and love to be out of doors. Their constitution is rather sensitive and needs this activity. Any restraint put upon it can produce ill health. This sign has rulership over the hips and thighs, so those parts of the body require the most protection. The nervous system, hands, feet, chest, and lungs are also rather easily affected. It is when their nervous energy is depleted that Sagittarians are most likely to become ill. They are subject to accidents to the hands, hips, or feet. Their quick movements make them prone to accidents. However, their good judgment deters them from taking risks just for the sake of thrills. They have a good deal of reserve power because they can relax so easily and so completely, even for short periods. Because they tend to scatter their forces, they do not recover from sickness as quickly as people born under other signs. But, barring accidents, they usually live long lives. Their cheerfulness and calmness help them to stay young well into old age.

These people are especially clear thinkers, and their reasoning ability gives them foresight. They are direct in thought and always ready to argue a point. But they are usually willing to accede defeat rather than quarrel. They handle big problems well, but small annoyances give them trouble. They are sensitive to their surroundings and to the people with whom they are involved. They have a strong intuition and should follow their hunches.

They enjoy conversation and are good at it but may often digress from their topic for the use of humor. Their sense of humor is very fine and quite unpredictable.

Sagittarians are well fitted for the financial world as they act swiftly and usually hit the mark. But their generosity is great and they do not like people to pay for them at restaurants or public entertainments. They usually reach for the check first. "Give and spend, and God will send" is an apt motto for them. They make successful bankers and financiers. But they do have to guard against allowing their expansive ideas to lead them into overreaching themselves.

Their ability to seize opportunities, their good judgment, and their active energy make Sagittarians good in the business world. Commercial pursuits are good for them and they enjoy meeting the competition involved. But their dislike of small details and the monotony of the daily routine do not make them good clerks. Their good humor, optimism, and ability to get along with people make them good in politics. They are also well fitted for business partnerships.

Although Sagittarians may avoid people who they may feel are beneath them, in sports they will associate with all on the same level. They will lend a helping hand to those who are in trouble or who are being treated unfairly. Social reforms interest them, and they are useful in such activities. Their good judgment protects them from becoming involved in radical movements.

Sagittarians are interested in religion, the law, and philosophy. They enjoy learning and imparting knowledge to others. They make good teachers, lawyers, and professional people. Teaching comes easy to them, and they do best in the teaching of philosophy. College-level teaching is best for them because young children often arouse their impatience. In religion, they are more interested in helping their parishioners than in the strict interpretation of the Scriptures.

It is difficult for Sagittarians to be especially successful in love. Their frankness and sincerity too easily injure the feelings of their loved ones. They often begin relationships hastily and rush into engagements that they regret later. As they find it difficult to lie at the marriage ceremony, they are likely to break the engagement. But if his woman understands him, the Sagittarian man makes an excellent and devoted husband. A woman of this sign is like the deer: always ready to run away. It is difficult to pin her down to a yes or no answer.

The Sagittarian dislike for restrictions of any kind often makes them difficult partners. They cannot stand jealousy or feeling possessed and may become irritable and sarcastic. But they try to make the best of the bargain. Although they are not likely to enter into emotional relationships with others, they can cause scandal rather easily.

The positive qualities of these people are many, and one of the best of these is their ability to brighten up the lives of their associates. People who are depressed should associate with Sagittarians. Their cheerfulness helps to begin the day. Their directness always lets people know just where they stand and what they can expect from them. When they have the best of the sign, they are a joy to the world.

Their negative qualities are a bit difficult to take. They can be very irresponsible. They may make promises that are never fulfilled and may disregard important meetings. Their dislike of details makes them rush into activities without reading directions or making any necessary preparations. They can be very impatient over small matters. And they may be quite intolerant.

Sagittarian children are very active, both mentally and physically. They should be given pets at an early age, especially horses, if that is possible. They are usually healthy unless carelessly fed. They should be guided rather than forced and should be given plenty of freedom.

Sagittarians get along best with people born under the sign of Aries, Leo, Libra, or Aquarius.

They are not happy when in association with people who were born under the sign of Gemini, Virgo, or Pisces.

Capricorn

People born under the sign of Capricorn are noted for their tremendous energy, industry, and attention to detail. As this is the most ambitious sign of the Zodiac, Capricorn people are willing to put forth every effort to fulfill their goals. They have the patience to work long hours and to accept responsibility. They are scrupulous and conscientious and know how to take advantage of every opportunity. Sometimes they lack imagination, so they do not use the daring moves that are often necessary to success. They have a great deal of initiative and may leap over obstacles instead of trying to force them out of the way. They get along on very little and know how to use and reuse whatever they have. Capricorn women usually buy clothes for their lasting quality and know how to make changes in them to keep them up to date.

Capricorn rules the bony parts of the body, especially the knees, so that people born under this sign are subject to rheumatism. This makes it necessary to avoid colds, if possible. Also, their liking for hot, spicy food can affect their digestion. Sometimes, when obstacles seem unsurmountable and they become depressed, they may drink too much. They have to fight depression. But their strong constitution helps them to resist disease. They can stand a great deal of physical hardship. As with Leo and Sagittarius, they usually live long.

In financial affairs, Capricorns are very careful and seldom take any risks. Sometimes they are penny wise and pound foolish, so large amounts may slip through their fingers. As they do not like to gamble, their fortunes are usually built on hard work and savings. They are the best people to handle money for others, if protection from loss is the most important factor. But they are not likely to produce any large or spectacular gains. They always make full reports, and every penny is accounted for.

Capricorn people are usually quite domesticated and are not the sort to leave home early in life. They go along with the rules and regulations laid down by their parents as the natural course.

The materialistic side of their nature quite often clashes with their romantic feelings. They are inclined to seek some advantage to their personal goals in addition to affection. Capricorn people need and want affection but have difficulty in showing their true feelings. They are more mental than emotional in romance and always very conventional. They are not the sort to dabble in love but are serious and determined. Once they have chosen their life companion, they will lose no time in marrying.

To outsiders, they may seem rather cold in the home, but they have a depth of affection that restrains them from outside affairs. They show their affection by what they do for their loved ones more than by what they say. Sometimes they seek to dominate in their families, and their restraint in demonstrating affection may make their children feel unloved. But they will make sacrifices for their loved ones and never neglect their wants or needs. Capricorn women need the security of a home, and once it is obtained, they expand and all their good qualities come to the fore.

Capricorn people are likely to have trouble in business partnerships. Their intelligence is usually greater than that of their partners, and they find it necessary to make the important decisions, which they expect to be followed. They are all business, which makes them seem unsympathetic to their partners. They always do their best work when they do not have to rely on others to explain their actions.

Usually, Capricorns measure the success of a venture by the money it brings. They like the power of money and will work tirelessly to obtain it. Starting at the bottom does not dismay them, as they know they have the ability to reach the top even if it takes a long time. They thrive on responsibility and are always given more of it as they move upward. Their ability to handle routine affairs and their grasp of details make them valuable. They are not bothered that their close attention to work does not make them popular with co-workers; for Capricorns, career comes first. It is more important to be popular with the people in power. They are never daunted by tedious or difficult tasks.

They are well fitted for political careers. They can be very diplomatic and have a fine memory. But they do have some difficulty making voters like them. They do best as the political power behind the scenes.

Capricorns have a great many positive qualities that help them to be successful. Their persistence, honesty, and determination are usually easily recognized. Without any rocking of the boat, they go about their work in a practical and serious manner. Their good points inspire confidence. They make fine administrators and executors and carry out whatever rules are laid down without argument. They have an ability to avoid many of the pitfalls that less intelligent people fall into. Many of the leaders of the world have a strong Capricorn influence, especially some of the most wealthy. And, in spite of their serious nature, they have a good sense of humor, which often comes to their aid.

Perhaps their most negative quality is the danger of allowing their ambition to make them cold and inconsiderate of others. They can be overcritical and bossy. They may be very disagreeable to people who they feel are beneath them. They should learn to show more warmth and friendliness. When their finances are involved, they can be stingy and bent upon acquiring a fortune under any circumstances. Capricorn people can avoid many problems by cultivating kindness, consideration, optimism, and generosity.

Capricorns get along best with people who are born with the Sun in the sign of Taurus, Virgo, Scorpio, or Pisces.

There can be problems of a serious nature when they are in close association with people born with the Sun in Aries, Cancer, or Libra.

Aquarius

Aquarius is an air sign, like Gemini and Libra, and a fixed mode or quality, like Taurus, Leo, and Scorpio. It is active and courageous, masculine and forward-looking, with Uranus as its ruler and Saturn as its co-ruler. Symbolically the waters pouring out of the urn represent the flow of wisdom, knowledge, and love, with which the heavens enrich human existence. If humanity achieves perfection, many astrologers believe, it will come through Aquarius in one way or another. Aquarius is usually ready to give serious consideration to new ideas and revolutionary approaches, opening up new paths and new ways. In that, Aquarius is most of the time in advance of the normal pace of progress. This is especially true when considering innovations intended to help people, reduce hardships, or lead to greater justice. But *intentions* are not guarantees, and the Aquarian can be taken in by spurious Utopias that bring about the very opposite of what is sought or promised. If misunderstood, Aquarians can be seen as quixotic, unpredictable, eccentric, even fanatic. But considered with balance, compassion, and wisdom, they are ahead of the times, ingenious, and sincerely dedicated to the betterment of society.

Aquarius rules the ankles and shins and strongly influences the circulatory system and the nervous system. The relationship with the ankles suggests the Aquarian urge to move forward to the exploration and merging into a new age. How important this rulership can be may be realized by modern medical studies. "A person walks about three miles a day, landing some 20,000 times on each foot with a force triple that of the body weight," according to Dr. John F. Waller, Jr., head of the Foot and Ankle Department of the Lenox Hill Hospital, New York. "A foot problem can throw your musculoskeleton alignment completely out of whack and cause pain in almost every part of your body." The circulatory and nervous systems link every part of the Aquarian body and mind to the physical ability to move forward, to advance, even to imagine and visualize what lies ahead.

Physical and intellectual facets of Aquarius are intimately linked. Though moving from group to group, from situation to situation, Aquarians constantly observe social structures and behavior patterns. Manipulating people in a benign way is not unusual with Aquarians, and they have a talent for amiable fraternization. Inherent, too, is the giving and the accepting of unaffected and sincere friendship and companionship, particularly with a wide and contrasting set of individuals. Clear and honest communication is the key to such relationships, and Aquarians are gifted in this area. Generally, Aquarius people are popular, well liked, and respected. Insincerity, snobbery, and sham are very rarely found among them. Motives are normally pure, objectives altruistic.

All these qualities should make the Aquarian an ideal business partner or associate in some financial enterprise. But it does not always work out so, for Aquarians do not measure success in dollars and cents. Nor, in artistic ventures, do they attach much importance to the usual concept of fame and fortune and blind acclaim. Inner satisfaction in doing something good, something positive, something beneficial to others as well as oneself—such are the criteria by which Aquarians live. In a positive sense the Aquarian is an individualist who has developed certain high standards and rules to live by, and will do so in spite of outside pressures and temptations.

Aquarians are sturdy and strong, not only physically but also in an inner sense; this moral quality seems to maintain them in good health. They are wiry, energetic, hard-working, and constantly full of ideas and plans and ambitions—none of them in any sense reflecting selfishness or self-aggrandizement. Seemingly self-effacing, the Aquarian should not be mistaken for a weakling, especially where ideals, motives, and social problems are involved. Aquarians will stand up resolutely in defense of justice and their ideals. Indeed, they are ready to accept martyrdom for the good of humanity, as they conceive that social good. Certainly there are areas in which Aquarius is not to be trifled with.

Though Aquarius people are usually outgoing, cheerful, and optimistic in outlook, enabling them to establish good relations socially, quiet, pensive moods are not absent. But such spells are not sad. Aquarians are often thoughtful and concerned with social events or goals. Yet so much personal energy is expended in social interests that friendships and affectionate relations are taken for granted and not expressed openly. Thus Aquarians are often considered aloof, perhaps even cold, in person-to-person relations. They are far from it. Lacking most prejudices, they are more often warm and friendly and compassionate. Seldom do Aquarians make prejudgments; usually they remain loyal friends in spite of odds and make excuses for the shortcomings of others. They get along well with a wide variety of people. Often some of their associates may appear strange to the world. Aquarians, however, are usually blithely unaware of anything unusual about their friends. Admirable though this quality may be on occasion, Aquarians do get taken in by plausible "hard-luck" stories and are often victimized.

Aquarians in love may display an exciting surge of energy that invariably impresses the opposite sex. With unusually wide-ranging interests vying for attention, they may not always be consistent or reliable. Personal freedom is important in their life and outlook, and there is a natural, and normal, resistance to all kinds of pressures. The impression might be given that Aquarians are not the "marrying kind," but such an impression would be erroneous. Aquarians need a special relationship, one without any hint of coercion, based on affection freely given and accepted without any strings or qualifications. Though love can be passionate and intense, and marriage wholly dedicated and profound, Aquarian love always has a sense of nonexclusivity, always ready to reach out to love—in a different, less personal way—the rest of the world.

Happy associations for Aquarius people result from the ties that develop between them, and they do well with people whose Sun signs are Gemini, Libra, Aries, and Sagittarius.

Some difficulties may develop with people whose Sun is in Scorpio, Taurus, or Leo; but basically all relations may be what the Aquarian strives to make them.

Pisces

People born under the sign of Pisces are impressionable, psychic, and somewhat dualistic in nature. At times they are too easily influenced, but they do have an ability to fathom the motives of others. They may seem a bit discontented, as their success may never quite match their dreams and desires. They react through their emotions and may delve into psychic subjects and strange religious beliefs. They are artistic and enjoy beautiful and comfortable surroundings. They can be quite unpredictable, which makes them interesting and fun to be with.

The sign Pisces rules the feet, so such people are especially subject to gout or other foot troubles. But the fluids of the body are also easily affected, so that dropsy should be guarded against. They should not associate with people who are ill, as they too easily attract the sicknesses of others. It is best for them not to use strong medicine except on the advice of a physician. They need much reassurance when they are ill.

Pisces people tend to be careless with money, so their financial affairs are often quite troublesome. Their generosity is great, but they use it unwisely and people take advantage of them. They are trustworthy with the money of others, but their judgment is not always reliable. They have to use more discrimination in their use of money. It is quite difficult for them to save and to build up an estate. They do not seem to care enough about money.

These people make good speakers and writers, for they are eloquent and fluent. They create a great deal of pleasure for others and may be the life of the party. They are good storytellers and clever mimics.

Pisces people are especially domesticated and are often petted and spoiled by parents and friends. Their ambition does not lead them into leaving home early in life, and their adaptability makes it easy for them to follow the family rules and regulations. They are always pleasant and easygoing but may not be very helpful at home.

These people are romantic and have no trouble attracting partners who arouse their interest. They are very devoted and placid and may show too much affection for their loved ones. They do not start affairs very readily but are easily attracted by the charms of others.

Pisces people are contented and happy in marriage. They enjoy comfort and beauty in the home, but they may not make a very great effort to secure them. Their emotional quality is such that they are always ready for love. They are placid and never start trouble in their homes.

In business partnerships, they do best as silent partners, leaving the actual decisions and important actions for others to handle. They do not want to bother with details and are perfectly happy to put in their money and leave the rest to their partners.

They also tend to take public affairs with an easy lack of attention. They do not especially want to accept responsibility but can do so very efficiently when the need arises. They may not exert themselves in business and are often taken advantage of by their employees. They are too generous.

A natural sympathy and a desire to be of service to others make Pisces people especially suited for welfare work, nursing, teaching, and activities that bring help to troubled people. Their perception and insight into people are important factors in any pursuits they follow. All lines of work that require charm and the ability to get along with others can produce success for them. They can make good in television, the stage, radio, or the movies. Dancing and music are also important to them. They are fine entertainers. Their artistic talent and imagination help them to become fine painters. They often do not set any goal in life for themselves but allow circumstances to rule their actions.

In religion, Pisces people are inclined to mystical beliefs and ceremonious forms that appeal to the emotions. Their sympathy and desire to aid others make them good priests and ministers. They can be clairvoyant.

Pisces people make fine friends and usually have a great many of them in all walks of life. But they can be oversolicitious and too helpful when it is not necessary. They are the best of all people to cheer up their friends.

Pisces children should be taught to be more self-confident and not to allow their playmates to take advantage of them. They should be taught to fight for their rights instead of just feeling hurt. They are good and truthful and easily surprised when their companions are not. They have to learn to assert themselves and not allow others to influence them. These children should be given a good education and college, if possible, as this will teach them to learn their importance in the world.

Some of the fine qualities of these people are their sympathy, their desire to help others, and their insight into the problems of others. They are tolerant, broad-minded, and seldom critical. Sometimes they are too generous. They can make others feel good, and their cheerfulness is inspiring to troubled hearts. They are trustworthy and not likely to betray a confidence. They love home and family and tend to spoil all for whom they are responsible. They make the most interesting companions for all the signs.

What few negative qualities Pisces people have work to their own disadvantage. They can allow themselves to be too easily influenced. They are ruled by their feelings and emotions. They can become sorry for themselves and become takers. Once their self-confidence is strengthened, they can be successful.

Pisces people are happiest when in association with people whose Sun signs are Taurus, Cancer, Scorpio, and Capricorn. People with the Sun signs Gemini, Virgo, and Sagittarius can create problems for them.

(V)
Love and Marriage

ARIES WOMAN—ARIES MAN

A tempestuous relationship in the stars. Two people who can't help wanting to be the boss, full of energy, full of ideas and enthusiasm, full of themselves. It is likely to be pretty wearing on the participants and anyone else in earshot.

And there isn't much chance that either of these high-strung people will give in, settle down, and play second fiddle. As the years go by, experience will mellow the partners, but not a lot! He's not impressed by pushy women; he needs encouragement and love, but this woman is of course unlikely to provide them, except in bursts when she realizes that if she doesn't let the brute have his way, then life will be total chaos instead of only half chaos.

The energy of his partner will stimulate, excite, and challenge the Arian male. The biggest problem is that neither has much humility. They rarely admit to being wrong and are too busy living to actually settle down and discover what life can really be about.

Sexually, they will have no trouble, lots of excitement and variation, and real passion at times. Financially, watch out! Arians like to make money fast—not for them the plodding methods of some of their colleagues. They must learn to keep a watch on the family finances if it isn't to be bread and cheese at the end of each month. They can be remarkably thrifty—they don't really care what they eat as long as they can wolf it down and feel full—but suddenly they will do something unbelievably extravagant. It's fantastic fun at the time, but it doesn't exactly make for a stable life style.

The Aries woman isn't much more tactful than her male counterpart. In fact, she can be downright rude, highly critical, and im-

155

patient in the extreme. He wants the world and he wants it now! But he's passionate, loves physical exercise, and needs it. There's a lot of generosity, humor, and empathy in this partnership, and it could last, but in the long run these two Arians had perhaps better seek their soulmates elsewhere. Sticking together could prove just too much when there are so many other exciting men and women in the world just waiting to be loved and bedded—at least that's how our "heroes" see it in their heart of hearts.

To begin with it's just like soulmates meeting—how else could it be?—but the sheer intensity of the loving probably won't last.

ARIES WOMAN—TAURUS MAN

A recipe for disaster—but who knows, this relationship could just turn out to be the exception, the miracle that confounds all the experts.

The slow, steady, responsible, honest, romantic Taurus man will be swept off his feet by the dynamic, restless, intermittently passionate, demanding, bossy Aries woman. She'll drive him wild and he'll drive her to distraction. He's jealous, at times very difficult, but this lady couldn't care less. She'll leave him standing there fuming while she seeks new pastures and new ideas and challenges. What can poor Taurus do but love her? She's so different, so stimulating, that his poor old head will hurt; he'll wish he could find a nice quiet girl, but when she's not around he'll be bored and continually looking over his shoulder.

Sexually, things could go well. Taurus is demanding and earthy and enjoys the best. Aries can match him in short bursts but isn't really built for a marathon—and we're talking about life style, now, not just about sex.

Both are likely to have artistic aspirations, and he may have a real talent for interior decoration, home design, and that sort of thing. His partner is likely to be too busy to stay at home much and she wouldn't be found dead making curtains or knitting. This is not pleasing for Taurus, who puts great emphasis on a strong, reliable home life. Meals—so important to this man—are unlikely to be ready on time if she does the cooking, although when the food does eventually turn up, it could be remarkable, not least for its ingredients but occasionally for its excellence.

The problem is that Taurus easily gets set in his ways, in fact *wants* to get set in his ways. This lady is unlikely ever to really settle down; there's too much to do, experience, be—too much to learn and enjoy in the great wonderful world. She might get hooked on a steady guy like this on the rebound, but in most cases both partners would be well advised to think very carefully.

It could just happen these two will fall for each other and nothing on earth will shake the relationship one iota. He'll think she's the greatest thing that ever moved and she'll wonder how she ever managed without him. The implication is, of course, that two worldly, experienced people born under these signs have a much greater chance of making things zing than young lovers who will be too selfish.

ARIES WOMAN—GEMINI MAN

It could work—it could be great fun, and for a change Aries is the one who's going to have to do the catching. The Gemini man is mentally like a will-o'-the-wisp. Routine is death to him, and that suits her. He'll be tremendously impressed by her energy, forthrightness, and honesty of emotions, but at the same time she's going to have to put up with his capriciousness, occasional nastiness, and charm. The charm is spread around pretty liberally in most cases, and Aries will have to resist her urge to walk out and never come back—provided, of course, that she's made up her mind this fellow is for her.

He's very good for her because no one else in the Zodiac is going to force her to face facts, resist her intolerant nature, and put up with so much. She might just finish up a much more rounded, tolerant, nice person—if she survives it all.

Gemini is industrious, in his way, which means he concentrates in short bursts and cannot stand routine. This goes for his woman too, but she can be more practical when it is necessary—and it is certainly going to be necessary with this fellow.

He's so gay, amusing, and clever that she's a pushover. Arians aren't exactly backward when it comes to bedtime, but don't be too disappointed if he doesn't take you seriously enough. It can be quite an experience for a passionate Arian lady to be trapped by a cunning Gemini. Aries isn't too good at understanding other people—mostly she doesn't have time for it—but this guy is a born psychologist, even if his final conclusions are a trifle light on logic. This is the sort of man who has exam technique rather than really knowing his subject.

Aries is a sportswoman who loves the outdoors and competitive games, and loves to win. Gemini will probably walk off court, throw his golf clubs in the stream, or give it up to study a cloud or flower that takes his fancy. It's no contest—after all, how can anyone play with someone who just won't compete on fair terms?

Don't underestimate this man. He's very smart, and he knows it, but he isn't built for a long haul; he's a sprinter. Understand this and the secret of a successful relationship with him is half revealed. The other half? Only experience brings understanding; that's something even the stars can't provide. If it turns out to be a short-term relationship, at least it'll be fun while it lasts.

ARIES WOMAN—CANCER MAN

This is potentially a difficult partnership because the Cancer man will demand more than the Aries woman is likely to be prepared to give. He's a really rather nice person, sensitive, defensive, dreamy, romantic. No one's ever called *her* nice. She's demanding, infuriating, and difficult—but utterly fascinating.

This man is a poser. He pretends, camouflages, retreats, backtracks, and deliberately confuses. The forthright Aries woman is likely to find gamesmanship much too much for her. Her idea of winning is to charge in, head down, and sweep away the opposition. He'll circle the target, weigh up the pros and cons, and only after a great deal of procrastination slip in with a knife.

He's emotional—not a great thinker but a great feeler. He's bright, gay, amusing, charming. He's also the home-loving protective type, and Lord knows Aries doesn't need that. She can look after herself better than any other sign in the Zodiac. Oh, by the way, he's moody too, a brooder who mulls over suspected insults for days. Aries couldn't care less unless she's hit by a brick, and even then the brick will probably crumble. She isn't exactly sensitive, although there's nothing vindictive or small-minded about this lady. She loves a scrap, and Cancer isn't going to give her one. He's possessive and strong in his love of tradition, but if he really cares, he'll go a long way to hell for his woman.

She should try to get him out of his dream world of art, music, and books, and get him interested in something—a hobby, building something. He isn't ambitious really, not the way she is anyway, so he's got to be gently pushed into things. And he's very sensitive—not in a make-believe way—and might well drink too much to cover his inferiority complex. But he is likely to be a deeply satisfying, very considerate lover.

Aries should add up the pros and cons, and then decide that unless he's rich or it's quite impossible to live without him, perhaps he's not for her. Incidentally, he'll probably hate her clothes, buddies, home decoration, mother, and smugness. Quite a few Aries ladies become bitchy in their later years because although they seldom get discouraged by life, they do get a bit cynical. This lady looks good, but in fact she isn't quite the bargain she believes she is. Cancer is probably too sensitive to tangle with her—or is he?

ARIES WOMAN—LEO MAN

Wow! Fire meets fire in what could be a head-on conflict—or very possibly a terrifically successful and rewarding relationship. At the very least it'll be stimulating, dynamic, and passionate.

Attraction is likely to be instantaneous. Leo is the man for this lady. Proud, commanding, demanding, generous, egotistical. Aries is arrogant, full of life, restless, infuriating.

What's it all going to produce? That depends on whether Aries is prepared to sublimate some of her energy to him. If she can surrender at times, accept him as the boss, then all will be well. The problems will arise when he doesn't quite live up to her expectations—what man could?—and then he'll feel her scorn. Leo won't like that; he'll respond and bingo, a fight that would leave most people prostrate for weeks is in progress. And amazingly both partners as often as not will emerge from it unscathed. In the long run this lady is just a bit tougher than her man, but they understand each other pretty well.

The way to get round Leo is to flatter him. It doesn't matter how outrageously. He'll know what's going on, but he'll still lap it up. He'll positively beam when he's complimented on everything from his tie to his genius. He knows it's all true. Aries is going to find it difficult, but if she wants him, then she has to put a little work in. He's got to handle her restlessness delicately, keep her occupied, dream up things for her to do, and every so often express profound appreciation. She doesn't want flattery, but she does want to be appreciated and loved and told about it from time to time.

Lovemaking is likely to be on a big scale; there's nothing petty about these two. Both are leaders. But she should keep a close rein on him when other women are around. He doesn't mean to be unfaithful; he just can't resist an attractive female. Be a little tolerant; he's probably worth it.

Aries selfishness is well known—how could the first sign of the Zodiac be anything else?—but with practice it can be disguised. He should realize that it isn't necessary to keep telling people he is the best.

This will be a hell of a relationship whether it lasts a short time or forever. And woe betide whoever comes between a pair like this who really care.

ARIES WOMAN—VIRGO MAN

On the surface this is not too promising, but in fact these two could make a formidable combination. The Virgoan precision, devotion, modesty, and honesty might just combine well with the Arian generosity, excitement, need for experience, and, quite honestly, rather selfish nature.

This pair is likely to enjoy traveling, and if he looks after the cash and makes the arrangements while she intuitively heads for the high mountains or persuades him that the desert is just the place for sunbathing, then trips could be decidedly stimulating.

He's a thinker; she's a doer. He's cool and methodical. She's aggressive and spontaneous. Of course, they could drive each other wild, but with a little common sense, each might see the other's virtues without taking too much account of failings and foibles.

He can be critical or even cruel at times, but he is a giver. If he loves the lady he really will want to serve, to be there to mop her fevered brow and put away her shoes cast aside by the bed. Sexually, he may well be more loving than passionate. He'd probably make a lovely monk, whereas Aries would make a terrible nun. She'd try to run the convent in no time flat and would be certain to get booted out.

The difficult time is likely to come when this woman wants a new dress and Virgo decides they can't afford it. She'll probably slip out—Arians like to think they're sneaky and cunning, while they're so obvious it's ridiculous—and buy the dress anyway, and Virgo will do his nut. She'll tell him where he can go, and he'll sulk. Making up will be fun, and he's certain to forgive her because secretly he admires her free and easy ways, which he'll never be able to emulate. But—and it's a big *but*—there are going to be some pretty heavy times for this loving couple.

Aries has to resist flying into a tantrum when things don't go just as she wants. She has to learn to listen to him—he doesn't miss much, this guy—and he is a most balanced character, partly because he does see both sides of things. Really there would be a better chance of a successful partnership for a Virgo woman and an Aries man; but if the Aries woman and Virgo man get over the first period, then there's no doubt that they make a most attractive combination.

She should try to tempt him to take part in sport or activities that draw him out of himself. He'll probably win too, because Virgos are pretty good at most things they take up.

ARIES WOMAN—LIBRA MAN

Libra men make great lovers but are not noted for their faithfulness. They live life to the full, are very attractive to women, and play around. Libra has a lot of virtues, but a relationship with this sort of man may be rather one-sided.

Aries isn't the easiest character in the Zodiac to get on with because she's restless, dynamic, difficult to pin down at times. But Libra is going to really give her a taste of her own medicine. He isn't just a playboy, though. He's easygoing and charming, and hates fighting with his partner. He's a romantic, hearts-and-flowers type, artistic and poetic. He's also a great believer in fair play and justice for the underdog. Usually he is a well-mannered individual, dresses nicely, and responds to reason. There's no way this fellow is going to be bossed around, and of course Aries is one lady who likes her own way and likes to run everything. She is a great organizer—it comes naturally; it's not forced as it sometimes is with Leos.

If she's going to make things go smoothly, then she is going to have to read between the lines of Libra's blandishments, his sweet talk, and his promises, and in turn she's going to have to be careful in her treatment of him. That's not easy for an Arian, who is often blunt to the point of rudeness.

Both partners tend to rush into things, so these two should think carefully about a long-term relationship. Librans are great for summer romances and for holding hands in nightclubs. Only some of them are ready to settle down—and he might not be one of this breed. He's a great one for experienceing everything that's going. But he's also a bit of a coward. Aries will never walk away from a scrap, verbal or physical. Libra is likely to walk out on her because he doesn't like anyone to be unhappy or unpleasant. He isn't a coward, but he just might not be there when she needs him. However, if anyone really tries to down his woman, watch the sparks fly.

Sexually, he plays at love. He can't resist that elusive thing called glamour, so he might just find it somewhere else. Aries shouldn't plan to settle down with Libra unless he's actually bought the wedding ring, paid for the honeymoon, put all the rest of his money down as a deposit on the house, and invited his mother to the church. And even then, don't be too sure—he might meet someone he fancies on the way to the altar.

ARIES WOMAN—SCORPIO MAN

This is likely to be a real slap-bang affair with not much quarter given or granted. It's likely to be a heavy scene when Scorpio starts to take over Aries and she puts her foot down, probably heavily on his hand.

He's a man of strong passions, a jealous, at times vindictive type. He is deeply sexual, often in the best way, but when thwarted his passion runs so deep that he won't be able to control it. Real love will make him turn all his attentions on his woman. And he wants her to look good, feel good, and be good. Aries is strong enough most of the time to keep enough independence. The one thing she must not do is get under Scorpio's thumb—she has to tread a delicate line between being subservient and flighty. Can it be done? Who knows? All things are possible in love and war, and this partnership may well be both at the same time.

Scorpio is a deeply faithful man with a strange mystical turn of mind. His home is most important to him; it's where he can collapse after a trying day. The problem is that Aries is no homebody—she's one for getting out and about. Not many Arians are caught at home for long, and they have an unfortunate tendency to forget to cook meals—Scorpio, like Taurus, doesn't like that sort of thing. Aries doesn't like to be pinned down too much, so this could be a distinct problem. He'll admire his woman's drive and stamina, but he isn't too good at complimenting the Arian woman, who responds much better to encouragement than criticism. Some Scorpios are past masters of the wounding word or phrase. If he tries it on Aries, he might just get his dinner in his face. But it'll be fun making up afterward when the fury has gone and the passion remains.

He's a complex sort of guy, probably too much so for the basically simple Arian. She hasn't the time to be cunning or vindictive. Scorpios are good at games like chess. They plan their conquests coldly and logically and realistically. She won't understand what the devil he's on about half the time.

On the whole this seems likely to be a difficult relationship; it could be rewarding if both partners can put up with its intensity, but it would be a lot easier leavened with a little humor and just plain everyday niceness. That could be too much to ask for, however, and in that case life might be more fulfilling apart. Perhaps this pair should take separate vacations, although Scorpio will resist the very idea.

ARIES WOMAN—SAGITTARIUS MAN

Things will never be dull when this fellow is around—and that suits the Aries woman to the ground. She's a person who loves change, novelty, and excitement, and he can't help exuding it the way some men ooze charm.

There's little doubt that these two will get on famously. He needs lots of freedom—he hasn't the time to be jealous—and she is ideal for him, provided she uses her basic common sense to limit him to just one crazy idea a day. He's endlessly stimulating, but she'd better keep her fingers clutched tightly on the family purse.

He's fun, charming, exciting to be with. He probably knows lots of people and has lots of contacts. He could be artistic in a revolutionary sort of way—not many Sagittarians like to be trapped in the conventional artistic mold. And many of them finish up doing remarkable jobs in the sense that no one else would have thought of earning a living that way or been nutty enough to make a success of it.

This is the sort of man who'll casually mention on the way out one Saturday that he's going sky-diving, and he'll be gone before his partner can even start to wail. It's impossible to be angry with him for long too, because he performs with an innocence and honesty that are just too beguiling. And this after he's been flirting and behaving outrageously with every pretty girl around! He's quite a challenge. Aries might just decide she's going to tame him. She probably won't succeed, but then if she did, she'd be sure to move on fast. The only way to beat this guy is by being subtle, and that's something Arians take a long time to learn even the rudiments of. On the whole she's too nice for this guy, but Arians are sometimes a little masochistic.

He could be a gambler—and what's worse, a lucky one. He won't be as interested in sports and physical activity as his partner, except in bed, but he won't try to stop her from doing what she wants.

One of the nice things about Sagittarians is that they seem to be at home just as much in a mansion or a palace as in a garret or a cellar. Everything they touch seems to end up with their own style imprinted on it, and this isn't the same as the way Aries turns everything to her will. Sagittarius has a lighter, more delicate touch. When comparing these two, it's a bit like watching a butterfly and a bird, and no prizes for guessing who is who.

ARIES WOMAN—CAPRICORN MAN

Capricorn is a cautious fellow, so this is much more likely to be what the world calls a serious affair than a flirtation. This may not suit the lively Aries woman, but then again she might just love the guy. If that's the case, there's a good chance that despite the inevitable battles this would be a good relationship.

He's ambitious, serious, and industrious. He might find this lady too extravagant, too independent, too . . . well, too everything! But this is a smart guy—if a strifle slow and stolid at times—and he's likely to recognize a good thing when he sees it.

He's a direct, straightforward type, and Aries is nothing if not basic. At times he might start feeling a bit sorry for himself, so this is where his lady can come in to cheer him up and spread a little light and joy around. He'll admire her drive and initiative, her interest in the new. He likes things organized so he can understand them, and the speed with which Aries moves at time will leave him bewildered. He's likely to be a direct, possibly rather unspontaneous lover at times, but he really does mean well. He'll keep this lady on the straight and narrow—as much as anyone can.

Every so often there'll be a terrific quarrel, a real beaut, but things will cool down and in the long run both partners will see that it was necessary to clear the air.

She's going to respect his ambitions but not his clinging to the past and his determination to do the right, noble thing, the legal thing, whatever the cost. In this way the volatile Arian woman is in fact more practical than her man, strangely enough. If both partners are prepared to appreciate the other's virtues and to make excuses for each other's faults, this could be an ongoing relationship. This pair could make a formidable partnership, not least on the tennis court or bridge table, because there is a real chance that they will complement each other. Incidentally there aren't likely to be many compliments from them for each other or their friends or opponents. Aries in particular tends to learn by experience, and sometimes that experience comes hard.

One thing is certain: He expects his woman to be interested in his career, and it doesn't matter whether he's a banker, a garbage man, or a film producer; he expects support and encouragement. Any holding back in this area will be fatal to the relationship.

ARIES WOMAN—AQUARIUS MAN

There's a curious lack of emotion about the Aquarian man, and Aries is likely to see him more as a challenge than anything else. That isn't to say he can't be damnably attractive. He's cool, almost hip, eccentric, sometimes even bizarre—but he's also fascinating and at times dreamily withdrawn. He wants to make the world a better place for everyone, and when his missionary zeal is aroused he can be a bit impractical and decidedly extravagant. The extravagant Arian is going to have to rein in her own spendthrift nature if finances are to be kept within even striking distance of what they should be, judged by earnings.

There is a tendency for him to change jobs, move around. He loves traveling. Even more than Aries, he looks to the future, demands originality. Even in the humblest home there are likely to be sudden rare and strange touches of brilliance. This element of detachment won't be easy for his woman to put up with. She is impulsive, not only in love and sex. She wants things to happen, to surprise her. This guy will certainly do that, but probably not in the way she expects or even wants.

He won't be easy to live with, but then Arians rarely expect or want an easy life, so this relationship could be successful, provided neither expects the other to be at home when he or she arrives. Meals unprepared or uneaten could be a continuous bone of contention. And she's going to have to put up with his remarkable friends dropping in at any time of the day or night, his curious failure to be on time for a date or meeting, and his refusal to get as involved as perhaps she wants on anything but his own terms.

Home life is not likely to be a rest cure where this pair is concerned, but it is going to be mentally stimulating, though at times others will wonder what happened to the emotion. Aquarius is highly inventive; his mind works fast. He isn't as good as Aries at appearing to know everything about everything while in fact knowing practically nothing about everything, but he's got his pride and isn't going to be put down by her.

This fellow is no snob and certainly not a prude. If he can be taught to be just a little more discriminating when it comes to friends or emotions, then she will probably put up with his coolness. In turn Aries has to slow down a bit and take things at walking pace sometimes—and he'll be there smiling in a friendly, unassuming way.

ARIES WOMAN—PISCES MAN

An intriguing, infuriating, and potentially successful relationship is likely to blossom from a meeting between these two. On the surface it should probably be a disastrous contradiction of characters, but in practice Pisces will be drawn even against his apparent will to this lady, and she will be continually delighted and exasperated by him—just the thing to keep an Arian lady interested.

She's never going to understand his dreamy, otherworldly, mysterious romanticism. But neither will he ever quite believe that anyone can be so confident, pushy, and excitingly stimulating.

The Piscean needs lots of compliments—never, never criticize—and a lot of understanding of his incredibly rapid change of moods, the way emotion sweeps him away, the churning he gets in his stomach while Aries soldiers on. It's no use expecting to reason out how he is going to act in any situation—he himself doesn't know. He's intuitive, possibly inclined toward religion or the occult, and often so right that the blunt, bombastic Arian had better shut up, listen, and learn. But that, of course, is not easy for her.

Maybe he's too sensitive, too sentimental, too attached to old hair ribbons, diaries, and love letters. There's something indefinably feminine about him, and yet he can also be hard and tough. It's as though he's continually acting—different roles. And that can be hard when Aries is feeling sexy and wants things straightforward, uncomplicated, and passionate.

Pisces is above all a dreamer by day and night. Take away the dreams and you have only half a man. Understand this and the relationship is halfway created or saved. And of course he has sexual fantasies that might make Aries' hair curl.

It's no use trying to change him; everyone's been trying since birth with total lack of success. Accept him as he is and love him for his virtues, his gentleness, his otherworldliness. He'll let his woman make the big decisions, and fight his battles too. He certainly isn't even going to try to push this formidable woman around. She should try to keep him off the drink and drugs. There's a tendency for the weaker Piscean breathren to take solace wherever it can be found, to drown the neuroses and complexes. But above all, she should share love with him and he'll worship and adore her. Life can be so comforting with this man, provided his lady has no illusions about what it will be like.

ARIES MAN—ARIES WOMAN

What happens when the tempest meets the whirlwind? There might just be calm. But will the sheer intensity of the initial contact prove too much for the partners?

Here we have two people who can't help wanting to be the boss. Both are full of enthusiasm, energy, life; a bit selfish, definitely self-centered but generous with worldy things; greedy for experience and love. Neither is prepared to play second fiddle for long, but each has much to offer the other and the world, provided that energy can be channeled into constructive areas. It's rare, but if this doesn't happen, Arians can be just about the most destructive people in the Zodiac. Mostly they end up constructive.

The Aries woman is quite a girl. She's likely to make the sexual running because she's not backward about coming forward when she really fancies a guy—and that might happen quite often, truth to tell. However, there's a good chance that these two will be convinced they're soulmates, and it could be true. Probably they'll find out later that the fires are going down despite plenty of stoking!

The problem is that although there'll be plenty of stimulus in this relationship, plenty of humor, plenty of physical sport enjoyed by both, and plenty of sex, there won't be all that much peace and quiet.

The house and meals are likely to be neglected, forgotten—too many other things are more important with these two. Neither should be first choice to paint the ceiling or mend the gate. They're rather accident-prone, and it isn't exactly unknown for Arians to collect scars all over their bodies as they plow through life. Aries does like to make money—fast—but his woman likes to spend it—fast. Both are more practical than it may sound, and no one's going to starve while these two perennial optimists are around; but sudden bursts of extravagance are going to strain the finances pretty close to the breaking point.

Not too much tact is likely to be displayed by this pair. The Arian method of winning an argument, a race, or anything else is to lower the head and charge in. Most times it works, but just occasionally someone sidesteps and uppercuts the Arian as he or she blunders past.

What it all amounts to is that experience and advancing years make Arians easier to live with, a bit mellower. But will the relationship last that long?

ARIES MAN—TAURUS WOMAN

The odds are against this partnership. Of course, there's always the exception—but mostly these two are so opposite that even brief contact is enough to suggest to the intelligent that things aren't quite gelling.

Taurus is often a very attractive proposition: practical, careful, shrewd in worldly things. But Aries is moving too fast for her. He's about as cautious as a charging elephant. He'll be fussed over, caressed, and pampered by this lady, and that might appeal to an Arian who's got the wanderlust out of his system. But two strong-willed people are going to have their differences even if their relationship is a big success in the bedroom. They should have a long affair before tripping to the altar.

Aries is pushy, impatient, spoiling for a fight. He needs change and chance the way some signs need air! Taurus is much too sensible to go tearing around the world. She needs real stability, a beautiful and expensive home, quality clothes, and proof that she's loved—proof like minks, diamonds, boxes of expensive chocolates, and the best seats at the theater and opera! Aries is unlikely to provide all these things, although he isn't stupid enough to discount their importance.

Taurus is likely to be a bit lazy, which certainly can't be said about her effervescent lover. She probably loves to lie abed in the mornings. He has no objection to a little cuddling as the sun goes up, but deep down he probably feels a bit guilty about lying there while so many things are happening in the great wide world that he could be sharing in.

No one pushes this guy around. He can be led and persuaded, and he'll horrify her sometimes by sticking bitterly to his point of view, popping out for a moment, and then calmly announcing on his return that he's changed his mind. There'll be much grinding and gnashing of teeth from his faithful woman. Aries is proud, and so is Taurus. And she might well have a tendency to nag and bitch. Aries won't stick around for that. One thing that could keep this pair together is the Taurean stubbornness and refusal to let go. Once this man is hers, she's going to dig in, and he might just decide it's easier to stick in there than risk the claws and the venom if he cuts loose. They should think very carefully about settling down together, and then try a period of separation—maybe several hundred periods of separation—and then, if it's still on, it's very clear that nothing on earth is going to separate these two.

ARIES MAN—GEMINI WOMAN

This relationship could be a bit like a continual contest of assorted mental and physical games. A continual challenge for both parties to see who's going to get the upper hand. And in the long run Aries will dominate. But he'll have to battle to pin the elusive, fascinating, charming Gemini.

Really she's too subtle for him, just too damn smart. So if she decides he's the one for her, then he hasn't a chance. But it may take her a long, long time—if ever—to get around to deciding. His sporting interests, his incessant activity, will bore the pants off her, but she will be fascinated by his drive, enthusiasm, and get-up-and-go. And that's a problem, because he might just get up and go from time to time.

However, he'll be back. Nothing fascinates an Arian so much as something or someone he can't beat—mainly because Gemini won't play. Her needlelike jabs at his ego will infuriate and capture him. He might accuse her of being too cold, unfeeling, distant—and it'll be true at times—but the relationship could be a good one. Both have tempers that when unleashed are extremely destructive. They had better not unleash them or the neighbors will call the cops, the fire station, and the hospital, thinking a major disaster has occurred.

Aries is a great one for new ideas, innovative things. The Gemini woman is likely to pour scorn on most of them. After all, this is a very smart lady. Just occasionally she'll say, "That's a brilliant idea, lover," and then he's going to have to decide whether she means it. There's likely to be something pretty deep about a relationship between these two. Communication isn't going to be easy between two people who are proud in different ways, but it'll probably be worth making the effort. He has to somehow get over the Arian indifference and tell her he loves her, very often. And she has to accept that he's the boss while continually cutting him down to size without totally antagonizing him.

This lady has artistic leanings. She's really rather civilized and appreciates genuinely refined things and people. Aries could be a little too obvious, too crude at times; frankly, he could be too damn rude. Despite all the contradictions, or possibly because of them, this couple has a great chance of a really rewarding relationship, provided they're not too tired at the end of a day of contest activity to roll into the hay and gaze lovingly into each other's eyes. Friends and relatives always take second place for these two.

ARIES MAN—CANCER WOMAN

These two have entirely different viewpoints, but this need not be a bar to a happy and fruitful relationship. Cancer is a complex sort of lady, emotional, cautious, often mixed up. Aries is direct, dynamic, opportunistic, great fun. She could be overpowered by this guy, swept off her dainty feet. But she's a bit moody and needs careful handling, particularly when life or someone has hurt her. He hasn't time to worry about such things; he just rumbles on like a tank, overpowering everything around him by sheer force of personality.

She longs for love and is terribly loyal. She's probably a great cook. She understands physical things and she has her own type of stamina, which the Aries man doesn't have. He likes to get stuck into a job and can amaze others by the amount of work he does in a short time, but he gets easily bored and wants to move on. The number of unfinished things Aries has been involved with—and that could include love affairs—is nobody's business. And actually that's the way he likes to keep it!

Cancer is a sensitive lady, make no mistake about that. She needs a strong man to provide security, a nice home, the pleasant things of life. Aries isn't too good at settling down until middle age—or perhaps never—but there is likely to be a powerful sexual attraction between these two.

It's always hard to forecast about a relationship, because of course almost anything goes when love takes over, but really this is a risky combination. If Aries can be restrained from tearing around the world and Cancer avoids vegetating, then it may work. But it is fatal for her to have expectations of this guy. He'll do wonderful things, but they'll be spontaneous, a reaction of the moment. She's part dreamer, part homemaker. She isn't nearly as selfish as he is, but she's much more mixed up. Both of them can have a great time straightening out her neuroses—or making them a damn sight worse. It's a tossup which will happen.

It's no use mothering this guy. He just won't respond. He deosn't want flattering and babying. He wants his woman to stand on her own feet, shoot straight from the shoulder, and so on. He sometimes seems to think in platitudes. But for all this, he's got sterling virtues. He's honest (not something that can always be said for the Cancer woman), but he needs taming. Is she the one for the job? Could be—but she'll probably need a little help from life and a little luck too. A fascinating contrast here, promising a restless, difficult relationship.

ARIES MAN—LEO WOMAN

This is probably the best partnership these two can make. She's going to be the driving power behind all that Aries initiative—and when she flutters her eyelashes, he'll go all gooey.

This really can be a formidable team, sexually compatible, fiery, dynamic. It'll probably be attraction at first sight and love at second. And of course nothing stops a Leo lady when she sets her heart on anything as important as a man. Aries is probably the only person who gets away with telling her what to do. She takes a lot of winning—at least that's the way she likes it to look—whereas really she's running the show.

He'll bow to her superior knowledge at times and he won't be worried by her occasional fit of temper or arrogance. He knows how she thinks, and she goes along with his impetuousness because it usually works. He's the sort of person who arrives home in a new car and, when questioned about it, announces it's hers—moments after she's criticized the pink bodywork and yellow upholstery. And then he'll beam with pleasure while she winces. Aries can be a trifle insensitive but is undeniably generous to a fault.

The Leo woman needs lots of flattery. She has to be told she's wonderful, looks terrific, smells gorgeous, is brilliant, and so on. She'll lap it up—after all, it is true!

Aries is pretty good at playing the flattery game when he takes the trouble—and this woman is worth playing with. Sexually, it's a terrific relationship. Aries is fiery, and Leo is more calculating but nevertheless romantic and demanding of love. Both these fire signs are desperately honest, although Leo might bend the rules a little more than her partner if need be. The one thing this lady must never do is battle her man into the ground. It can be done because Leos are terribly one-pointed in their desires and they hate to lose an argument. He has to win sometimes, and then all will be sweetness and light. If she keeps bouncing him, he'll leave her for someone he can dominate.

Leo is most efficient. Her home will have style and almost certainly little touches of luxury. Her meals are produced with panache, and they taste good too. She's a very stylish lady from the tip of her nails to her toes. She has to look good or she feels miserable. And her man has to look good too to feed her somewhat oversized ego. He's certainly the man for her, and he's going to have a tough time saying no to this formidable lady.

ARIES MAN—VIRGO WOMAN

This is one relationship that depends very much indeed on the lady, for she's the one who's going to have to make it work. Most of the time Aries is easygoing, easy to handle, kind, generous, and romantic. She's a decidedly reserved lady who is not going to throw herself away on any bum. He's a terrific optimist, while she plans, calculates, figures, and schemes. Get the message?

The bold, imaginative, lively Arian will have to come to terms with her Virgoan reserve, and she's got to take him as he is. He takes a lot of changing and a lot of living with too—when he's home and not tearing around the world, that is. Everyone will expect the relationship to end tomorrow, but this may not be the case—it depends how much Virgo is prepared to work at pretending that she's ready for love at the drop of a hat and that she doesn't mind moving every month and a half as Aries leaps from job to job.

This girl is not easy to understand or come to grips with. This is partly because she's almost a split personality. She has a highly developed monastic complex and at the same time is actually surprised when her emotions burst through in what she sees as an embarrassing way and everyone else see as a relief from the tension of her criticism and tight-lipped disapproval.

She's attractive to this guy, that's for sure. He wants to grab her and carry her away. Chances are Virgo wouldn't like that. She has fixed notions about romance, and subtlety pays dividends with her. Aries has to learn that this slightly prudish lady demands cleanliness, neatness, and decorum above almost anything else. She's not selfish, and he is, so there are certainly grounds for a relationship here. In fact, he could be just what she's been looking for to devote her life to. Will Aries devote his life to her? Probably not, in all honesty, but he invariably means well in his heavy-handed way.

Aries loves a fight; he needs the challenge in his life. Virgo considers that sort of thing demeaning and definitely not nice. He should either find another lady who'll kick back or take this fascinating woman in the full knowledge that at times she's going to be an enigma and at other times she's going to need love desperately—because Virgo gets frightened from time to time.

ARIES MAN—LIBRA WOMAN

Libra is an attractive proposition for most men, but she's going to have to be particularly lively to satisfy Aries. There will be a tendency for him to dominate, and she isn't going to like that. She's a strong-willed lady, idealistic and elegant, and this man could prove too basic for her romantic, rather traditional ways.

There is likely to be immediate attraction. Both are impulsive, but she's sentimental while he just doesn't understand all that hankering back to an era that has gone forever. Aries looks ahead; he can't help it. He's the eternal optimist. Knock him down a dozen times and he'll come springing back, while his woman can only gape at this remarkable show of courage and perhaps sheer foolishness. Life with Aries will never be dull. He'll astound and horrify her, trying to lead her into things she really doesn't want to know about.

He's a bit secretive too, mostly with his plans and aspirations. Libra is likely to resent this. She's very independent, but a partnership to her is a total partnership. She wants an equal share of everything. In bed it is likely to be a partnership in the best sense of the word. What he has to sort out is how it can happen that one minute his woman is a helpless kitten and the next a roaring lioness. If nothing else it'll keep him on his toes.

She gets involved helping others in trouble. Aries, being the first sign of the Zodiac, is strictly out for number one. He'll help out generously with time and money when called on, but he doesn't care to be dragged into things that demand his compassion and understanding for very long. It's not that he lacks stamina, but he needs continual boosting and stimulation. Libra would be wise to remember to buck him up occasionally. And he'd better learn a few romantic endearments to whisper in her ever receptive ear.

The opinions of others don't matter much to this fellow, but his lady can easily be hurt by a thoughtless word. A big problem is her old-fashioned sentimentality. She has a natural grace and dignity, and almost always looks delicious, but she does have expectations, and her man is expected to live up to them. If she's prepared to put up with Aries, then he's a lucky man. He might even settle down and realize that this thoughtful, gentle woman is his guardian angel after all. However, it is vital that there be physical compatibility—and Libra may have to work at this just to please her man.

ARIES MAN—SCORPIO WOMAN

Initially this will be a stunning, overwhelming relationship, but the odds are against a long-term, happy union. Both partners are fighters. Neither knows when he or she is licked, and the Scorpio woman is particularly stubborn.

She's a sexy lady and she wants to be dominated, but not forever. Aries is usually a bit short on tact, and although he has stamina, he needs continual stimulus and challenge. There are times when their sex life will be terrific, satisfying, perfect. But then at other times it'll be a mess; there'll be anger, recriminations, battles.

Scorpio will go along with her restless man, putting up with his crazy ideas and his changes of job and environment. The one thing she won't put up with is his infidelity. He's her guy, and he stays that way. She's probably the most dangerous woman in the Zodiac when crossed, and an unfaithful Arian would be wise to treat himself to a bulletproof vest, or better still get a food taster to test his meals for poison.

There's something slightly mysterious about this lady. It's hard to pin down what it is, but this is the thing that makes her a bit moody at times and produces the occasional burst of really bad temper or spitefulness. Scorpio is usually sorry soon after and is hard to resist when she gets in a romantic mood. Aries certainly doesn't have the equipment to fathom her wiles.

She will admire this guy's aggressive enthusiasm and love of life, and she'll help him go out into the world—provided he comes back regularly to report what he's discovered. The secret of this is that Scorpio knows that the really important things all happen when she's around. She's basically oriented to the inner things, while he will keep looking out into the world. It irritates her not to be his all, and this will be hard for her to accept or understand.

It'll be a difficult relationship to sustain. She's not likely to be as admiring, gentle, and supportively enthusiastic as Aries expects his lady to be, and when she finally strips him bare with a few well-chosen and brutally honest phrases, he'll have a job to shrug it off as he is accustomed. He'll probably shrug *her* off—Aries is a proud man. And she might just breathe a sigh of relief as she discovers there are more appreciative, subtle men in the world.

ARIES MAN—SAGITTARIUS WOMAN

This is almost certain to be a happy fruitful relationship. Two fire signs together are great fun and understand each other. The biggest problem will be her grasshopper mind, but these two are going to find it's much more fun to be together than apart, despite their very distinct tendencies to hardly ever be at home.

Sagittarius is impulsive, tolerant, flirtatious, impetuous, and frankly often a bit randy. But she means well, isn't nearly as pompous as her Arian mate, and seems to enjoy almost everything she does. He's going to have to put his foot down sometimes. She'll laugh but will take notice. Aries is usually so easygoing that when he does put his foot down, she knows it matters. He has to work at being a little less self-centered than he is by nature, and she'll help him. There's likely to be a lot of laughter when these two get together. Both have plenty of friends and contacts, particularly Sagittarius, who positively blossoms in company even though the approval of the world means not a thing to her. She can be extraordinarily unconventional, and even the independent Arian man will sometimes gasp at her sheer effrontery.

As both get a little older they'll start to limit their regular activities to only two or three dozen a week; they might even get to the dinner table at the same time one day—but, no, that's probably asking too much.

There will be conflicts, probably over money because neither worries too much about it until it is often too late. But the splendidly optimistic Arian will usually sort things out—he can be pretty realistic when the occasion demands. Initially Aries is likely to make a terrific impression on Sagittarius. Love at first sight is not unknown for these two, even though she is more subtle and in many ways more intelligent than he is. She may look totally disorganized as she juggles half a dozen balls in the air at once, but every so often a penetrating shaft of sheer genius will make it clear that she knows what's going on. Watch a Sagittarian in the kitchen. It looks like chaos, but the end product is really good, and only she knows how it is managed. That's originality—and Aries certainly appreciates this rare quality.

He's a basic, simple, uncomplicated guy, even though he'd like everyone to think he's a cunning monster. This lady knows all about him, his failings and his virtues, and is likely to love him for them all.

ARIES MAN—CAPRICORN WOMAN

The Capricorn woman makes a very suitable mate for the volatile Arian man. She's ambitious both for herself and her man, she is honest, and she's eminently practical.

Aries certainly has his faults—he's egotistical, hasty, extravagant, and occasionally petulant like a small boy. But he is exciting, loving, demanding, stimulating, and great fun. He will in fact be good for the cautious Capricornian, who sometimes takes root if she stands still too long—which she is apt to do.

She is a real woman, make no mistake about that. She's proud and independent, but she does want a dependable man, not a total show-off. It is likely that she'll see beneath the Arian exterior to the steel beneath (in some cases it's a mighty thin sheet of steel), and if she decides this fellow is for her, then she will be so loyal and so dedicated to him that he's bound to succeed—he just can't fail.

She's cautious insofar as she doesn't believe in love at first sight and all that fanciful nonsense. She'll keep the house or apartment spotless because she's a worker. She can't help it. Physically she may be just a little prudish, rather set in her ways, sexually and otherwise, but he will soon shake her up. She's a good saver too, and she'll need to be with this man. But she also admires his sheer confidence, his get-up-and-go, and the way he can't be bothered with detail. This irritates her, but she secretly respects it.

This woman is a born banker. She's the sort who has fifteen bank accounts, three piggy banks, and a dozen hiding places for smaller amounts. Aries has to learn to harness his knack for making money to her ability to make money work for her. All that's needed is a little humility on his part—that comes hard for Arians—but it'll be worth the effort and he knows it.

Lucky is the Arian who hitches up with a Capricorn woman. It won't always be easy because she can be calculating and cold, but equally she is most likely to be loyal, faithful, and honest.

One thing to watch is the Capricorn lady in friendly company. When she lets her hair down, she can really have a ball. Her lover might get the shock of his life when he sees that she's actually flirting—and it'll do him a world of good.

ARIES MAN—AQUARIUS WOMAN

Arians tend to be lucky—no one knows why—and falling in love with an Aquarian may well be even more luck than even this guy deserves. On the surface things shouldn't work out too well, but in practice her coolness and his fire go well together.

Aries is selfish, while Aquarius is just the opposite. She's everybody's friend and everyone gravitates to her. She's a great traveler and doesn't like to be tied down too tight, and that suits the wandering Arian. In fact, if he lets some other guy get her, he's making one hell of a mistake.

His possessive streak might cause problems, as might her extravagance. It isn't that she does not understand the value of money—she just doesn't care. She likes the best even if it is decidedly unconventional. In fact, Aquarius is the least ordinary type in the whole Zodiac. Modern art, unusual clothes, the fastest car, the exotic place, all appeal to her—but don't think she's going to be conned. She's far too smart for that. In fact, she has almost a mania for improving herself, quite possibly has a gift for languages, and has a very good mind indeed—which she uses sometimes to dramatic and quite brilliant effect.

This pair may not be as passionate as some, or even as much as Aries would like. He has to remember that she's a dreamer, at least at times. She believes in true love, meeting a stranger across a crowded room, all that sort of stuff. She has humanitarian ideals, provided of course they don't involve too much contact with actual people. Aries has a habit of rolling up with some underdog he's picked up. The poor underdog will probably get short shrift from Aquarius, who doesn't like losers of any sort.

She can't be expected to be house-proud, to dust the books, wash the curtains, that sort of thing—for her, life is too important to waste on trivial chores. If nothing else, this lady thinks big.

The thing to grasp about her is her unconventionality. She cannot be treated like any other woman, for her responses are not predictable even if they eventually prove to be devastatingly logical. She's her own woman, but if handled right (give her one red rose, not a bunch), she'll be so fascinated by Aries that all the other men who buzz around her won't stand a chance. She's an altruist looking for *the* man. Let's hope she's found him when Aries looks deep into her eyes and tells her he loves her—he's probably said it before.

ARIES MAN—PISCES WOMAN

Fascination—that's the secret of a relationship between these two opposites. It'll probably be love at second sight. Her dreamy, otherworldly, gentle, totally romantic attitude to life captivates this guy. She is overwhelmed by his enthusiasm, his daring, his sheer bluntness. She quivers with horror half the time he's around and with barely concealed passion the other half.

Pisces is passionate—she wants to be carried off by a knight on a white horse, to be whisked off to a harem in the exotic desert. She needs romance, protestations of undying love, the way some women need diamonds. She'll cheerfully die for a man who needs her and keeps on telling her so. But under it all she's a lot tougher than she looks and sounds. In fact, these two make a remarkable combination.

At times she withdraws into herself. It's not unknown for a Piscean to weep with joy and frustration at the same time. The bullish Arian has to learn to be just a little more tender and gentle with this lady. Her career won't matter a damn to the selfish Arian, and she'll go along with this because she longs to give herself, all of herself, to her man. She isn't too good with money; if she has a small amount, it will be gone in no time. But give her a big sum and suddenly she's cautious, sensible, and mercenary to a degree that even surprises her.

She isn't too good at taking responsibility of any sort. Much of the time she'll be his little girl in her little print dress and her hair in bunches. And then suddenly she's there in satin and silk with her hair over her eyes, and she's all woman, the sexiest thing around.

There's something about her that attracts Aries and keeps on drawing him back. One moment she treats him like a child, the next she needs comforting and loving. The sheer changeability of this lady is part of her fascination. She's all emotion. The knots in her tummy are part of her life. She's very shy, and Aries is never going to understand her embarrassment when he is gauche or rude. But her touch of mystery and her beauty will continue to excite him even though he may know she isn't going to make life easy for him.

This man is easy for Pisces to string along. Half the time he doesn't know what is happening. Indeed there is something in her makeup that is just a tiny bit sneaky, even though it's carefully hidden most of the time. This will be a joyous relationship for both.

TAURUS WOMAN—TAURUS MAN

Two stubborn natures could make this relationship a difficult one, but there is a lot going for it. Taureans are physical, straightforward, and not easily moved, but they respond to the artistic side of each other's natures. Music, good food, and a pleasure in entertaining are vital for this relationship, and if the Taurus woman can prevent her man from becoming bored, they can have a lot of fun.

Both are practical when it comes to finances, and she'll win his admiration for her business sense, not only when shopping but also when dealing with friends, guests, and business colleagues. However, there is a chance of jealousy, a little spying, and sometimes unreasonable outbursts on both sides. But this is better than the boredom that can creep in when two Taureans get together and refuse to move. Strong physical appetites that both of them continually exhibit can be wearing on even close friends and buddies, so there has to be some sort of compromise.

Marriage for Taureans is certainly a better bet than an affair—neither really likes the thought of instability—and she'd better be around when he gets home from work. Incidentally, he'll still be looking pretty smart—he likes to look good, and it won't hurt for his wife to notice this from time to time.

Taureans have a tendency to get stuck in the same house or town or job, as indeed these two can get stuck in a comfortable relationship. He is unlikely ever to be a hero in her eyes, but at least he'll be looked after, and with a little luck and effort, sex will be good, although it would be wise for her to be adventurous from time to time. But she mustn't overdo it or he'll be sarcastic, not to say rude. But if they handle it right, the romantic side of Taurus will show itself. He might even surprise her with a display of excessive generosity—probably at a favorite restaurant. The Taurus lady should be aware of her weaknesses—any box of chocolates left around will be finished fairly fast, and she might even finish a couple of boxes. But if this greed for life can be contained, Taureans are reliable and occasionally surprisingly intuitive. They are earthy, yes, but sensitive about physical things and often fanatical about cleanliness. Tell a Taurean that something is dirty or may have germs on it, and he or she won't touch it for life. Tell a Taurean that someone is a bad egg, and he or she will have nothing whatever to with that person, even if initially attracted.

TAURUS WOMAN—GEMINI MAN

A quiet domestic life isn't what the Gemini man is likely to be looking for, so the Taurus woman does have problems with this relationship. He's quick—and that's an understatement; his mind does work almost as quickly as even he thinks it does. He's unpredictable: one moment a wonderful communicator, the next moody and mischievous. But if his moods can be put up with, life with this guy could be very stimulating indeed, and marriage could be great in a way that even closest friends are unlikely to understand.

This lady needs stability in most relationships. She's a great hostess with an organized, efficient mind and is sure of herself despite lapses into sulky laziness—but these are rare. He admires this efficiency, but he'll still make big dents in her ego. He'll be late for dates, might even forget about them altogether, and he isn't very impressed by the artistic temperament. He will come back, though—probably many times—before a marriage decision is made.

In a sense the Taurean lady is a port in the storm of life for him. He's so versatile, changeable, and often talented that he really can appreciate steadiness and perseverance.

Taurus will rarely really know quite where she is with this guy. He'll drive her mad. But he is so imaginative, charming, undependable, and stimulating that she'll almost certainly forgive him as she would a willful child.

Perhaps it's up to her to make up her mind whether she wants this whirlwind man—because if Taurus is really serious, she'll have to make the important decisions, and Gemini will be happy to go along with it. She's the one who is going to have, and to want, to work at this relationship, and it won't be easy all the time.

She'll have to think long and carefully about cementing a relationship with this man, because it's likely to be awful wearing or even just plain awful sometimes. It isn't of course, all one-sided, because he'll get irritated by caution, good sense, and a determination to get things right—all the things Taureans have to do and indeed manage so well. He'll do dreadful things to her ego, but if she can avoid being his doormat, prevent him from making a convenience of her all the time, and have a quiet cry to herself rather than when he's around, the gods may just nod quietly and let Gemini and Taurus get on with their very special sort of irritating, infuriating life.

TAURUS WOMAN—CANCER MAN

A passionate combination with every chance of a romantic, satisfying relationship. Taurus will be flattered by Cancer's attentions, and she is no shrinking violet when she knows what she wants. He'll be loving and faithful, but she has to be prepared for his moods. He's insecure one minute, in control of everything the next, and withdrawn not long after. It can be confusing, to put it mildly, so this lady has to hold the relationship together at times. Cancer will make her feel good, and he won't take her for granted, but if and when she's tactless and clumsy, as Taureans can be, he'll do one of his disappearing acts—probably physically as well as mentally.

If she's wise, Taurus will take all this in her stride. Basically both partners are passionate and emotional. The physical side is likely to be good—things will really hum at times, make no mistake about that. The one thing these two have to remember is that they must work at the relationship. Neither one must take the other completely for granted, and the Cancer man will be more responsive when Taurus is soft, subtle, and yielding.

There is enough togetherness here to last a lifetime, if that's the way the partners want it. He's a home builder and a dreamer, but this woman has his measure. By the way, he'll fall in love quickly and easily, so it's up to her to tell him he's strong, masterful, and a great lover. He'll believe it and will reward her by working for her.

He's fun, complex, and childish at times, but he's protective and truly will worry about his woman. Her job is to project all the virtues he expects her to have. And she'd better have plenty of plausible excuses ready when his expectations are just too high. He'll believe almost anything—when it suits him to do so.

Taureans are good cooks, wordly-wise, cool on the surface, uninhibited when aroused, ready to give much of themselves—but woe betide the lover who oversteps the mark or makes her really jealous. Taurus takes a lot of upsetting, but she certainly can be pushed too far, and when and if this happens, Cancer's sensitive nature is likely to be crushed for hours or even weeks!

Working at a relationship takes a lot of time and trouble. But it has to be done, and Taurus's confidence is likely to be rewarded by this man later in life.

TAURUS WOMAN—LEO MAN

Leo thinks he's a big wheel, and he may well be, so Taurus is going to have to go along with this. He'll always be number one in everything. But he's quite a guy: strong, warm, generous, demanding. He's a hard man not to fall for in a big way, and he knows it.

Taurus is a much more sober, sensible customer, so she may well find herself swept off her feet—not only by his grandiose plans as he maps out their future, but also by the grandiose restaurant he sweeps her into and the way the staff treat the two of them.

The way to handle this man is to flatter the hell out of him. Taurus should tell him he's stupendous, wonderful, magnificent. He'll know she is hamming it up—but it won't matter; he'll love it *and* her. In fact, he'll lap it up forever if he can find a woman who can keep the flattery coming forever. It doesn't matter how outrageous his lady is.

It won't be a complex union. It will be simplicity itself so long as she doesn't let him down. He'll want to show her off, of course. If money runs to it, there'll be diamonds, minks, big black limousines, and all the trimmings. And even if cash doesn't go that far, he'll probably rent them for her a couple of times a year. He'll want to reorganize the home, the garden, the kitchen, everything—he can't help it; that's the nature of this great big splendid beast. But he's big enough to admit when he's wrong, and most likely he'll eventually get the message that the one place he stays out of is the kitchen. That belongs to his Taurean mate. Another thing he might learn is that he belongs to her. He's got a roaming eye, but he's so obvious about it, like a great big greedy schoolboy, that his lady can usually cut him off before his ego gets to work on the blonde, brunette, or redhead he's just spotted across the crowded room.

In truth, Taurus is likely to be there before any other woman gets her hooks into Leo, but just occasionally, he'll get loose while she's visiting her mother. When and if she finds out, all hell will break loose. He may never be forgiven—but several dozen bunches of roses, boxes of choclates, and earnest speeches of endearment muttered from the bended-knee position will eventually have the desired effect in most cases.

Many Leos are oversexed, overwhelming, and overdo things, but life isn't likely to be boring for this pair. Taurus should just remember that he's the boss and it's always going to be that way.

TAURUS WOMAN—VIRGO MAN

This could be a nice sensible relationship. Note that word *sensible,* because it has to be the cornerstone of this pair's deal. Virgo is a perfectionist, very good with money, rather fussy, and awfully precise. He may well be a bit of a prude. She's earthier and blunter, particularly about sexual matters, so she has to break down this reserve.

Taurus is pretty practical too, particularly when it comes to the home, kitchen, money, and dealing with the myriad problems of modern life. She'd better not go planning anything without deep and reasoned consultation with Virgo, or he'll be very upset. In fact, he'll be genuinely hurt because he loves to organize, rationalize, and quantify.

If that all sounds like too much, don't worry; he really will love her forever—if that's what she wants—and since they both want security, the crazy dreams and often crazier actions of some other signs of the Zodiac aren't going to worry this pair too much. They'll be too busy sitting in front of the TV warming the brandy gently between their palms while the maid clears up. The maid? Well, there's a good chance they'll have one, because money tends to stick to this pair, and although he'll be generous with his lady, he's not going to chuck it around when it could be gathering interest in the bank.

He could be too cool for her—at times, anyway—but don't expect perfection. Remember, he's honest, loving, vulnerable, often charming in an innocent sort of way. He's a little too well organized, and although with some men the best way to snap him out of his habits would be by suddenly doing something outrageous, it won't work with Virgo. He'll hate it and curl up inside. He's a slow maturer, so don't ever make fun of him.

Taureans do need a little excitement from time to time, but this lady had better find it somewhere else. This doesn't mean she should go looking for a Leo or an Arian, but she should get some outside interests, anything from skiing to bridge. Taureans are pretty good at almost everything they touch anyway, so this shouldn't be too great a problem.

And when she gets back from wherever she's been, Virgo will be there, everything will be running smoothly, and she might reflect to herself that things could be worse. There's a lot going for a Taurus-Virgo relationship, so she shouldn't worry about his criticism— laughing it off would be better.

TAURUS WOMAN—LIBRA MAN

He's an awful flirt, and she's not the type to stand by and let him run riot as his nature would have him. If Taurus can take this in her stride, though, it could be a beautiful relationship. Both have genuine emotional warmth, and Libra can bring out the very best in the otherwise rather passive (not to say at times dull) Taurus woman. Usually this man is not one to rely or lean on, but he is capable of making a commitment, even though he's a ladies' man. Librans always have problems making up their minds—they seem naturally to gravitate to a point somewhere between yes and no but then insist that they're not sitting in the middle.

Taurus has lazy spells—or, more accurately, periods when all that scurrying about gets to be too much and she just puts her feet up and nibbles on a candy or three. He has phases when he does an incredible amount both at home and at work—but then suddenly drops right out and does nothing. He hates routine almost as much as an Arian does.

Sexual attraction is likely to be strong. Librans are good-looking people, and Taureans are patient and persistent. Usually Libra will be able to put up with Taurean jealousy and outbursts. He's terribly honest—it never really occurs to him to go to the trouble of inventing a pack of lies—and in fact it would almost certainly help the relationship along if he did take the trouble. But if and when he settles down for one lady, he'll respond well to more adventurous sexual overtures. Yes, he'll get bored, but then he's so used to getting bored with just about everything that with any luck he'll find the lady at a time in his life when he's ready to settle down.

If that sounds a bit confusing, it's simply because Libra is a puzzle—to himself, that is—she'll get his measure remarkably fast if she hasn't already. He'll postpone any decision for days, while this is something a sturdy Taurean could never abide.

She should express appreciation for his virtues—there are quite a lot—because he's artistic, affectionate, and likely to acquire possessions even if he doesn't value them as much as she does. Both love going out to concerts, the ballet, the cinema—anywhere, in fact. He is most likely to see the other person's point of view, too—that is a trifle strange for an apparently selfish person, but then the Libra man is quite a puzzle at times.

TAURUS WOMAN—SCORPIO MAN

A tempestuous affair seems a virtual certainty—really more like a battle than a partnership—and if Taurus should by any chance want a life that is full of chaos, excitement, and fire, then she'll certainly get it with a Scorpio man.

Love can sometimes be so near to hate, and there is a fair chance that this could happen when Scorpio and Taurus get together. There'll be a lot of sexual chemistry in the air when these two snuggle close—there won't be time or strength for outside affairs of the heart. Scorpio has a frightening temper when aroused, and Taurus is as stubborn as they come. Others should beware of getting caught up in the battle—a stray shot might just come from the direction of a well-meaning friend or relative.

This is a magnetic guy with an air of mystery about him. He knows she needs him even if she herself is not so darn sure. A ruthless Scorpio might play with her like a spider with a fly, and then leave her cold and lonely as he storms on by. But a Scorpio who's been hurt himself a few times might just be able to restrain himself enough to make a go of it with a lady who loves him and is prepared to put up with his tricks, his possessiveness, and even his cruelty.

He is an astonishingly passionate man, tender at times, clever at knowing her moods. But he does need a challenge, and in all honesty Taurus might decide not to rise to the occasion the twentieth time around and the twentieth time her ego has been bruised. But there are exceptions, and with some sort of compromise that brings a sense of tolerance into the relationship—maybe age and experience are part of the answer here—this could be a strikingly attractive, fascinating encounter.

The big difficulty for Scorpio is that he's gentle and cruel, mean and kind, tough and tender, all at the same time. He doesn't know where he is half the time, so how can he expect her to know? But he's also got a very keen, knifelike mind. This lady may find all this just too much to resist, and the attraction may well be fatal (not literally, in most cases).

The Taurean steadiness, honesty, earthiness, domesticity—gift for homemaking, cooking, entertaining—will all appeal to this man. Even he needs his fevered brow soothed from time to time. But she'd better not start flattering him. Scorpio is one sign that won't stand for it.

TAURUS WOMAN—SAGITTARIUS MAN

A great friendship, but these two should try not to fall in love. If it happens, then the independent Sagittarius man is going to have to give up some of that independence, and the jealous Taurus woman is going to have to realize that he's the free-wheeler of the Zodiac.

He's so happy-go-lucky that some people will forget he can be hurt. He keeps so many balls in the air, has so many things going at once, does so many jobs, knows so many people, that he has to really want her before he'll accept even a long, long, apron string tied to him. He'll certainly broaden her interests. He's a sportsman, a competitor, an outdoorsman, a guy with a zest for living that could prove too much for the more sensible, steady, but stubborn Taurean nature.

If it is love, then for Taurus it's going to be hard work to change her nature—only he will be able to change his own—and she's going to need all the enthusiasm she can muster for his enthusiasms and nutty ideas. Sagittarians are great at bouncing back—not quite in the Aries class—but he's almost certain to be better read than she, probably speaks twenty-three languages (to his satisfaction, anyway), used to know Mozart well, had lunch yesterday with the President, and is so greedy for experience he'll make her feel positively dull.

Taurus does have one advantage: Every so often Sagittarius stops gyrating—though not for long—and announces that he's worn out, and then's the moment for Taurus to hint that his bachelor existence may not be good for his health. A new idea like that might just hit him so hard that he'll fall gratefully into her arms.

He does have a sense of humor, while this lady has—to put it delicately—only half a sense of humor, so a little work is needed to laugh, not scream. Taureans are pretty sexy, while Sagittarians are inventive and innovative, so he could upset her once too often in this area.

Taurus is stubborn, and this is an aspect of her character that the experienced lady can do a lot to disguise, but she meets her match in Sagittarius—not because he is more stubborn than she is, but quite simply because Sagittarians haven't time to recognize stubbornness.

TAURUS WOMAN—CAPRICORN MAN

One of Capricorn's main needs is a steady, sensible, harmonious home life, and since this suits Taurus down to the ground, this seems to have all the right ingredients for a compatible relationship.

He has a lot of virtues. He's responsible, industrious, good with money, loyal, trustworthy, and loving. The Taurus woman is devoted, romantic only when it isn't too inconvenient, and jealous. Jealousy could just be the undoing of a relationship for some. She must resist the urge to check up on his every movement or he'll strongly object—unlike some other signs, who would be rather flattered.

This is a pretty deep guy in many ways. He's not nearly as sociable as he might appear at first. He's proud and he needs to be proud of his woman, his home, his children, his achievements, and so on. He's not vain, but he knows his own value and won't be sold short by anyone. This can make him much more domineering than either he or his partner suspects at the beginning of a liaison. With Taurus he has to resist demonstrating his occasional bouts of depression, because she might just poke a little ostensibly harmless fun at him, and that'll go down like a lead balloon.

In other words, emotional rather than mental compatability is likely. In many ways it will be a business relationship, but every so often either party will do something genuinely nice, loving, and generous that will make up for a whole lot of rather stodgy organizing, planning, building, and cooking. Not that the kitchen is likely to be anything other than a splendid meeting ground for this pair. Romantic Taurean ladies need plenty of hugging and kissing, but they might not get so much from practical Capricorn men. She should persuade him to work at it a little more. He'd never dream of spying on his woman—in fact, there is a distinct streak of asceticism in his nature. Capricorn is usually not fat—at least when he's young; she might just feed him too well later—and he rather likes tightening his belt both physically and economically when it comes to saving for a rainy day. Taurus has this sort of practical streak, too, so no one's likely to starve when these two are around.

Oh, by the way, he's very ambitious and he does like to give the orders. She should restrain that Taurean will—no mean demand— and all should go swimmingly.

TAURUS WOMAN—AQUARIUS MAN

The difficulty here is that Aquarius is unconventional, unpunctual at meals, and uninterested in being a big worldly success. Taurus wants money and influence and wants to show the world that she's made it in a big way. His being late for meals may sound trivial, but it is the sort of thing that builds into the cornerstone of a divorce.

Aquarius is not going to sweep her off her feet; he's much more likely to be somewhere else when she wants him to. She might even decide he's a bit crazy, though fascinating. To him anyone who acts possessively the way Taurus does is being ridiculous, rigid, reactionary, and conventional. Maybe friendship would be the answer for this pair, but life doesn't always fix things up that way, so if the die is cast, she should try to let him know that the budget is in good hands and that he isn't to worry.

One of his most endearing characteristics is that he gets on with almost everyone—in fact, he's a great lover of company. He's more likely to go out in the evening than to sit at home. He is likely to be a great storyteller, and after a few drinks he'll loosen up in a surprising way. He doesn't give a damn about convention, although he may well be a little vain of his appearance, almost dapper when it comes to clothes; he has a good sense of what suits him and his lady.

Taurus might well decide to settle for someone she can understand. The trouble is she's not likely to be appreciated for her virtues: homemaking, cooking, sport, and all the rest of the practical, sturdy activities she engages in. Aquarius is probably wondering why Neptune is a cold planet while she's struggling to move the furniture.

One other thing. He expects honesty, frankness, straightfor-
wardness in all things, and mostly he'll get it from this lady. He'll
do almost anything for someone in trouble, but he might just forget
that his woman is at home moving the furniture. Oh, well, at least
his "abandoned" mate will know he isn't just wasting time. He can
indeed be industrious, particularly about improving his mind. Bed is
more than likely to be for sleeping when this fellow is there, but
don't dismiss him as hopeless—his virtues are often the very ones
that the Taurean needs to complement her own.

TAURUS WOMAN—PISCES MAN

Pisces is a rather special guy. Don't imagine that he is all gentleness and charm. He's unpredictable, independent of public opinion, and intuitive, but he's also terrific fun, and at times remarkably
sure of himself.

It's the other times when Taurean strength and common sense
will be needed—when Pisces is dreaming while the house is burning,
or fantasizing while his lady is fixing the car. Sexually he's very sensitive and he'll try to keep her happy, but she's going to have to dig
the garden, wash that damn car, and sort things out while he worries
about whether goldfish really like waterfalls.

Pisces does think big, however; he can't help it. He'll be solving
the world's problems or philosphizing about the nature of beauty,
truth, and black holes while somebody—guess who—is getting the
dinner.

If it is love, then he's going to need his Taurean's strength of
purpose, good sense, and industry. He's going to rely on her and yet
worry more about the underprivileged. Like the female Pisceans, this
male is tougher than he seems at first, bigger physically and yet apparently slim and graceful in most cases. He does give in easily to
drink, drugs, and just about anything else that can give him confidence, solace, and confidence. Maybe the stronger Taurean lady can
fulfill this need so that he won't be tempted to drown his sorrows
in drink.

But it won't be all doom and despair for this pair. He has a nice
sense of the ridiculous—even if he's the one being ridiculous—and
he's great to cuddle up to. He'll probably be torn between two or
even three women when he enters her life, and she'll have to decide
he's worth saving. Pisces will be too busy dreaming of conquests, la-

dies in moated castles, cloud-capped Himalayan kingdoms, and success beyond anyone's wildest dreams. Sometimes all these things will come true. It's incredible, but Pisces has an astonishing gift for making the improbable happen, for turning his private world of ghosts and elves into reality in quite practical ways. But he does care intensely what his lady love thinks. He doesn't give a damn what anyone else says or thinks about him, but he'll cheerfully die for his beloved—provided it involves a grand and noble gesture, she'll have to find her own way in traffic jams. Nevertheless, Pisces has a certain style, a true elegance that everyone recognizes.

TAURUS WOMAN—ARIES MAN

It's no use trying to boss Aries about, because it just won't work—it would be a bit like putting hands up to stop a typhoon. Aries likes to give and be appreciated for his giving. This woman is going to have to train him to receive gratefully whether it is love or presents.

These two are both pretty strong-minded characters, and both are inclined to be a trifle selfish (although not with things) when anything interferes with what they want to do. This man is a great one for starting new projects. He doesn't need much stimulation, but someone else might have to pick up the pieces and sort out the chaos he has left behind because he couldn't be bothered with details. Confronted with Taurean criticism, he might turn vicious—something usually alien to his nature. And Taurean jealousy may be a problem. It may prove impossible for Taurus not to be jealous when Aries flirts with the neighborhood beauties, even though he says he doesn't mean it.

He's a pushy character, while she's more steady and even placid. He lives for a challenge—which is probably what he saw Taurus as. He needs excitement and may not get enough of it from this lady.

On the other hand, a more evolved Arian may be poetic, sympathetic, loving, generous, and selfish at the same time—on second thought, Taurus should think very carefully before saying yes to this guy.

Differences will tend to be rather dramatic. Neither will draw the line at a knockdown fight in a restaurant or department store—the sort of thing that would make a Pisces woman die on the spot. But equally all can be sweetness and light again, because neither of these two holds a grudge for long—and neither would stick the knife in. However, they'd better not leave a bludgeon around—that would be a favorite weapon for whichever of the two got to it first.

Aries is something of a fitness fanatic. When he isn't playing at some sport, he feels rather guiltily that he ought to be. Taurus would just as soon cuddle up with him, or with a romantic novel, in front of a nice fire with a glass of wine and a box of chocolates. Aries likes his food, but he isn't going to consume as much as this ravenous lady. Success is important to the Arian—or at least he believes it at the time—but he may not be around to garner the fruits of victory. Taureans, take this as a hint!

TAURUS MAN—TAURUS WOMAN

Everyone will say that this is an ideal partnership, and on the whole it's true. There will be arguments, jealousy, and differences of opinion from time to time, but these two are pretty tolerant and will almost certainly be friends as well as lovers.

The Taurus woman is passionate in her own way, and the Taurus man will be proud of her virtues, her homemaking, her cooking, her general air of competence. There is the problem that both of them can become stick-in-the-muds, one waiting for the other to make a decision or to suggest where to go on vacation, but a relationship can very easily drift into marriage because it's just too inconvenient to be parted.

This rather admirable Taurean stability and dependability is something a few other signs of the Zodiac could do with. The Taurus man should try not to settle too deeply into that cozy rut or another suitor might just appeal to the Taurus woman's more romantic side, and if he's dynamic enough, she might be off with him before her Taurus friend has realized that the relationship is threatened. But this possibility is relatively slight.

There won't be any problems in the bedroom. Two sexy Taureans with strong feelings and an emotional bias in all their activities will have a great time. Food and sex are the cement of this relationship, and both partners are likely to enjoy music, opera, theater, and such things. Two cheerful, possibly slightly overweight, honest people do incidentally make good friends and can be relied upon to know what is right and wrong, even if at times they choose the wrong.

He shouldn't question her too closely about where she's been, what she was doing at 9:30 last Tuesday night, who was the tall man she was seen with in the jeweler's, and so on—some signs would be flattered by this evident concern, but she won't. It's more than likely that she'll tell all about it anyway, because she isn't really secretive.

All the portents are good for financial success, too—provided he doesn't get stuck in a rut. He should remember that the lady loves flowers, chocolates, little gifts and, if they can be afforded, big and expensive gifts too. The way to a Taurean heart is through the checkbook or the stomach!

TAURUS MAN—GEMINI WOMAN

Frankly, this is not the most promising relationship. This lady is likely to drive the dependable, reliable, sturdy, honest, and cheerful Taurean man absolutely berserk.

He'll never know what to make of her flighty, moody, scintillating, exciting unreliability. Taurus operates through his body, while Gemini has a mind like quicksilver and an absolute need for mental stimulation. Although she'll admire his seriousness and loyalty, she will probably be somewhere else when he's being loyal and serious.

Of course, every relationship has a chance if the right people are involved. If she's prepared to let him be the boss, marriage could work, but the odds are against it—he's probably just too blunt in everything, including sex, for this sensitive lady. Nevertheless she attracts him because she's just about his opposite in everything.

Taurus is slow, conservative, and generous. He loves good food, and wine, and probably likes watching sports as much as playing them. Gemini can be awfully glib and superficial at times, like a butterfly flitting from flower to flower helping herself to the nectar. Of course, she's going to slow down from time to time, and Taurus might catch her on the rebound, but he's going to have to work almost as hard as she to make a go of life together.

Gemini is likely to be intrigued by Taurean response, the way problems are mulled over and decisions are final—no one ever got a Taurean to change his mind once he decided something was right or needed doing. The sheer stubbornness he displays almost defies description. This is what is meant by really getting one's own way. Just watching a little Taurean cry his way to what he wants is enormously instructive, not just about his nature but about human nature in general.

It isn't all gloom, though. Taurus could do a great deal to unloose neuroses shielded from the light by the restive Gemini. This earthy sexuality could be just the thing for her, provided she's still around after his first approaches. If she is still there, then it could be love, although Gemini might well take quite a time to realize it herself. One thing she has to do is improve her cooking, get a big comfortable sofa instead of those Queen Anne chairs, and remember he loves flowers—Taurus is a sensualist and not ashamed of it.

TAURUS MAN—CANCER WOMAN

A compatible pair. He'll love being the center of her world, while she'll find him a wonderful, attentive, reliable mate. Neither likes to leave the hearth of a home they've built; security is very important for these two.

Taurus is a stable sort, so there won't be any need to worry about where the next meal is coming from. He understands the importance of being comfortable, and a little flattery won't go amiss.

Cancer does have emotional problems. She thinks with her stomach in the sense that she can get into an emotional tangle that produces turmoil and even physical pain in the stomach area. But she has a lot of love to give, and Taurus is going to want it all. Sexually all should be well, but he will be terribly jealous even if she just looks at another guy. And if caught in a compromising position, that's the end. Taurus is a proud character who knows his own worth, and he isn't going to play second fiddle to anyone—at least not when his possessions are involved, and his woman is a possession to him. That's where there could be a little trouble. Cancer rather likes to be "owned" and supported and needed, but this man could begin to take her for granted, almost oppress her, and even the worm will turn under such circumstances. Cancer has a good idea of her own value, too, so she might just up and leave one day if he doesn't treat her with the respect she deserves.

It's a good match. The emotional irrationality and turmoil that Cancer feels from time to time will be soothed by Taurus, and she'll forgive him the odd sarcastic comment.

There will be lots of physical activity in and out of the home, alternating with periods when absolutely nothing happens. If he keeps telling her he loves her and needs her, she'll be putty in his hands; she'll do anything for him and love him forever. It's so easy to keep such a nice person as Cancer happy. The Taurus man should work on his imaginative powers and try to anticipate what she'd like him to do.

This guy is logical, positive, and sure of himself. Cancer is not nearly so certain that everything is for the best in the best of all possible worlds. If he can persuade her to take up flower arranging or yoga or anything, she'll blossom!

TAURUS MAN—LEO WOMAN

Two strong characters could make this a stormy relationship—but it could also be very satisfying. Leo is a confident, fairly dominating lady who likes to get out and about. She's worldly, sexy, straightforward, and honest. Taurus is much more of a stay-at-home, full of common sense and good with money—and that means careful at spending and earning it.

Both are ambitious for nice things, a house or two, good clothes, quality food, and so on, so there is a compatibility. Leo and Taurus understand each other through and through. She can be recklessly extravagant, and that might just turn his hair gray overnight, but really he understands.

They're stubborn; both know darn well that they're right all the time, so there could be some friction. If they can get this side of their natures under control, then they might just agree to disagree on some things, count their blessings, and have a really great time together.

Leo loves to be flattered, and Taurus is likely to be good at it, because he really will appreciate her most of the time. He could be overindulgent sexually, but Leo is no slouch; she's probably had or is going to have plenty of experience. Leos have to try everything, while Taureans are more cautious. He'll probably think this lady—and *lady* is the right word, because Leos like quality—is too sophisticated at times, too worldly, too much of a show-off, particularly with her dresses. But catch him in the right mood and he'll pay the bills.

This Leo impulsiveness probably has to be tempered with a little caution if the relationship is to last. But even if it doesn't, both have a lot to give. She'll lighten him (not least in the pocket), and remove some of that Taurean lugubriousness, and he'll make her appreciate that life isn't always a game. Leos should watch out for the occasional Taurean who is greedy, vicious, and totally selfish—but most Leos have too much common sense and experience to fall for that sort of guy.

Taurus is a man who can be depended on. He might well take over the kitchen from time to time and serve superlative food, but mostly his lady will feed him like a prince because she likes things done well. There's a good chance she loves flowers and will fill the home with them. She has excellent if slightly flamboyant taste in decoration, and he likes it.

TAURUS MAN—VIRGO WOMAN

Potentially a beautiful relationship. A compatible pair almost certain to be the envy of friends and relatives who enjoy visiting and entertaining this twosome.

Virgo is neat, precise, really rather fastidious, very conscious of the importance of hygiene, and at times appears a bit cold. Taurus is patient, honest, comfortable to be with and steady as a rock, but frankly sometimes has some of the less desirable characteristics of a rock—he's hard to budge, and this could cause a little friction with the anxious Virgo woman. He'll bring her the security she needs in order to blossom. There's something of the eternal virgin about her, and the earthy Taurean is likely to do a lot to balance the convent potential of his lady.

Taureans value tradition, perhaps too much. But both these two are likely to appreciate art, music, and the finer things. She shouldn't rebuff his compliments or he'll feel entirely rejected. Nor should she make fun of him—that isn't the way to treat Taurus. He likes good food, wine, and plenty of cuddling. And he's jealous if his lady so much as looks at anyone else. It's a bit trying, but he isn't perfect— just possessive and at times a little bit greedy. She should help him watch his weight—a dog might be just the thing to persuade him to ease himself out of his favorite chair (but even then he'll probably need a little prodding).

These two are likely to make an enviable team. She's not likely to give him much cause for jealousy once they are settled. She's a conscientious lady with her fair share of neuroses, but he'll soothe them. They should try to persuade each other to get up and join some social or sporting activity—it doesn't matter what it is, as long as it means leaving the kitchen and living room. This will help to keep the relationship fresh and interesting. Boredom is a possible problem where genuine compatibility is found. She should not criticize him even when he makes a fool of himself; instead, she should mildly suggest that what he has just done that made everyone cringe was a mild lapse of taste. He'll be like putty in her hands.

Virgo is hard-working and could get a little upset at times by the well-known Taurean tendency to laziness, hence the need to get him off his bottom. But honestly there's every chance it will be roses all the way.

TAURUS MAN—LIBRA WOMAN

The Libra woman needs romance, and the Taurus man may well be hard pushed to "ham" it up enough for her, but this could be a tender, loving relationship.

This guy is jealous of his woman's time, affections, and appearance—in other words, her flirting with attractive men will infuriate him. But Libra likes men, so unless she can restrain her impulses, there's going to be a storm brewing from time to time.

He'll look after her, make no mistake about that. She'll be expected to wait on him, keep the home spotless, and churn out gourmet meals. That isn't going to be easy for Libra, who likes her freedom, rarely counts the cost before buying, and is impulsive to a fault. Taurus is careful with the cash, doesn't squander his emotions either, is slow to move, but could well provide the sort of anchor that Libra really needs. Emotionally he could be ideal. He isn't the sort to get depressed, whereas she gets all worked up about the injustices of life—not just the way it is treating her and hers, but the way the Chinese, Africans, Eskimos, and so on are being ill-treated. She's a soft touch emotionally and in the pocket for any plausible charity, while Taurus is definitely not.

Both have a weakness for luxury and good living and appreciate art they can understand (not too much of the modern stuff, please). At times he'll treat her more like a naughty child than a highly intelligent grown-up person. But that's his way, and he's a difficult man to change. Perhaps this is the crux of any difficulty this pair might have. It's just no use trying to change this fellow. He's so stubborn and proud he'll make her weep, but on the other hand, he does appreciate everything done for him and usually says so. He can make his partner feel very good. He's so practical he'll make her scream, but secretly she admires his strength and almost certainly needs it in her muddled, emotional sort of Libran existence.

Physically these two are likely to make sweet music because Librans are fundamentally nice people. There's every chance the storms will be weathered. She should not compliment Taurus on his appearance, although that's a pretty good ploy for every man, but should admire his ability and something that he's done well—he'll beam just like a Leo, and love will positively blossom.

TAURUS MAN—SCORPIO WOMAN

There's not too much going for this relationship—on the surface anyway. Both partners are greedy, jealous, and stubborn. But precisely because of all this there is a chance that the Taurus man and the sexy Scorpio woman can each understand the impulses and compulsions the other suffers from and can make enough allowances to keep love alive.

It won't be easy because these Sun signs are opposite, and none of the friends and relatives who watch the relationship with undisguised amazement are going to expect it to succeed.

The biggest difficulty is that both know they're right and are likely to get set in their ways, refuse to budge, and make even the silliest minor disagreements resemble a pitched battle in the Napoleonic Wars. The home is likely to be crucial. A pleasant, comfortable, private sort of place without too many visitors is essential. But Scorpio is emotionally demanding, and Taurus likes things taken more gently, logically, realistically. She's going to have to take time to educate this guy in bed. He's lazy and rather unimaginative at times, but he's got a number of virtues. He's honest, trustworthy, hard-working when he wants something or is threatened, and jealous. That last one isn't exactly a virtue, but strangely enough Scorpio would probably be resentful if he wasn't. She certainly isn't lazy; she's probably fascinated by the occult, the mysterious, the dark side of human nature. He isn't going to understand that, but if it's love, he'll put up with it—provided, of course, that his breakfast, lunch, supper, and bedtime snack are served on time.

Scorpio does need respect, although she probably wouldn't phrase it like that. One thing she will get from this man is just that.

He's very sensitive—when it comes to his own feelings—and it's well known he can ride roughshod over others; but fundamentally he finds his Scorpio lover a bit of a puzzle, and as she's unlikely to enlighten him about her emotional involvements with the mysteries of life, he's always going to be a tiny bit scared of her. After all, familiarity does breed contempt. The boot of course could be on the other foot; Scorpio could decide she knows him just too well and opt for a little excitement elsewhere. And she might be wise to do just that, harsh as it may sound.

One thing about Taurus, he doesn't hold grudges, but that is most certainly not true of the Scorpio lady!

TAURUS MAN—SAGITTARIUS WOMAN

This is unlikely to be a successful relationship because Sagittarius is a roamer while Taurus is a stay-at-home. This doesn't mean that opposites won't attract. Both partners can be very attractive—but in truth the attraction is likely to be superficial. These two should think hard before starting a serious involvement.

She's humorous, cheerful, likes to keep several balls in the air just as the juggler does. He's serious, not to say gloomy, steady, responsible, stubborn, and at times sexually most attractive. He's a very possessive guy, and she's a firefly who doesn't care a fig for convention, money, or an easy life. Sagittarius is interested in the things of the mind, needs constant stimulation, and loves travel and often the more esoteric sports and activities. It could all be terribly wearing, unless each partner develops masochistic tendencies.

He'll want to know everything she does—he's the sort who keeps private detectives in business. And she'll resent him even asking her where she had lunch. If he can get the message that this lady is never going to be one of his possessions, then the relationship has a chance. And if she will settle down and cultivate the garden a little more than her nature indicates would be pleasurable, then she too might make a go of it with the sturdy, honest Taurean.

He's good with money, knows the value of things, and isn't going to be taken in by anyone. He'll provide a sheet anchor for this woman if—and it's a big *if*—she's prepared to let him. He'll probably be in a permanent state of jealousy when he sees his woman making eyes at the other males at a party. Taurus would do her a lot of good, but it could be frustrating and contentious before the hatchet is finally buried (take comfort from the fact that Scorpio would probably bury it in his head).

He's good husband material, at least that's what he looks like, because he isn't stingy and needs a good woman. But a major sacrifice of independence is required for anyone who's going to live with this fellow.

In this relationship there is likely to be a good deal of hurting and making up, loving and hating. Sagittarius might rather enjoy this, but it is unlikely that a Taurean will be able to stand it for long.

TAURUS MAN—CAPRICORN WOMAN

Neither partner is likely to do better! The Capricorn woman and the Taurus man were made for each other—and everyone will tell them so. There'll be plenty of physical attraction and a very strong need for a soundly based home background—and if that sounds a bit formal, then it could well be the way this relationship will go.

There's nothing flippant or "crazy" about this pair of earthy characters. Both like their food, probably plain, not too much of that fancy foreign stuff; they like elegant things and are prepared to work for them. Capricornians tend to be worriers, particularly about future security, but Taureans are sunnily self-confident about such things.

The only danger is that this happy pair could get so set in their ways, so comfortable, and even so boring that they might forget that the rest of the world exists. Nothing is likely to persuade these two to leave home pastures. Capricorn is probably more ambitious than her partner, who tends to take things as they come and deal with them practically without fuss. He'll be better than any other sign at satisfying her slightly prissy sexual needs. There isn't going to be all that much fire in this relationship.

Both have a nice sense of humor. Capricorn is a great manager, thrifty, sensible, and industrious. All this appeals to Taurus because he has a tendency to be lazy and to live off the fat of the land. He can be extravagant at times, and she shouldn't discourage this—let him have his fun. It's the nearest he's going to get to real excitement, and she can always go and exchange his gifts for something more practical the next day.

Capricorn had better not flirt when he's around; he'll likely go berserk. Taureans have a pretty exaggerated idea of their own importance, and for him to see one of his "possessions" tripping the light fantastic is likely to be too much of a blow to his pride. Taurus is, however, the ideal partner because he needs this lady's encouragement and drive behind him. And in return he'll love and cherish her and tell the world how proud he is of his beautiful woman. She should just smile as mysteriously as possible. It won't fool anyone, but it'll make him ecstatic.

All in all, there's every chance of a happy union. It's likely to be blessed by prosperity, sobriety (although Taurus does like his booze), and probably plenty of friends. One suggestion to Taurus: Do try to understand those moments of Capricornian coolness.

TAURUS MAN—AQUARIUS WOMAN

Taurus is going to get the best of this deal—provided he can somehow persuade Aquarius that she needs him.

If that sounds a little complex, it's nothing like the inside of an Aquarian's head. This is the most independent and stimulating woman in the Zodiac, but she may be a bit cool for the earthy Taurean. She's a great one for company, visiting new places, and doing exciting things, but through it all she stays strangely detached. She's an enigma even to herself. One moment she's all over her man, the next she might be a thousand miles away. It could be just too much for the simple, loyal, trusting, honest, diligent Taurean. But if he can get it together, she'll broaden his horizons and force him out of his comfortable lethargy like nothing and no one else can.

She's extravagant, although she likes top quality. She's forward-looking in everything, unconventional, and unambitious in a worldly sense, although she demands nice things. Taurus is just the guy to provide the nice things, though he might prefer a couple of Rembrandts to a dozen Impressionists. The communications gap could just be too much for this pair, but who knows?

One difficulty is that the Taurean's home is really his castle: It's number one in his life, and it has to be right. He'll pay all the bills even if he moans about the cost of the best mahogany and Persian carpets. What he'll do when he comes home one day and finds she's thrown it all out in favor of plastic chairs and bare boards, only God knows.

The odds are that Aquarius isn't going to succeed in changing this guy as much as she'd like, but he will keep her down to earth.

Sex could be an on-off business, but when she's in the mood, it'll definitely be "on." Aquarians are desperately intelligent people who probably know too much for their own good. Taureans feel with their stomachs rather than think with their brains, so this could create a nice complementary sort of relationship, even though he is going to have to revise his ideas about expecting dinner to be on the table every evening when he gets home. His lady might just be figuring out where Einstein went wrong when he arrives.

TAURUS MAN—PISCES WOMAN

The emotional insecurity of the Pisces woman seems likely to present problems for the Taurus man, who likes things simple, stable, and secure. Her intuition, vulnerability, charm, and allure are very attractive to him, and she senses in him someone she can lean on who will make the decisions she seems incapable of. But although there is an obvious attraction of opposites, Taurus could find the relationship more than his earthy nature can bear.

It's a bit of an oversimplification to say some people need looking after and others need to look after, but although Pisceans are a good deal tougher than they often seem, they are often very difficult to live with.

One of the problems is that this very ladylike lady is a dreamer. Her whole life revolves around her romantic dreams of knights and princes. Physically these two will do nicely, but mentally they're a whole world apart. He's practical, is good with money (she, too, can be surprisingly efficient at making money), and demands a fine home. She'll go along with that, seeking elegance and style, probably preferring traditional buildings to modern ones, but at times she's going to find this just too rough, stubborn, sensual, and thoughtless for her fundamentally delicate, rather high-toned and nervous disposition.

She's a possessive person, make no mistake about that, so these two will be totally wrapped up in each other even if the world falls apart around them. Pisces loves music, art, anything that engages her very fine senses. She may have a spirituality about her, too, that will bewilder her man. He won't be able to catch her—it's a bit like chasing clouds—but nevertheless she will fascinate him, just as a moth is fascinated by a flame.

If this sounds a bit morbid, it isn't meant to be. Both of them are fine people, in their way. He could give her the stability she needs, and she could help him spread his muddy wings, but in all honesty the pressures all this creates seem likely to be too much. Her romanticism will probably survive the Taurean jackboot—although that makes it sound too grim. He won't like her sudden moods and withdrawals, her flashes of temper and remarkable intuition. Pisces will need to get away from her man pretty often to recharge her batteries in the sunshine, even if it's only the "sunshine" of a dress shop or a park full of flowers.

TAURUS MAN—ARIES WOMAN

Most astrologers feel this match is likely to be a total disaster, and in most cases they would be right. But just occasionally it can be a miracle combination.

Aries is a stunner: exciting, demanding, impatient, bossy, adventurous, stimulating, infuriating, and often egotistical. She's everything Taurus dreams about but in practice finds he just can't put up with. For her this guy is likely to be just too slow, logical, and possessive.

In fact, he's probably just what Aries needs to stop her tearing off in thirty-seven different directions all at once. And she will certainly brighten his life. But alas, human nature being what it is, it'll probably be just too inconvenient for these two to make a go of it. He's very jealous, while she has no time to be jealous, so in practice they'll probably never meet. One Arian lady described her ideal man as a busy brain surgeon who's also a politician and on the weekends sails a yacht. She wasn't exaggerating. But it's unlikely that Taurus will be in this category—he likes to take it easy at home with a glass of wine and his favorite TV program. She'll probably be reading a book, doing a crossword, planning the next vacation, dreaming about her ideal man, and watching TV all at the same time. And Taurus won't even notice because he'll be wondering if the '58 vintage was better than the '59.

Lots of Arians have artistic gifts that rarely come to anything really remarkable, simply because life is so exciting and there are so many things to be done, so much to experience. There just isn't time to settle down and study only one thing! Taurus, of course, can't understand this. He'll do anything for the right woman who loves him, tells him so, and looks after him. Aries is unlikely to butter him up, and although she is a great entertainer, she will take far too much notice of her guests. She may love him, but she's darned if she's going to keep telling him so.

In most cases it just won't work. Aries can't be bothered to admire her man's possessions, even though they may have been gathered with flair and determination.

There are a lot of things militating against a successful relationship, but just occasionally it happens that an Arian slows down, a Taurean speeds up, the sun shines, the birds sing, and a lifetime match is made. No one knows how it works, but it does. Hallelujah.

GEMINI WOMAN—GEMINI MAN

Together these two could be just about the most fascinating and extraordinary pair in the entire Zodiac—or the relationship could be a disaster from the second week onward.

The difficulty is that neither of the partners is ever going to be able to make up his or her mind. That isn't to say that there won't be a lot of fun—it's just going to be frustrating a lot of the time. Both are flirtatious, easily bored, mentally hyperactive, lovers of games— mental games, that is—and hopeless at getting down to the nitty-gritty of living together.

When the partnership does work, it works in a big way because each has clearly decided to let the other take the lead, to sublimate personal interests and respect the other for virtues and not despise him or her for faults. There won't be too much routine in this relationship—indeed, these two might behave like twins at times in actually thinking alike, responding alike, and surprisingly even growing to look alike.

There will be terrific quarrels. But although outsiders may scurry for cover, the protagonists will be curiously detached; there won't be any malice when the storm is over—it's almost as though they've been playing games, as indeed they have.

Both will behave childishly and petulantly from time to time, more likely the male Gemini because he's likely to have an even more active mind and temperament than his lady love. They're both great fun to be with, exciting, and sexually compatible most of the time, but there's more than a fair chance that the sheer chaos of the relationship could make one or the other partner give up and look elsewhere for a stronger, simpler, more straightforward (if less overtly compatible) partner.

If the partnership is going to work, flirtatious impulses have to be curtailed and joint interests have to be developed, especially if they involve getting out of the home together. If the partners start going out alone regularly, then the end is in sight. But two genuinely grown-up, emotionally mature Geminis are a delight to watch and be with. True love was never more obvious or more charming.

GEMINI WOMAN—CANCER MAN

There are temperamental problems ahead for this pair, and it is doubtful if they are going to weather the storms. The Cancer man is sensitive, rather shy, and emotional. The Gemini woman is short-tempered and vivacious. He needs stability, peace, and domestic bliss. She is sociable, friendly, and mentally active.

There will be clashes, but they can be overcome. He's certainly going to admire this lady's quicksilver responses and her sense of fun. But he'll sulk when things aren't perfect. He expects an awful lot from his woman.

He's a good businessman who knows the value of money. He is also a good traveler and enjoys it, but his home is of vital importance to him. He doesn't really want his lady to interfere in his working life and arrangements; he wants her there at the end of the day. He probably loves antiques and old houses; he may well be an inveterate collector. He's appreciative of the things she does to beautify and organize his life because he's a pretty efficient fellow. But he responds to situations with his guts rather than his brains, and this is most certainly not the way Gemini acts. He's pretty deep at times, and this lady is inclined to dismiss his serious moments as just another one of his moods—that's a mistake. He doesn't like to feel insecure. He needs to be frequently complimented on his taste and his achievements, and he needs reassurances that all is going well. Gemini can do this easily if she chooses. But will she?

Sexually he is serious. He is deeply aroused, while she is more playful, perhaps too playful for him. She flits from idea to idea and may well be having erotic dreams of someone else when they are together. It won't be an easy relationship but it can work if Gemini determines to talk openly and frankly and if Cancer can restrain his morbid instincts and understand that his lady sees much more light and joy in the everyday things of life than he does. He might even speed up in his responses, given time and encouragement.

Neither of these two is a fool, make no mistake about that. Gemini can be changeable and moody too and can certainly give as good as she gets in an argument, although her lively temper is quick to dissolve. Cancer will have trouble returning to an even keel after a quarrel, and frankly there'll probably be quite a few of these, often about trivial things other signs would not even notice. But then life can sometimes be a battle—with no winners.

GEMINI WOMAN—LEO MAN

This is a fascinating combination, and there's a very good chance that it will work out to the enormous satisfaction of both parties. Leo is a real powerhouse of ideas and emotions, a born boss. Gemini is so smart, she'll twirl him around her little finger, tie him in knots, and untie him—and he'll love every moment of it. He's straightforward, simple, uncomplicated, demanding, intolerant, and huggable. She's quick, often moody, temperamental, flighty, and fascinating, and he finds her ever so desirable.

Leo is a great big booby, really. A little flattery is all that's needed to handle him. A *lot* of flattery, no matter how outrageous, will have him eating out of anyone's hand. He knows what's going on—he isn't stupid—but it doesn't matter because he has a lovely big ego. One thing he isn't is small-minded. He's big-hearted, often noble, generous, and surprisingly efficient. He's sexy, likes to eat and drink well, and doesn't like pain. He easily feels sorry for himself, and this is where there could be a problem. Gemini might just decide to be a bit vindictive and to put his ego through the grinding machine. He can't stand that, and he'll hit back blindly and possibly walk out. Leo isn't going to stand for competition in anything he's running—and he thinks he's running this relationship.

Gemini can be rather fickle. She loves novelty, new things, stimulating ideas and people. She might be bowled over by Mr. Big. In fact, the way to get her is to hit her with new ideas every ten seconds, never give her time to think, and then propose before she has time to reconsider. Unfortunately, he could get just too bombastic, self-important, and pompous. And no woman will stand that for long, certainly not the vivacious, charming, and often rather unscrupulous Gemini woman.

Nevertheless, this relationship has every chance of success because of the very oppositeness of temperaments. These two can make a formidable partnership, and woe betide anyone who gets caught trying to muscle in. Unless of course the interloper is really attractive; then it'll be too much for either Leo or Gemini and the split will happen so fast that no one watching will believe it.

GEMINI WOMAN—VIRGO MAN

There's not much chance this relationship will last. Of course, there are always exceptions, but the sensible onlooker isn't going to bet on these two making a go of it.

The problem is that Gemini moves like greased lightning, mentally at least. Virgo is precise, irritatingly exact in everything, and a born perfectionist, and Gemini hates to be tied down as tightly as he is going to want her to be. He's cautious to a fault, fussy, and very practical; habits comfort him. He thinks like a computer and often acts like one. He seems rather cold, and he'll try to deal with this woman logically. It just won't work—his computer will break down, and he'll go crazy if he tries to apply logic to the actions and ideas of the Gemini woman.

She's going to decide he's a boring stick-in-the-mud. She'll quickly tire of being corrected and criticized, and will eventually look elsewhere for friendship, understanding, and love. She will be attracted by his punctuality (not exactly a Gemini virtue), his neat and stylish clothes, his solicitude, and his very evident desire to please. But he's careful with cash and will never understand her violent changes of mood and her occasional petulance.

Sexually things may also go well at first, but the differences between these two are probably too great. A short, beautiful affair seems to be the answer, or, if it can be done, a life together spaced out like chapters in a book, with lots of fresh beginnings. It could work if both partners are intelligent enough—and they *are* an intelligent pair—to realize that each has to step back from time to time and see the other as though he or she were an entirely new person.

He will be attracted by the Gemini intelligence and vivacity. This lady could do him a world of good—or drive him insane. Perfectionists are always difficult to live with. He seeks profundity and despises the superficial. When he's depressed—and it will happen—he needs to be assured that the world is really an efficient and carefully organized place; that'll cheer him up because he expects efficiency all around him. OK, so he'll be disappointed, but at least his dream still remains. If she tells him the world is a mess and he's a mess, he won't be around long. But he is prepared to work at being devoted and he's a soft touch for someone who genuinely needs help—but make sure it's genuine.

GEMINI WOMAN—LIBRA MAN

This could be a good, lasting relationship with every chance of happiness. Libra has a lot of style. He wants and expects a full partner, not a servant or a lapdog, and Gemini is likely to give as good as she gets and appreciate his character and his charm.

He isn't the strongest or toughest of men, but he will certainly show respect for her feelings. He's sophisticated and yet at the same time there is often an unspoiled, little-boy character peeping through, saying "Hey, look at me!"

Gemini likes his romanticism and his free and relatively easy attitude. She likes to go out to parties and other stimulating functions, and he'll happily tag along. She isn't usually possessive, but equally she isn't as logical a lady as she might be. She can be prey to sudden, short-lived enthusiasms that stimulate her mentally. If this fellow is wise, he'll bring a book of difficult crossword puzzles or brain teasers and his chess set around when he invites himself to her place. She'll love it and probably him too.

Sexually both are affectionate and might well be passionate. He's a fine, sensitive lover, and he'll probably be given plenty of chances to use his talent by the mercurial Gemini lady. Life certainly isn't going to be dull for this lively pair. She may have to work at the union more than he does because things don't come quite so naturally to her; she's used to walking out of situations that bore her or no longer come up to her fertile expectations.

Their first meeting is likely to be very important. Indeed, if there's no "click," there probably won't be a second meeting. She shouldn't nag or criticize him too much. He won't stand for it—it's the one thing apart from jealousy that Libra despises and that really disagrees with his delicately balanced system. A lot of the time these two think alike, even though his emotional apparatus is more important to him, while her mental apparatus is both her strength and her weakness.

Oh, one more thing: Libra can't stand displays of temper and temperament. Gemini has the ability to avoid displays like this if she chooses—or, if she decides to, she'll really let herself go and upset everyone. If she values this guy—and she ought to—she'll keep things calm and nice and easy.

GEMINI WOMAN—SCORPIO MAN

This is likely to be a real "tingler" of a relationship. Everything is going to be charged with emotion and meaning for these two. They probably won't be able to let each other alone, physically or emotionally or mentally. In some ways it will be a battlefield rather than a union, but it'll certainly be stimulating.

Scorpio gets abominably jealous, and Gemini won't be able to understand why. There's likely to be a lot of excitement about first meetings. He's intuitive, attractive, and charming when it suits him to be so. He's also a bit moody and a trifle mysterious even to himself.

What he really wants and needs is a calm, settled, undemonstrative home life. He isn't likely to get it from this bundle of energy, who has the most active mind in the Zodiac. If it were to work, it would be a remarkable relationship, but the odds are stacked against it. He won't be able to play the boss with this woman; she will find his attempts in that direction screamingly funny and will tell him so. He'll probably lose his temper. Unfortunately Scorpios have a capacity for storing up grudges and an undeniably sharp tongue—a nasty combination.

Scorpio is, however, an attractive man. He is a strong man, make no mistake about that, and he's a trier; if he wants this lady, he isn't going to take no for an answer. What might throw him is her repetition of "maybe." He's often pretty good with money too, and will probably need to be when she's around because she can be reckless and thoughtless when the mood is on her. Gemini can be funny, fey, and delightful all at the same time. Scorpio may not appreciate this. His grim silence isn't going to do a lot for the partnership.

He's a pretty intense sort of person. Gemini is just the opposite. Perhaps he should treat her as a refresher while pursuing some other lady. It's the sort of thing he might well be doing anyway, because he's a very sexy guy. In fact, it's his main motivation, though not necessarily in a lewd or earthy way; he does have a sense of style. But sex is important to him, and he likes to excel.

The trouble is that he wants to possess his woman completely, and Gemini isn't having any of that. Life together, however long it lasts, is likely to be a remarkable series of ups and deep, deep downs for this pair.

GEMINI WOMAN—SAGITTARIUS MAN

These two are alike in many ways, and the union might break up because of this very fact—or it could be a great success. It's difficult to predict what might happen when these two bump into each other. Whatever happens, it's likely to be a fun-filled relationship.

He's an attractive, lively, flip sort of guy. She really appreciates his charm, his ease in all sorts of company, and his apparent frankness and honesty. He's so restless that at times he might even make the volatile Gemini lady wonder what's going on. These two might just stimulate each other to a dead stop—and that could be very good for both of them.

Everything this man does is an adventure. He takes awful chances, gets in a terrible tangle, and then suddenly extricates himself with a stroke of genius. He may seem woolly, disorganized, and hopeless—and then suddenly he demonstrates with a remarkable intuitive comment that really he's got it all together. He's a great persuader too, a born optimist, but sometimes his promises turn out to be just that. If this woman wants him, she'd better buy the wedding ring herself.

He wants a woman who is a constant source of amusement and stimulation. That's precisely what Gemini is likely to be. He's a flirt and needs to do just what he wants. She demands to go her own way, but she can be more stubborn than he would ever dream of being.

Their sex life is likely to puzzle even them. Anything could happen at any time. Is he worth hanging on to? Decidedly, but it is going to be a big effort for this lady. And his remarkable collection of contacts and friends isn't going to make it much easier.

Gemini will need a lot of determination to put up with him at times, but at others he's so delightful that she'll forgive him anything—and that includes all the other women, real or imaginary, she thinks he's surrounded by. There are evident weak points in a union between these two, but neither is fundamentally selfish or demanding, and this makes a big difference. If they can learn not to act on impulse all the time, then things will work out fine. Another big plus is that neither will try too hard to change the other.

GEMINI WOMAN—CAPRICORN MAN

It would be difficult to find two characters who were more dissimilar. But opposites do attract, and these two could make a go of it provided they are prepared to really work at the relationship rather than expect things to drop smoothly into place. Indeed, there's a lot to be said for such a relationship, in which the partners have to really watch their step.

The difficulty is that Capricorn is reserved, serious, reliable, and practical and has a deep need for security. He's a good saver, a good manager of finances, and happiest when he's working hard with a particular goal in mind, whether it's the need for a better job or a better house or a bigger bank balance.

Gemini is capricious, stimulating, mentally active, and full of fun. She lives for the moment. She spends money like water, given half a chance. Capricorn is a great respecter of the past, of traditions and law, but he can get rooted in his job or home or way of life if he's not careful. He likes order and balance, and this is good, but of course these things can produce stultification, boredom, and sheer lethargy if someone like Gemini doesn't come along to shake him up.

He loves stylish and beautiful things and may well be a collector of anything from postage stamps to gold plate (encourage the latter). She is going to have to make a real effort to live up to this side of his nature. His home is the place where he can relax—and plan his next business coup. Well, that's not quite the right word because this fellow is much more likely to make it to the top by sheer hard work than by a stroke of genius or something slightly risky. There will certainly be major problems for these two, particularly when he watches her cavalier and free-wheeling attitude. Geminis aren't worriers, and Capricorns are. One thing is that he'll worry about and for her—in fact, he'll do enough worrying for both of them. If at times she seems a little cold, distant, and sexually unresponsive, then that's the way Capricorn will also appear at times. This relationship is very much a maybe one.

GEMINI WOMAN—AQUARIUS MAN

This is potentially a very attractive union. The major problems are likely to be physical ones because these two could run out of sexual steam. Whatever happens, they're likely to remain close, dear friends. They could well end up staying together because of the sheer fascination each has for the other.

Things certainly won't be smooth all along the line. Life will never be dull for these two. He's often brilliant, often infuriating, often cold, often warm and charming, often a bit of everything, if that is possible in one human being. He is forward-looking, is fascinated by new things, and loves to travel and see new places, meet new people, do stimulating things. That suits the agile, vivacious Gemini lady, who is even more easily bored than he is.

He's going to respect her intuitive and logical response to situations and her ability to concentrate in relatively short doses. There'll be probably too many friends and acquaintances buzzing around this pair, but Gemini knows how to handle them better than Aquarius does. If she values him, she'll keep these friends at arm's length, or the female ones anyway.

Aquarius can be amazingly undemanding, honest, and practical at times. But he can be pushed over the top, and Gemini could do it if anyone can. She has to avoid creating a furor over trivial incidents—this can happen to Geminis—and to remember that her man is a rather special one. He's terribly interested in the future well-being of the planet and in humanitarian and charity projects—at times it may look as if he's bidding to take all the world's troubles on his shoulders. However, there is something dispassionate about his responses that saves him from the emotional stress that deep involvement with others can produce. This is something that Gemini understands well because she also is mentally rather than emotionally oriented.

This is where there might be problems. Sometimes these two have to have a good old-fashioned quarrel to bring them closer together. They could just drift too much into other avenues of life and interest and out of each other's path. That would be a great pity because these two have much to offer each other and the world if their strange and sometimes enigmatic energies can be harnessed to work in tandem. It's going to be an unpredictable but possibly very satisfying relationship.

GEMINI WOMAN—PISCES MAN

This will be a decidedly shaky sort of relationship, with both partners likely to exhibit ninety-two facets of their remarkable and different characters at any one time. The sheer unpredictability of these two will make this union desperately difficult to maintain.

Pisces is almost totally emotional, while Gemini is mentally oriented. They almost live in different worlds. Of course, it can be fascinating and enormously stimulating to meet an "alien," but communication can be decidedly tricky. Can the relationship work? Of course it can; nothing is impossible when two people fall in love, but it's going to be pretty tough going most of the time.

The sheer insecurity of living with a partner who can't make up his or her mind is extremely wearing. Living with an emotional dustbin is a daunting prospect for Gemini, and Pisces will think she's so superficial that she must be deeper than she seems. He'll be fascinated by her mind, her responses, her ability to penetrate to the root of a problem. But this is so alien to his sentimentality and his romantic nature that he'll cut off sooner or later. This man is a dreamer. He's not aggressive or pushy, and he's really attractive and fascinating despite all his faults. Gemini is likely to be a short-term pushover for him because she just won't be able to fathom what's going on at all.

But it won't last. These two will be so busy making plans that nothing will get done. That isn't to say they cannot be practical, sensible, and realistic when they have to be. It's just that such practicality is so much less fun than planning and dreaming and arguing and living in the moment. Mistrust is bound to creep insidiously into this relationship, through the Piscean's tears and protestations of undying love and the terse, sometimes aggressive responses of this Gemini when she can't make him understand that a bucket of tears won't pay the rent. He's probably pretty good at his job, even if his stomach churns around all the time as emotional responses leave him a quivering jelly—but Pisces has met it all before, so no wonder he is tougher than he looks.

GEMINI WOMAN—ARIES MAN

The Gemini woman will be enormously attracted by the way this Arian takes control of things, makes the decisions, and organizes her life. But he's never going to really understand how this mercurial lady thinks and why she acts the way she does.

Life together is going to be a continual battle—not a major war, but a battle of little irritations and misunderstandings. There is compatibility at a deep level, but there could be all sorts of barriers to break down and overcome before these two can get down to basic honesty.

All this doesn't mean that life together won't be fun. The stimulating Arian, with his dynamic and at times overbearing manner, will clearly be the boss and will expect his love to be an active sporting lady. This won't suit Gemini, who rather despises brute force. Her temper is going to show from time to time, but still she is fascinated by this fellow. There is a danger she'll refuse his amorous advances once too often and he'll be off—but that danger exists anyway, for Aries doesn't like to stay too long anywhere; he begins to worry that he might miss something of what the world has to offer.

Gemini needs mental stimulation. She's subtle, artistic, and elegant. She's probably too quick for Aries when it comes to an argument, but she's likely to change her mind from moment to moment and drive him berserk. When an Arian finally loses his temper, it is something to behold—or maybe it's safer not to be around to behold it! She'll try him sorely, but he'll forgive her. He is quite incapable of holding a grudge; life's too short for that. Gemini is unlikely to relish staying at home. She wants a challenging job, with plenty to keep her active mind working, and fortunately this gives her the opportunity to work off steam out of the home environment.

Gemini has one great advantage in this union—she is able to understand how her man thinks and operates. She may not fully understand her own responses, and *he* certainly won't understand her, but this gives the partnership an outside chance of being a terrific success and a good chance of being at least a workable relationship. She should just remember that he likes to be number one and should string him along if he matters to her. He's probably worth the effort and the trouble because he's fundamentally one of the good guys of the Zodiac.

GEMINI WOMAN—TAURUS MAN

Not a very promising relationship. Taurus is slow, reliable, honest, home-loving, and at times boring. Gemini is mercurial, mentally active, argumentative, and fascinating. She wants freedom, while he's a born jailer. She loves to tease and stimulate, and that's the last thing a Taurean wants.

Basically she's moving too fast for this guy. He usually reacts with his body first and his mind second. She's all mind and expects to control her emotions and body, although of course it doesn't always work out quite that way. He's a very jealous sort too, and although the quick-thinking Gemini lady will probably set him straight, it won't make life easy.

He is a strong man, and this is where the attraction could come in. Sometimes she's going to stop whirling around and have a good cry because life isn't working out for her the way it should. Taurus has big broad shoulders to cry on. He has artistic appreciation, too. He wants a comfortable home above almost everything else, and he loves his food. Will Gemini be around long enough to share his dream? It depends on whether she's prepared to sublimate her own interests for him.

He has a healthy sexual appetite too, and his pretty basic advances and demands could turn the fastidious Gemini off. A little subtlety would do the relationship a world of good here. However, his deep sexuality could help Gemini to experience life instead of running around and around in circles inside her own admittedly brilliant mind.

He does have a nicely developed sense of humor, and he tends to dress well, if a trifle conservatively. He wants his woman to look good, to reflect his own prosperity and social standing. Gemini must curb a tendency to extravagance, good businesswoman though she undoubtedly is at times. He isn't a stingy guy, but he is careful with money, and she will have to learn to understand this part of his nature as well as put up with his other faults. It won't be an easy relationship, particularly if he should happen across a really snooty Gemini—they do exist—although even so she's still approachable because all Geminis are suckers for an argument or a mental challenge. These two should try an affair before even starting to get serious—and should try to keep even the affair lightweight. Taurus probably won't be able to do even that, and the lady will realize what she's up against. Good luck.

GEMINI MAN—GEMINI WOMAN

The problem with these two is that neither partner is ever going to be able to make up his or her mind. The relationship could be a frustrating experience that will end in total disaster, or it just might be an extraordinary and fascinating one. The Gemini man might seem ideal at first, and his partner might be all he has ever dreamed of, but will it last?

The flirtatious Geminis are easily bored, tremendously alive mentally, and frustrated emotionally. They love games in which the mind has to be used tactically or positionally, and are pretty hopeless at getting down to the nitty-gritty of living together unless they make a really special effort.

Of course there will be quarrels, but when they're over, these two will just smile and carry on as though nothing had happened. It will seem as though they've only been playing at arguing—and because these two always have a certain detachment from reality that acts as a sort of self-defense mechanism, that's likely to be how it was.

Geminis are great fun to be with. Sexually they could make a great pair, but their relationship will be so chaotic that she may well go looking for a stronger, more stable and reliable partner—and then wonder if she's done the right thing. But that's the sort of quandary the Gemini woman is likely to find herself in often. When the partnership does work, it works very well because it means that each has decided to sublimate personal desires and interests for the sake of the partnership. This could be very amusing at times, but flirtatious impulses will have to be curtailed. Two genuinely mature, responsible, loving Geminis are a sight to behold. True love is surely never more charming or courteous.

There won't be much boredom when these two are around; there'll be so much going on that outsiders are likely to shake their heads in disbelief. There may, of course, be tensions simmering below the surface, and certainly neither will tie the other down when it comes to contact with the other sex—though they would be better off being a little more possessive if they want their partnership to continue. When Gemini temper tantrums happen, they are not premeditated or harped back on. In most cases this will be a short-lived partnership, but there could be some very special exceptions.

GEMINI MAN—CANCER WOMAN

This won't be an easy relationship because the Cancer woman is emotionally oriented, while the Gemini man is mental in his responses. There will be some stormy sessions before balance is achieved—if it ever is.

Cancer enjoys traveling but prefers to have a stable home environment she can return to. She's moody and romantic at times, and she needs security. Gemini is as fast as they come, in more ways than one. He needs security like he needs a hole in the head. He's lively, vivacious, charming, exciting, and fascinating. This lady could fall for him in a big way. He's almost her opposite. She's serious, while he's flirtatious. He is playful sexually, while she can be deeply aroused and deeply hurt.

Cancer may well be a good businesswoman, and Gemini will admire this, just as he will her efforts to make their home cozy yet elegant. But will he do his part? That's the big question, and in all honesty it isn't likely. These two could be awfully good for each other. Cancer's worrying and emotional chaos can be lightened by Gemini's zany ways. He can be taught that sometimes things have to be taken more seriously and that life does sometimes throw up responsibilities that cannot be shrugged off.

But make no mistake, neither of these two is a fool. Gemini will give as good as he gets in an argument and shrug it off as unimportant, while Cancer will brood for days over imagined slights that others might not even notice. Life with these two might seem very much like a battle at times—and there won't be any winners.

It's a fascinating combination if it can be made to work, and it can if Gemini will restrain himself and talk openly and frankly and if Cancer can overcome her suspicion that life is not the best possible thing to happen to anyone! She must learn to see more light and joy in the everyday things. It's long odds that these two will make a successful union unless they are pretty experienced. But it can work if they are prepared to make the effort.

Cancer will look after the care and feeding of her man. She needs praise and reassurance, and unfortunately, this fellow tends to pounce on people for their mistakes. She mustn't retire into her shell when the going gets rough, but must sometimes lash out; he'll respect her for this.

GEMINI MAN—LEO WOMAN

There's every chance that this relationship will be a good one, with the bossy Leo meeting her match and being outwitted every time by the temperamental Gemini.

Leo is easily handled. She has to be flattered outrageously—although of course she'll know it's all true. She is beautiful, talented, charming, brilliant, and so on. She's also impulsive, fiery, domineering, and great fun. She's certainly not small-minded. She's very sexy, is fairly resilient, likes to eat and drink well, and, given half a chance, lives in real style. She has an excellent design sense and may dress exuberantly, if not extravagantly.

Gemini is flighty, brilliant, sometimes moody, fascinating, and difficult, but inventive and clever in bed. Leo will let him go his own way until he strays just a little too far—as is the Gemini style—and then she'll pounce like a lioness and haul him back to base. Most times he won't mind; he likes to be wanted and needed. Just occasionally he'll be vicious or petulant, and that's where there could be trouble because Leo is a proud lady and won't take too much of that. She'll walk out, and he will suddenly realize what he's lost.

There'll be lots of excitement with these two around. He'll really be good at charming her and flattering her, and a lot of it will be sincere. She's going to have to learn to sublimate her straightforward "whack 'em on the head" behavior and play it a little subtle with this guy. He responds well to sudden changes of plan, mysterious phone calls, and the like. Sometimes he thinks he's part of spy movies anyway, so keeping him on his toes is a legitimate part of the relationship game.

Gemini is getting the best out of this relationship, but he can offer his woman a good deal provided he's prepared to be serious. She'll always try to go one better, whether it's at tennis, driving, or car maintenance—she can be a very useful lady to have around. But he just won't compete; he's not interested in proving how good he is. This can be a frustrating experience for the competitive, ambitious Leo, but if she really wants the guy, she'll get over it and learn that although she may be the boss, she must never tell him so.

GEMINI MAN—VIRGO WOMAN

The problem here is that Virgo tends to have fixed opinions about almost everything, while Gemini doesn't like to commit himself and tends to vacillate. Clearly the stage is set for some resounding clashes of temperament.

Nevertheless, the relationship has a chance, albeit a relatively slim one, if the lovers can accept each other's limitations and capitalize on the good points. Gemini is bright, vivacious, stimulating, quick-witted, charming, and fun to be with. Virgo is sensible, efficient, honest in most cases, and persistent. It's not an easy combination, although there will be plenty of attraction to start with. She'll want to help or even mother him, and he'll be attracted by her caring, warm, genuine interest in him and his activities.

Virgo does have a reputation for being cold, analytical, and critical. She certainly can be excessively critical and fussy, but at the same time she can be too giving and forgiving of those she loves. She's likely to be imposed on by Gemini selfishness, and frankly she would be better off without this. It has been suggested that few Geminis ever grow up, and there's some truth in this in the sense that all sensation-seekers are immature. But life would be so much duller without the Gemini sparkle.

Sexually, Virgo expects deep passion, while Gemini likes to keep things playful and light. He doesn't want drama in his sex life, although he certainly isn't averse to it in his love life (kindly note the difference). Gemini likes to see the results of his actions, so he doesn't make a particularly good social reformer. Virgo, on the other hand, has in many cases a highly developed social conscience and often feels for the underdog.

This lady will have to control her tendency to nag and grumble if she wants to keep Gemini around. Incidentally, she has pretty fixed and straight ideas about love and courtship; she might even seem rather old-fashioned about such things. Does a burningly romantic heart lurk somewhere deep within her breast? Not really, but she does need the strength and love of a good man. She'd probably better look elsewhere despite all the razzle-dazzle and at times brilliance that Gemini brings into her ordered and efficient existence. This man attracts a lot of women, so Virgo be warned.

GEMINI MAN—LIBRA WOMAN

There's a lot going for this pair: sexual attraction, a distinct possibility that temperaments will complement each other, and a fundamental understanding. Libra wants equality and appreciation. She's likely to get it from Gemini, who wants his freedom—probably too much so—and refuses to be bound by conventions.

Sexually both are affectionate and could well be passionate. Both like excitement and novelty. There could be financial problems, but they won't worry him too much. She needs someone who understands her occasional moods. She probably won't get this under-standing from him, but he will be very appreciative of her efforts in the home and to make herself attractive for him.

Gemini will certainly stir things up, doing things like whisking her off for surprise trips and vacations. Sometimes even the not-too-serious Libran will wonder why she married a zany, maniacal, flip-pant, and infuriating man like this one. But life won't be dull. She's going to have to work at the union, but fortunately, he isn't too pos-sessive. She likes parties and flirting almost as much as he does. One way to a Gemini's heart—if there is such a thing—is to present him with lots of intellectual puzzles and games and challenges. The smart Libran will make things a bit difficult for her Gemini lover.

She shouldn't criticize him too much, however. He won't stand for it; he'll argue and get angry. But for him to criticize her is death. The way to end a relationship with a lady Libran is to pull her to pieces (verbally). Her delicately balanced organism just won't take it; she'll be gone so fast it won't seem true. But enthusiasm for her ideas and projects, that's a different matter. No jealousy either—not that it's likely from Gemini; he isn't likely to be there enough of the time to notice anything to get jealous about.

It's a lucky Gemini who finds himself a nice Libran lady. She communicates well with him. She does get tied up in emotional knots from time to time—indeed, she may even be in an emotionally cha-otic state a lot of the time, but it won't often show. But she is fun-damentally a lady, and that can't be said about all the signs. If she can stand him, then she's going to do him a lot of good by making him more responsible and reasonable. There'll be a whole lot of fun and joy in this relationship.

GEMINI MAN—SCORPIO WOMAN

The serious Scorpio woman should give this man a wide berth. There isn't much chance these two will be other than ships in the night. Of course, anything is possible when love comes along, but the clash of temperaments is likely to be too much for a lasting relation-ship.

Gemini is smark, quick, charming, and flippant. This lady wants more than that from her lover. She needs financial security and, even more important, emotional security. She can be very jeal-ous indeed, and that won't suit the fast-moving Gemini man.

Sexually there could be a degree of compatability, and lots of initial passion, but it won't last. She's a deep one, a little mysterious, possessive, and strong. She hates being contradicted and enjoys a fight. This guy just isn't up to that. He's fundamentally a lightweight out of his class with this lady. She has her black moods too, and although he would seem to be just the one to drag her out of them, she's more than likely to tell him to push off and get things sorted out herself.

He might even come to think of her as neurotic. Scorpio may well be dramatic and even a little vicious at times. She's all woman and fascinating to Gemini. And she certainly is sexy. Not only does she need sex physically, but she is mentally and emotionally equipped to deal with and understand sex and all its implications in our society. This gives her a terrific advantage over this fellow, who will frankly never understand what makes her tick. (She may never come to understand it herself, it must be added.)

She can be a heavy number. Not many signs can deal with a real Scorpio, but fortunately these are rare. No one is a fully fledged member of the Scorpio clan, since there are always other planetary influences at work. But in case this makes her sound unbearable, she also has a real creativity and she appreciates the sheer brilliance of Gemini's mind when it's working on something worth concentrating on (this may be rare). And she may be frighteningly loyal.

She's a fascinating woman who is probably looking for a real cause to give her all for. It isn't likely to be Gemini, because she's going to see through him and his playful flippancy. It's likely to be a battle rather than a union. She wants to possess and be possessed completely, and Gemini isn't equipped for this. Life together, no matter how long it lasts, is likely to be a real series of ups and deep, deep downs for this pair.

GEMINI MAN—SAGITTARIUS WOMAN

This is an attractive pairing with an excellent chance of developing into a strong, exciting relationship. Perhaps the biggest danger is that because these two are so very similar in many ways, their restless, stimulating relationship will break up.

Sagittarius is charming, sociable, optimistic, and fun to be with. She is outgoing, likes to keep on the move, and won't be tied down to the home and by too much responsibility. This suits Gemini. He respects her independence and her sense of humor, and her mind is almost as quick as his. She will understand his capriciousness, his failure to make the books balance at times, and his superficiality. Both are good-natured, stimulating, and a bit zany at times.

Gemini could make the mistake of being too critical of his lady's weak points, and that won't go down too well. Sexually anything could happen and probably will. These two are unpredictable, but they are not possessive or jealous, so most of the time things will be sweetness and light. One thing that must be moderated—and hopefully will be by experience—is their impulsiveness. It's fine a lot of the time, but not all the time! Every union needs its quiet, reflective moments, and these two have to work at that.

They'll have plenty of friends and acquaintances. There could be job problems, as both are prone to move on. Six months is a long time in any one spot for either of these gadabouts, and of course there is always the danger represented by the pretty blonde at the office or the handsome guy at the tennis club.

A lot of the things these two share are going to be magical, terrific, intuitive. They could begin to think alike. "Darling, I saw this terrific ceramic monkey in an antique shop and couldn't resist it." "You're kidding. I bought one in the market an hour ago." And so on. It will be an endless source of fascination, of course.

Sagittarius can get in an awful mess, and there's a fair chance her desk or private corner at home will be chaotic. She'll know just where everything is, though, and woe betide anyone who moves things or tidies up. The mess could well be emotional too, but then suddenly she'll do something quite brilliant, proving that she's been "with it" all along. Gemini will be truly appreciative of this display of virtuosity. If these two are emotionally mature, then theirs will be a very special partnership.

GEMINI MAN—CAPRICORN WOMAN

Don't take any heavy bets on this relationship working out. It would be hard to find two more opposite characters.

Love won't be a bundle of fun for these two. Capricorn needs security, and passion related to a steady home and social life. She doesn't want the excitement and stimulus that the lively, charming, unpredictable Gemini man brings into her life. But he could be very good for her. He'll get her out of her rut as no one else will—provided she hasn't gone screaming mad before it happens.

He is an attractive guy, there's no denying that, and opposites do certainly attract. He might catch her on the rebound. It isn't exactly unknown for Capricorns to end relationships. She is a worker, and she needs encouragement to build something—a bank balance, for instance. She isn't likely to get it from Gemini, who'd rather spend her cash than sit there figuring out the interest that's accruing.

Some of his sexual behavior might well embarrass this lady. She is decidedly conservative in many ways. He's just too flippant, flirty, and devil-may-care. The sensible Capricorn lady is going to take one look and shake her head. But of course, not even Capricorns can be sensible all the time, and Gemini is so attractive, after all. If only he would face up to reality as she sees it. . . .

One additional danger is that he may come to regard her serious approach and her jealousy and interest in social causes as just a great big bore. She's a collector too; she loves quality things and her home is something to be proud of and enjoy and relax in. Gemini isn't going to be able to understand this even if he says he does. His trouble is that he's always paying lip service, saying how he understands and loves and feels deeply. He just doesn't do any of these things deeply. It's all just too too frustrating for Capricorn.

If the mercurial Gemini and the worrying Capricorn can reach some sort of truce, there is a chance for their union. But honestly the chances are slim. They should have a good old-fashioned fling and stay friends. Too much proximity might make them hate each other. Perhaps they could have several divorces and remarriages to each other, and incredibly the whole thing might just be a miracle that no one else will ever understand.

GEMINI MAN—AQUARIUS WOMAN

Lucky the Gemini who finds and falls for an Aquarian lady—provided, of course, that he can fight off the horde of admirers already there before him.

This woman is pretty special in that she is undemanding, forward-looking, serious, and yet almost certainly highly intelligent. She works on her mind, studies hard, and, although she's not necessarily talented, has a thing about improving her mind. This suits Gemini down to the ground—it's paradise for him. His volatile, mercurial, stimulating mind will certainly be appreciated by this lady. Neither of these two is particularly sentimental or romantic in the hearts-and-flowers sense. But sexually there is likely to be a lot of initial passion that might later become real affection.

Aquarius is a dreamer; she thinks big—never doubt that. She can be unpredictable too, but Lord knows she's met her match in this man. She's very easy to get along with, but he's going to have to try to create a base for her. She isn't really equipped to do all the homemaking herself.

There will certainly be mutual respect. And she will teach him a lot if he'll just listen sometimes. She will fascinate him and he won't know why. Geminis can easily get out of their depth when things get serious, but there is a lot of affinity between these two that can really be capitalized on. She may have to look after the finances. He knows something about everything—or thinks he does—but she's going to have to put her foot down at times. That won't be easy for her, but it may be good for her development. She can be pretty impulsive too, but mostly she's a practical sort. He certainly needs her basic common sense.

There'll be plenty of fun in this union. Both love travel and seeing new places and new sights. One big plus for this relationship is that she is rarely jealous or too demanding. There's something dispassionate about her responses that saves her from the emotional stress that living with a Gemini could produce in so many other signs.

The Gemini mental orientation can sometimes be excessively critical or wounding. Once in a while a good fight will help these two to clear the air. Aquarius won't like it at the time, but it will bring them back together if they should start to drift apart, as might well happen. This is certainly going to be an unpredictable relationship.

GEMINI MAN—PISCES WOMAN

Pisces is tougher than she looks, but this is going to be a decidedly shaky sort of relationship at the best of times. The awful unpredictability of these two certainly gives them a common bond—but who can live with it? Maintaining a loving relationship or even a speaking relationship will be difficult for this remarkable pair.

Pisces is emotionally oriented—and how. Gemini is mental. They inhabit different worlds most of the time. Of course, it is fascinating, exhilarating, and stimulating for "aliens" to meet, but communication is not always the easiest thing in such circumstances.

Pisces is very possessive—she wants exclusive rights—and this guy isn't likely to fall in with her plans. His lively mind and his need to demonstrate his brilliance and individuality militate against the cozy relationship she has in mind. She is a dreamer, a romantic, a sentimentalist, a nostalgic, forever expecting knights in shining armor and sultans with long mustachios to whisk her away from the mundane chores. She really does expect such things to happen at any moment. Her imagination makes her an ardent lover, and Gemini will certainly turn her on—but he just isn't stable enough to counterbalance her emotional insecurity.

This union does have a number of things going for it, because these two are very attractive in their different ways. He'll certainly stimulate her—sometimes almost to despair. There'll be plenty of unexpected trips, friends dropping in unannounced, surprise presents, that sort of thing. But it will make her even more insecure than she normally is. She has extraordinary intuition at times and can come up with remarkable moneymaking schemes that actually work, but Gemini is not really the man to carry them through to a successful conclusion for her.

Financial difficulties might well prove the rock on which this relationship finally founders. These two are just as likely to be tucked up in bed while the creditors remove the furniture. But where do they go when the creditors also remove the bed?

There is likely to be genuine affection between these two, but life together will be just too insecure. She's all feeling and needs emotional security. He is too self-centered and critical for her.

GEMINI MAN—ARIES WOMAN

The Arian woman doesn't have time for games, so Gemini is going to have to work hard to stay in touch. If he wants to, he can certainly attract this lady—she's a sucker for an amusing, stimulating guy, and he has the remarkable ability to make light of her attempts to run his life the way she wants.

She'll be irritated by the fact that she can't pin him down. Mentally he's a will-o'-the wisp. But both are independent and not prone to jealousy, so there's every chance that a lively encounter could gradually turn into something more serious.

She will need plenty of patience and determination to make a go of things with him. He can be terribly infuriating at times, but he will certainly appreciate her lively sexuality although he won't be nearly so enthusiastic about her sporting activities. She likes to keep in shape and expects her man to tag along. She's a lady who fears nothing. She piles in where every sensible being in the Zodiac sheers off. And she just doesn't know the meaning of the word *tact*.

Gemini is going to be very attracted by this powerhouse, but he won't like her sudden displays of temper or irritation when life isn't behaving as she thinks it should. He's going to have trouble if he plays her up too much; she'll be out of the door and gone. But she's so exciting to have around that it's worth fighting to get her back.

There is mutual attraction. She's more ambitious than he is likely to be, but he can be battered into submission and obedience, and she is the one woman to do it. Neither is likely to get bored in the bedroom, but he can get into a spiral of moodiness. She's going to have to pull him out of this by the scruff of his neck.

Perhaps the one thing Aries has to learn is to temper her drive to dominate her man with a little cunning. She may never learn this and lose him to someone a bit wilier. But experience can teach even Arians, and if this happens it could produce a formidably intelligent and lively union. At times Gemini will be too superficial, too lightweight, but he is fascinating. He wants a real partner, not a slave, and this suits this woman. She is a bit selfish at times in a rather innocent "grab it" sort of way, but he understands this because he's no saint himself.

GEMINI MAN—TAURUS WOMAN

Potentially this is just about as bad a partnership as is possible, but there are always exceptional couples who overcome all obstacles—a bit like prisoners who emerge alive after forty years in the salt mines. This is likely to be how the relationship will feel to the participants at times.

Jealous, slow, reliable Taurus is really out of her depth with this vivacious, charming, unreliable man. And he is more than likely to decide that despite her sexual appeal she is boring and firmly stuck in the mud because she wants to be there.

Total incompatibility can, however, create attraction, sometimes of the masochistic sort. The last thing this guy wants is a homebody building him a nest. Unfortunately it's what Taurus badly needs to be. She is an excellent and creative hostess, but she is going to get horribly jealous. Gemini isn't going to like that, even if he is misbehaving himself. His problem is that he desperately needs to communicate his often brilliant, if slightly superficial, ideas and thoughts. Someone once suggested that a Gemini should marry a tape recorder. There's just enough truth in it to make it worth bearing in mind.

His moods and changes are likely to remain totally incomprehensible to Taurus. She is likely to lose her temper eventually and that's worth watching—from behind a bulletproof screen. It won't often happen, but when it does, oh boy! She hates being teased too, and Gemini loves to do it. If this lady is half as smart as she ought to be, she'll take one long look at this fellow and head for the nearest exit. If she really must, she can take *two* looks, but that's it.

He moves a bit too fast for this lady to cope with, but if by chance she could stand it, he would do her a world of good by opening her up and letting the breeze blow through the musty rooms of the Taurean mental processes. This isn't to belittle the lady; she can be great fun, but she is bodily oriented, and needs physical love much more than this gent. Her healthy sexual responses and offenses could in fact turn the fastidious Gemini off. That would be a pity. These two should try an affair if they must, provided they realize just what the problems are. By the way, Geminis make fascinating friends.

CANCER WOMAN—CANCER MAN

Two very sensitive loving people may get on each other's nerves at times, but a deep relationship *can* develop.

Of course, these two are alike, but this need not be a problem as it can be with some signs. There will certainly be a domestic tendency, a need to make the home cozy and charming, a desire to share meals at home rather than eat out. Cancerians are romantic and loving and need to be needed. There is a danger that everything said, sometimes in the heat of the moment, will be taken literally and remembered and brooded over. But if this tendency can be played down, then the partnership will blossom.

The Cancer woman is perhaps more emotionally oriented than her male counterpart, and it is not unknown for her to have a stomach full of butterflies and emotional knots and hangups half the time. She needs a strong man to throw her weight behind, to labor for, and to respect. The Cancer man is going to have to work at this. He won't need to be bossy, but at times he is going to have to lay down the law and make the final decisions.

There will certainly be petty quarrels and arguments and bickering, but petty they are likely to remain. Neither holds a real grudge for long. They both hanker back to more elegant days and are prone to nostalgia. Both are generous and tender. Mood music is made for Cancerians. Deep understanding can develop, and sexually things are likely to go well provided the criticism is kept to a minimum. Maybe togetherness rather than deep passion will mean more to these two in the long run.

She will expect compliments and presents from her man—even

when he's out of sorts or life has been steadily kicking him in the
teeth all day. He may want a little love and she isn't in the mood
to give it. But this isn't really emotional selfishness; it's more a case
of a couple of overactive egos impinging at times.

Compared with so many other couples in the world, these two
should daily count their blessings, for life is likely to come up trumps
for Cancerians—not just when it comes to possessions, but also with
loyal friends and the all-important feeling of being needed and loved
by each other. Occasionally both partners have to loosen up and take
things a little less seriously, to analyze rather than react to situations.

CANCER WOMAN—LEO MAN

If Cancer is prepared to accept this man as the boss, flatter him
outrageously, and at least on the surface defer to him, he will be little
better than putty in her skilled hands.

He loves to be petted, looked after, admired, and wanted. He's
like a great big baby at times, but in return he is generous to a fault,
steady, reliable, passionate, and genuinely grateful for his mate's attentions. He is a sexy guy and this could prove too much for a Cancerian, who tends to blow hot and cold. At times she wants his total
attention and will get it. But when he is preoccupied with something
else and doesn't give her what she thinks she deserves, then she will
go decidedly cold and will feel emotionally rejected.

Both these two are romantic. Leo loves the grand gesture. He
positively demands a luxurious home or at the very least a nice car.
On the surface this relationship would not be an easy one, but in
practice all it needs is a little low cunning from a woman who decides this man is worth having. He might well stray because he's not
going to look the other way when an attractive woman catches his
eye. But he'd better not admit it to Cancer afterward or all hell will
break loose.

Cancer would be wise to keep a restraining hand on the finances. Leo can pinch pennies for weeks, grumble about minor ex-
penditures, and then blow his savings on new carpeting for the entire
house. If he is guided, it will at least be that and not a bronze statue
of the winged mercury that will involve taking half the roof off to
get it into the house. Incidentally, he's likely to be a great talker. He
can be very persuasive at times, so his lady had better look impressed
even if she's heard his favorite stories and jokes before.

All in all, he's a nice man to have around—and he knows it. Leo is not given to undervaluing his virtues and his strengths. Just occasionally—not too often, it must be stressed—Cancer is allowed to cut him down to size with a well-chosen bit of sarcasm. He'll sulk for at least ten minutes before he admits she was right and grabs her. If he provides the emotional security she needs—and he probably will—this is likely to be a satisfying and successful union. But she has to be prepared to meet him a little further than halfway most of the time.

CANCER WOMAN—VIRGO MAN

Virgo is a perfectionist. He is practical, sensible, and reliable and is good for the more emotional Cancerian woman. He is a thinker rather than a feeler and at times he may be too cool for this lady, but he is generally faithful and honest, and she could do a whole lot worse in a partner.

The relationship could get a bit boring if both partners don't whoop it up a bit sometimes. Virgo is cautious with money, though often talented at making and using it, and he needs a secure and nice home. If Cancer is prepared to provide this, as she will almost certainly want to, then things are off to a good start.

He has a tendency to be critical, yet he doesn't take too kindly to criticism himself. Still, he can be very loving, particularly when something goes wrong and his help is needed. She will confuse him with her Cancerian moods, but she can help him by keeping him from overworking. He does tend to be a worrier, and he will bring his work home. His lady can do a lot to prevent its taking him over completely. He is unlikely to pay her extravagant compliments and would be wise to make an effort to admire her new dress or shoes—but it will be an effort for him.

Sexually these two are likely to get along well, although both have a tendency to play it straight, or even to make love at fixed times so that they will feel secure about the whole business. There is every chance that a loving relationship will quickly develop between these two, who might just find that life is so much better together than apart. Neither is envious by nature, and jealousy will only rarely intrude. He does have the highest expectations of his woman, and at times she won't be able to live up to them. At these moments he needs a swift kick in the pants to remind him that we do not live in a perfect world. He's intelligent enough to get the message, although that same message may have to be delivered every few months. He isn't stingy but he is careful, and he makes an ideal employee—he's rarely the boss. Virgo is not given to thinking big, but he deals with the day-to-day business of living better than almost anyone else.

This guy is not really a strong, secure character, and Cancer understands this, but he offers her a great deal provided she does not hanker to share the peacock throne. He badly needs her love and encouragement and admiration, and if he gets them, he might even surprise himself.

CANCER WOMAN—LIBRA MAN

These two will have difficulties making decisions. Libra is easily bored, and Cancer will be hard pressed to keep him interested.

He is a charming guy, self-centered but great fun to be with. Most of the time he is easy to get along with. He knows when to be light and playful and fun, and he counterfeits seriousness most convincingly; but he is rather a lightweight when it comes to emotion. He will certainly have scant sympathy for Cancerian moods. He remains detached, and this will make it difficult for her to relate to him at times. He is definitely attracted to her seriousness and her emotional tangles. He feels that he can cut through all the sentimentality and romantic nonsense to the very heart of his Cancerian. He is unlikely to be successful—using intellect alone, anyway.

Cancer is affectionate and loving, and he won't mind that. Sexually he is inventive and something of a perfectionist, and he will understand her pretty well. But it is doubtful if he'll be prepared to work hard enough at the relationship to make it work well.

If she can learn to relax a little more, stop worrying, and enjoy herself without any guilt feelings, then the partnership can work well, even if there are tensions simmering in the background. One thing about this man is that he expects his woman to realize he's the world's greatest lover. He is pretty good, but he isn't quite as great as he thinks.

In fact, the Libra man may not be strong enough to satisfy a Cancer lady. She needs plenty of reassurance and a firm base to return to at times to recharge her emotional batteries. He needs a wide circle of friends and plenty of stimulus. Decisions do certainly have to be made, and he will make them when forced to, but he'd prefer to leave most of them to his partner, while she'll be expecting him to take the lead. It could get a bit frustrating.

He may become a trifle exasperated with his beloved when she gets into one of her moods and decides that the whole world is ganged up against her and there's nothing to do about it but open her arms and submit to the will of inexorable fate. He just can't go along with that sort of thing—he believes in himself in the last resort. It won't be an easy relationship, but potentially it's a good one, provided that both partners show a little maturity and common sense.

CANCER WOMAN—SCORPIO MAN

Potentially an excellent match. Scorpio strength is just what the Cancer woman seeks and needs. His passion will be deeply satisfying to her, and his undoubted jealousy will almost certainly be given few genuine opportunities to show itself. She is likely to be very loyal to this man.

These two are emotional and intuitive. He is efficient, demanding, and sexy. He works hard and seeks a pleasant home that will be his. She will respect him, look after him, help him put weight on, and generally overdo things—and he'll love it. All she asks in return is his love above all. There will be a great deal of passion in this relationship. At times it may even seem as though these two seek to devour each other in the strength of their passion.

There is likely to be instant empathy for these two—almost a feeling of having met before and even loved before! There is every chance that the bond on all levels will become a deep and satisfying one for both of them.

Scorpio is a masculine guy, and he does appreciate femininity. He doesn't want his lady trying to give him orders. He'll make the running, and she'd better remember it. That doesn't mean he cannot be corrected or argued with, but he does demand loyalty. Given this, he'll go along with her romanticism, her occasional extravagance, and her moods.

His jealousy will, of course, still show itself even when there is no cause—it makes him very possessive. He wants to be everything to his woman. He needs to know everything about her, but she would be wise never to show him her all—a little mystery that he cannot quite fathom will intrigue and attract him. He will respect her privacy while trying to break it down, and this will possibly be a source of slight friction. The wise Cancerian will laugh this off even while he fumes. And then when she is tender, he will be ardent.

Given this basic understanding of his nature, Scorpio is a desirable "property" for this woman. He won't have many friends, although he is likely to have plenty of acquaintances, and this is one reason why he will need his woman more than people of other signs who have a gift for making buddies. He is pretty intuitive too, so things certainly won't be dull. He does hold a little something of himself back in any relationship—perhaps as a safeguard in case things go wrong—and yet he demands her all. Be warned.

CANCER WOMAN—SAGITTARIUS MAN

A dim prospect for a lasting relationship. Sagittarius seems determined to stay a rover all his life, while Cancer needs security and steadiness and passionate love. She won't get the security from this guy, that's for sure.

If she really wants him, she'll get plenty of stimulation—probably enough to make her tear her hair out—but if she enjoys a good fight, then the relationship could just work out. He likes to keep a dozen balls balancing on top of each other at once or juggle with a dozen options. He will have trouble holding down a steady job, and Cancer won't like that. But he is great fun, is often astonishingly intuitive, and, although easily bored, is often loving in a selfish sort of way.

Cancer is a giver, so this might be one area of meeting. He is lucky too, and generous to a fault when called upon. Sexually he's pretty active, and with a little effort he could do her a great deal of good, although he will never dominate her. Actually he won't even try.

He is charming, make no mistake about that. And he knows it. He may also be extremely intelligent and artistic. He appreciates the good things of life from a cigar and a glass of French wine to Mozart, the opera, and the best hotels. There's a good chance he likes luxury cars too. He loves traveling and is a good conversationalist. There's no way that any partner of a Sagittarian can vegetate.

He will be attracted by this lady's femininity, her apparent vulnerability, her emotional tangles, her appeals for help in sorting out her emotional problems. That's one way to hook the guy if that's the way things are to be. His promises may not always stand up, but he is generous, and although there is a good chance that there will be money troubles at times, he always seems to land on his feet. At the darkest moment a sudden stroke of brilliance or a chance encounter will set him off again, enthusiasm written all over his face, even when he's seventy-five and trying to shake off the effects of his third ulcer.

Despite all this, Sagittarius is a nice guy. Cancer could do a great deal worse. But frankly, a short-term relationship is much more likely than a lifelong romance. Whatever happens, he'll probably remain a friend.

CANCER WOMAN—CAPRICORN MAN

Capricorn will provide the security this woman needs, but he can be pretty exasperating as he concentrates on building his career.

Cancer is going to have to understand her man's drive and occasional lack of intuition and indeed spirituality. In return he will provide her with the security and home life she needs, and he will prove himself strong and caring. These are no mean virtues, so this relationship does have an excellent chance of being a good one.

Sexually Capricorn might be a bit withdrawn at times, but there is strong attraction, and he will appreciate her warmth and femininity and need to be comforted when the going gets rough. He will long to get home and probably stay there. At times he may even have to be pried out of his comfy armchair. With a little luck the insecure Cancerian will find the sort of atmosphere where she can blossom and where her sensitivity is not overwhelmed by the masterfulness of some of the other signs.

She will have to give way to this man even when she finds him a bit of a bore, and of course this applies to his career aspirations. At least financial problems are not likely to trouble these two very much—the biggest problem they are likely to face is when they can afford to move to a bigger house.

Cancer does at times have extravagant impulses, and this won't go down too well with Capricorn. He isn't tight-fisted—but he is careful. He knows the value of things. He works to cover his insecurities, but don't tell him so. He's a serious fellow, though occasionally, after a few drinks, he lets his hair down and surprises even himself.

By the way, he isn't going to settle for just any woman he comes across. If his eyes light on a Cancerian charmer, he will be faithful and probably contented. There will be arguments, probably over her impracticality and flights of fancy, but he is worth a lot of trouble. She should try to understand his complexes and neuroses. She'll need plenty of stamina to keep up with him at times, but above all she must keep him active at home or he might just take root as he grows older and begins to realize that there are other things in life besides office work.

CANCER WOMAN—AQUARIUS MAN

This is likely to be a thorny relationship because Aquarius uses his mind first, while Cancer relies on her emotions. It may well be that she's going to have to make the romantic running because the best way to get this guy is to grab him fast before he has time to start adding up the pros and cons.

Sexually things are likely to go well, although she may think he lacks tenderness at times. The romantic Cancerian needs plenty of loving and comforting and admiring, and she isn't too likely to get it from this fellow without a good deal of coaxing, which she will certainly find demeaning.

He's a very forward-looking guy indeed. He thinks big. Worries about whether the inhabitants of Sirius are getting on all right. Wants to know why it rains, all that sort of scientific stuff. He isn't quite as good at paying the doctor's bills. But he can be a fascinating guy, he's rarely if ever jealous or too demanding. He's fair, honest, charming, unsentimental (which doesn't mean he won't like a nice present on his birthday), and at times a bit moody. But these are things that Cancer understands even if she will try to change them.

He's likely to be attracted to her sensitivity and her artistic impulses, but he will try to improve her mind. He often has a thing about intellectual improvement—he takes courses in all sorts of profound subjects and may well have a gift for languages. He's honest emotionally, which isn't always the case with this lady, and he likes to travel and meet with friends to discuss, argue, and philosophize. This isn't going to suit Cancer, who may well sulk. She might even nag, and this could provoke an argument.

Aquarius is logical and straightforward. Cancer often relies on hunches, which are right a disproportionate amount of the time—and that is irritating to him. One thing he will do is look after her with tenaciousness and real compassion when she is ill or in need. This guy is a reformer and sympathizer with the underdog, and he respects fair play. She should keep him stimulated—that shouldn't be too difficult for the changeable Cancerian.

CANCER WOMAN—PISCES MAN

A definitely compatible couple, even though they might decide to stay in bed with the covers over their heads while the whole world falls apart around them. They are likely to get very wrapped up in each other, but they get away with it because they are affectionate, sensitive, delightful, and totally exasperating to friends and relatives.

These two will be perfectly happy to stay at home for ever and a day. She won't mind cooking and sweeping and washing and doing all the rest of the chores for such an appreciative guy. He'll bring her flowers, poems, and gifts and lay them and himself at her feet. Who could resist such evident passion?

These two are incredibly imaginative and at times impractical with money. She is a dreamer, and he is the dreamer to end all dreamers. His life is a perpetual dream with moments of supreme happiness and depths that few others can even imagine. Cancer can do a great deal to comfort Pisces when he gets the blues, as he surely will. Sexually there will be lots of attraction; he is a good deal tougher than he may seem at times. Sex may even be one way to get him out of his periodic depressions.

There may well be immediate empathy when these two meet. Both are so intuitive at times that it will seem ludicrous; they might even be clairvoyant. Certainly their interests and enthusiasms are likely to be remarkably similar, and they will grow even closer as the relationship ripens. Security is important for both, and this is probably the only thing they are prepared to really work for. Emotionally things will at times seem chaotic—their sensitivity will put remarkable strains on both partners and their friends. But despite all the difficulties, this can be a genuinely magical sort of relationship—great fun for everyone around and joyful for the lovers. What does it matter if he spends the housekeeping money on a sculpture he found at an art gallery and she blew the rent on a crate of champagne? Life's too short to worry about such mundane things—or is it?

Lucky is the woman who finds a Piscean man she can love and cherish. Life together may not be roses all the way, but it will be most of the time, and even when the roses are not blooming, there'll still be the wine!

CANCER WOMAN—ARIES MAN

This could be an excellent relationship provided Cancer knows what she is getting herself into. This dynamic man can also be a trifle insensitive—and that's putting it mildly—and she needs careful handling at times.

He will be great for reassuring, protecting, and organizing his lady, and she'll soothe his ruffled pride and stem his impetuousity when it threatens to get out of hand. He can be a blunderer, there's not doubt about that. He's blunt, often charming, sometimes immature. He'll have real difficulty understanding why she gets hurt by the things he says or does. She can be so sensitive. But he can also count on her loyalty in a crisis, and this means a lot to an Arian. He demands reliability and is himself just about the most reliable in the whole Zodiac.

There will be plenty of sexual attraction at first, although he could, by his very independence and willfulness, provoke her to jealousy. He can be rude too, and must learn to curb his tongue if he wants to get on with Cancer. These two are very different but are quite clearly attracted. She will be restful and gentle with him, and if he's lucky she'll persuade him to settle down a bit.

There is a danger that if she fails to at least try to keep up with him, he will drift away. He can't be bothered to understand her deep frustrations and feelings. That is a distinct pity. Directness and complexity can certainly rub each other the wrong way, but the odds are that love will produce an accommodation!

One thing that is certain is that this relationship will be an exciting and stimulating one. He can be terribly impulsive, so it is up to those who love him—and there may well be a few of them—to make him see sense. A moment's hesitation usually works wonders because he is an intelligent fellow. Aries has a lot of love to give; he wants to serve. He doesn't want to be fussed over and petted. He wants to do the seducing. This doesn't entirely suit his lady, who will certainly want to mother him and to look after him. A more mature Arian will take this in his stride, while a sensible Cancerian will count her blessings, not least in bed. These two are very good for each other, although it may not always seem that way. There'll be lots of fun and passion and problems—and beneath it all a compatibility few will understand.

CANCER WOMAN—TAURUS MAN

A most suitable relationship. There will be plenty of passion here. The sensitive Cancerian approach to life will almost certainly be matched by the courteous way the Taurean treats his woman. Both seek a stable, steady, restful life and value their home almost too much. These are two serious people. He'll appreciate her cooking and domestic skills and admire her gifts. She'll positively blossom when he compliments her. Taurus is a sexy, earthy type, and it suits him very well to be the center of his woman's whole world. He will take all the fussing, mothering, and loving that Cancer can provide. He values the so-called good things of life and expects his lady to enjoy them too. Of course, there's a danger that things will become almost completely material for these two—but forewarned is forearmed. Boredom can be prevented by the use of a little imagination from time to time.

He will be surprised and a little resentful of her moods, which are sure to descend from time to time, upsetting the smooth flow of his life. In fact, this will probably be good for him—it might even shake his complacency now and then. This lady cannot help worrying, and he won't understand that either—but so long as he isn't given cause for jealousy, he'll be there in the background, good old Taurus. Okay, he is a bit slow, sometimes overcautious, sometimes a stick-in-the-mud. Nevertheless he's got a lot of virtues, and it's a lucky lady who finds a nice Taurean. She should try being his anchor; that's what he really wants.

The biggest difficulty for these two is likely to be coming to terms with Cancer's emotional troubles. That's when Taurean kindness and generosity and nobleness will be most needed. Let's hope he will not fail her then.

These two will settle for a cozy couch in front of the fire, and perhaps some nuts and chocolates and a bottle or three of champagne. So it's no use friends stopping by at such times—the door will stay bolted; the lovers are at home together, and they're quite enough for each other without any other stimulation.

All in all, they are a splendid combination because each has so much to give to the other. He's practical and sensible and likely to be successful, and she's charming, sensitive, and a bit willful but very loving and sensual at the right times.

CANCER WOMAN—GEMINI MAN

Emotionally these two are not really compatible, and the relationship will need a lot of hard work if there is to be any chance of success. It is unlikely that Gemini is going to be prepared to make the effort to ensure a happy union.

The difficulty is that he is mentally oriented, while she is emotional. She is insecure and needs a steady, reliable man. But he is volatile, restless, fun-loving, and flirtatious. All this is likely to cause severe frustration in both partners.

Of course, love might conquer all. There will certainly be fascination when these two meet. They are so different that he might just decide he needs her very badly, and yet she will take a lot of convincing. Cancer understands how changeable and restless and nervous he is and that he needs her calm, tolerant approach. But is he worth the great effort it's going to take to live with him? There's something rather superficial about this fellow, which will irritate the deeper Cancerian, but he is quite charming and a great talker. If she really wants him, she's going to have to first appeal to his mind, test him, contradict him, stimulate him, and then keep him interested by varying her emotional responses.

The relationship is most likely to be enigmatic: on one minute, off the next. He is a very curious fellow. He wants to know everything about his woman, and he isn't going to get it all from Cancer. He wants to experience everything, the good and the bad. He should be intelligent—because he has a superb mental instrument of great range and clarity, if not depth—but sometimes it is his very intelligence that lets him down because it is just not enough to put up against real emotional honesty.

The sensible Cancerian will run a mile when she sees this guy coming, and if he values his sanity he won't follow his old path after her; he'll head for more compatible soil. Does it all sound too depressing? It's just that the friction and irritation and volatility of this union—his laughter when she is serious and her tears when he wants to play—make the relationship too risky and too hurtful.

A good old-fashioned fling will help him to understand that he, too, is an emotional being and will show her that there are things in life besides family, home, and kitchen. Cancer might try to hang on—it's her style—but she'll be hurt if she does.

CANCER MAN—CANCER WOMAN

There are likely to be petty quarrels and arguments, perhaps because these two sensitive people are so alike. But most of the time this will be a loving, satisfying relationship and a good union.

There will most certainly be strong domestic tendencies, a need to have a cozy, charming, perhaps elegant home, to share meals at home rather than go out to restaurants. These two may well develop genuine togetherness.

Cancerians are certainly romantic and loving, but they both need plenty of reassurance that they are needed and wanted and appreciated. Both partners are going to have to work at this, perhaps a bit dishonestly at times to encourage the other. But it's all in a good cause, and the flattery certainly doesn't have to be outrageous. Some of the advantages of this match are that Cancerians don't hold grudges, they are rarely sharp-tongued, and they are not selfish.

Both are sensitive. Emotionally they can get into real knots. Stomachs can churn and there can be a buildup of frustration inside. But both are generous and tender, quick to apologize, and understanding. Things are likely to go well sexually, as long as she uses her imagination at times. She will be moody from time to time, but so will he. She needs someone strong whom she can put her undoubted loyalty and determination behind. Cancer wants to do much the same sort of thing, so he's going to have to learn to lead and organize rather more than he wants to.

There is certainly a danger that things said in the heat of the moment by one partner will be taken literally by the other and remembered and thrown back at a later date. But this is not really vicious—it's more the response of someone who is thin-skinned and easily hurt. From time to time both partners are going to have to learn to loosen up and take things a little more easily. They should just enjoy the present moment rather than worry about what might happen and probably won't.

Both also have to learn to analyze and reflect rather than react to situations. This doesn't mean that recklessness always goes with the sign of Cancer, but it can sometimes be a danger.

CANCER MAN—LEO WOMAN

Not too promising. Leo needs a very strong man, and this fellow is unlikely to retain her respect for long in a close relationship. Cancerian moods and need for appreciation and encouragement are unlikely to be met by Leo understanding. Indeed, she demands a very great deal from her man. She expects things to be organized, she expects to live well, and she doesn't like to have to pinch pennies, because she is generous with her money and her emotions.

Cancer is emotional and a romantic at heart despite his sometimes bold exterior. He will certainly idolize his woman, but this won't go down too well with Leo, who'd rather have a night out on the town and then a passionate clinch.

He is always a sensitive man, probably too sensitive for this powerhouse of a lady, and perhaps too inventive sexually at times, because Leo lives by her own morality and draws the line at some funny times. An additional problem will be Cancer's appreciation and need to relate to the past, his family, and his experiences. Leo finds all that sort of thing soppy most of the time.

There is likely to be more instant attraction than long-lasting love for these two. One thing he will appreciate is her excellence as a hostess. Her style is balm to his soul even if he grumbles at times about her sudden extravagances. Her need to be independent, possibly financially, could provoke endless arguments and irritations. If Cancer can be the boss in this relationship, all could be well, but it's unlikely to happen, and he is likely to look elsewhere. He can at times be a dreadful show-off, particularly if she crosses his emotional needs. Leo, who is rather given to the grand gesture herself, will despise him for it.

This is the sort of relationship best dreamed about rather than entered into. They should make it short and passionate if possible. Of course, love might conquer all, but they'd better be prepared to work hard at sustaining the union. One thing about Cancer is his need to discuss things late into the night—maybe she should buy him a tape recorder. Leo can be faithful to ridiculous lengths, but suddenly she'll get the message and be gone without a word—she's all woman and needs to be told so, often.

CANCER MAN—VIRGO WOMAN

Virgo lives by logic, while Cancer lives by his emotions. Things will get pretty hairy if these two team up. The moody Cancerian will drive the sensible Virgoan around the bend at times, but he could be good for her. She can be cold and a bit unfeeling. His lovingly romantic approach to life might just melt her icy detachment.

She's shy and often withdrawn, but she'll appreciate the Cancer warmth and lovemaking when she's in the mood. When she isn't—forget it! However, real warmth and understanding *can* develop, although they are going to have to work at seeing each other's point of view. Sexually Cancer could go too fast for this lady, though she is not really cold when her emotions are aroused.

The home will be important for these two, and both are usually pretty good financially. He is more of a worrier than she, but a determined provider. He will certainly need lots of reassurance and loving, and this may not always be forthcoming from Virgo. She could lose respect for him if he tries to put her on a pedestal, and that would be fatal because she has highly developed ideas of loyalty and law and the rights of the individual.

Cancer, being introverted, will expect his woman to understand how he is feeling. She will be expected to appreciate his mania for collecting, his love of antiques and the like, and he wants her there when he gets home after his working day. If she wants to hang on to this guy, she has to convince him that he is a winner and can do anything better than anyone else. His inferiority complex will take a lot of converting into positive strength, but it can be done—probably not by Virgo, who is likely to give him up as a lost cause and seek consolation in a convent. Those last few words are exaggerated, but they get the message across.

When things go wrong, as they will at times for even the nicest Cancerian, he retreats into himself and mulls things over for a year or two. If she treats him with gentleness and understanding, with luck he'll become a more easygoing fellow, and will be deeply grateful to his woman.

CANCER MAN—LIBRA WOMAN

Despite the difficulties, this is likely to prove a good relationship provided that both partners show some common sense and maturity.

Cancer will certainly be attracted by this lady, and he does promise much—he's domesticated, smooth, charming, romantic—and often emotionally a mess. This won't suit Libra, who's more sensible and stable. She, too, can get into an awful emotional turmoil at times, but basically she is reliable in a crisis.

The well-known Cancerian moodiness and need for encouragement, love, and reassurance all the time could make Libra more insecure because she herself needs these things too. However, she is able to detach her mind from her emotions if necessary, and Cancer might have a hard time catching her. That might be a good thing for all concerned.

She likes to look good and can be decidely extravagant. He won't grudge her the money for this; but although he is a good provider, he can also be rather extravagant at times, so don't expect the finances to be easy or a point of total agreement. She needs to be told she's beautiful every other hour—and he is pretty good at doling out the compliments. Both are sensitive and caring. Libra can do quite a lot if she chooses to help Cancer to maintain a sensible emotional balance instead of being swept away by gusts of passion, greed, and all the rest. This lady is independent, refuses to be bossed, and likes her own career and money whenever possible. She can also be fearfully stubborn, even more so than Cancer.

This man needs a stable home life. He loves his food and his cozy little home—at least that's how he sees it. He's a worrier, but he's a worker too, even though his Libran lady would prefer to get out to parties and have more fun than he thinks seemly or wise. However, there is likely to be plenty of empathy, and there aren't likely to be any sexual complaints, so there is more going for these two than seems likely on first glance. There will be trying times when neither is prepared to make a decision, but there'll be plenty of fun. In the last resort, Libra believes in herself—which is something Cancer has to learn or never really understands—but if she's prepared to weather the difficult times and share the more frequent good ones, there is no reason why these two should not be splendidly happy.

CANCER MAN—SCORPIO WOMAN

A very suitable pair in many many ways. Scorpio may prove to be the driving force of this relationship, but Cancer understands well enough what is going on and will play his part.

Cancer has a deepseated need to give and keep on giving, and this suits Scorpio, who is basically a taker. She is a strong lady, and his love and devotion are just what she needs to prevent her jealous nature from showing through. She is passionate and he is sensitive, so sexually they will get on well. They also have every chance of creating a long-lasting and deep partnership.

Neither like getting into debt, and the home is very important to both. It is not only a measure of financial or worldly success but also a place to share and cherish. These two are likely to do things together—even if it's staying quietly at home.

Cancer should avoid giving his woman reason to be jealous or unsure or disturbed. Actually, this is precisely the sort of security that he is able to offer her. Scorpio can be very good at soothing ruffled feelings when it is necessary. Frankly, she's a nicer person than her male counterpart. And she's sexy, too. There is always something slightly mysterious about both Cancerians and Scorpios—at times neither really understands his or her own responses. But this sort of thing may only deepen and draw the relationship even closer.

Scorpio demands a lot from any man—and is likely to hold a little of herself back in any situation. Perhaps this is part of her charm. Cancer won't mind this. He knows a good deal when it hits him between the eyes.

Given a chance, she could play the field a bit, while at the same time expecting absolute fidelity from her partner. It's up to Cancer to keep his beady eye on her, and then she'll always come home.

Lucky is the Scorpio who finds a nice Cancerian, and vice versa. Not everyone gets on well with or appreciates the Scorpionic virtues, but this is one lady who can make a success of the relationship if she makes the effort.

CANCER MAN—SAGITTARIUS WOMAN

Almost certainly a disastrous union. Cupid would have to work overtime to keep this pair contented and together.

That isn't to say they aren't nice people—it's just that they are radically different in too many ways. Sagittarius likes to get around. She has lots of friends and contacts, isn't too sensitive, and needs her freedom. She's great company and enjoys a joke. But she's death to the moody, home-loving, emotionally unsure Cancerian. He wants a woman who'll be at home to hand him his slippers, or who'll at least be at home when he gets in. Sagittarius probably won't be there. She resists being tied down. She's flexible, easygoing, and generous, but she won't be able to take the thin-skinned Cancerian seriously much of the time. That is a pity because he has a lot to offer a woman. He's devoted, kind, gentle, passionate, and home-loving, but not nearly as competitive as this woman.

Cancer is a good and stimulating traveler and he likes a warm climate. He can't resist a romantic setting, even though red roses don't do an awful lot for Sagittarius. She'd probably prefer a set of golf clubs or water skis. Mentally she's very quick. She may well have artistic inclinations—even if she hasn't quite decided which art she's going to excel at. And she appreciates the good things of life.

Cancer would be well advised not to fall for such a lady because he's likely to suffer quite enough without having her around to poke fun at him when he's feeling particularly down or when she thinks a little harmless fun will cheer him up. Sometimes this lady is about as sensitive as a bus speeding downhill with no driver.

Life certainly won't be a bed of roses for these two. Quite a lot of Sagittarians have a number of affairs and even marry several times. It's partly because they are so changeable emotionally.

Maybe it won't be quite as bad as it sounds. But unless this partnership was made in heaven, the lovers would be well advised to keep things brief and friendly.

CANCER MAN—CAPRICORN WOMAN

There is sexual attraction here, but the practical Capricornian woman may become irritated by the way this man needs continual encouragement, affection, affirmation, and reassurance.

When Cancer sulks, this lady just won't be able to understand why. She is a sensible sort of lady. She's ambitious for herself and her man and expects the finances to be sorted out and life to be regulated and organized.

She is also a busy lady and expects those around her to be busy and efficient. She can be sadly disillusioned by Cancer, even though he is a worker when he has an aim—which may well be to provide a home for his woman and ensure security for his family. All this implies a secure financial future with a good deal of shared sentimentality.

Cancer is a dreamer with a distinct streak of obstinacy and a tendency to get into an emotional turmoil from time to time. Capricorn could be a big help here. She calls a spade a spade, and of course this may upset Cancer sometimes. He'll brood, imagine all sorts of insults, and sulk, but he'll survive.

He'll have to come to terms with her drive and her withdrawn periods and indeed her love of comfort and good food. At times she'll need to be pried out of her favorite armchair.

To make any sort of a success of this relationship, the career-conscious Capricornian is going to have to sublimate some of her desires and demands for power and success. Cancer is then going to find himself with a lady not averse to giving him both a helping hand and a helping boot when she thinks he needs a little encouragement to climb the career ladder. He won't like it, but he's going to have to accept it if he wants this lady.

The other thing is that she's a woman who isn't going to settle for just anything in trousers. She has set ideas about what her man should be . She'll probably settle for someone other than Cancer, and she'll be right to do so.

Quite a lot of the time Capricorn will think that Cancer is disguising or hiding his true feelings. This isn't really true—it's just that, like the crab, he has a hard shell and a rather soft interior, and he hurts rather easily, so experience has taught him to be self-protective.

CANCER MAN—AQUARIUS WOMAN

Not an easy relationship. Aquarius will probably fail to respond to the emotional "cries" of Cancer, who needs a lot of togetherness and reassurance and affection.

Although not a cold woman, Aquarius tends to keep people and things at a distance. She is efficient and works well, and this will certainly impress Cancer. But she isn't exactly a homebody, and cooking and cleaning don't really enter into her idea of how life should be lived.

Cancer will put up with quite a lot of this as long as he knows she is happy, but eventually he will start to make demands, and Aquarius won't like that too much. She isn't likely to spend too much time bothering about money—she'll just spend. Cancer will not be amused, and she is unlikely to really appreciate his love of old things and his collecting instincts.

Sexually he is very sensitive and romantic, while she is more detached, although not lacking in warmth for the right guy. He is, however, rather vulnerable, and this lady needs a tougher man if the union is to succeed. She is extremely forward-looking, free-thinking, and at times impetuous and adventurous. He is cautious and reserved.

Aquarius has the gift of being able to relate to more Zodiacal signs and personalities than probably any other woman, but she will eventually feel uncomfortable with this fellow and his insecurity and need to have tangible success. She cares nothing for power or influence and she certainly doesn't see herself as the little woman at home billing and cooing with her man fresh home from a hard day at the office.

The relationship could work, and work well in exceptional cases, if Cancer can overcome his neuroses and if Aquarius is prepared to give up some of her independence. Having work that brings them together would certainly be a very good point of contact between these two, who are likely to make a quite impressive team. But a long-term relationship needs a lot more thinking about and certainly a lot more careful planning to balance the formidable differences of temperament that these two signs demonstrate. Incidentally, Aquarius is a sucker for a cry for help.

CANCER MAN—PISCES WOMAN

Almost certainly a sensationally successful partnership—although Lord only knows how these two will actually survive in a cold, cruel world.

Actually it isn't going to be that hard. Pisces is tougher than she seems, and Cancer can be a very good provider once he knows where he's going and when he has a woman supporting and encouraging him all along the way.

Sexually this is likely to be a good match, for they are both loving and will reassure each other. Arguments aren't likely to last long, although they could be decidedly stormy while they last. There will be real rapport on all levels for these two. Pisces is a hopeless dreamer who actually expects a knight in shining armor to be waiting for her around the next corner. Cancer isn't much better. A bowl of roses, a glass of champagne, a warm starlit night will send him into ecstasies. He's ready for a whole lifetime of love—and he might just get it with this lady.

Yes, there will be emotional crises and lots of stomach churning and worrying. But the togetherness will be so much more important and worthwhile than being alone that there's little chance of either of these two straying. They should try to cut back on the daydreams and the fantastic projects and face reality, so that life will blend more smoothly. He will demand a lot from this lady. Cancer can be a bit selfish, but Pisces has so much to give (she probably spread quite a lot of it around before she met him) that she'll go more than halfway to meet him.

There'll be plenty of romantic fussing for these two, who love to be wanted. They'll stay at home and she'll do the chores with meticulous and almost disconcerting thoroughness. He will be appreciative. The empathy, the intuitive togetherness of these two, will be positively startling at times. It will be disconcerting to others, as will their sensitivity. A casual word is likely to be built up and mulled over and finally assume gigantic proportions in their minds. But all will quickly be forgiven in each other's arms.

CANCER MAN—ARIES WOMAN

The cautious Cancerian could get several shocks to his sensitive system if he tangles with this lady. But he will be immensely attracted by her enthusiasm and drive.

A long-term relationship does demand more than sexual attraction (although let's not underestimate this little matter), and Aries could prove too much of a handful for this quiet man. However, he could do a lot for her—calming her down, providing a base for her wandering and her need for stimulation and excitement.

Sexually Aries might prove too "fast" for this fellow. Later he could get jealous of her independence and occasional biting sarcasm. She does not suffer fools gladly, and this all makes for a difficult relationship. In fact, at times these two might seem to be living in different worlds. Cancer is very sensitive and easily hurt—and Aries doesn't have time to be considerate. He needs lots of reassurance and confirmation that his work and his talents are both appreciated and respected. She can't be bothered with caution and niceness. Her idea of meeting a man she likes is to march up to him and hand him her door key. Real subtlety.

Cancer is a homebody. He wants his woman to be there when he gets home to hand him his slippers while the romantic music is already playing in the background. Aries won't be there; or if she is, she probably heated the oven and forgot to put anything in. To be fairer, she's a pretty efficient person, and if she says she'll be somewhere at such and such a time, she'll be there come hell or high water. But, and it's a big *but*, there's no way this lady is going to be domesticated—even by the man she loves.

Cancer is imaginative and needs stimulus, and he'll expect it from his Arian lady—but she'll look elsewhere for her additional stimulus. He's one of nature's sufferers, and if he settles for this lady, he'll have plenty more practice. When he casts his protective cloak over his kith and kin, Aries will promptly start cutting holes in it, and Cancer will be deeply hurt and brood and sulk and imagine the worst. Aries won't even notice this, and that'll make things even worse. She'd be well advised to leave this charming dreamer to his own devices.

CANCER MAN—TAURUS WOMAN

There's quite a lot going for these two if they concentrate on the advantages of a union rather than the disadvantages. Taurus is jealous, fairly uncomplicated, honest, and passionate. Cancer is much more subtle, loving, and romantic.

That makes for a rather nice balance of qualities and a rather complicated balance. There could be emotional difficulties at times, particularly when Cancer gets moody and withdrawn and his lady can't understand what it's all about. But she is a tolerant woman, and if things are going well financially—as they are likely to be—and the home life is consistent and good, then she will put up with his difficult periods.

This is likely to be a loving relationship. There won't be any sexual complaints. His romantic and deep responses will be matched by her tendency to respect and almost worship the man she loves. Nothing will be too good for him—after all, she fell for him!

Domestic bliss is likely. This is an easy-chair, afternoons-in-the-garden and drinks-on-the-terrace sort of relationship much of the time. And with a bit of luck everyone around these two will feel more secure and wanted because of the stability of the relationship. Indeed it's the sort of empathetic relationship that improves and deepens as the partners mature. The dreamy Cancerian can be practical when he wants to be, and he won't ever take his woman for granted. He will really appreciate what she does to make him more comfortable and successful in his business life. Certainly Taurus can be a trifle tactless at times, but she has so many other good qualities that even Cancer will forgive her—eventually.

One thing that must be avoided is noncommunication. A wall of silent resentment could build up because both have their pride. Just a tiny bit of humility rather than stubbornness—and this lady can really be stubborn at times—will make life so much easier. Cancer wants to give and protect. Is it so hard to give way to him sometimes?

This man expects kindness, understanding, and gentleness. He really cannot understand why anyone should be unkind and cruel. All he needs is a little love and appreciation—or rather, a lot of love and appreciation. Taurus can do much to help this complex, often delightful, mixed-up, emotional man. He's worth taking a little trouble over, and when he gets talking he'll make it clear that he, too, thinks this is the case.

CANCER MAN—GEMINI WOMAN

Not a very promising partnership. Gemini is all mind, whereas Cancer feels rather than considers. Her insecurity and uncertainty are likely to be aggravated by his flirting, his rapid switches of thought and mood, and his undisciplined sexual energies.

She will find him jealous and unreasonable. He expects her to conform to his expectations, to be there when he wants her, to encourage and reassure and love him. She will certainly be attracted by his domestic tendencies, his artistic sensibilities, and his real need for a loving and affectionate woman. But she will feel that he wants to imprison her bodily, emotionally, and mentally. She just won't stand for being his "little woman." She likes to get around. Whatever he does, this guy will respond with his feelings and emotions rather than his mind. This certainly doesn't harmonize with the careful balancing of ideas that Gemini does with such rapidity that at times she seems to be responding intuitively and emotionally herself.

Sexually he is deeply aroused; he is very sensitive to changes of mood. Communication is going to be the big problem here. If these two can find the common ground that undoubtedly exists, then they will make a go of it. But it is a big *if.* She isn't able to understand his moods and insecurities. There will be a sort of emotional Russian roulette going on much of the time that these two are together, and that can be decidedly wearing on sensitive people, if not fatal.

She is a great talker, believes in initial impressions, but isn't too impressed by the Cancerian mania for collecting and the way he loves antiques and things that have a romantic background. If Gemini is determined to settle for this man, she has to come to terms with this and his need for a stable home life. He is no fool, and may well turn out to be a shrewd businessman, so financially things are not likely to be too difficult. But the other emotional-mental difficulties are likely to prove too much.

If these two can put aside their masks and their hangups and talk together rather than chat or hedge around and sweep things under the carpet, then the partnership has a chance. Objectively speaking, they would be wise to have a long affair or engagement before settling down together.

LEO WOMAN—LEO MAN

It's heaven or hell for these two—with a fair chance that it will be the former. What happens when the king meets the queen? Either they get on famously or they carve each other up, split the kingdom, and hate each other for ever.

The difficulty is that with this pair there are likely to be no half measures, no pussy-footing around, and not much subtlety either. It is impossible to say what will happen when two impulsive, passionate, demanding, generous, infuriating, charming, extravagant, splendid people fall in love.

The Leo man can be absurd. He knows everything, is an expert on everything, and hates being corrected or contradicted. He has to be the boss in almost any circumstance, and yet at the same time there is a part of him that wants to be directed by someone he respects. He can be extremely efficient. He probably works hard—and plays hard too. He likes his creature comforts—good food, plenty of booze—and he likes the ladies. He's pretty direct about it too, rather childishly at times. But his self-confidence usually helps him get away with things. He's competitive—he likes to win. At his worst he can be an egomaniacal bore. At his best—and he does enjoy being told what is his best—he's fascinating, charming, and rather noble. The way to handle this man is to flatter him outrageously. He isn't stupid; he knows what's going on, but he likes it nevertheless.

The Leo woman is not an easy lady to live with. It's the mature Leo that knows when to give way. Until that maturity comes, she's liable to boil over, throw plates, and curse.

Sexually, Leos are romantic and very good for each other. Their quarrels will be stupendous and so probably will the making-up afterward. Emotional immaturity is a Leo problem—but a determination to focus internally and to develop detachment will work wonders even for the Leo ego. The Leo man wants a feminine woman, so he may at times consider the Leo woman a bit too assertive. There will be ostentatious displays and tantrums, but fundamentally these two have so much going for them that it would be a shame if they stopped talking—even if it's only about sex—and did not become the formidable partnership they could become. The Leo man plays for high stakes, but even when he fails, he seems to land on his feet. If the initial difficulties of living together can be survived, then there is every chance that the world will benefit from two more Leos living happily if stormily together.

LEO WOMAN—VIRGO MAN

A difficult relationship. Virgo will find it difficult to understand the extravagant emotional gestures of this lady, and her need for expressions of love and for flattery is not likely to be satisfied by him.

Virgo is generous with his time but careful with cash. Leo is just generous, and she doesn't worry too much about the future. She loves to have friends around and to entertain royally. Virgo prefers a quieter life and won't like paying the bills for what he is likely to see as unnecessary expenditure.

If the partnership is to work at all—and of course that is possible—then both parties will have to practice tolerance to a degree that is rather alien to their very different natures. Sexually some Virgos are decidedly inhibited, while others are more loving and warmer than many people are led to expect.

Virgo will find it hard to dominate this woman the way she really wants and expects from a man. He may well become critical and then sarcastic, and she just won't take that. He could, of course, be completely swept off his feet by the undeniably exciting and flamboyant Leo—he'd be wise to regain those feet pretty fast. And she'd be better advised not to play around with the serious Virgoan's affections.

Virgo does appreciate a little luxury, and this lady certainly has style both in the home and in her dress. She can make a little money look as though it's going a long way when she tries. Even the perfectionist Virgo, the born accountant, will at times enjoy just basking in reflected glory. He does have a good brain; he's quick and hardworking. Leo could teach him to unzip a little and enjoy life more. Another difficulty is that Virgo is logical and organized and sometimes lacking in humor. He will hate the way Leo throws her clothes around, spends too much on out-of-season flowers that he never liked anyway, and always heads for the best restaurants. He can't understand this sort of approach to the serious business of living, even if at times he himself has been known to take a drink too many to drown his inferiority complex.

What it all boils down to is a bad risk. This man is kind, very loyal, and gentle at times, but his passion for order will be too much for this lady, who is emotional and intuitive rather than a great thinker. She hasn't the time for nitpicking and grumbling.

LEO WOMAN—LIBRA MAN

There are serious drawbacks here, and insecurity and unhappiness are a distinct possibility. Libra is a flirtatious, charming, often lovable companion. But he needs his freedom, doesn't like to get involved in arguments, and goes all funny when in the presence of beauty, either human or in nature.

Leo is romantic and passionate, but she has her feet more firmly on the ground than Libra. She will lose her temper pretty often with this dreamy, erratic fellow—and he'll do almost anything to avoid a scene. She's just too fiery and extravagant and forceful for him.

Libra is a born psychologist. He certainly isn't opposed to luxurious living, but he needs a harmonic balanced life, and he doesn't like to make decisions, particularly if they are going to upset someone or the comfortable status quo. Neither of these two is lazy, but they will tend to work hard at very different things and fail to appreciate each other's good qualities. Sexually, Leo is straightforward, basic, and demanding. Libra fantasizes and needs continual stimulus, and if she won't provide it, he will look elsewhere without a qualm.

He is romantic, make no mistake about that. He understands love and inevitably does the right thing; he doesn't want anyone to suffer, least of all his lady love. There is a chance that if his roving days are really over, this could be a successful union. But will she ever be sure and secure? One thing he will do is treat his woman as an equal—or even as more than an equal—at all times. She'll never be taken for granted or treated as a doormat. Anyway, that's hardly the sort of thing Leo would put up with.

There is every chance that they will find jealousy creeping into the relationship, and Libra will strenuously resist clearing the air with a good quarrel. He might even become secretive—and that's the beginning of the end because he won't be too good at that. Both these two like traveling, having fun, and sports. He has a nice sense of humor and will often prevent her from becoming boring or pompous. But they should make strenuous efforts to find someone else to love before settling down. It's really sad to see two splendid people in their entirely different ways making each other miserable when life has so much to offer to talented, clever, charming people. They should stay friends and stay apart.

LEO WOMAN—SCORPIO MAN

A decidedly stormy but potentially successful relationship. Two strong, emotional people, proud and independent, don't make for an easy partnership, but they could achieve something many other couples fail to even approach.

Scorpio can be a jealous, possessive fellow. He's passionate but also strangely secretive about his own feelings, while wanting to know everything about his partner's feelings and thoughts. The difficulty is that he's likely to get as good as he gives from this woman, who has a mind of her own. She is a generous, warm, loving woman who may certainly be attracted to a Scorpio man. Her need to have an independent life at times could cause problems, but not if she finds a mature sort of Scorpio who is prepared to give a little more and be a little more reasonable than some of his brothers.

He will provide security and almost certainly a nice home. Sexually, both are pretty active and both want to dominate, so the sparks will fly in what will probably be a very satisfying relationship once this couple get to know each other a little better.

Scorpio will expect his lady to admire his undoubted gifts. This can be a little tiring. He would be wise to remember that the way to Leo's heart is definitely through flattery, and the more outrageous, the better. She's far too bright to fail to realize what is going on, but it won't matter because she'll still love it—after all, isn't she the most beautiful, desirable, charming, intelligent woman around? Who could deny such self-evident truths?

Scorpio can't help being jealous—he's a complex man, even he doesn't understand the murky emotional depths of his psyche, and he complicates simple things because he really does read more into them than the situation demands or allows. But he's fascinating despite all his faults. He isn't an easy person to love. Attractive, yes; lovable, no. When Leo flirts elsewhere, as she surely will, watch out for the sparks (or even the odd murder). He's selfish and egotistical and sometimes power-mad. Can Leo accept her lesser role?

That depends on her. If she wants him enough, she'll fight him on the small things and he'll give way, but on the important issues this man never budges an inch. That, of course, is the problem if his lover does indeed seek some independence. He can't stand it and will wear and tear her down until she either gives up or moves out.

LEO WOMAN—SAGITTARIUS MAN

Almost certainly a superb partnership. Sagittarius is so stimulating and lively and outgoing that Leo can't resist him. Certainly there'll be times when she wonders how she got herself into such a madhouse, but most of the time life together will be at the worst fun and at the best bliss.

He'll organize her unmercifully, even though half his arrangements will go wrong. His flirtatious efforts with other women will drive her wild, and his total failure to arrive on time except in the direst circumstances will strain the relationship at times. But what the hell, no one's perfect, or at least that's what he'll say.

Sexually both desire freedom and there is a very good chance that they will develop a seemingly strange balance of togetherness and freedom. She should use her Leo practicality and try to stop him from gambling or taking outrageous chances. He certainly won't try to prevent her from contributing to the family finances. And he won't be jealous or vicious. He's a very nice guy in a sometimes otherworldly sort of way. Some people think Sagittarians are too nice for this planet, but others know they can be a bit penny-pinching at times and then extraordinarily kind at others.

This man loves to keep twenty-seven balls in the air at once—and he's very good at it. Ten to one his desk is a terrible jumble and muddle—but he knows where everything is. Move a thing or tidy up and he'll be decidedly sarcastic, as near as a Sagittarian ever gets to losing his temper. He doesn't like to be pinned down and he isn't too good at giving precise instructions. But he does appreciate initiative. He creates his own life patterns, his own unique style; it's terribly difficult to categorize him. He has lots of contacts, friends, buddies. Leo might just finish up as one of them.

But he is responsive rather than innovative, very quick to seize a half chance, a fixer rather than a doer, a schemer who doesn't quite have the ruthlessness to be nasty.

Leo will try to dominate the relationship, but she won't succeed. As soon as she begins to get too heavy, he'll be gone, if not physically, then emotionally and mentally. It's like trying to be angry with a will-o'-the-wisp. She should put up with him, because he's worth it—life will be a ball with this guy.

LEO WOMAN—CAPRICORN MAN

These two are likely to annoy one another, but the relationship could work out as a blend of different emotional characters. Things aren't likely to be easy because both are passionate in very different ways.

Leo can be rather extravagant; she loves good things and price comes second to quality in her eyes. Capricorn demands the best too, but he counts the money very carefully and worries a lot about the future and avoiding destitution, which in fact is seldom the lot of those born under this sign.

Emotionally he is often in a turmoil, though he seems calm on the surface. Some think him cold and aloof and proud. Actually he longs for love and togetherness, even though sexually he will dominate—he knows no other way. He is a serious guy; he isn't really amused very often. Perhaps it would be better to say he was intense rather than serious. Leo can take things a bit easier despite her will to power. She is self-indulgent too, whether it be chocolates, booze, or sex.

If she can put up with his telling her what to do all the time, criticizing and organizing, then the relationship can work. But this won't be easy for the Leo lady. It has been suggested that if Capricorns stand still too long they may put out roots. This is hardly fair, but they do have a tendency to settle happily into a rut and vegetate in a nice sort of way. Leo will probably not let this happen, and to this extent will be very good for this man.

He's rigid and tenacious and fanatically hard-working. He loves to fill his house with collectors' items of all sorts. He's good with money, so no one starves when he is around. His possessions are to him a direct measure of his success; Leo measures success in different ways. This guy is usually honest and careful and a bit slow for Leo. But he has a lot going for him, even though her bluntness will upset him. With any luck he'll have her going for him too, because she can soothe his troubled emotional nature and encourage him not to be too rigid. This is likely to be very much one of those count-your-blessings type of relationships rather than one in which the partners are complaining all the time—at least it should be this way.

LEO WOMAN—AQUARIUS MAN

There are fascinating possibilities for these two. On the surface Aquarius could be too detached for this passionate and demanding lady, but she could bring out in him the gifts that he so often hides.

This man is a detached thinker; his emotions are seldom allowed to impinge on his logical thought processes. Leo is practical too, but she is also emotional and she could teach her man to accept this other side of his nature. His aloofness will certainly be something of a challenge—the thing these two have to take pains to avoid are fixed ideas and opinions. Both can become rigid in their approach and Leo in particular may become bossy and difficult if Aquarius cannot retain her respect. She needs a strong man, and he may not be big enough for her.

Sometimes she may feel she's married an automaton, but he is a very considerate guy; he certainly wants an equal partner. In bed she is likely to prove more than an equal partner, and Aquarius could at times withdraw into his more comfortable fantasy world.

His interests, humanitarian principles, and artistic and cultural preoccupations could prove too much for the simpler Leo woman, with her powerful desires and drives that she wants to fulfill on the spot. She respects and understands tradition, while he is forward-looking and fascinated by the possibilities of the future. Often there is something rather selfish about the Aquarian approach to life, but it is a selfishness created more by lack of interest than by greed.

The one thing this lady must do if she wants to keep him is never to reveal all of herself. He responds to the mysterious but loses interest in the things he understands and can analyze and evaluate and pop into convenient compartments of his mind. Life with

Aquarius will be a challenge, not so much a battle but a constant effort to keep up with his changing ideas and to make him relate to the basic practical requirements of life. This guy thinks big but his actions don't always quite match his thoughts. He's an observer more often than a doer as he evaluates and compares. He'll certainly do that with Leo, and he might eventually decide he likes her. He's going to need all his strength and courage to tame this formidable lady, to convince her that he really cares and later that she is not his jailor but his partner. It's all a bit confusing, but then that's the way this union is likely to be a lot of the time.

LEO WOMAN—PISCES MAN

A complex, difficult union that only the most determined will manage to make a successful partnership. The introverted, shy, intuitive, and emotional Piscean is likely to be affronted by the sheer ebullience and bluntness of the Leo woman.

He could well attract her because he seems to need her love and protection. But he is basically an unstable type, one minute groveling with self-pity and the next standing on the mountaintop confident and alone. Sometimes he will simply withdraw into himself mentally and this will be very frustrating for the more simple, loving, and caring Leo, who must almost above everything communicate with her man.

Leo likes to get out and about. She has a healthy appetite for life and its pleasures and usually manages to enjoy herself. Pisces will make her brood and worry about her role in their relationship and her place in life. This isn't too good for her. She might lost her patience, and Pisces will give as good as he gets in an argument. He's tougher than he seems, although he is not nearly as ambitious, dramatic, and demanding as this formidable lady.

Pisces is above everything else a dreamer, a day and night fantasizer. Everything is to him romantic and special. He doesn't want to know about the humdrum things of life, although when pushed he can be practical. The family finances are likely to be in a permanently strained if not totally collapsed state because both are impulsive, generous, and extravagant. But Pisces does want to give of himself. He is deeply sensitive and wants to create a perfect union, peace, and contentment. Leo wants a little more excitement and drama. Often she is little more than an actor, but a big-hearted one.

This fellow needs to know that his woman is on his side, supporting and worrying for him, so this is what Leo must do if she wants to stay with him.

Frankly, the odds against a successful partnership are stacked high. It can work if both partners can come to terms with their romantic aspirations and the reality of their situation—but it's going to be hard work all along the line for these two to overcome their particular hangups. The way to his heart is probably to wash his socks!

LEO WOMAN—ARIES MAN

When fire meets fire what happens? It will probably be love at first sight. There could be instant sex, and very rewarding it should be. Both need to be the boss, but strangely enough Leo will take orders from Aries and he will bow to her wishes very often. Certainly there will be enormous quarrels, but togetherness will be much more fun.

Aries will respect this woman's qualities, her honesty, frankness, bluntness, passion, courage, and almost overweening confidence. She will admire his resilience, enthusiasm, and massive drive and energy. Leo has greater staying power but in a head-on clash is no match for this guy. She should let him win the short games and then take over to sneak the match away from him. He won't mind; Aries is much more interested in being competitive and playing well than in winning—and this applies to life too. He moves on sometimes before collecting his prize. Seldom do Arians complete courses of study. Often they can't be bothered with details, but they are very reliable. If an Arian says he'll meet someone at the North Pole at 10 A.M., he'll be there fuming because the other person is fifteen seconds late, delayed by a thunderstorm over Hudson Bay.

As a lover he is straightforward and yet inventive. There shouldn't be any complaints about sex in this partnership. But do remember that there is something curiously boyish and immature at work in this guy. However, he doesn't hold grudges and is hardly ever jealous—which isn't true of Leo—or impulsive. She is much more calculating, but not in a cold way. She has a lot to offer any man and none more than an Aries.

There'll be a terrific amount of excitement and stimulus in this relationship. He's strictly an "I want it *now*" sort of person, while Leo thinks more clearly and, although dramatic and extravagant at times, will prove a splendid sheet anchor for him. Strictly speaking there should be money worries for these two, but in practice things seem to work out surprisingly well. This pair could be found living happily in a castle or a hovel, and in either case their characters will quickly become stamped on their environment. One thing's certain, wherever they go these two cut a dash and leave a long deep wake behind them. Lucky the Leo who finds a nice Arian to hold her hand.

LEO WOMAN—TAURUS MAN

When two stubborn people get together, anything can happen— it could even be a very successful relationship. Physically these two are definitely compatible, but he is a bit slow-moving; he's very practical but not too imaginative. Leo is dynamic, extravagant, and apt to resent this man's lack of fire—except when they get into an argument and he shows that he wants his way.

If both partners are prepared to sublimate their desires and determination to run the relationship, then things could be both stimulating and passionate. If not—well, who knows? Taurus can be a trifle stingy at times, and Leo will resent this because she is extravagant, and it certainly goes against the grain for her to have to keep checking her purse.

He is a strong man, make no mistake about that, but he's conservative and sober and very willful. Frankly, there isn't going to be too much subtlety in their relationship. He has a definite horror of overspending and ending up in the workhouse, and perhaps this is why he has a tendency to overeat—who knows when the next meal will come along!

He is also an extremely jealous guy. But then Leo won't have her man playing around. Too much of that and she'll be off. He will expect to be the sun and moon and stars of her life with everything subordinated to him. In return a fine home, good living, and worldly success are a distinct possibility. Leo would be good for him, shaking him out of his comfortable materialistic rut, if she's prepared to keep after him and keep digging him in the ribs. It could be hard work.

Things certainly won't be easy. He'll want his woman at home, while she'll need to be out and about at all hours of the day and night. And she's a perfectionist in many ways; things have to be just right to satisfy this lady. She isn't going to settle for second best un-less, of course, she slipped into this man's clutches on the rebound, as can happen with volatile Leos. She needs to look and consequently feel good. Taurus will find this all a bit overdone, but if he's wise he'll accept the reality that he's married a glamour puss or that he's living with someone a bit special.

Will it work out for these two? That really is in the stars because two strong-willed persons under one roof can do very much what they want—for good or ill.

LEO WOMAN—GEMINI MAN

Leo is not the easiest woman to live with, and Gemini is very different from her. He's mentally oriented, charming, quick, often charismatic, changeable, fickle, and often lovable.

He needs an awful lot of entertaining if his interest is not to be lost. To keep this guy, Leo is going to have to learn gamesmanship. It's not a question of beating him—he won't really be playing the same games—but he needs to know. His knowing may be superficial most of the time, but he has a terrible need to understand more than his mental apparatus can take, quite simply because there are more things in life than those mentated by anyone.

If that all sounds a bit formidable, it's meant to be. Gemini has a lot to offer any woman, but he must be made to respect his part-ner's mind. Emotionally he has no idea what is going on, and it may well seem as though he has no true feelings, or at least feelings that can be recognized as such. This isn't true; it's just that they change as fast as the clouds on a windy day. He isn't insincere or notably dishonest, just unique.

Gemini's natural instincts are to gather his rosebuds while he can, so Leo could find herself deciding whether his philandering or flirting are too much to stand. But with any luck he'll just about hold the relationship together if he wants to. As Leo is the stronger per-sonality, a lot will depend upon her will to continue with this unde-niably fascinating fellow.

He is a great communicator and a fine talker, and he does ap-preciate genuine gifts and merit. He will quickly learn that the way to this lady's heart is through flattery. However, the sensible thing for these two is to take their relationship rather slowly. This will probably prove impossible, but don't say the warning hasn't been given. Leo has to learn to be almost as tricky as Gemini, and she might decide that she's too proud to bother. End of partnership.

If she can be a little humble and is prepared to become a master gameswoman, both in playing actual games like backgammon and in the more serious matter of running a relationship, then these two could become a remarkably effective team. Each can complement the other and they will certainly keep each other busy. There isn't much in the way of peace and tranquillity ahead for this pair, but that's the way they'll want it.

LEO WOMAN—CANCER MAN

Potentially a very stimulating relationship indeed, but likely to be short-lived. Cancer is very sensitive and serious. He demands total commitment from his loved one, and it is far from certain that Leo will be prepared to go that far.

He has a tendency to put his woman on a pedestal and worship her, and this might well suit Leo because she isn't exactly without an ego. She could, however, become a shrew if he overdoes this. This woman above all has to respect her man, not necessarily for being stronger than she but because he is better than she at some things and knows more about others.

Cancer could fit the bill nicely, provided he doesn't get home drunk too often. She'll tolerate a lot in return for flattery or, better still, genuine appreciation of her many virtues.

Cancer is a romantic soul; emotionally he positively throbs. He wants to give himself and his possessions to someone who appreciates and loves him. That's all he asks. Is it so much to ask? Actually it is, because it really is harder to receive properly than to give. Leo should try to restrain her temper and to avoid becoming rigid in her mental expectations and structures. In return she has much to offer this man, reassuring him, comforting him, and at times mothering him. Will she do all this? Probably not, but that's life.

Sexually the relationship depends on Leo's responses. If she holds too much of herself back, then this couple will drift slowly apart. If initial problems can be overcome, then this could be a remarkably successful partnership in the best sense of that word.

The way to hook Cancer is to play it cool. Let him work up a romantic steam. Play hard to get and he'll go berserk. He can't help being dramatic and he'll probably threaten or at least hint at suicide or mental breakdown if she doesn't go out with him. Leo won't really be impressed by this nonsense, and if she has any sense she'll keep avoiding the wretched fellow. Once he gets his hooks in, she'll have a much harder job dislodging him. He's too moody and sensitive for a nicely brought-up Leo girl. It's too late? OK, but do please warn the guy that he's getting a real live flesh-and-blood woman and not a cross between the Mona Lisa, Joan of Arc, and Greta Garbo. It won't make any difference, but at least he was warned.

LEO MAN—LEO WOMAN

This can be a heavy number, but if the natural Leo combativeness can be diluted with a little sweet reasonableness, then it can be a spectacularly successful pairing.

The problem is that there are likely to be no half measures when these two are around. There won't be much subtlety in what promises to be a passionate, impulsive relationship. The bossy, demanding, extravagant, charming Leo man won't play second fiddle to this lady, but she in turn won't be ordered about. Either these two get on splendidly or they tear each other to bits. When the leopard meets the lion, anything can happen.

Sexually these two can be very happy. Their arguments will be earth-shattering and the making-up will be equally soul-stirring. The Leo man must watch that he doesn't become too rigid, too set in his egocentricity, one-pointedness, and demands. The Leo woman, if she wants this guy, must learn to moderate her combative instincts and possibly her extravagant requirements for the best in everything. She should subordinate her independent willfulness and get right behind her man in his career endeavors.

The way to handle him is to flatter the hell out of him. He must learn that he won't get what he wants by browbeating or criticizing her—she'll just flare up. Both can be efficient—coldly practical when it suits them. They play hard and work hard, love their creature comforts, dote on good food and wine, flirt outrageously, and can both be immature at the silliest times. Stubbornness can be a virtue but it can also be a grievous fault when carried to ludicrous extremes. The Leo man is if anything slightly less prone to generate a fixed position than his female counterpart. He can usually be corrected and will rapidly change his mind if approached gently and sensibly.

He certainly wants a feminine lady, and she'll have no trouble playing the part. There will be tantrums and displays of conspicuous waste and ostentation from time to time even in the humblest environment. She is just as likely to come home with a basket of roses as the whole-wheat bread he wanted. And woe unto him if he complains. She isn't his servant and she'll let him know it in no uncertain terms.

This guy plays for high stakes, may be a gambler with a lucky streak, and doesn't lack self-confidence. He may never be really satisfied with what he is doing—he thinks big—but he has a habit of landing on his feet. Yes, both these Leos will upset and irritate a lot of people—but equally many will love them.

LEO MAN—VIRGO WOMAN

This is not too promising—Virgo is likely to resent the dominating Leo man who has—as she sees it—gotten her in his clutches. The rather unsure, critical Virgo may well be attracted by the smooth, forceful, generous Leo who knocks rather than bumps into her. But she's going to have a hard time facing up to his demands.

There will be a definite tendency for her to nag and scold and become introverted. He needs lots of flattery and loving and affection, and she is not inclined to bow down whenever he wants her to. Really these two are incompatible. Financially he is extravagant, thinks big, and is generous to a fault, while she pinches pennies. This is likely to be a most difficult area for Virgo with her accounts book, slide rule, and purse with a padlock on it.

She is, however, a hell of a worker. She never stops. She probably did well at school, where she was regarded as quiet, industrious, and unimaginative. That last point is not so: She is not unimaginative; she is just disciplined. She despises waste of physical or mental effort. She's too sensible for the Leo man.

Sexually she may be rather withdrawn, and his blunt advances may upset her. That doesn't mean that she can't be passionate when everything from her hair to the candlelight and music is just perfect. She hates dirt and dust and grime. If she finds a grease spot on her gown, she'll stay at home rather than go to the ball. She's a thinker, ruled by her brain rather than her emotions.

Strangely some Leos and Virgos do get on rather splendidly. This is because some Leos need to be mothered and badgered and reminded to clean their shoes and so on. She'll probably drive her man to drink—no hardship for Leo—but she'll serve him as no other Zodiacal personality will. Leo likes that, provided he can escape sometimes. What these two must do is take things gently. Virgo must resist his outrageous advances, send back his tickets for the opera at Monte Carlo, and tell him she's washing her hair, so skiing in the Alps is out—for the moment, anyway. This guy needs plenty of reassurance. Tell him he's really not a great lover and it's the end. His ego will just fold up and he'll get vicious. It's the little-boy complex showing. She should either love him or leave him alone—and think very carefully before falling for this splendid monster.

LEO MAN—LIBRA WOMAN

A good partnership. Libra's knack of getting around Leo will be a major factor in the success of this relationship. She's a born fixer who cannot fail to attract this manly fellow because of her femininity. Both work hard and are pretty extravagant, so a tenuous balance will be kept in things financial.

Sexually Leo isn't as romantic as this lady—she's all hearts and flowers. She is a fine hostess but demands equality in everything, and this is where a particularly dominating, egocentric, demanding Leo could come unstuck. She won't be able to face the Leo temper—so he'll have to restrain such outbursts. This woman, despite her outward calm, can easily become neurotic. Butterflies in the tummy are not exactly unknown to her. Emotionally she can get into some dreadful internal tangles.

She is a negotiator, and that's good because confrontation with Leo is too wearing for most people. Indeed it's a lucky Leo who finds a beautiful Libran to spend his life with, load her with jewels, and show her off at the best restaurants and travel spots. She's good for his ego. She may bore him stiff at times, but she'll make up for it in so many other ways.

Keep the compliments flowing and both partners will positively beam with joy and fulfillment. A compliment a day (or hour) keeps the divorce court away for these two. Incidentally, Libra has lots of friends and is going to have to resist spreading her favors around as she may have done before she met her lion. He will go berserk with jealousy if he finds out that she's still carrying on. He might even use physical violence, and that will appall the sensitive Libra, the humanist and champion of the underdog.

Certainly there will be conflicts from time to time, probably over some underdog she's championing and he's decided is a sponging rat. Libra sometimes has trouble making decisions. Leo doesn't, even when he's woefully wrong. He'll hand out the orders, and she'll question them and refer them back and mull them over and then infuriate him by starting the dialogue all over again. With time and maturity he may become less dominant and willful—but don't bank on it.

These two have a great chance of a lasting and fruitful partnership. When Leo is at his most difficult and unreasonable, she'll just turn off and dream about something else while muttering agreement with everything he says. It's effective and practical.

LEO MAN—SCORPIO WOMAN

A challenging relationship—one way or the other. Scorpio is a lot of things that Leo is not—she's intuitive, mysterious (even to herself), intense, intelligent, and passionate. She's also strong-willed, intensely jealous, and, just like Leo, she knows best.

She is also all woman; she isn't afraid to experiment with men or anything else. There's a fair chance she's had a few boyfriends and rejected all of them; will Leo be the exception? She will certainly be attracted to this warm, generous, dominant man. She works harder than he does and then expects him to match her. The occasional total laziness that Leo indulges in will upset her. She is careful with cash, and his extravagances—even if they are infrequent—will drive her wild. Sexually these two could have a fine relationship; without this there is little chance of their staying together.

This lady can be withdrawn and aloof—she's a real enigma. She is secretive and withdrawn a lot of the time, while Leo is one of the great talkers, one of the persuaders, a man with a deep need to be appreciated, loved, encouraged, and pampered. She isn't likely to be impressed by Leo in his bombastic moments, but she could be drawn to him in his quieter periods when he's not trying to impress anyone. He's a nice man in many ways, if a trifle immature. This can't be said of her, although she clearly has her faults. In fact, there isn't much chance that Leo will ever understand how this remarkable lady functions. She's the biggest challenge that is ever likely to enter his simple, basic, often comfortable life.

By the way, she does appreciate the good things of life, but she expects them to turn up rather than having to work for them—which, paradoxically, she is quite prepared to do. Is it all a bit confusing? That's right, that's just how Scorpio is.

Emotionally these two are both intense and at times dramatic, in slightly different ways that could complement each other. Leo demands a lady who is always elegant. Scorpio certainly makes the grade when she chooses to, but much of the time she prefers the anonymity of comfortable gear and walking shoes. Is she prepared to resist the impulse to tell her man how to really do things properly? Can she take second place much of the time? It's all a mystery—just like Scorpio.

LEO MAN—SAGITTARIUS WOMAN

A compatible relationship seems assured for all but the most unreasonable Leos and Sagittarians. Both are charming, passionate extroverts, with Leo providing a firm base for the more excitable and fickle Sagittarian to return to.

Leo will have to move fast to catch this lady, to wrestle her away from her admirers—but he's well able to do that and she'll be hard put to resist this dominant, aggressive, demanding, and probably successful man. He could be jealous of her interest in other men, but that may be no bad thing. In Leo's eyes her "value" goes up, although woe betide her if he finds her flirting later on in the relationship.

The way to handle Leo is to flatter him outrageously. It's no secret—he knows it too—but it doesn't matter because he still loves it and can't help responding in his nicest way. He's a generous, warmhearted man, and Sagittarius is unlikely to do much better with any other guy.

Sexually these two will really get it together. Both are far from backward in their appetites for food, booze, and sex. Both are extroverted and fun-loving. She is a great traveler, both physically and mentally. She loves the spirit of adventure. Leo is going to have to accept that at times his meals won't be on the table; in fact, they won't even have been thought of. He won't like this, but when Sagittarius gets a bee in her bonnet everything is subordinated to her enthusiasm. She loves competitive sports too. She is an enthusiast in everything, although she may be a master of nothing. She's witty, bright, and sometimes superficial. Some suggest that Sagittarius will always be superficial in everything, but this isn't quite fair. Her vitality is refreshing and is good for Leo, who can become a little jaded when his normally healthy appetites are overworked, as they are at times.

Sagittarius may also be a health nut, and this could eventually get on her fellow's nerves. Most of the time, however, he'll tolerate her waywardness because he can't help loving her for her good qualities.

The finances may prove a problem with this extravagant pair and all their friends. But with any luck Leo will make a million and solve that little problem. Emotionally Leo can become fixed—and this could cause rifts and serious problems. But if Sagittarius can persuade him that life is to be lived joyously and that he isn't quite as pompous or important as he likes to think, then this is likely to be a fruitful and enviable partnership.

LEO MAN—CAPRICORN WOMAN

Many experts think this is a nonstarter, but in fact these two have a lot going for them, and there is a good chance of a fruitful and enduring relationship.

Leo's generosity, dominant nature, and passion are certainly attractive to the practical and sensible Capricorn woman, who, if she can be pulled out of her rut, is both loving and passionate herself. It is unlikely that the level-headed Capricorn will see this man in quite the role he would like—lord of the universe, no less! But she needs security and a nice home, and the affection and trust that he offers. She is unlikely to stray when her man needs her.

Capricorn is careful with money, if not downright tightfisted. She'll be horrified by Leo's sudden extravagances, but since she will also be very supportive and will expect him to be successful in his career, this may be no bad thing. She is not too impressed by bouquets of roses and passionate wooing. She is much more impressed by a large bank balance. She always seems to look good. Even the plainest Capricorn lady has something about her. But she is serious. Not too many jokes or Sagittarian-type games, please, or she'll be off.

Once her love is given—even though at times it may seem like a computerized decision—she is faithful, trusting, and honest. Certainly she needs reassurance, but not nearly as much as Leo. He has to be assured every day that he is the greatest, the noblest, the most wonderful. Who said flattery? Never heard of it, says Leo; just the plain truth—and keep it coming!

At times Leo will be totally lazy. This will upset his Capricorn mate. She is a hard worker and she expects everyone else to be too. There are very few Capricorns on the dole, although quite a lot are—not to put too fine a point on it—rather boring individuals.

What it all boils down to is that if Capricorn is prepared to make a real effort to stay out of the rut she can so easily get into and to cultivate her romantic side (yes, it's there), then Leo will be so contented he won't even need to take his superinflated ego to conquer pastures and blondes new. One thing about this lady, she never ducks a challenge. She plays it straight and is certainly no coward. Leo appreciates this. He's no slouch at appreciating the virtues of his "property." Note that last word, because it could characterize one aspect of the relationship.

LEO MAN—AQUARIUS WOMAN

There's a stormy relationship in the stars for this pair, but it could work out surprisingly well in the long term. These are two very different characters, but Aquarius is pretty adaptable and actually gets on with more of the other signs than anyone else in the Zodiac.

This woman is unique. She has a mind that at times Leo will think she inherited from outer space. She is friendly with a whole host of people; she's loving and charming and yet impersonal and decidedly cold all at the same time.

She'll drive the practical, passionate, demanding Leo crazy. One thing though, it'll keep him from getting rigid as some Leos are inclined to do. He'll never know what to expect. One moment she's sexy and romantic, and the next she's just the opposite. One moment she's caring for the little boy next door, and the next she's off on some cosmic mind trip. She's fascinated by new things and new ideas. She has to respect her man's mind—she'll forgive almost anything but dullness. She also has real style when it comes to dress. It may be outrageous, but it's recognizably style.

Leo won't know what to make of her detachment, the way she cuts off and thinks logically. He won't like this, but he may come to terms with it. What he won't be able to forgive is if she shows no interest in his career, because by definition that means she shows no interest in him. Leo's ego can't stand that and he could turn nasty, pompous, and unkind, which is not really like him at all. He'll realize he's being monstrous and that will make him worse. The end.

Sexually he could do a lot for this lady. With any luck he'll unlock those dammed-up emotional floodgates, but she'd better show her appreciation of his ardent lovemaking. Leo wants a fine home, while Aquarius couldn't care less. She's a great traveler and has lots of friends and contacts; he'd rather go out to his favorite restaurant, where the waiters call him "sir," pamper him outrageously, and earn a huge tip from him. They understand him even if his woman doesn't!

Both are extravagant, Leo to make a splash and Aquarius because she doesn't like to be limited in her spending. She doesn't like to count the contents of her purse; there's something demeaning about being poor for her. In the last resort he is conventional or even reactionary, while she is unconventional and at times brilliant. She has to exercise her mind, probably to study Urdu or ichthyology or the symbolism of Tantric yoga. Leo just stares.

LEO MAN—PISCES WOMAN

A decidedly unpromising relationship in all but the most exceptional cases. Pisces is all emotion; she thinks with her body; she is the great dreamer of the Zodiac. Leo is unlikely to be tolerant enough to appreciate this remarkable, irritating, and at times neurotic woman.

Sexually there is likely to be a lot of physical attraction. She wants to be taken, to give her all. Leo likes that—after all, he knows he's worthy of anyone's love. Pisces is not ambitious, but he is. She is shy; he is extroverted. He expects her constant admiration and praise. She sees his faults. He expects her to create a beautiful home for him. She will do this but not so much for him as because it is something she feels needs to be done in humility for life. She is not good with money and this could also create tension.

Pisces has something of the actress about her, a deep and genuine sensitivity that she may or may not cover up. She prefers to remain quietly at home, while he loves to trip the light fantastic, to feed his giant-sized ego. He is a generous, big-hearted guy. He needs lots of admiration and appreciation. The little boy in him needs plenty of reassurance that he is a big wheel. He probably dresses well, sometimes loses his temper, to this lady's horror, and will do his best to drag her into the world away from her ivory tower.

If this relationship is to work at all, Leo has to understand that Pisces is a romantic. She does believe in knights in shining armor, and the extraordinary thing is that they—or their modern-day equivalents—do turn up at times to rescue her from situations that only she could get herself into.

She is moody at times, supersensitive, and loves the moonlight rather than the midday sun. She's probably too passive for Leo, although he revels in a conquest. She has difficulty making up her mind and then, when she's made a decision, she goes back over it all again even if she made the right choice. She's the sort of person who, when she has made a right decision, wonders if she should have made the wrong one! And she has a propensity for the mysterious, occult, spiritual world. She is tougher than even she thinks, but Leo has to realize that she is still very easily wounded by a thoughtless word. In all honesty life would be a lot easier for these two if they found someone else to love and cherish and fight with. Or would it?

LEO MAN—ARIES WOMAN

Boom! When fire meets fire, there'll certainly be excitement, passion, and trouble. These two are likely to have a terrific time together. Will the relationship last? Quite possibly, because these two are going to find life apart so boring.

Aries has so much enthusiasm and aggression that even Leo, who isn't exactly backward when it comes to going forward (if you follow the meaning), is horrified. She'll certainly inflame his passions, and they probably didn't need a lot of inflaming anyway. Her idea of egging him on during their second date is suddenly to tell him she's great in bed and asking how he is making out.

She is independent, irritating, headstrong, and irresistible, but she needs a constant challenge. She's a great game player but she doesn't play to win; it's just for the fun of competition. She's the sort who'd win an Oscar and not bother to go and collect it. If Leo can (1) catch her, (2) keep her, and (3) avoid being pompous, self-righteous, and mean, then there's no other woman for him.

Sexually there'll be fireworks. Both are passionate. Aries is a leader; Leo is a ruler. Physical togetherness will help to get these two through many an emotional black spot.

Both are proud, active, unvindictive. Leo will get jealous—probably with good cause—and then the sparks will fly. He is no saint hinself, but he does expect his woman to behave herself more than he does. That's what's called ego. Both are almost frighteningly generous at times. Money is not important to them, but the things that can be done with money are. And yet, perhaps strangely, there probably will be enough money to let them do the things they want. The biggest difficulty will probably be Aries' refusal to admire and fuss over and pamper Leo in the way he badly needs. He has to be continually assured that he's the greatest. She knows *she* is the greatest!

To keep this guy—and he's worth the effort—Aries has to learn a little humility. She has to become a flatterer against her nature. She has to learn a little low cunning of the sort her sister signs have been practicing for thousands of years. She won't like it, but in fact it will be good for her. One thing she can console herself with is the knowledge bordering on certainty that she was born for only the best; with a little luck this guy could both be and provide her with what she wants.

LEO MAN—TAURUS WOMAN

Taurus could suit the more earthy Leo very well. But he's going to need plenty of sexual energy and a good appetite for her undoubtedly substantial meals, and he must make an effort not to overdominate this lady.

She is going to look after and flatter and generally mother her man—and this suits Leo quite nicely most of the time. But when he steps out of line and flirts, he's going to get into hot water. She's almost as jealous as Scorpio and she just won't stand for it. She knows she's a good catch and woe betide the man who does not give her due appreciation.

She is likely to fall heavily for this dominant, passionate, and forceful man. He in turn will appreciate her femininity, her efficiency in the home, and her general air of elegance. He is likely to get pompous and overbearing at times, but Taurus will probably ignore him at such times—the best way to deal with him anyway.

She's good with money, and although she likes to have her own way, she will take second place in the bedroom. Leo will irritate her by being extravagant at times; she is very security-minded from both a physical and emotional point of view. She likes her diamonds big and her flowers in large bouquets. She wants to get married because she needs the security of a steady, ordered relationship. This may or may not suit Leo—it probably depends on his age. She certainly isn't above checking up on her man's whereabouts and irritating him very much—probably because he'd like to be misbehaving even if he isn't.

She will brood a bit at times, but not for long. She's a serious lady, but a little romance usually turns her around rapidly. She's a sucker for the hearts-and-flowers routine. In return she will wrap Leo around her little finger by flattering and cuddling him. He loves it.

At times Leo will try to treat her like a slave, and this may not always suit her. She could rebel. Things are rarely as simple and straightforward as we would like them to be. It's the same with Taurus. Most of the time she's as good as gold and then suddenly she gets difficult. These are the times when Leo must refrain from exploding and he must demonstrate a little of the tact he really has, even though he rarely uses it.

LEO MAN—GEMINI WOMAN

Leo is likely to be baffled by the moods of this lady, but the relationship has a good chance of success because he will certainly be fascinated by the aspects of her he cannot understand.

Gemini can be superficial. But she is smart, and this is important with a Leo. She will almost certainly be able to keep one step ahead of him because of her mental orientation. She thinks so fast she even goes cross-eyed herself sometimes. In fact, she thinks so quickly it sometimes seems as though she's being emotional even though she isn't!

Most of the time Leo is easygoing, generous, and reasonable. But his rather large ego will be definitely hurt if he sees her flirting—as she is likely to do—and then there will certainly be fireworks. He is a much stronger character than she is, although he'll probably never really understand what makes her tick. Sexually her ups and downs and changes of temperament will sometimes irritate and sometimes fascinate him. She'll certainly test his loyalty—but most of the time he'll forgive her because she is a lot of fun.

She is a sucker for every new novelty, and she really doesn't want to have to accept responsibility. However, it will come, so she has to learn to make the best of it and not always expect someone else to make the decisions. Not, of course, that Leo is averse to deciding everything and anything even if he doesn't know a damn thing about the subject!

She loves games and new projects and is good at them too. Leo will certainly boss her around, and she'll resent it but in most cases do as she's told. All she has to do is flatter him, convince him he's the greatest (that won't be difficult), and remind him that not everyone thinks or performs as he does. He'll be surprised to be told this, but he is a big-hearted sort, and this little ploy should work far better than with any other sign of the Zodiac.

Gemini certainly seeks experience and excitement—and usually manages to find it. Life with Leo would be good for her because it would bring a little order into her crazy, chaotic life. That doesn't mean she isn't efficient when she wants to be. Some suggest that Geminis are Jekyll-and-Hyde characters—this is far too simple. They are not really so extreme, and besides, they are likely to have not just two but a dozen different personas.

LEO MAN—CANCER WOMAN

This will be a difficult relationship because Cancer wants to know everything about her man, have his total allegiance, and serve him completely. If it all sounds a bit intense, that's precisely how it may well be.

She makes very considerable demands on her man. Emotionally she needs reassurance, affection, and security. She needs the sort of secure home life Leo is likely to want to provide. He will enjoy showing her off, and at times this may not suit her. She could be sulking when she should be simpering or brooding when she should be bright and cheerful. Leo will have a lot to put up with if he takes this lady on, but equally there is a chance she will open his eyes to a whole new world of feeling and deep passion.

Leos are dominant, but they are also gentle and kind and often considerate. This is the part of this guy that will appeal to Cancer. She herself is often an actress, casting herself in the roles she thinks she ought to be playing. This doesn't make it any easer for Leo to come to terms with her temperament and nature.

The difficult thing is to treat this woman as she really is. She has to discover who she is for herself, and it takes a sensitive and caring man to help her do this. There is a fair chance that Leo will just throw up his hands and move on to new pastures. He may well decide it's too much like hard work when all he wants is a comfortable, basically uncomplicated existence with a loving woman. Emotionally this woman is likely to be tied up in knots a fair portion of the time. The way he spends money won't help, but given time and experience it should be possible to coax him into being sensible and a bit less extroverted. This may be wishful thinking, but it's only fair to give Cancer the hope that she and Leo can make a go of a relationship.

This is very much a relationship made or broken by how much Leo cares as well as loves. He falls in love rather easily and, although not a fickle man, is attracted by many women. This union will need that very special extra little sparkle or indefinable plus that makes it seem inevitable that these two should be together. If it isn't there, then both partners are going to have to work hard to develop a tolerance that may not be there naturally. But don't despair. Whether it turns out to be a short or long affair, both parties will learn more about human nature than they would with almost anyone else.

VIRGO WOMAN—VIRGO MAN

Virgos believe in complete participation in every aspect of life together. Of course, this can be pretty wearing, but every detail is of genuinely deep interest and importance to these two.

Friends—if any remain—are likely to be driven slightly insane by the pernickety perfectionism of these two, but they are a decidedly intelligent pair who can certainly make a go of a relationship. There is a danger that boredom will set in, but there is clear compatability. This twosome will be looking for togetherness as much as sex, if not more so.

There is a curious idea around that Virgos are not sexy. This is not so, but they are particular. Everything has to be right for love: moonlight, music, flowers, and champagne. Virgos are sexually reserved and dirty jokes and porno movies do not amuse or interest them, even though they may pretend they do at times. Virgos are often very critical indeed, but they extend this to their own life, which is why they are so often dissatisfied not only with the life around them but with their own work and play performance.

Together there will be agreement on many many things. The Virgo woman will be forever organizing and tidying up, and the Virgo man will also be tidying and planning. Both are sensible with money, if a trifle cautious. Both are good savers and have plenty of common sense. A nice, tidy, very clean home is likely to be produced. If you tell Virgo children not to touch something because it has germs on it, even if they have no idea what germs are, they won't touch it—probably ever.

Virgos just cannot be less than thorough. Both are likely to enjoy exercise and sport, possibly walking or camping. Whichever one of them is making the arrangements had better get them right. The other one isn't likely to forgive someone who makes them miss a train or ferry. But since Virgos usually go over arrangements fourteen times beforehand, they won't have much to worry about.

Both work hard and have humanitarian instincts, provided those being helped are prepared to help themselves. The difficulty with this relationship is that the magic can go out of it and it can become routine and habitual. Virgos must try to avoid being insular and start giving a little more of themselves to the world—which badly needs some of the Virgoan virtues. "Let it all hang out sometimes" is good advice to this pair—it won't be for them, but they should try.

VIRGO WOMAN—LIBRA MAN

The charming Libra man should do the Virgo woman a great favor—leave her alone! She is too serious, demanding, sensible, shy, and faithful for him. He's great fun, a mixer, friendly, loves a good time. He will be unfaithful, unthinking, and thus unkind without meaning to be. Virgo will certainly be attracted to him because he is many of the things she would like to be but cannot. She will forgive a man who loves and needs her a great deal—and she'll have a lot to forgive if she takes Libra on.

The relationship can work if Libra loves her enough to give up his mental and physical wanderings, and if she is a little less rigid, takes life a bit more as it comes, and enjoys herself. It won't be easy for this couple. Sexually, Libra will consider Virgo cold and critical. She will find him loving rather than passionate. He needs lots of stimulation and excitement and may not find this lady ready to turn it on for him. He falls in love too easily and is too easily swayed by emotion. Too often he is superficial and yet he is a fair man who hates cruelty and injustice.

He hates displays of anger or having arguments. He will walk away rather than respond. He will expect his woman to be an equal partner in everything, so there won't be any need for liberation when this guy is around. This may extend to equal shares in the restaurant bill, which won't go down too well with the feminine Virgo, who also believes in old-world charm and courtesy when it applies to her. She likes to be elegant and sophisticated and she expects to be treated suitably. Libra will appreciate this and want to show her off, but there might be trouble deciding which restaurant or night club to visit because he can be rather indecisive. Really this fellow prefers someone else to make up his mind for him, and Virgo isn't going to like that too much either—she needs a stronger man than Libra.

Don't run away with the idea that Libra is just a social butterfly with good intentions. There is more to him than that; the trouble is that Virgo is likely to bring out the worst in him. He is ruled by his emotions and feelings, while she has a mind of discerning quality that she uses all the time. His constant changes of mood will disconcert her. Unless it's love that has weathered a few ups and downs and lasted a good while, think hard before settling down.

VIRGO WOMAN—SCORPIO MAN

A difficult relationship that could be a great success. These two are very different characters, but there is likely to be a strange attraction that may not be immediately obvious even to them. For instance, there is quite a good chance that they met at work or in a work environment. He is likely to admire her efficiency and she his aggression and will to win.

Sex is a matter of deep and abiding interest to Scorpio, for that is an important indication of his power and influence. His sexual ardor could prove too much for a faint-hearted Virgo, but most of them will love being wanted and needed and told so. Scorpio understands the yes and no of life, the dark and light, all the contrasting elements that make up the whole vital sexual area that impinges every day on all of us. Does he sound like a heavy number? Too true. He is, but he's all man, jealous as no other sign in the Zodiac can be. That's OK with Virgo, except when she wants to cut off, turn off, and think her own thoughts for a while. Scorpio will want to know everything about her and yet retain his own secrets. He's a difficult man but a fascinating one.

Certainly he will attract the Virgo woman and his questing, inquiring mind will suit her well. She too is curious. She is a mind-orientated person who weighs and calculates and is not jealous. This will be a problem because it is difficult for her to realize why he is always checking up on her. It won't be easy for her to relax with this man around—but at least it will be stimulating. There is a good chance that she will put her skills at the beck of his ambition, and together they could be a formidable combination, particularly if they decide to make a million or two.

Financially, things are likely to go well. Scorpio wants money because that means power in this world, or most of it, and she is careful with the cash. She does not like waste or conspicuous consumption, and he admires that. At times he will suddenly be extravagant, but she'll be hard put to complain because she is likely to be the recipient of his generosity. At other times he will be stingy. Yes, there will be disagreements and problems, but on the whole these two will make it, and he might even be able to open her tight emotional doors and let a little of life's breeze in.

VIRGO WOMAN—SAGITTARIUS MAN

The stars are not likely to shine too brightly on this combination. Sagittarius is a charmer, attractive in many ways, outgoing, imaginative, vivacious, impulsive, and quite unsuitable for the serious, calculating, prudent Virgo woman. He is just too different in temperament.

He charms everyone, but it's only skin deep. He'll take dreadful advantage of Virgo and then let her down. Although she is not a jealous person, his flirting and carrying on are just the things to produce such symptoms in her. His devil-may-care attitude to money will profoundly upset her, even though he usually manages to get by. He doesn't worry about paying the bills; she certainly does. She's the sort of person who pays bills before they arrive!

However, Sagittarius has a lucky streak with money, and he likes a little gamble from time to time. He doesn't really believe in working too hard, while she certainly does. Sagittarius relies on intuitive strokes and intermittent effort to make his fortune. He isn't lazy but he isn't too good at detail and likes to keep plenty of balls in the air at once. He has too many contacts and friends for the more reserved Virgo.

Sexually, Virgo needs security and regular attention. Sagittarius is too selfish to understand her and is likely to look outside the relationship for solace when she turns difficult. Life to him is full of fun and excitement and interest. Virgo is not the prude she is often thought to be, but she prefers quality to quantity, while he is self-sufficient. These two are heading rather rapidly in opposite directions. He will give his love to this woman if he wants her, but he cherishes his freedom of action even more. He is a great traveler too. As he gets older, he'll slow down—possibly because of the ulcer he has generated—and might even get religion. But don't bank on it.

These two would be advised to think very carefully before venturing into a serious relationship—and a brief liaison is not likely to be good for this lady. If she decides it must be Sagittarius, then she will have to work very hard to develop the lighter side of her nature and to count the blessings, not the failures. He in turn will have to strive to be at home when she needs him and really try to limit the superficial bent of his character. He must take this sensitive and practical mind-orientated lady seriously or he will hurt her dreadfully. And she deserves better.

VIRGO WOMAN—CAPRICORN MAN

There's a lot going for these two. Capricorn is not the most exciting guy in the world, but he is practical, sensible, and ambitious. Virgo is just the woman to support, succor, and comfort him. When these two give their love and trust, it is likely to be permanent, and that's just what they want.

There is likely to be a good strong physical attraction, and financially these two are similar in temperament. They are careful and good savers. No one starves in their household and both are likely to tuck money away in bank accounts and piggy banks and under the linen just in case a rainy day comes along. Virgo is more changeable and must resist a temptation to nag. She needs the security that Capricorn will provide and in return must attempt to lighten his occasional gloomy, self-destructive moods.

He is possibly a bit of a snob and she will happily accept this. After all, he chose her! She is sensitive and particularly vulnerable to criticism. She has an excellent mind, and he will certainly appreciate it, probably failing to perceive that its range is somewhat limited. Virgo is a worrier, not just about finance but about almost everything. This is why she needs continual reassurance that all is well, that she's pretty and he loves her. Mutual trust and faithfulness are likely to be steadily built up as the union matures.

Virgo is likely to make this man the center of her world. His hard work and ambition, however, could become too dominant in all the affairs of both home and work. She would be wise to work at taking his mind off his career and possible failures when he gets home. The best way to cheer him is to make love to him. Sex is a natural thing for a healthy Capricorn, who doesn't usually have too many hangups about it. He will be good for this lady in drawing her out emotionally and fulfilling her. He is likely to enjoy adventurous pursuits like skiing or sailing and to expect his woman to take part too. If she backs off, he will take it badly because he expects his other half to really be just that. He has high expectations, which he often masks under a proud smile. Capricorn never likes to admit that he is either sensitive or hurt.

Perhaps the biggest difficulty—and it isn't really too big when compared with the problems many other couples face—is for Virgo to persuade Capricorn to take part in stimulating and meaningful things as he gets older. There is a distinct possibility that he will vegetate and become set in his ways.

VIRGO WOMAN—AQUARIUS MAN

Aquarius is not the easiest man to pin down, and this is what Virgo will keep trying to do. She will keep failing and ultimately wish she'd never started.

This guy is not likely to be sympathetic and understanding enough for the sensitive Virgo woman, who needs lots of reassurance and affection. He's not too worried about money—or anything actually. She will resent this because she is a great worrier. She likes things neat, tidy, and spotlessly clean and positively relishes nice rows of accounts that all add up perfectly. Aquarius can't understand what all the fuss is about. He doesn't expect his accounts to balance because he doesn't like checking up on his bank account, and he certainly doesn't expect his home to be spotless. There are far more important and exciting new things happening in the world and he wants to be out there exercising his perceptive mind on these rather than worrying about the washing machine or the garden.

He loves a party or entertaining friends, thrives on travel and new places, and can be a most attractive and charming man, although he inevitably holds part of himself back. The best way to keep his attention is to be a trifle mysterious. He needs to respect his partner's mind, and Virgo, who wants to give all of herself to her man, will be hard put to provide enough mental stimulation. She does have an excellent mind, but its scope is rather limited compared with the Aquarius breadth of intellect and curiosity. As to who actually achieves the most, that is an entirely different matter. Virgo is a master of the pragmatic, the possible.

This is certainly not going to be an easy relationship. Sexually, these two aren't going to set the world on fire. He is likely to consider her unresponsive unless everything is just perfect. She may well decide he isn't interested enough in her.

Virgo needs a nice home, the security of loved and cherished possessions. Aquarius is quite likely to regard them as junk and throw them out—or alternatively he could be a hoarder of things that he feels might be useful for his researches into the religious life of the Potomac Indians or the economic history of Latvia in the twelfth century. He's certainly an interesting man and he's unpredictable and slightly unpunctual unless there is a real crisis on. He also has a highly developed social conscience, which will probably irritate Virgo, who reckons charity begins at home. Play this one cool.

VIRGO WOMAN—PISCES MAN

These two are very different characters, but this could prove a strength rather than the expected weakness if the partners are prepared to make a lot of compromises.

It won't be a smooth union because the Pisces man is all emotion and the Virgo woman is mentally orientated. Pisces is a dreamer, deeply sensitive, vulnerable, fascinating. He will drive Virgo wild because she is efficient, practical, sensible. She needs warm, affectionate, loving companions, while Pisces is more dramatic, romantic, intuitive, and daring.

He will understand every nuance of her moods, including the cold and critical part of her nature. He won't be too good at making decisions and doesn't much like saving or planning in a financial sense. He's likely to leave the accounts to her, and she will do the job beautifully. Pisces will retreat into his fantasy world at the drop of a hat, and this won't make a real partnership easy. Sexually, Pisces may well astonish Virgo by the depth of his passion. She is rather more disciplined and will be unable to match his needs.

The secret of Pisces' functioning is his romanticism. He doesn't really want to face up to everyday boredom and reality. Virgo will try to force him to face facts and he won't like it. He will do so when pressed hard enough because he's tougher than even he thinks, but it's no use expecting him to become a tycoon or as efficient as this lady.

Pisceans are more wordly than many think, because they enjoy luxury and elegance. They are almost certainly historically orientated, preferring old buildings to modern bungalows. He quite possibly believes in reincarnation and has an interest in the occult and the mystic and spiritual. Virgo is less sympathetic to such things because she expects to know. She was probably good in school, sweet, unobtrusive, and a bit withdrawn. She needs a strong man, and this Pisces certainly is not. He has many virtues, but his changeability and his almost otherwordly outlook at times make this partnership very hard. This lady expects things to run smoothly, likes to get on with things. She is certainly sensitive—particularly to criticism—but the sensitivity runs in different grooves from that of this man.

These two will be much better as loving friends than partners. They have things to offer each other, but the drawbacks are likely to prove too great for a regular relationship.

VIRGO WOMAN—ARIES MAN

It is not terribly likely that these two will hit it off, except for the time that he sweeps into her life and carries her off before she gets that Virgoan mind working.

When she does come to her senses, she'll wonder what on earth happened, because he's so very different from her. He's impetuous, audacious, imaginative, and confident. She thinks about tomorrow, worries about the finances, and needs lots of reassurance and affection. He is much more likely to want to grab her for a quick love-in on his way to the airport or another date.

He doesn't worry too much about the future. He works very hard in relatively short bursts and may have worked at many different jobs. The Virgo woman will find that irresponsible. He'll see it as the sensible way to garner experience.

He falls in love easily; she doesn't. Sexually, he needs passion, while she seeks consistency and security—which isn't to say she is a poor lover. When the right man comes along, Virgo is as loving as they come. But perhaps there's some truth in the old adage that she prefers to talk while he prefers to act. He's a fighter; she's a diplomat and strategist. He likes to be with people and usually gets on well with them. He will certainly respect the way she runs the home or office. He will want to issue the orders, to challenge—and Virgo would be wise to find something for him to take on even if it's only the next-door neighbor over the noise. If he isn't fighting a worthy opponent, Aries might decide to fight his woman. Enough said.

It isn't likely that Aries will ever understand how Virgo thinks or responds. He hasn't the time to delve deeply; he's too busy experiencing and rearranging the world. After all, he knows best. He looks out for number one, but he isn't selfish or nasty about it; it is simply the way things are, and his woman is going to have to accept it. He's generous, unvindictive, and boyishly charming. In some ways he will always be immature. Some say Arians are frustrated Leos.

He probably loves sports of the competitive one-to-one type. Team games are unlikely to appeal as much. He's great fun, remarkably reliable, and not for this lady except in the most exceptional circumstances. Virgo would be good for him because she'd slow him down and teach him to be less selfish. In return, life would always be exciting and unpredictable. The Virgo shell might crack, but on the whole these two should try a short, stimulating relationship rather than a lasting union.

VIRGO WOMAN—TAURUS MAN

An excellent relationship with a good chance of real and rare teamwork. The qualities that these two display are likely to be both complementary and appreciated by the other partner. Taurus is cheerful, patient, and honest, a bit of a stick-in-the-mud, but nothing will be too good for his woman. Both appreciate the value of money and want a secure, comfortable, cozy nest of a home. Virgo will run the home or the office efficiently, and he will respect her for her agile, practical mind.

He is jealous, but she isn't likely to give him much cause. She's a hard-working woman who will support her man all along the line. One thing he must avoid is criticism. And she must make allowances for his occasional spell of laziness and lethargy.

Both could become rigid and conservative in their approach to life and eventually bored with each other—but this is a relatively small risk when balanced against the togetherness. Sexually, Taurus is an active man who takes sex seriously but doesn't make it a problem. Virgo will suit him very well.

Taurus will encourage and reassure his partner, protect and cherish her. He can, of course, be dreadfully stubborn, but Virgo will either learn to live with this or learn a few tricks to get her own way while he thinks he's still making the running. He is definitely body-oriented, while she has a cerebral approach to life and its problems.

Both value tradition and probably prefer old houses to new. He will appreciate Virgo's responsiveness to art and music and poetry. He wants and intends to own things—including his woman. This is his form of security. He will cook, probably well, and appreciate his lady's culinary efforts. And it's ten to one he enjoys the odd dozen glasses of wine. He is more outgoing than she, more prepared to enjoy company. She'll settle for her man and her needlework.

There are not likely to be too many moments of ecstasy for these two, but they do display many of the more stable virtues. And more important, there is likely to be a developing harmony in the relationship as the years go by. These two will almost certainly be prepared to give and take, smile and weep, and stay together. Since Taurus is an old sentimentalist anyway, he'll like that last sentence. Lucky Virgo who falls for a Taurus partner.

VIRGO WOMAN—GEMINI MAN

This is one of those relationships that depends purely on what the partners make of it. That may sound a bit vague, but bear in mind that some signs have to work much harder at a relationship than others.

Gemini is a flirt. He is a good communicator, restless, stimulated by challenge. The serious Virgo woman could find him rather immature and superficial. He in turn could find her restrictive and possessive and overcritical. She is a perfectionist.

What this means is that these two are more likely to drift apart than stay together. Certainly he is attractive. He has a chameleon character and blows hot one minute, cold the next. But he won't be able to resist the caring, loving Virgo. He needs lots of stimulation, plenty of games, and—until he grows up—a stern boot on the seat of his selfish little pants. He's selfish, while Virgo is giving—so there is some sort of accord, but it's likely to be a bit one-way.

Sexually, they could get on well enough, until Gemini starts to stray. He will, however, demand his freedom in no uncertain terms, and Virgo, who wants exclusive rights, won't like that. She wants total commitment and the security and continued reassurance that this should naturally bring. She will put up with a lot for the right man—but is this fellow good for her?

There will be plenty of clashes as he disrupts her well-ordered life, but paradoxically, when all starts to go well, Gemini is likely to lose interest. He could become bored with her, and that is bad in almost any relationship (though some signs call boredom "stability").

It really does seem that this partnership will be either a good one or a total failure; yet no astrologer can be certain where Geminis are concerned.

Gemini is a very fast thinker; indeed, he thinks so fast it sometimes seems as though he is moved by emotion. This isn't so. He thinks like a computer, and if a display of emotion helps him, he'll outperform anyone. Life to a Gemini is a joy and a delight—or at least he thinks it should be, and that everything within life should be fun. He is rather surprised when things don't always work out quite the way he reckons they should. He is a sensual man with a flair for organizing and improving any organization or company. He certainly isn't as bad as he may sound—but he is too excitable and skittish and highly strung for the nice Virgo lady in most cases.

VIRGO WOMAN—CANCER MAN

This could be a most successful relationship, provided the Cancer man is not one of the minority of this sign who are truly supersensitive. In most cases these two will make a good partnership.

He is a romantic, while Virgo is a realist. He will look after, romance, and cherish her. Half the time she'll love it, and the other half her puritan instincts will rebel and she'll wonder if this is really how life ought to be led. But Cancer will get something of enormous importance to him from this lady—emotional security. And he in turn provides emotional security for her. Virgo will protect and cosset him, and he will stimulate her and at the same time seek to please her.

Cancer is ruled by his heart, while Virgo is ruled by her head. At times his emotional intensity can be deeply disturbing to the cooler, more logical Virgo, but at the same time it can do a great deal to release her repressed emotions and make her less calculating. Both are financially shrewd and seek a settled home life. His caring and loving approach will at times irritate her, but all she has to do is go away for a while or withdraw into herself, and on her return she will hopefully appreciate his sterling qualities.

A supersensitive Cancerian is a problem. Every word can wound and a silence can hurt even more. He is impossible to live with despite his charm, his manners, and his sense of fun and play. He, even more than Virgo, can build a crablike shell around him as a protection for his vulnerable interior.

But in most cases these two can understand each other and

make allowances for weaknesses. At times Virgo can mother or treat her Cancerian partner as a child. He in turn must make allowances for her puritan instincts, which are likely to show at the most inappropriate moments. Together they can make a most sensitive team. There may be problems in making decisions because both are inclined to worry. Despite his glossy exterior, cancer is insecure and shy at heart. He needs a trusting and affectionate woman, and with a little luck he will find just that in Virgo.

If at times Virgo finds it difficult to relate to a man who intuits and feels things, then she must learn that logic and mental application can go only so far, and that there are other areas of consciousness whose existence she only barely realizes. She will be far better suffering a little and fighting a little with Cancer than as a frustrated single woman.

VIRGO WOMAN—LEO MAN

A stormy relationship seems likely for these two. The dominant, arrogant, and at times insensitive Leo is likely to upset the Virgo woman. His need for outrageous flattery and for her to recognize his genius is likely to be just too much for her to stomach.

Of course, these two can get on—if they want to. But there's going to have to be a lot of give and take. Leo is the boss, make no mistake about that. He's generous, passionate, and demanding. He tends to make snap decisions and then, if things don't work out, blame someone else. He isn't likely to apologize too often. Not many Virgos are prepared to be a doormat for Leo's ambitions or ego trips.

If this makes Leo out to be some kind of a monster—that's right, he is. But he is for the most part a benevolent monster. He is usually highly sexed. He prefers a roll in the hay first and questions and recriminations later. He has an earthy quality about him, and Virgo may well be attracted to him because of the way he sweeps her off her dainty feet, brushes aside her objections, and bundles her into bed. Later she will wonder what on earth happened.

Virgo is practical, sensible, and hard-working for the most part. She is an introvert and a giver. She's a nice person, and Leo is certainly going to realize it. She's also a perfectionist, and so in a different way is he. She won't like his financial extravagance because she is cautious and a great saver for rainy days which probably won't come. She could well start to nag him, but he'll brush it aside. If she really fancies him, her job is to remain feminine and to try to accentuate her gentle and loving side. No man wants a computer or just an accountant for a lover or wife.

Leo is ambitious, and this lady will certainly approve of this and do what she can to support him. She believes in the virtues of hard work and thrift. Leo can overdo the food and booze, but Virgo is likely to try to turn him into a health-food addict. Nice if she can do it. She hates dirt and grime and germs, and she is almost certainly excessively tidy.

In many ways Virgo is ideal for Leo. He needs a lot of looking after—or at least that's the way he sees it. And although he may not be the most faithful guy around, he certainly wants his woman to be. Remember that his bark is invariably worse than his bite, and despite all his faults he's quite a person, worth taking a lot of trouble with. Don't disapprove too much of him for his fun-loving ways.

VIRGO MAN—VIRGO WOMAN

Virgos are perfectionists, so they will expect a great deal from each other and from themselves. They also believe in complete togetherness, so there is every chance that this partnership will work well.

There will be difficulties because concentration on every little detail can be most wearing, even though this pair will find continued fascination in everything they do. They are both intelligent, but there is also a distinct danger of boredom setting in as the relationship ripens and they get to know each other just a bit too well. It would be a good idea for the Virgo man to do something unexpected and illogical sometimes. It won't be easy for him, but it will certainly keep his lady interested.

Naturally there will be agreement on most things. These two are practical, sensible, organized, and tidy, but often too critical. It would be a good idea to try to moderate this critical instinct, even though the partners will understand well enough what is happening. Virgos are very thorough in everything they do. They will probably want to play sports or exercise together. Both work hard and have humanitarian instincts, their compatibility can be as much a strength as they care to make it.

A neat, clean, comfortable home is likely to be one result of their endeavors. She will be forever tidying up, but as he won't be leaving things around much either, she could become just a little too pernickety and fanatical. Ashtrays swept away while the guests are still smoking could be a possibility, as well as deodorant spray being pumped around him and the windows opened. Hardly the sort of thing conducive to keeping friends or making them welcome. But this would be the extreme. Mostly Virgoans are much more loving than many people think. They rarely enjoy dirty jokes or anything in dubious taste. They are nicer people than they sometimes sound.

The Virgo woman is well able to concentrate on her home or her work. She makes an excellent mother, for she will rarely lose her cool. The Virgo man is also calm, at least on the outside, but he is more likely to fly off the handle if things are not running as efficiently as he likes. And life being what it is, he is likely to be in a semi-permanent state of irritation with his less efficient colleagues. This is where a little soothing and cooing from his mate are invaluable.

VIRGO MAN—LIBRA WOMAN

These two are rather incompatible, and a relationship will be pretty frustrating. Both have keen, inquiring minds, but Virgo is not an easy man to live with because of his critical instinct and his expectation of efficiency.

Unfortunately, Libra is far from efficient, and criticism of any kind will just make her curl up and die or walk out—more likely the latter. She will certainly admire the way Virgo suffers and agonizes before making a decision, but she won't understand why it is so difficult for him. She rarely makes decisions at all—she just waits for life to get on with it, usually in the shape of someone who will decide for her.

She is a gracious lady, possibly sophisticated and elegant, certainly extravagant. Virgo will have a hard time trying to explain to her that money doesn't grow on trees. She loves luxury and fun and doesn't mind admitting it and indulging wherever possible. Unlike Virgos, she lacks both emotional and mental discipline. Under such circumstances there are bound to be communication problems. Virgo will get furious with her flirting and she'll promise anything just to get him to stop yelling at her.

She has a habit of involving herself in other people's problems, of genuinely caring for others. This is an endearing quality that makes up a lot for her woolliness and lack of firmness. Libra is not too difficult to bundle into bed—that's putting it delicately. Sex is enormously important to her, almost too important. She needs love and can be a deeply sensitive lover—she's probably too emotional for the more introverted Virgo man. He has to have things perfect. A fly wandering across the ceiling as he cuddles up to his mate is likely to disturb him. The point being that he probably thinks flies are dirty and she should have seen it and chased it away beforehand. He can be a difficult guy.

He makes love as much by doing things for his woman as in bed. She wants to talk and whisper about life and love as well as caress him. Virgo is honest, while Libra does tend to see things her way. She's going to decide that he's too fussy and busy and interested in his work. He will decide that she likes parties and her friends more than him. Virgo will have trouble convincing himself that he is (1) right for this woman and (2) right for anyone. He has a built-in insecurity and inferiority complex that even this woman isn't going to be able to shift. After a while, she's likely to give up.

VIRGO MAN—SCORPIO WOMAN

This could be a lethal combination—or, strangely enough, it could work out. It depends on the partners and, in this case, a little help from the gods.

Scorpio is desperately serious, sensual, and emotional. Virgo is serious too, but he responds to situations mentally, analyzes and only then reacts. Scorpio knows she's perfect, so how could Virgo possibly criticize her? But he will, and usually he'll be right to do so. She won't like that. He will want to care for her, to show his love by fussing over her. She'll resent this, and thus emotionally there will certainly be problems. The only thing they will probably agree on immediately is finance. Both are very industrious, sensible, and practical, and she will very much appreciate the efficient way he looks after money.

The biggest problem is likely to be in the area of their sexual responses. Scorpio is all woman, deeply passionate, terribly jealous and moody. She's very sexy and needs lovemaking like some signs need security. In a way this is her security. She will keep trying to make the clinical Virgo man more open and sensual. Don't get the idea that he is the cold fish he is sometimes made out to be; it's just that few signs can match the sheer intensity of physical passion that

Scorpio feels and radiates. If this lady decides she wants him, then poor Virgo hasn't a chance. She is tenacious, determined, and ruthless. Scorpio wants power and that means when she wants something, she gets it by hook or by crook.

Scorpio's extraordinary jealousy will drive Virgo to distraction. He just won't be able to understand why she wants to know where he is every moment of the day and night. She's the sort of person who knocks on the bathroom door to see if he's all right!

But all this can, given the right vibes, create an astonishing (to an outsider) union that defies logic and yet works. The Scorpio woman can satisfy some deep desire hidden behind the cool Virgo facade, and he in turn can provide for her the security and balance she needs—particularly if she's had her fling and is ready to settle down and work at the relationship. If Virgo will just can the criticism, the partnership will have a much better chance of working out. These two should be patient with each other and count the blessings, not the beatings.

VIRGO MAN—SAGITTARIUS WOMAN

A challenging relationship, with the partners more than likely driving each other crazy because of their very different approaches to life.

The happy-go-lucky Sagittarius approach contrasts strongly with the more disciplined, serious, and practical way that the Virgo man looks at things. He is usually guided by reason, while Sagittarius is emotional and impulsive—often with some success, it must be added. Sagittarius is forever on the move; she has lots of friends and contacts and she likes to keep things light and cheery. She likes to get a response and is playful and flippant. She enjoys sex and wants plenty of it. She is probably pretty untidy but actually knows where everything is. Virgo will be infuriated by this—he likes his house and office clean, tidy, and clinically efficient.

This woman will upset, stir, and mystify Virgo. In many ways she'll be good for him, but this somewhat rigid man may not see it that way. She loves trips and parties, while he prefers a quiet time at home, although when there he is likely to get caught up in gardening, home improvements, or sport. He likes to be active and is a good worker and provider for his loved ones.

Sagittarius doesn't worry too much about money and can be rather extravagant at times. Virgo is just the opposite. These two will have some fine old quarrels in this area of their partnership. Sexually, Virgo has a much less brash and easy attitude, and this won't help the relationship. Problems for most couples begin either in bed or at the bank!

It needs a mature, sensible Sagittarian and an experienced, more reasonable Virgoan to make a go of togetherness—although of course this doesn't mean they have to be in their eighties. The friendships and enthusiasms of these two are likely to be markedly different. He wants to give and she is a taker, selfish, and much more superficial in her emotional and mental responses. That doesn't mean Virgo acts like a bookend most of the time, but he isn't too wild about crazy romantic plans of the sort this lady comes up with—even though one-tenth of them prove brilliant and successful. He's going to hate her friends anyway. A lasting relationship will be difficult but not impossible. He should try going out with her sister if she's got one—or her mother. If that doesn't work, he should move to another country—or else give in; love just might conquer all!

VIRGO MAN—CAPRICORN WOMAN

A fine, constructive relationship between two people who will understand each other well. Both might finish up as workaholics, but both appreciate discipline, effort, and tenacity and Capricorn will give plenty of support to Virgo's ambitions and his hard work to make a success of his career, whatever it may be.

Both are practical and sensible and will be able to rely on each other. Sometimes Capricorn might get a bit down in the dumps, but her reliable Virgo mate will try to cheer her up. He will fail miserably and then they'll both probably have a good laugh over the whole thing. Love is likely to grow steadily between these two, even though at times they will be inhibited from expressing it. Virgo is a thinker, calculator, and helper, and Capricorn and he have uncomplicated sexual needs that are unlikely to make either hit the roof but that should produce an affectionate rather than passionate affair.

The home is bound to be very important to these two, and they might also enjoy some sport or recreation together. They naturally tend to be faithful once they have given their heart. They are far too sensible to mess up their cozy union in any way. Some signs would say this was because of sheer lack of feeling, and others might well find this pair dull—but it's fine for Capricorn and her Virgo mate.

Whatever this lady does for her man will be appreciated, and she will want to share books, art appreciation, and travel. There is certainly a danger that the rest of the world will be excluded when these two get enmeshed. New ideas would be welcomed at times, and occasional changes of environment will do wonders for this pair. Capricorn won't be as interested as Virgo in social schemes to help the underprivileged. In fact, someone once said that Capricorn believes in lame dogs carrying their own stiles rather than being aided to climb over them—but that's a bit unkind.

Both are proud and as they get older could become lonely, but since they are likely to be set for a marriage rather than an affair and since children are a distinct possibility, then the more they are drawn into a family atmosphere, the better. It would be wrong to underestimate the good will that these two feel for others, even if they don't wear their hearts on their sleeves as much as others might. It's a lucky Virgo who finds himself a Capricornian woman.

VIRGO MAN—AQUARIUS WOMAN

Aquarius will not be a comfortable partner for the Virgo man, but the relationship could be a stimulating and fruitful one. She is essentially a free spirit who will not be bound by any conventions or expected behavior patterns.

Virgo will certainly want to look after this woman—but it won't work; she will always have an essential detachment that he will find irritating. She will respect his agile brain, and since both need to communicate, there is certainly a basis for togetherness. Both are reformers who see things in the world that need improving and in their different ways set about doing things. If this partnership is to work, Virgo must learn to encourage rather than criticize his Aquarian woman. Neither is vindictive, and although Virgo can be a bit jealous, this need not be too much of a problem.

There could be problems in that Aquarius is never going to be much good at or have much interest in housework. Virgo won't like that because his ego will be affronted by anything less than perfection, even though he himself may not be able to achieve the perfection he espouses. Aquarius also refuses to penny-pinch or even budget properly, and this will also irritate if not infuriate the careful Virgoan. Sexually, Aquarians are much more relaxed than rigid Virgoans, but these two could be well suited because they are more passionate in the moment than many people seem to think and yet are certainly not obsessed with sex or their own attractiveness. Virgoans can become frustrated in later life, but that will have nothing to do with this woman.

She is not particularly ambitious, while he certainly is, even though he is often better in a supporting role than being at the center of the stage either in business or in politics.

Aquarius will often demonstrate her interest in the future, in new ideas and the development of consciousness. In other words, she is forward-looking and hence a little detached at times from what is going on around her.

The Virgo man has a genuine ability to sift the dross from the real—and he's likely to realize that this lady is honest if a trifle off-beat at times. There are Virgo-Aquarian partnerships that work very well and they are usually based on affection and respect rather than passionate intensity. Aquarius could inspire her man in many ways, but he would be wise to recognize that she is and will always be independent, elegant, and a trifle mysterious.

VIRGO MAN—PISCES WOMAN

Virgo could be too rigid in his responses for this passionate and yielding woman. She could certainly be very attracted to him, because he can be charming and caring and romantic and at the same time maintain a certain curious coolness that will more than likely fascinate her. She might even see him as a sort of challenge—someone to crack open to reveal the warmth and loving nature beneath.

She is totally emotional; she longs for every kind of emotional stimulus and usually gets plenty. He is practical, sensible, and mentally orientated. They are total opposites in many ways. He's a perfectionist, and she knows that no such thing as perfection exists on this planet.

For Pisces, love and sex are all-important; for Virgo they are just one part of his life. She could come to think he is incapable of deep and true love, but this might be only one of the problems this couple encounters. Financially, Virgo is a bit tight, or at least careful. Pisces is generous to a fault and at times rather irresponsible with both her own and other people's cash.

Pisces is a dreamer, both by day and night. She believes in true romance, and even when she's old and gray (if that ever happens), she'll be expecting Mr. Right to pop around the corner. This is part of her charm, but she is changeable, flighty, extraordinary, probably mystically oriented, and deeply sensitive to criticism. Never tell a Piscean that she's wearing the wrong dress or is looking less than perfect. She'll go back to bed or at the least mull over imagined insults for weeks—and probably pay back fourfold any real slights that come her way. Virgo is critical and honest and straightforward and will certainly upset this lady many times.

If the partnership is to work, then there must be a lot of give and take. Both are sensitive but in different ways. He will want to sort out all her problems, put her right. She will be deeply grateful but will soon realize that he has no idea how to go about solving her emotional difficulties. All this will create complication upon complication. He'll begin to wish for an ordinary woman, even though Pisces creates a charming and neat home. He wants to influence and guide his woman, but Pisces will cut off and almost be absent when he tries. There is certainly a good chance that a "stranger" will move in on these two. They should be friends rather than lovers. Or if necessary, he should look for a Piscean mistress; she'll be ideal.

VIRGO MAN—ARIES WOMAN

Not an easy relationship. The Arian woman lives life at quite a pace; she grabs what she wants while on the move and only slows down at bedtime—and even then only when she's exhausted!

Virgo is likely to be intrigued by sexy Aries, but she is likely to prove too domineering and adventurous for this more serious, slightly rigid fellow. Virgos love to talk, while Arians believe in action. And this makes it unlikely that this relationship will work unless there is a real commonality of interests, hobbies, and activities. Of course, this is possible, but the relationship will still need a lot of working at.

Most Arians love to travel, as do Virgoans, and sporting interests could be important to these two. One difficulty may be that Aries will decide that Virgo is too cold, too critical, and too mental in his approach. But if she gets ill, she'll appreciate his efficient loving care. She really couldn't be in better hands—even though she'll want to be up and about the day after she's shoveled into bed in a crumpled heap.

He is careful with money, while she likes to make a splash. He'll certainly want to serve his lady, but she requires her freedom, and she isn't exactly a wilting violet when she spies a man she fancies. She does have a tendency to take things to extremes, but she is nothing if not exhilarating. She'll certainly blow the Virgo cobwebs away and possibly blow his mind too. She's an extrovert while he's an introvert who worries quite unnecessarily. She won't understand this even though she could learn a lot from him if only she'd sit still long enough.

Aries is selfish; it will always be "me first" for her, but at the same time she is not vindictive, is not particularly critical, and is kind to lame dogs—when she finds the time, that is. The sticking point of this relationship will come when Virgo is really critical. She'll regard this as vicious, and if she doesn't throw a temper tantrum, she'll walk out, probably for good. A lot of patience is going to be needed to keep this partnership on an even keel.

Virgo is more affectionate than passionate, the Aries woman needs to be dominated in every way. There could even be something masochistic about her response, because in many cases Arians lack true maturity. If Virgo is prepared to put up with this firebrand, then half the battle is won, the other half is too chancy to predict.

VIRGO MAN—TAURUS WOMAN

A very promising relationship between two people who are most likely to understand each other well and to appreciate each other's virtues.

Both are practical, particularly where money is concerned, and both expect a nice, comfortable, and possibly elegant home. Virgo wants to make a fuss over his partner, to care and provide for her. This will probably suit the Taurus woman, who'll let him get on with it. His critical streak will have to be curbed, but she'll make more allowances for it than most signs. Taurus is sexy and basic and will do her best to loosen Virgo's inhibitions; she'll be as successful as anyone is ever likely to be. At times, as with all relationships, patience will have to be used, but all the ingredients are here for a successful and loving union.

Virgo is a perfectionist in a world where perfection is rather rare, so he will get frustrated. He will work like a maniac for his family and also simply because he knows it's the right thing to do. He'll rarely demonstrate the flair that gets people to the very top in their profession, but his precision, common sense, and willingness to work long hours are likely to produce the cash to produce the physical comforts that the Taurean wants and expects.

At times he will seem repressed and withdrawn and a bit cold—he's probably criticizing himself and minutely examining his failings—but a warm-hearted, generous Taurean can do so much to reassure and comfort and even mother him that his inferiority complex is unlikely to reach dangerous proportions. At times he's going to have to be cajoled into taking a vacation or going to the theater or ballet. Most times he'll be grateful, until the next time, that is. These two must, as they get older, avoid becoming stick-in-the-muds, content to sit at home with the wine, the TV, and their memories. In fact, they could become remarkably boring. Taurus would be wise to keep her man physically active, and not just in the bedroom, and he must make every attempt not to be too critical. In many areas there is considerable compatibility fo these two—minimize the differences and maximize the togetherness. They won't set the world on fire, but they'll have their share of quiet, honest fun. There are a lot worse things in life. It's always interesting to see a basically physical woman and a mentally oriented man get it together—they probably will.

VIRGO MAN—GEMINI WOMAN

The volatile Gemini woman will certainly find Virgo's more placid—at least outwardly—approach attractive and encouraging. In fact, they are very different characters and will need to recognize this early on if the relationship is to have a chance.

Virgo's predictability, efficiency, and common sense will both attract and irritate Gemini. She'll probably decide that he is dull and much too cautious and possibly a bit boring—but it will take a while for this opinion to be formed. Virgo will come to think she's crazy, totally irresponsible, chaotic. Both viewpoints are biased and inaccurate.

The changeability of Gemini will certainly be a major problem. She needs excitement the way some other women need peace. She is not logical. Plenty has been written about Geminis being split personalities, Jekyll-and-Hyde characters. This is much overdone, but truth to tell, there might be facets of a dozen different characters emerging at any time from behind the Gemini facade. This makes these people a trifle superficial at times.

Virgo is a bit too careful with money for this lively lady. He'll try hard to understand her sudden unpredictable moods and changes and he could be overcritical—this won't help. Sexually, they'll get along OK even though this lady is more impulsive and refuses to be dominated. As soon as Gemini feels her man trying to take her over, control her, dig into her psyche, she'll close up or push off. She won't stand constriction of any kind, and this makes a partnership decidedly difficult.

By the way, Gemini is a highly intelligent, enormously quick-witted woman. She thinks so fast it sometimes looks as though she's being emotional. But she's a calculator who needs lots and lots of mental stimulation. She can be very efficient when it suits her. Virgo is so much more thorough in everything he does that he will seem slow and steady compared with her. These two are certainly going to test each other's constancy and patience; but she is a loyal person despite her changeability, and he is very patient and honest and wants to give himself to someone he loves, so there is more of a chance of a real union than might be suspected. Some people think Geminis are neurotic (and certainly some of them are), but in the right circumstances they are charming and fascinating as well as irritating and irresistible. Are these the right circumstances? Maybe yes, maybe no—or just maybe!

VIRGO MAN—CANCER WOMAN

This is likely to prove a sound, enduring relationship even though Cancer's emotionalism and her moods will bewilder the Virgo man a lot of the time.

She is an affectionate, deeply sensitive woman who needs love and encouragement. She is romantic, while Virgo is more practical and sensible. There would apparently be considerable differences between these two, and yet there is a very good chance that the union will gradually become sounder and more steady, because each is likely to respect the good qualities evinced by the other.

The implication is that certainly at first there will be plenty of minor differences. Virgo is logical and mentally oriented, while Cancer is much more emotional, but both are more introverted than they might seem at first. Both are shrewd when it comes to cash and business. He will provide a nice home, which will be good for Cancer—

she needs to be anchored firmly or she could go decidedly quirky or even to extraordinary extremes (which is a nice way of saying she could become unstable in certain circumstances).

Virgo will thus be very good for this charming, often delightful woman who worries almost as much as he does but only in patches, and can be rather voluptuous in her enjoyment of luxury and even vice. She's all woman, though, and there is a chance she'll penetrate the Virgoan reserve and make him more loving and sympathetic. Sexually, things should be good because Virgo will protect and serve while Cancer will seek to please and comfort and reassure. Both are likely with luck to cast off their reserve and enjoy life together so much more than even they at first think possible.

One other aspect of Cancer's character is her love of her home and her instinct to run for cover when attacked either emotionally or verbally. This, of course, is where Virgo will be ideal because his instinct is to help and placate. He won't be there to do this as much as she would like—she needs lots and lots of attention—but neither would any other sign in the Zodiac.

So here we have two nice people with every chance of getting it together. There are faults on both sides, and Virgo can be woundingly critical at times, but they have an undoubted appeal for each other and a great deal going for them. She might even convince him this world isn't meant to be a perfect place—or she might fail to convince him of this and yet enrich his life greatly.

VIRGO MAN—LEO WOMAN

This relationship is likely to be either a complete disaster or a remarkable success that no one else can understand. There are unlikely to be any midway points for these two.

Leo is likely to sweep the Virgo man off his feet, dazzle him, and have him at her mercy in no time. Later he'll probably wonder what on earth he saw in her, until the next time she sweeps into his life and does it all over again. She will find him withdrawn, cautious, critical, and possibly fascinating. He's not the sort of guy she usually has around.

She is extravagant, generous, a great hostess, a flamboyant friend, a buddy, a mate, and sexually rather demanding. Virgo is going to have difficulty satisfying her in bed. Perhaps she should take a lover—but of course Virgo wouldn't like that—it would be an untidy arrangement, with too many loose ends for his taste. There will be massive arguments, possibly over money because she likes to cut a dash and he is decidedly cautious, if not downright tightfisted at times.

She is however susceptible to flattery, no matter how outrageous it is. This is the way to get around her, but Virgo may well decide that nothing on earth will make him a flatterer. Well, that's one way to end the partnership quickly. He is a hard worker who expects rewards to come from diligence. She is often more successful with her flair and initiative in a quarter of the time. Both have to learn tolerance; if they don't, then the relationship won't last long.

It's no use expecting Leo to be a little housewife—that isn't how she sees herself at all. She sees herself more likely as a cross between Cleopatra and Mata Hari, and criticism will induce her to display the famous Leo temper in all its technicolor glory.

Virgo does have a good mind and is efficient, and these two can make a formidable partnership. It all depends on how much they can avoid the rigidity that could quickly set in when they are together. If they are able to interact, then Leo will teach Virgo to enjoy life much more and he will persuade her to limit her overdramatic impulses.

One thing to remember is that Leo needs to respect her man. Virgo isn't going to gain this respect by blustering and bullying as a Leo man would. Instead he must earn that respect by his caring attitude, his incisive mind, and his earnest desire to understand and then share love with this endearing, delightful, formidable and usually highly desirable woman.

LIBRA WOMAN—LIBRA MAN

These two make a romantic couple, but are they mature enough to really make it work? Probably not, though it's certainly going to be fun while it lasts.

These two will of course know how each other operates and understand each other's need for luxury and need for togetherness. Life together will certainly be affectionate and romantic, rather than deeply passionate. Librans like to be out and about rather than at home, but as they get older this couple might come to value the less provocative and evocative pastimes. What does that mean? It means Librans are often in love with love—and that naturally means lots of lovers.

However, each has a real sense of justice and fair play and is quite likely to take up some lost cause with genuine vehemence and not too much sense of logic. Librans are not lazy, so efforts will be made to make the home more elegant. They are very sensitive to impressions and the feelings of others, and they love parties and friends dropping in. Life could easily become a three-ring circus.

Sexually there could be tremendous initial impact. There'll be bliss, flowers, theaters, restaurants, and fun—but almost as rapidly the letdown. Reality obtrudes and our loving Librans find they are not quite as mad for each other as before. There's nothing cold-blooded about it; it's just a gradual dawning that marriage may be out and friendship in.

Librans are a bit difficult to pin down. The Libra woman needs a tougher, stronger man to look after her and boss her around. She expects to be an equal partner in every sense of the word, but paradoxically she also knows her weaknesses and will respond to gentle but firm direction.

Friends and relatives will consider this good-looking couple an ideal match. What they may not know is that the Libra man has a lot of top show. He can act the he-man, the sharp executive, anything that takes his fancy—but he isn't going to fool his Libra mate. She knows he's a rather superficial guy at times, a little boy at others, and a sensitive lover at others. He does understand sex and has a gift for pleasing, but a long steady relationship for these two is difficult. Incidentally, don't take bets on how many months or years it will take him to get around to proposing marriage.

LIBRA WOMAN—SCORPIO MAN

This is likely to be a stormy partnership with a very good chance of lasting.

Scorpio is a very possessive, jealous, demanding fellow, and this could well be just what Libra needs to keep her in line. He is a strong man, and Libra will irritate him considerably at times, but he certainly loves her and she will know it. Sexually he is going to keep his woman busy; there may not be as much time for her to flirt as she would like. There will be plenty of passion at times with Scorpio calling the tune. As long as he doesn't get too bossy and plays it sneaky as he can, then Libra will be blissfully happy.

She will provide her man with a more balanced outlook on life and a deeper appreciation of beauty, and he might even learn to have fun. This is a serious guy; he gets moody and works hard because he is ambitious and wants power. He won't share as much as she will because there is something slightly secretive about him even at his best. But, and it's a big *but,* this lady is just what Scorpio needs and wants.

He will probably want to look after her. At first he will think she is cuter and sweeter and softer than she really is. He'll chase her around the world a dozen times when he's made up his mind he wants her. This guy is determined and intelligent.

Libra will keep demanding her independence and failing to achieve it. Does she really want it? Only she can answer that. Don't be put off by his cynical worldly look or conversation. He isn't that jaded or that wicked. Scorpio can become disillusioned and bitter, but no more so than any other sign in the Zodiac. One thing, though, he's a bad enemy. Love him, but if the time comes to leave him, make sure he's ten thousand miles away, and even that may not be enough.

This relationship can blossom despite the mental and emotional differences because both partners are intelligent and can come to understand their own limitations. If Libra carries on too much, Scorpio will cut her out suddenly and cleanly. If he gets too cruel or sarcastic or fails to look after the finances, then she will drift away like a cloud until suddenly she's over the horizon, and he won't ever understand how it happened. This lady does need mental stimulation, whereas, to put it crudely, all he needs is a body. A safe, middle-of-the-road relationship is not likely for these two.

LIBRA WOMAN—SAGITTARIUS MAN

This pair is much more likely to have a wild fling than a lasting partnership. There's something charmingly juvenile about Sagittarius, and Libra is very likely to respond positively to him rapidly and passionately. No holds barred on the first date is possibly the scenario.

The fun-loving Libran will certainly be charmed and attracted by this happy-go-lucky guy who does his own thing. He doesn't have much sense of responsibility, but he sure is stimulating. Libra isn't likely to resist him, even though deep down she knows she needs a more serious, committed partner.

He's a great one for crazy schemes—an eternal optimist—so he's perfectly likely to come up with a plan to dig gold in Argentina or start a company importing flying boats in the Philippines. Libra might go along with this nonsense until the pale light of dawn breaks in. Both are too selfish to really make this partnership work, although Libra seems to be a much more giving person. She wants her independence as much as he does, so of course there is a common denominator here; but they're better off having an affair than a marriage.

This guy has a short memory when it suits him. He is generous and stingy by fits and starts, mostly the former. These two certainly aren't going to be bored. Sexually they'll be fine, but Libra will want to place much more importance on the home than he will. He'll probably say he's never been jealous in his life—but he will be when his woman flutters her eyes at the handsome surgeon she meets while out jogging. There will be lots of interests in common. Both enjoy traveling. He'll take the risks and the gambles (possibly on the horses or at the casino), and more times than can be reasonably expected they'll come off.

Certainly there will be problems. Sagittarius won't be at home as much as he should be—and this could well persuade Libra to get on her bicycle to find a little of the fun she suspects he is having. With luck she'll cycle home and he'll meander in a little the worse for wear—but is it a basis for a lasting relationship? Keep it light and gentle is the best advice these two are likely to get, count the blessings, don't get too serious, and stay friends when the curtain comes down at the interval. Don't expect Sagittarius to provide an engagement ring anyway—buy one for him and present him with the bill, and at least someone will have something to have and hold.

LIBRA WOMAN—CAPRICORN MAN

Libra could fairly quickly become disenchanted with this man's rather rigid style and his rather serious practicality.

On the other hand, she will certainly be attracted by his stronger personality and what at first seems to be his security and stability. In fact, Capricorn isn't nearly as secure as he seems, but it will take time for this facet of his personality to show. One of the difficulties is likely to be her determination to do her own thing and live her own free life, which will conflict fairly violently with this fellow's idea of how his woman should operate. He expects his meals on time, his house cleaned, and his loving woman waiting to fall into his arms when he staggers home—probably very late—from the office. Please note the use of the word *his*. Capricorn is pretty possessive.

He will have difficulty with the Libran capacity to spread money around liberally, to enjoy parties and going out and about. Capricorn's idea of a good time is distinctly staid compared with hers. He's a worrier, a planner. She just takes things as they come. But he is a hard worker. He can get nervous if he feels he hasn't done a fair day's work. This isn't likely to worry her very much.

Sexually Capricorn can be attractive, and as Libra is very good in bed—she understands male sexuality and male demands and wants to please—things can go well. But their social life is much more likely to be where the cracks in this partnership appear.

This guy will try to organize his lady's life, often to the last detail. In a sense this is the price she will have to pay for living with him. She expects his reassurances of undying love—but they probably won't come frequently enough. Tension will build up, and although he has the ability to stick things out, it is unlikely that she will stay around when the going gets too rough. There are a lot of men in the world, and she'll find them; she does like an appreciative audience.

He's ambitious and a good saver, so there aren't likely to be any money problems despite his complaints about needless extravagance—or possibly *because* of these complaints. He's too set and rigid in his ways for this lady, but this is a pity because she could bring a little light and gaiety and joy into his gray life. Libra in turn could certainly benefit from a little discipline. It'll be an interesting affair, but don't start making long-term plans until awareness has dawned on the real character that each hides beneath the charm.

LIBRA WOMAN—AQUARIUS MAN

This looks like a good partnership because neither is too demanding and both are prepared to see the good points rather than the bad.

Aquarius is a busy guy who enjoys travel and stimulus and fun. He's forward-looking, well ahead of his time in many ways, and seeks a real partner in any relationship. This suits the lively Libran very well indeed. The opinions of other people don't matter a fig to him, but she is more easily bruised. Yes, she is a romantic, affectionate lady even though she has a calculating streak, and this guy might be just a little too cold and distant for her. However, in bed he's fine for her, and the Libran desire to give and satisfy will have plenty of scope with this adventurous fellow.

Libra tends to think with her body and emotions, while Aquarius is mentally oriented. This doesn't mean he is cold, merely that at times he will seem a little distant and withdrawn—and yet he is great in company and often has a magnetic sort of attraction simply because he doesn't ham it up and is naturally himself. There's a very fair chance these two will meet at a party. He'll be humming "Strangers in the Night" and she'll be whistling "Some Enchanted Evening" and bingo!

All right, let's admit it, he's eccentric in some ways—but he is rather delightful. If things get a bit on top of him, he'll withdraw to

the bedroom or the bar or take a walk through the night—then he'll
be back and everything will be fine again. Any sort of restriction upsets these two, so of course there is a chance that they'll just drift
apart. The important thing is that they talk together and keep sharing things all the time. Self-reliance is great, but an effort to create
togetherness will sometimes be needed.

These two have a whole lot in common. Libra's sentimental and
romantic streak complements Aquarius's will to improve the world,
make it a nobler, better place—cleaner, neater, and less dramatic. He
isn't going to succeed, and he doesn't care whether he's popular or
successful in worldly terms. There's a good chance that worldly success and money will come as a by-product of his interests and endeavors. He's quite a strong man in his strange way, and if he isn't
quite as elegant as Libra would like at times, then she'd better weigh
his virtues against her wish to observe the social graces.

LIBRA WOMAN—PISCES MAN

This is likely to be a difficult but very possibly rewarding combination. Pisces is all feeling, romantic, sentimental, traditionalist, in
some ways a rather feminine person. But he is tougher than he at
first seems and he is certainly attractive. He's quite likely to persuade
Libra to join him in his very special dream world.

He certainly makes any woman feel good, but he is moody and
deeply sensitive and easily hurt by a thoughtless word or action. Living with him is likely to be a fascinating experience, but at times a
little of him can go a long way.

Libra really needs a stronger man to keep her in order. The fact
that he so much wants to share himself and his things in a truly loving way with a woman goes a long way to make up for his deficien-
cies. But Libra is going to have to learn to make at least some of the
decisions—and she won't like that because she herself needs plenty
of admiration and appreciation (which she'll get), leavened with gentle but firm direction.

Sexually this partnership could be really fantastically close. But
will it last? Who knows? It depends on whether these two are prepared to pool their need for dependence, their weakness, and in a
strange way create their own strength. At times this won't be easy
because Libra likes to get out and about, while Pisces will probably
disapprove of her interests that take her out of the home environ-

ment. He expects—and it's true—that looking after, and being with him will be a full-time occupation. He is sensitive to home atmosphere and he wants elegance and scrupulous cleanliness. He's prepared to work for it himself.

This guy is never likely to be a captain of industry, but it is surprising how well many Pisceans seems to do. They are intuitive, and often their intuitions prove right, and they have the happy knack of being at the right place at the right time. But making decisions can be agony for them, and emotionally they are usually unreliable in the sense that logic is rather foreign to them and they are quite likely to change their mind in a twinkling of an eye and then be truly surprised when others resent this.

He is nevertheless a deeply caring and sympathetic man; there's nothing phony about this aspect of his personality. He could be jealous at times, but he's always fascinating.

LIBRA WOMAN—ARIES MAN

This is likely to be a difficult but fascinating relationship. Odds are that it won't last because these two are so very different, but both are extraordinarily attractive in their different ways.

He is a dominant, demanding guy. She believes in equal shares. The relationship will certainly be exciting. He'll be very impressed by her elegance and unforced charm. And she's pretty sexy. He is a great communicator in an arrogant sort of way. Libra will probably think she's found a man who will look after her and give her the security she needs. But he's a man of sudden interests and enthusiasms. He needs excitement and new challenges.

He isn't the easiest man to live with because he certainly is not sentimental, and he isn't really romantic either. He's quite likely to make a dive for Libra, and she'll find his action coarse and unromantic. She herself is more sensitive and prepared to please. Sexually things should be fine, but socially things will not be nearly as straightforward. This partnership could quite likely begin on impulse and end on exactly the same note almost as quickly. Arians usually make good friends and are surprisingly reliable.

Sometimes Aries is likely to lose his temper. Libra will visibly blanch. The last thing she wants is such displays of what she sees as quite unnecessary emotionalism. She likes things on a nice even keel with everyone being nice to each other. Life's too short for nastiness, she thinks. Aries finds life too short for niceness. He can't be bothered being nice to people he doesn't like; there are too many exciting things to do in the great big wonderful world, and there are a lot of women too.

This guy will always be a "me first" person, but he is generous, unvindictive, and fun to be with. Sure, he has his shortcomings and plenty of them, but notice the way the word *exciting* keeps cropping up. These two like to get out and about, they both love company and travel, and this lady will surely be accepted as an equal partner in this relationship in every sense of the word. This is terribly important to the socially aware and sympathetic Libran. The opinions of others don't matter much to this guy, but she can be hurt. She's sentimental and he isn't. They are very different people who can get it together if they really want to.

LIBRA WOMAN—TAURUS MAN

Don't expect this one to be an exciting relationship, though it could have a lot of the old-fashioned virtues and last pretty well—provided, of course, that Libra is prepared to settle down after having her fling.

It probably is important that Libra does her thing before settling for this rather jealous, immensely reassuring, and home-loving guy. He is likely to be good with money and to want to provide a lovely home for his woman. He expects substantial meals, wine, and candlelight. OK, maybe he lacks a touch of sensitivity, but Libra can do a lot in that department to loosen him up and make him aware of beauty.

This may make Taurus sound a bit like a clod and that isn't fair. He often has artistic interests. However, he is a traditionalist, slow to change, and a man who genuinely appreciates the value of laws and old customs. Libra will irritate him by the way she spends first and counts up later, but he is likely to be proud of her attractiveness and the way she wants to serve him. The biggest problem for these two may be her need for independence. She wants to give herself and to please, but at the same time she expects to be treated as an equal and to go her own way at times. Taurus will resist this. He will see unnecessary complication and paradox. She'll see it too but still go her own way.

Taurus does lack flexibility, but physically they should be in tune. He's a terribly stubborn guy, though. Once he makes up his mind, there's nothing in the world that can change it—but you can try that well-known Libra power of persuasion.

There will be fun and games when Libra starts flirting. This is a strong man, don't forget that, but he does need a woman prepared to lean on him and take advantage of those strong arms. The Libran who wants her Taurean had better learn this and be a little more helpless than she really is.

One way to the Libran heart is through expensive restaurants, theaters, and trips to exotic places. She isn't a materialist in the way Taurus is, but she does like to live it up a bit. He will value a woman who "costs" him a lot more than one who slips easily into those strong arms. Don't expect him to be a knight in shining armor; he's more likely to be a kind uncle or an excellent chauffeur—but bear in mind that the virtues of the latter two types can be rather nice when knights go out crusading and nights get cold.

LIBRA WOMAN—GEMINI MAN

This could be a very good partnership, although things could get pretty hectic at times in the "mad" whirl created by these two. He's an attractive guy, rather selfish and changeable, and he probably just doesn't understand why he is the way he is, but Libra can do a great deal to help him.

Libra, the flirty, flighty, emotional soul that she is, needs a strong man. He isn't exactly that, but he isn't a weak one either. He is mentally oriented; in fact, he thinks so fast he sometimes even surprises himself. He needs continual stimuli of all sorts. She is likely to provide that stimulus because she likes to get out and about; she can't bear routine, and there will be something slightly mysterious to Gemini about the intuitive way she sometimes responds to situations and people.

Sexually these two have love to spare—and might well spare a bit for someone else. But they will have a good time. Both are passionate but neither is overjealous or demanding or possessive. In many ways this is an ideal partnership. Theirs will certainly be a stimulating and exciting affair both in and out of bed. And don't underestimate the physical. Most unions go wrong either in bed or in the purse.

Libra has the ability, if she cares to use it, to adapt to circumstances and people as much as anyone. If she truly cares for this charming guy, then she'll make a big effort. In return he'll appreciate her creativity and the way she puts up with him. He's modest enough to know that at times he's difficult to live with because of his change-ability and zest for life.

One way for Libra to keep this man interested is to purchase the biggest compendium of difficult games and crossword puzzles and brain teasers she can find. When he announces a few days later that they're all too easy, she can then reveal that she is a chess grandmaster and actually compiles the crosswords herself. He'll probably propose on the spot.

Both enjoy a good time, so sometimes the finances will be a little strained, but what the hell, you can't take it with you. The important thing to recognize is that Gemini is high-strung, restless, always ready for a challenge. Libra likes to think things over, but she'd better not think too long or he'll be gone to Patagonia to hunt the rare wild blue ibis.

LIBRA WOMAN—CANCER MAN

Two rather insecure people do not look as though they would be a good bet for a real partnership, but strangely enough these two can do very well together if they are sensible.

Cancer is a devoted, practical, and home-loving type with a whole mess of romanticism stirred in there somewhere. He is essentially a gentle, kind, guy who worries too much and may well become a bundle of nerves and neuroses. Certainly he is a creature of intense and often artistic sensibility. He will be moody and a bit gloomy at times, but a couple of drinks will liven him up.

Libra will get plenty of attention from him. He isn't averse to pitching in with the housework or cooking, but he is rather more careful with cash than the slightly irresponsible and sometimes extravagant Libran. He'll grumble when she blows a week's money on a new outfit, but mostly he'll take it well and even make the occasional not-too-funny joke. This sensitive fellow is vulnerable and can be hurt quite easily, though he'll try to hide this. He needs security, and this is perhaps where there will be difficulty.

Libra believes in sharing as equal partners, and she likes to get out and about. She's a lightweight in many ways—and she is not likely to provide the sort of secure, steady, home atmosphere that Cancer craves. There isn't all that much compatibility here. He can become overcritical, and the impulsive Libran will shock him with her inconstancy and inability to concentrate enough on him.

The affair will reach its turning point—one way or the other—when Libra starts going out on her own, particularly if Cancer starts to brood on it. She is a little too sophisticated to take part in sports and probably prefers the art gallery to the football stands. She is less of a traditionalist than Cancer and needs more mental stimulation. He gets his kicks on the emotional plane. But they can get by if they are determined that all these things will not prevent togetherness, although clearly it won't be easy.

Incidentally, Libra can be remarkably stubborn too, not so much over things like the color of the walls or the house she wants, but over ideas and situations where she is sure she is right. For instance, if she decides she wants a Cancerian, then nothing on earth will change her mind—not even the Cancerian! And she can do a lot to loosen her guy up with a cuddle or a bit of fun. She may be irresponsible at times, but she is fun to be with.

LIBRA WOMAN—LEO MAN

This looks like a good one, provided Leo doesn't try to totally overpower his Libran partner—and he might just do that. It would be a bad mistake because she believes in equal shares and real togetherness in the best sense of that overused word.

This is a big-hearted, domineering, generous, larger-than-life man. He loves to be complimented and flattered (some say this is the way to get to his heart), but so does Libra, so there could be a whole pile of play-acting going on. If he has money—and he probably will—then he'll certainly spoil his woman. He loves the big gesture, the best restaurant where the maître d' knows his favorite table, and the best box at the theater. Libra ain't gonna complain!

Leo is passionate, while Libra will do her best to supply his needs. This is a sexy partnership at best, torrid at worst. There will be quarrels, but mostly she wants to avoid unpleasantness at almost any cost, and she'll succeed because she's a strategist. She'll quickly realize that the way to get what she wants from this fellow is not by a frontal approach but by low cunning and stealth. He won't even realize what's been happening until it's too late, and even then he'll probably tell himself that he wanted it that way anyway. Leo has a considerable capacity for self-deception.

He wants a feminine woman and he'll get one in Libra. He's a bit of a hypochondriac, so he'll need mothering at times. When he really does get ill, this guy flakes out totally. And he'll have to resist her impulse to overspend at the drop of a catalogue.

Leo will make a mistake if he treats this woman as one of his possessions. Sure, he'll look after her, baby her, and want to show her off to his buddies. When she resists this, he'll show a little of the Leo temper, which can be formidable, if short-lived. This lady had better learn to ride with the storm because at first he'll scare her stiff. Really these two are not likely to find more compatible companions, and he'll even put up with Libran flirting and irresponsibility—most of the time, that is. But don't push him too far.

As the relationship progresses Leo could become bored with this lady. It's up to her to hang on in there—and she should keep the outrageous compliments and flattery coming because this guy will put up with an awful lot if he thinks he is really appreciated. And after all he is the greatest! He'll give orders like a drill sergeant and then get irritated when questioned about them—but he'll be right, half of the time.

LIBRA WOMAN—VIRGO MAN

If this partnership is to work, then Virgo has to become less rigid and sure that he is always right. In a way he has to become less cerebral and more impulsive and responsive. Libra can help him to accentuate this other part of his nature that he is not accustomed to giving free rein.

Virgo can be finicky and demanding, but he can also be charming and sympathetic. He has to resist his overcritical nature as it applies both to others and his own actions. He's a worker both at the office and at home and he wants to create a charming, spotlessly clean world where everyone behaves as he should, nothing breaks down, and all is perfect. He's probably going to be disappointed! In fact, he could become paranoid.

He does have tremendous personal discipline, and Libra will respect him for this. He will enjoy the Libran grace and elegance but will be most irritated by her irresponsibility and the way she handles money in such an open-handed way. He doesn't need the sort of luxury she does, but both are good communicators with sharp, observant minds. Libra likes to go about more and enjoys sharing with friends (with any luck she'll have shared enough of herself before she met

Virgo). He is mental in his approach and some see him as cold, a subtle sort of computer. This is not quite fair, but certainly this guy calculates his effect and because of this sometimes fails to make the top in his chosen profession simply because he is not too intuitive and believes that hard, detailed, and steady work is so much more valuable than a leap in the dark or a gamble. Virgos make great accountants or secretaries.

Sexually things could be difficult because Libra believes in tenderness and togetherness, while Virgo sees sex as only one part of life. She might start looking elsewhere for a little consolation while he's at the office studying the way tin is moving in Malaysia. Virgo is a serious type who doesn't believe in the sort of games this lady likes to play. She must try to loosen him up, and he has to appreciate her less intense way of living and understand that he doesn't have to live on his nerves all the time.

Virgo isn't going to rush into a relationship. He'll want to discuss and rationalize everything. He wants the truth and every bit of the truth every time—rather wearing, rather puritanical—but that's the man. Is he worth the effort?

LIBRA MAN—LIBRA WOMAN

Sometimes it may be possible to know just a little too much about how one's partner thinks and responds. This could be the case with these two, particularly because both often seem to lack the maturity to ensure that a relationship becomes and then stays meaningful.

Meaningful is a much overused word but it implies that togetherness is not quite enough. There has to be mutual respect as well as making allowances for faults. Libra has to respect her man, and she knows that although he is romantic and caring, he is also a wanderer, one who requires his freedom—and he has been known to cast an eye over other women!

They make a romantic couple, and it will be fun while it lasts, however long that may be. Librans love to get out and about. Parties are the stuff of life to them, and money takes second place to fun. Which means that money will at times be short. Both can be crazily extravagant and resent criticism. They revel in luxury, the best restaurants, the best seats at the opera, perhaps a winter cruise, and so on. However, Librans have a nicely tuned sense of justice and fair play, and they have a genuine appreciation of beauty and elegance. They may play-act a lot, but they do have class.

Sexually this couple can reach remarkable intensity, but after the initial impact they could find themselves wondering what they saw in each other. The Libra man in particular may be difficult to pin down. He will accept his mate as an equal partner in every sense, but she may have trouble getting him to the altar if that is her intention. Everyone's going to look at this couple and beam; they seem ideal. But do they have the maturity to make it work? Frankly, the odds are loaded against them simply because they are such attractive people and others find them so too. They are a trifle selfish, and although each truly wants to please the other, they may find there's little to talk about or relate with once they are out of the bedroom.

There's nothing cold-blooded about Librans, although they sometimes seem tougher and harder than they are. They are soft and yielding most of the time and will do almost anything to avoid an overt quarrel or unpleasantness. This failure to face facts is a problem, not least with money. The occasional infidelity will be overlooked, but more likely is a gradual drift apart. And that's a shame because these two relating properly have a good deal to contribute to any society or environment. They are two sensitive people with perhaps too many gifts!

LIBRA MAN—SCORPIO WOMAN

This is likely to be a difficult relationship, although there will be plenty of initial excitement and attraction. An amorous, charming Libran will certainly attract Scorpio, but really she is too strong for him.

Scorpio is a complex woman, even to herself, and this will attract Libra, but their very different views on home and social life will create difficulties. Libra believes in a free and easy relationship. He won't be too good at giving orders, and he likes to flirt and play games of all types. Scorpio despises this; it is fair to say she runs a tight ship. She's a very jealous lady and makes a bad enemy. She has a touch of vindictiveness about her and she wants always to win. She seeks power even if she's never really admitted it to herself.

Don't assume that Libra is all fun and joy; he has his serious side too and may have artistic talent. And likewise Scorpio likes to enjoy herself; she doesn't play the "heavy" all the time. She is a sexy lady and there will be plenty of healthy lovemaking when these two get together. This will be a passionate, often stormy union.

Libra likes to feel he's learning something new every day. Scorpio likes to feel something new every day. He won't become domesticated for her, and she won't tear around the parties and clubs for him. So there'll have to be a little more give and take than this pair might be used to in other circumstances. Scorpio will always be worried about achieving financial security, particularly with the extravagant Libran around. He won't worry too much about the finances, and she's too stubborn to change her ways.

Sometimes Scorpio will simply announce that this fellow is too superficial and charming for her, but she'll accept the flowers and champagne and homage as her due. Libra will never get to understand this lady, and her air of mystery and aloofness will infuriate and attract him. "Who does she think she is?" may well be the refrain at times. She knows she's special, and if she has this thing about suffering being essential to progress and success in any sphere of life, who is Libra to try to explain that he doesn't believe her? She'll just look straight through him and smile in a patronizing way. Libra will be appreciative of anything done for him, but really these two should think very seriously before tying the knot.

LIBRA MAN—SAGITTARIUS WOMAN

This could be a satisfying partnership, and neither party is likely to be bored. Libra seeks a partnership in every sense of the word, but Sagittarius likes to run around even more than he does, so there will be the occasional fight.

Sexually these two will get on fine and they will certainly have a very active social life. Sagittarius is a cheery, charming, fun-loving lady, but even she will get exhausted at times keeping twenty-three balls in the air at once and two hundred and seventeen friends and contacts happy. Then she'll scuttle home for comfort and find Libra out visiting.

Finances threaten to be in a permanently precarious situation. Neither worries much about cash; they like to splash it about, so somewhere along the line bankruptcy looms. Libra might even have to grow up and take command of the pursestrings.

This isn't really an ideal partnership, but they'll have an awful lot of fun together before they pack it in and seek someone more steady. On the other hand, life with someone more steady might be just too boring. Who knows, it could work out for this exuberant pair. Libra will truly appreciate her crazy ideas and tell her she's the greatest thing since grilled cheese. Don't be surprised if she suddenly announces she's off to see her aunt in Lithuania and on the way back she's going to stop at Kyoto and would it be OK to meet her under the great oak in Sherwood Forest, England, at full moon next month!

Libra is not exactly the easiest guy to pin down, particularly when it comes to a wedding, but he may get there eventually, more by default than anything else. He'll expect his woman to be very smart at all times, but he also expects things to just happen. He really doesn't like making decisions, and Sagittarius is usually too busy rushing around to consider the implications of practically anything she does, so in the end it may all boil down to how much he wants to keep the relationship going. It can break down in no time flat if he doesn't make a special effort.

One thing about this man is that he's a born diplomat and he'll go a long way to avoid a scene of any kind. Sagittarius is more straightforward in most things, less fussy, less ambitious, and often pretty disorganized. Have a look at her desk or dresser. Total chaos, or is it? Actually she knows precisely where everything is, and surprisingly she can be pretty efficient, coming up sometimes with the most intuitive comment or idea that proves she's no fool.

LIBRA MAN—CAPRICORN WOMAN

Capricorn could do a great deal for this guy, but he is unlikely to truly appreciate her virtues, and the odds are that the relationship will not stand the test of time.

Libra is a charmer when he wants to be, and Capricorn will be attracted by his easy ways, so different from her more intense approach and her need to work hard and support her man. Later on she will be upset by his partygoing and his need for company of all types. She will be irritated by the way he lets their relationship drift and seems to worry more about the troubles of complete strangers.

Capricorn wants to be loved—for herself. And Libra is unlikely to prove the rock on which she can build her life. That's a great pity because he could help her to loosen up. This is a reliable, devoted, and often dedicated woman—she'll stick to Libra long after many others would have quietly given up. He's too flirtatious and capricious and selfish for this lady.

If Libra can, perhaps as he grows older and more mature, become less superficial and restrain his instincts to laugh at her and tell her the finances will be OK when they patently will not, then the partnership could prosper. Sexually he can please any woman; he seems to have built-in expertise, but he isn't likely to last the course as this woman is. He's a bit lazy at times too, often a jack of all trades and master of none, and the busy Capricorn woman won't like this.

It is likely that Libra will take his time getting to the altar—rather a lot of time, actually—so this is in fact perhaps a blessing. Capricorn might have moved on to less obviously attractive grounds with a little more substance. He doesn't want a lady who will create an efficient and spotless home for him. He'd much rather have a pretty woman (or two), and though he enjoys his food as much as anyone, he's the sort of guy who goes to the "in" places rather than those that provide quality. This lady will pretend she loves the mad special whirl to please him. And although he will go miles to avoid a scene or an argument, he's not lacking in courage when it comes to protecting the weak or battling on behalf of those unjustly treated. This guy isn't just a social butterfly. Is he worth the pain he'll cause Capricorn? Well, that's for her to say, but she's been warned!

LIBRA MAN—AQUARIUS WOMAN

This could be a good relationship because both will stay independent and yet they can get together when it matters.

Aquarius is an easy woman to get on with, as many men have found, but at times she can be a trifle distant and reserved. Some will say that she lives in a different world from everyone else, but this is an exaggeration. She certainly is not a sentimentalist; she looks forward, probably has an excellent if rather analytical mind, and responds in a selfless way. Libra has considerable capacity for being selfish and egocentric, but he does want to please. He's more romantic than she is, but she knows even more fascinating people than he does and likes to get around just as much or even more—although she probably despises parties for not being meaningful!

What it all means is that Libra has finally met his match, his Waterloo, his downfall. Enough exposure to this lady and he won't know whether he's coming or going. She'll fascinate him, but he just won't be able to comprehend how she ticks. This woman will drag him off to a lecture on astrology one night, to a yoga class the next, and to a concert to hear an early fourteenth-century Piedmontese revival of madrigal settings the next. With all this mental stretching going on, there might not be time for sex. When it happens, it'll be fun, impulsive rather than grimly determined, and good.

Libra will certainly be attractive to this independent woman. They'll probably meet on top of a mountain somewhere or while deep-sea diving, anywhere exotic or unusual. Aquarius loves traveling, and Libra isn't too good at staying put in one spot for long.

Even if the partnership breaks up, these two are likely to remain friends. He doesn't try to take over his lady's life—he accepts her as an absolutely equal partner, and she likes that.

Aquarius is an innovative and often elegant dresser. She would be wise to work on the elegant aspect when this guy is around and play down her intuitive ideas about what women will be wearing next century. Libra can be rather sentimental at times, and some men of his sign do have distinctly soft centers, while others have become corroded in their selfish ways. She'd better keep an eye on him when a pretty woman comes in sight, or better still tie his pajama belt to the bedpost. Even when he's old and gray, Libra will have a roving eye, and it's surprising how successful even an aged Libran can be! He's certainly got something. If he gets an Aquarian, he's a lucky guy.

LIBRA MAN—PISCES WOMAN

There will be plenty of disagreements in this relationship, but the concord could outweigh them and help create a remarkable and lasting union.

It won't be easy because Pisces is the most emotional, romantic, dreamy, and tantalizingly irritating woman in the Zodiac. She's all feminity and yielding charm, but she's moody, changeable, difficult, and badly in need of reassurance and a strong pair of loving arms. Libra will seem like Prince Charming to her, and she'll probably daydream about him for months while he tries vainly to get some sense out of her. Which isn't to say that she isn't a sexy lady when she gets what can only be called firm direction. Is Libra the man to give her the security she needs? Frankly no, but he is enormously appealing, and she is faithful in the sense that she rarely bothers about any other man when he's around.

Financially the pair of them could do with a little more com-

LIBRA♂ - ARIES♀ (321)

mon sense. Intuition is fine and so is artistic appreciation, but some people prefer bread and butter. There'll be plenty of complicated games played at all levels when these two get together—and they'll love it. This is a lady who loves to give herself totally. Libra is more than likely quite willing to accept her sacrifice. Sure, there'll be tensions and some nasty little arguments, which both will hate and yet find themselves embroiled in. But a guy who's gotten mixed up with a Piscean finds it hard to get unmeshed even if he wants to. This lady seems to have tendrils all over the place; it's part of her charm.

He's a very understanding, possibly good-looking fellow. He truly needs a woman with taste and who dresses well. When he's happy—and he often is—the whole world smiles with Libra. This lady will at times withdraw into herself. She isn't a strong character, but she seems to need to recharge her batteries, perhaps by long walks in the country or looking after children. Her home is likely to be neat and spotless. She has a gift for creating harmony wherever she goes, and this will certainly be appreciated by all about her. She is loving and giving and often truly sweet, and is prepared to work harder than many give her credit for. She's tougher than she thinks.

Pisces is often a good and economical cook, but one shouldn't give her a free rein when she goes shopping for clothes. He may have to go with her and keep a firm hand on the checkbook. After all, she is emotional and romantic, and no one's good at everything. This relationship is truly worth working at.

LIBRA MAN—ARIES WOMAN

Aries is unlikely to put up with this fellow for long, and he will probably find her too aggressive for anything but a short, sharp, but decidedly passionate affair.

Of course, any two signs can get it together if the will is there, but some are going to find it harder than others—these two are in the latter category. Libra is charming and stimulating both in bed and out, and although he's interested in lots of girls, Aries could easily force herself onto page one of his little black book. He's an attractive guy and he knows it, but although he plays games he is also continually seeking to create peace and joy and harmony. He hates quarrels, whereas she thrives on them. She's always ready for a fight.

She'll be driven crazy by his indecisiveness and it'll show—the Arian temper when it finally erupts is something else again. She wants a man who truly appreciates her. She's a slightly arrogant person who is not easily flattered and can be pretty caustic when the mood takes her. But she's generous to a fault to anyone in distress and is always fascinated by new ideas and new people and new emotions.

Both are romantic, the difference being that Aries demands romance (a contradiction if ever there was one) while Libra lives and breathes it. Sexually there'll be fireworks and there won't be any complaints about bedroom technique. But there will be plenty of complaints about other things, not least finance. These two are very different in their approach. Aries is suddenly extravagant, while Libra is one of those people who can't be bothered with money—not too promising a situation, the bank manager will probably announce.

One thing in their favor is that Aries is not vindictive. She doesn't bear grudges; really she hasn't the time, there's too much else to do in the world. Libra doesn't hold grudges either—he believe in love and light and fun. He's not frightened of anyone or anything; he's just a hater of scenes and anything that disrupts his carefully worked-out equilibrium.

Incidentally, despite being a nice guy, or perhaps because of it, he cannot be bullied, and Aries, who often gets what she wants by this very stratagem, will have to quickly learn this. That is, if she's around long enough to care. They should try a short, sweet, passionate affair before really falling for each other. Do remember that Aries is incredibly impulsive when the mood is on her—and it's on her most of the time.

LIBRA MAN—TAURUS WOMAN

Don't take any bets that this one will work out. Taurus is a pretty possessive and at times jealous lady. She isn't going to put up with Libra playing around—and unfortunately that's just what he wants to do, even though he swears that he doesn't.

Physically they can play sweet music together, and emotionally they might come to understand each other. But Taurus wants one man who wants her, and Libra is just a little too fickle. He doesn't like to plan too far ahead—about twenty minutes is fine—while she likes to see things moving as she intended. Incidentally, she could have quite a job getting this guy to the altar—which may be a good thing for both parties. But being Taurus, she'll try. She needs security the way some babies need a comforter, and a ring on her finger (plain gold band, of course) looms large in her life plans.

This need for security implies a nice home, money in the bank, and a man with a steady future. There's not much chance of getting the latter two with Libra, although he isn't silly enough to not seek the former. In a way both are perfectionists, but they are looking for different things. He seeks harmony, while she seeks . . . well, never mind what she seeks, she'll settle for a real man, and she isn't likely to stray if she finds him.

She will do routine jobs without suffering, while he would rather die than get in a rut. The problem with this relationship is that Taurus just cannot rely on Libra as much as she wants to. Actually this guy is honest and might well explain in detail to his woman what his faults are. He will be great when it comes to visiting art galleries or theaters or restaurants. He's not quite so good when it comes to paying the rent or building a life together. Yes, he'll mellow as he gets older, but damn it, gray hair suits him!

He will expect Taurus to be an equal partner, while she would prefer to be the sheet anchor. He's a fair man in that he gives praise where it's earned and he responds to logical progressive thinking. Don't expect him to make the decisions. In fact, Taurus might do well to make one decision early on in the relationship—buy a one-way ticket to somewhere far distant! Yes, there'll be plenty of fun for these two, but she can't keep it light enough and he can't get serious enough.

LIBRA MAN—GEMINI WOMAN

These two are likely to fit together nicely. They are likely to respond like twins both emotionally and intellectually. Both need lots of freedom and want to get out and enjoy themselves either together or alone.

Both are passionate and enjoy sex, which they understand well, so a marvelous affair or a promising marriage is in the cards. Both can be a trifle superficial at times in their thoughts and responses, but the only real difficulty could come because the Gemini approach is mental, whereas Libra tends to respond emotionally and in a less calculating and selfish way.

Gemini will certainly appreciate her romantic lover—life isn't too serious a business most of the time when Librans are around. Libra will—if he's serious or as serious as a Libran is ever likely to get—realize that this lady responds to games, preferably intellectual ones like chess and then later the bedtime games. There'll be lots of fun for these two, lots of laughter, and everyone else—friends, relatives, the tax collector—will love having this partnership around.

It won't be long after a first meeting that these two find that it's more fun being together than with other people or alone. Libra will treat her as a real partner, not a slave or a goddess. She likes that; it's her style too. He's a charmer, not a strong silent type, so decision making could be agony. But's he comfortable and adaptable and has a good base of common sense most of the time. It probably won't happen, but Gemini would be very wise to resist any temptation to display jealousy. Libra can't bear a scene of any type, and he'll go a long way—probably around to a girlfriend's—to avoid a quarrel. And he hates tantrums, which is strange because sometimes he behaves like a little boy himself.

Gemini can be changeable, and Libra had better realize it. She's not exactly a creature of moods, but she does get irritated by the situations that life sometimes gets her into. Some people have suggested that Gemini is a Jekyll and Hyde character, but this is unfair. Most of the time she shows the same face in public and private. She doesn't? Oh, well, there are Geminis and Geminis; they're a wide-ranging breed. Seriously, she needs help to deepen her self-awareness. Libra is probably not the right guy to do this, but she'll find herself a guru or spiritually more aware buddy.

LIBRA MAN—CANCER WOMAN

These two unfortunately seem to inhabit different worlds much of the time—which is a pity because together they could make quite a team.

Cancer is very sensitive, particularly to artistic impulses and ideas. She is feminine and sympathetic and a bit moody. She is gentle and romantic and loving. Libra wants to take things a little easier and lighter. He wants fun, and she knows there are some things in life that are too deep for that sort of approach.

Libra is too selfish for this lady. She needs to be petted and told she's lovely a thousand times a day. He'll certainly be better than most signs at pleasing her, but somehow sometime she's going to sense that he isn't quite sincere in his protestations of undying love.

Cancer has a tendency to be critical and grumbly, and this is precisely the way to upset Libra and really turn him off. He likes to go out and enjoy parties, while she's much happier at home. He's extravagant and impulsive, while she's careful with the cash. She'll trust him far too much. But one day the truth will finally dawn. There will be plenty of tensions in this relationship, and although he is charming, Libra won't want to make the decisions. He wants to treat his woman as a true partner, while Cancer expects her man to take the lead most times.

The strange thing is that a small minority of Librans and Cancerians do live happily together. Even they probably don't know quite how their relationship works. Maybe they're just sympathetic souls who are not showing the more extreme characteristics of some other members of their sign group. As this guy matures, he may become easier to live with, but he will probably still have a roving eye.

When he gets bored—and it happens relatively easily—Libra and his roving eye get going. The thing to do is to keep him interested, and if Cancer can't manage that, then she should keep him too busy. He may refuse to build her a house, but he might be persuaded to follow in Cezanne's footsteps or even become the Mozart of the twentieth century. A little subtlety is all it needs, but Cancer may be too wrapped up in her emotional dilemmas and problems to even use a few simple ploys like this. Sometimes Cancerians seem to want to become martyrs.

LIBRA MAN—LEO WOMAN

This won't be an easy relationship, and it certainly won't be a comfortably boring one, but equally these two have a lot to offer each other, even though an affair is more likely than a marriage.

Both are warm personalities who want to please and be loved. Leo can be domineering and difficult, but she is generous and passionate and romantic. Libra is certainly romantic—he will shower her with roses and diamonds (if he can afford them) and she'll absolutely adore him. But Leo has quite a temper. She can be decidedly jealous and she likes to do her own thing.

Libra likes to flirt and play around, and this lady won't have any of that sort of nonsense. He is sensitive to beauty and really charming when he wants to be. She's blunter and more straightforward when it comes to sex. She tends to walk out and grab—or walk in and grab! Libra will be offended. These two are sociable and generous and loving, and physically things should be terrific, but both need plenty of stimulus and if it isn't forthcoming there could be trouble. Libra, for instance, will walk a long way to avoid a disagreement or a fight. Leo will walk a fair distance to get involved in one. She likes nothing better than a battle against overwhelming odds (such as the tax man), unless of course she's in one of her lazy, totally collapsed moods, when Libra will have to wait on her hand and foot until she comes around.

Librans don't worry nearly as much about their homes as Leos do, who given the choice will prefer a mansion or palace to a cottage. And they have been known to overlook such trivialities as the cost of upkeep, the lack of hot water, and the dry rot. Both can work very hard in rather erratic bursts and both can be critical—not a good thing to be when dealing with either partner. Libra will certainly want to treat his woman as an equal. She may decide she's a good deal more than equal, and despite all his virtues Libra might just fade quietly out of the picture if this happens.

Both enjoy traveling and sports and parties. But Librans are not too good at making decisions (and that's an understatement if ever there was one). They tend to see all sides and are often such reasonable people that they just can't force themselves to pick one thing over another. Leo, on the contrary, will just give the orders and then be astonished if and when she is not promptly obeyed. This is certainly going to be a stimulating partnership even if it doesn't last.

LIBRA MAN—VIRGO WOMAN

Libra has too many sides to his personality; he is too expansive for the more straight-laced, serious, honest and critical Virgo lady. She is shy and gentle most times, but this fellow could well bring out the worst in her. She needs a man she can trust, and Libra probably is not ideal in this respect.

He is basically too selfish for her, although certainly at first he will be so charming, understanding, and generous that she will really imagine that Mr. Right has at last dropped in on her slightly boring existence. She wants to give herself to her man, but the difficulty here is that Libra seeks an equal, not a worshipper. He wants an independent woman who will do her own thing while he sometimes has a little flirtation on the side. She is definitely careful with money, while he spends as he gets and incidentally enjoys himself much more. He'll probably start looking around for comfort elsewhere quite soon in the relationship.

Virgo has the choice of taking this man with all his faults and his charm, or of moving on. She'd probably be wise to take the latter course, but if she sticks around, then she could learn something from this guy about loosening up and enjoying herself more. But it's always hard work for a Virgo to enjoy herself!

One thing Libra won't put up with is argument or disagreement. He simply turns off mentally or walks away. He just cannot stand disharmony, even though he's quite capable of creating it himself. He might even come to think of this lady as crabby and petty-minded. She'll think he's a superficial playboy. Both views are unfair.

Yes, he's romantic, probably looks good, and dresses with taste and possibly even flair. He knows how to flatter a girl—any girl. He falls in and out of love, while Virgo is still thinking deeply about making the first move. But he is capable of suffering, for a while, anyway. Life and love are a game to Libra. He's emotional but also intelligent. He'll certainly be a test for Virgo's patience and stickability. She's going to have to be a bit of a masochist to stick around this guy for a long period.

If this all sounds a bit gloomy, then it must be borne in mind that there are no absolutely set rules in astrology, only tendencies and potentials. Virgo and Libra can get things together if they are prepared to make an effort and avoid criticizing each other aloud or to themselves.

SCORPIO WOMAN—SCORPIO MAN

The only word to describe this partnership is dynamic. It's certainly going to be wearing on the nerves but could be a tremendously deep and satisfying relationship between the storms and tears.

These two could go overboard for each other on sight. They have violent likes and dislikes—there's a great intensity about Scorpios and many of the things they do. And they are rather jealous people, continually prying into areas of each other's psyche and emotions that really do not concern even a lover. They are suspicious by nature, and it is not unknown for a Scorpio woman to check up on where her man went for lunch and who was with him, or for him to want to know whom she met at the supermarket. It's a bit irritating.

The Scorpio man is interested in power, and his career is important to him. He can be aggressive and has a violent temper even if it is rarely unleashed. The Scorpio woman doesn't give an inch either, so fights between them could eventually become physical. Neither forgets an insult or a slight, and when the time comes each might decide to pay back with interest. Both will be deeply interested in the financial side of their partnership, so there shouldn't be any danger of bankruptcy.

Sexually, things will be dramatic with this possessive pair; when quarrels take place, the neighbors had better avoid the firing line. The bedroom should perhaps be a place for gentle communion, but don't expect that when these two get together. It depends on the maturity of this pair whether their infatuation turns into a true and lasting love. Both will have to make compromises, which are certainly well worth making. He wants to be the boss, and a sensible Scorpio woman will go along with this because she wants the secure love he can provide. But in all honesty she's going to start smoldering, and if he plays the heavy too often, there'll be an explosion.

Scorpios can get moody. They are deep people and can hurt others deeply with words. There will be emotional ups and downs which can be controlled, but it's no use pretending that it will not take considerable effort. Scorpios might try taking some of their spleen out in energetic sports. If this partnership works, it will be very formidable, and emotionally and mentally these two will hone each other to pretty fine "fighting points." Together they could prove quite exceptional in many ways. Forget the sleepless nights, remember the love. Forget the pain, remember the joy.

SCORPIO WOMAN—SAGITTARIUS MAN

This is not an easy relationship, because the independent Sagittarius man will feel threatened by the possessive Scorpio woman, and she in turn will feel that he is too superficial and playful for her.

Don't get the idea that this is a weak man; he isn't. But his strength is channeled in different ways than hers. She is jealous and home-loving, intense, and at times difficult. He is much more outgoing, likes to do lots of things at once, has lots of friends and contacts, is independent, and will find it difficult to contain his wanderlust.

In many ways it may be seen that they are very different types, and opposites may well attract. Both are physical, but she just won't be able to tame him or control him as her nature dictates that she should. He is generous at times and can suddenly become a bit petty. He likes to take a gamble and is surprisingly lucky. He needs plenty of stimulus and adventure and doesn't worry too much about money most of the time. This lady could become a neurotic basket-case if she tries to keep up with him.

She is probably too intense in her loves and hates for him. She does nothing by halves and might well decide she wants to marry him. If she so decides, he hasn't got a chance despite his skill at fielding inconvenient questions or avoiding the issue when it suits him. It's really no competition. She may be doing better in her career than he in his, but this won't worry him. He won't mind if she decides she's going to keep him in the luxury to which he probably isn't accustomed. He doesn't bother too much about his home, but home is intensely important to her. Even if she can't find the security she needs in a man, she will expect it through possessions.

Sexually, there will be difficulties. Sagittarius is not easy to live with because he's always on the go, while she expects his undivided attention. This man has plenty of charm, can be great fun, loves outdoor sports and women. Scorpio would be wise to take one long look, just out of curiosity, and then announce that she's washing her hair, has a date, isn't feeling well, or has to work late at the office. This may not be enough to convince this guy, but at least she tried.

If these two should decide to make a go of it, then there'll be plenty of work and long sessions explaining where it went wrong and what has to be done about the relationship to make it better. It'll be hard work at times but lots of fun at others.

SCORPIO WOMAN—CAPRICORN MAN

This could be a very good relationship. The ambitious, industrious, and disciplined Capricorn man is likely to quickly get on the same wavelength as the intelligent, frank, and intense Scorpio woman.

Despite his exterior, Capricorn badly needs reassurance and security, and this essentially jealous but faithful woman could provide it. The myth that Scorpios are promiscuous is not borne out by the essential facts, although it is not uncommon for lady Scorpios to have difficulty finding the right man and thus to make a few mistakes. Scorpio does have quite a sex drive, but she is rarely romantic in the sense that a Libran can be. She is straightforward and yet at the same time there is something mysterious and slightly strange about her.

Capricorn must learn to spend more time with this woman even though she expects him to work hard and be successful. She has to be the most important thing in his life by far. Financially there should be few difficulties, because both are industrious and the Scorpio woman in particular almost makes a religion out of saving and economy, although she knows quality and will not stint guests or her man in any way.

The thing that Scorpio must remember is that she can make or break the relationship by her attitude to his need for security. If she fails to tell him she loves and needs him and appreciates his efforts

on her behalf, he could get moody—he might get moody anyway—
and even more insecure than he is naturally. This lady really holds
the reins of the relationship.

In return he is and will be totally devoted to her. He isn't likely
to play around unless she rejects him, and even if he fails to make
president before he's thirty, he might just be persuaded that there's
still time. In a way the Scorpio woman might be seen as a prize by
this guy. He often disguises his feelings and even his thoughts, but
he may well be very proud of his woman and her talents. If he's a
little cold and proud and withdrawn at times, then she can gently
loosen him up and persuade him he doesn't need that fifth drink to
calm him down.

It's true that he's pessimistic and parsimonious, but cheer him
up and he'll agree that his lady has to look extra smart for the meeting with the big boss. Pretend the mink cost half what it did and tell
him the rest of the money went for household necessities. It'll be a
relief to him even though his precious bank account is depleted. Remember that one way he measures success is by the way the bank
president greets him.

SCORPIO WOMAN—AQUARIUS MAN

Not a terribly wise partnership for all but the most determined.
The Scorpio woman is the opposite of the Aquarius man in most
ways and will call him cold and unfeeling and independent. He
might take this as a compliment!

He dislikes drama and scenes and arguing, and he likes to get
out and about with his friends to pursue intellectual and educational
interests. She tends to respond much more emotionally to situations,
and she wants exclusive rights to his mind, body, and soul. She is a
jealous lady who wants to know what he's doing, where he is, and
what he's thinking about (if not about her) all the time. This will create a good deal of tension.

Under pressure like this, Scorpio could take to booze or anything else from chewing gum up or down to alleviate her frustration.
She values her home and her possessions as an indication of her success and power. Aquarius is much too interested in the fate of the
world to worry too much about where he lives. He will appreciate
the sharpness of Scorpio's mind but will wonder whether it isn't just
a little too concentrated and gloomily serious.

Sexually, Scorpio wants and needs a lot of loving, while Aquarius doesn't need physical togetherness so much—which doesn't mean this woman cannot turn him on. But he won't allow her to dominate him in any way—that would be giving up his independence. To stay together, these two will have to understand each other—Aquarius is a thinker, while Scorpio is very emotionally bound up with feelings and responses. Aquarius is much easier to live with than Scorpio, although he might at times seem to lack her depth. She will want him to be a worldly success, and when he isn't—because he doesn't care enough about it—she'll be hurt. Aquarius is the least jealous fellow around, so she'll probably be upset when he doesn't ask where she's been when she rolls home plastered at four in the morning.

However, Aquarius is a faithful sort of guy. He does care deeply for the underdog because of his advanced social conscience. In some ways he's a few hundred years ahead of his time. Scorpio is probably a hundred years behind her time. If possible these two should try to avoid a serious affair, but life has a habit of thrusting unlikely couples together, possibly to make them learn and grow up, so be prepared for a long, hard haul to marital bliss. Yes, both will get frustrated, particularly Scorpio, but she is strong enough to get through the difficult patches.

SCORPIO WOMAN—PISCES MAN

This will be an emotional but potentially very successful relationship between two people who respond to things rather than think them out.

Pisces is dreamy, insecure, and very dependent. Scorpio will certainly be the driving power behind this partnership, but she will have to learn that even when her man is indecisive and shy, he does have remarkable intuition and is a good deal tougher than even he thinks he is. Pisces is good in company, and most people cannot help liking and sympathizing with him. He finds it no trouble to be a charmer.

He is easily depressed, so his Scorpio partner must resist her tendency to be sarcastic and critical. She's going to have to watch the family finances because he is extravagant and rarely ambitious.

Sexually, these two will fascinate each other. Pisceans are imaginative and warm and clinging. Scorpios are sexy, demanding, possessive, and determined. If she decides she wants him, then nothing on earth will deflect her purpose. He will at times wish she were a ghost and not a reality, but that's because he's a fantasizer who dreams of harems and desert sands and little maids from the high mountains. He's sentimental and romantic and nostalgic, while she's realistic and serious and practical. It sounds as though they could never get on together, but strangely enough their weaknesses and strengths are complementary.

At times this strong lady will reduce her man to tears, but then she'll comfort him and mother him and he'll smile through the sobs. It will be all so dramatic and exciting in a way that would drive some other signs right around the bend. Pisces is a mysterious fellow, driven by emotional intensities that he often cannot understand, sometimes effeminate and sometimes sturdily masculine, changeable and artistic, and then suddenly good with money and property. Life with him is disturbing but will keep this lady very much on her not-so-dainty toes.

Pisces will need time to dream and be alone and simply feel the wind or listen to the rain. Scorpio would be wise to go along with this, and she might even learn something from it. She's a restless soul, curious and jealous and deep. In this man she will discover the half of her that she tends to repress, and if she can restrain her impulses at times to cut his heart out and feed it to the dogs, then all will be well.

SCORPIO WOMAN—ARIES MAN

What happens when two people who know they're right bump into each other? Either they pool their genius and it's terrific, or war breaks out. That just about sums up how these two will get on. It will certainly be fireworks a lot of the time when this pair starts a relationship.

Both are fighters. It was once suggested that the ideal group to capture an impregnable fortress would consist solely of soldiers from these two signs: Arians would tear in with unbelievable ferocity and Scorpios would press on until the last man fell or the fortress was taken. The Scorpio woman won't even listen to people trying to put her right. The Aries man will listen, and then do it his way anyway. She believes in stability and the home and security and power achieved by persistent work. He seizes opportunities, takes risks, and leaps around like a maniac.

He doesn't worry too much about the finances—something will

turn up, he says. She does. Sometimes sex will be terrific, but at other times there just won't be enough togetherness and tenderness to make it pleasant. A short and stimulating affair rather than a marriage is indicated if possible. Don't get it wrong, these two are fatally attracted to each other. She's liberated and very sexy and ambitious. He's just as likely to emigrate the same day they decide to make him managing director, and he won't change his mind despite his woman's screams and entreaties.

Scorpio does not find it easy to forgive or relax and has even been known to be what must be called vindictive. Aries cannot understand that he hasn't the time to brood over insults, for there are far too many exciting things to do in the world and so many exciting women to meet! Her jealousy will drive him to distraction, and he won't put up with it for long. When Aries makes up his mind, he goes, and he goes fast with no nostalgic looking back. This applies also to his career because he needs stimulus and challenge. He'll grumble at times, but he needs to be there in the thick of things, at the point of the arrow pressing on and pressing on and pressing on.

Will this partnership work? Only if Scorpio makes an enormous effort and loves her man enough to let him do his own thing, and to be there as his sheet anchor, his shelter from the storm. He in turn must resolve to tell her she's right five times a day even if she isn't. He won't find it easy, but it will be good for him too.

SCORPIO WOMAN—TAURUS MAN

Despite a number of difficulties, these two are quite likely to stick together through thick and thin. Both can be awfully stubborn and rigid in their views, and obviously this can create considerable problems for two people inhabiting the same country, let alone the same house!

Financially, things are likely to be pretty good because both are conscious of the need for a nice home and cash in the bank. But they are certain to be intolerably jealous of each other, and from time to time Taurus needs a sharp kick somewhere to get him out of the deep rut he is likely to dig himself into. He likes comfort and peace, and he's sensitive—when it comes to his own convenience and feelings, that is.

All right, he's a bit slow, but he is reliable, honest, and loves his food and drink. His efforts to amuse his Scorpio partner will probably amuse her, but when all is said and done there's something essentially endearing about the guy. In bed there should be lots of fun and passion. Both need lots of sex and have the stamina to keep coming back for it. But sometimes Taurus is lazy and proud at the same time. Scorpio tends to despise a fellow who isn't a hundred percent with her all the time when it comes to ambition and determination.

The Taurus man is not aggressive, but he seems to be sure of himself. He'll be attracted by the Scorpio urgency and seriousness. They'll make excellent business partners, but it's more of a tossup in other life areas. There *are* some nasty Taureans and Scorpios around—they're in the minority, of course—so be careful not to catch one of these earthy characters who've probably crawled straight out from under some slimy stone left around for a million years.

Taurus may well be deeply interested in art, responsive in an emotional way to beauty, and this may be why he wants an elegant and charming home and is prepared to work for something tangible like that. Scorpio won't say no to a chateau or two or a beach house at Malibu for vacations. She's a sensible sort, except when the black moods get her. This will be less often than such moods get her Taurus partner. More important is the need for this pair to recognize their opposite approaches to life and to build on the strengths rather than dwell critically on the failures and differences. If they can't do this, then a cheery wave and a good-bye kiss are the answer—don't stick around to suffer more than is absolutely necessary.

SCORPIO WOMAN—GEMINI MAN

These two would be wise to think long and hard before even having dinner together, never mind living together. Scorpio is just too intense and serious for the Gemini man, who is changeable and irresponsible and delightful and loving by turns.

He's nobody's fool. He thinks like a supercomputer but is not emotional in the way she is. He wants his freedom and enjoys company more than she does. The way to his heart (if it can be found) is through stimulating his mind, although it must be added that he isn't backward in coming forward where sex is concerned! In bed these two will have no problems, but out of the bedroom Scorpio is likely to decide that he's a lightweight. She's a strong, intensely jealous woman with a need for security and love. He takes things much more easily and he won't enjoy her possessiveness.

Yes, he'll get very restless cooped up with this lady. He may seem to her to be going around in circles, but he enjoys himself, has a good time in a rather simple sort of way, and is too erratic. This may have something to do with his split personality, but only some Geminis exhibit this all of the time; most only demonstrate it ninety percent of their waking lives! This is a little unkind, but truly these two will not find it easy to tolerate their very different approaches to life and problems and fun.

He does have a nice sense of humor, quick, effervescent. He's the sort of guy to take to Acapulco for the weekend, but even the sexiest Scorpio—and that means a very sexy lady indeed—wants a little more than that. He'll be immensely attracted to her—there's something deep about her he wants to understand and never will (she probably doesn't understand it herself)—but he'll keep trying.

Gemini, given the chance, could leaven the Scorpio gloom and seriousness. He'd make an excellent business partner, but he has to be pinned down to make decisions. He has to be grabbed by the short and curlies sometimes so that his ideas are made practical as well as brilliant, as they sometimes certainly are. Both are creative, and he talks very well. He almost convinces himself sometimes. He works in jerks and starts, unleashing vast amounts of energy at unexpected moments. No one ever called either of these two lazy, but Scorpio believes in achieving power through steady, concentrated effort. That's just too boring for Gemini.

It might appear an awful relationship, and yet work to everyone's surprise—but that's the miracle of life.

SCORPIO WOMAN—CANCER MAN

This is likely to be a most successful teaming—of the sort that Mother would approve of. Emotionally these two should understand each other and respond in broadly similar ways in most instances.

Both are sensitive, and Scorpio will feel secure and loved by the way that Cancer becomes devoted to her and her well-being. She is more of a taker, more selfish, than Cancer, but this is complemented by his need to give himself. Most of the time he'll let her make the running and accept her extreme stubbornness. Both take care of the cash, so there should be no difficulties about making budgets balance and such trivia. The home is important to both of them and is likely to be a pleasing place for relaxation and work.

Sexually, the passionate Scorpio woman will find the Cancer

man prepared to go along with her whims and fancies, and for the most part this will be a caring and balanced union. Even the well-known Scorpio jealousy will not worry this guy most of the time. Indeed, unlike some signs, he might well be flattered by her deep interest in him and what he is doing. He will keep coming back to draw on Scorpio strength and determination. She expects her man to succeed in worldly terms, and why not?

Cancer can be hurt by thoughtless words, so Scorpio must rein in her critical comments, but she can be sure of his loyalty. When things get rough he'll come running home, and if Scorpio is there to mother and reassure him that all will be well, he'll scuttle back to work again with renewed enthusiasm and determination to work for such a wonderful woman. All this suits this lady, who must, however, avoid the tendency to turn her man into a serf. If she does that, she will be the loser because her own respect for him will diminish. Some Scorpios are not averse to taking a lover, and this could happen—but that's one thing he won't stand for.

These two are unlikely to find more compatible companions. To outsiders things might seem a bit dull at times, but romance will always be there in the little things even if at times he seems too shy and withdrawn for such a strong lady. Remember that Cancerians are more intuitive and intelligent than they sometimes seem. He will understand Scorpio rather better than she thinks he does. And as she has a tendency to dramatize and become too intense in some situations, it is good to have a sensitive and gentle and possibly artistic man such as this one on hand to cool her down and kiss her troubles away.

SCORPIO WOMAN—LEO MAN

What happens when two power-mad people meet? There could be instant accord in the interests of world peace, or there could be a horrendous explosion of temperament.

That's the choice these two face. Leo is a warm, generous, demanding, and sometimes irritating megalomaniac. Scorpio is just as strong and determined, and when he realizes this he might become unyielding and arrogant and pompous. She'll laugh at this and he'll get worse. The Leo man can become rigid in his viewpoint. He will resent the way she always seems to know best, and naturally there will be terrific arguments, with neither willing to give way. He wants a woman who will let him take the lead, but this woman isn't likely to fancy that sort of placid life.

She's a highly industrious lady who won't appreciate his sudden extravagances, even though she might well be the recipient in many cases. She doesn't relish the grand gesture as he does, and she is not likely to provide him with all the outrageous flattery he thrives on. She's too honest and critical for that, and her sarcastic asides could prove too much even for a less volatile Leo. Financially, there will be conflict unless he is prepared to let her have a large measure of control over the budget—something she will handle very well.

This is an intense, serious woman who even takes her pleasures with a sort of resigned determination to have fun. It isn't really that bad, but Scorpios are self-critical too, whereas Leos are not. There's something slightly secretive about Scorpio that will certainly prove attractive to the prima donna in Leo. Sexually, it will be fireworks all the way because there is plenty of physical attraction, although Scorpio's jealousy will rear its ugly head quickly and Leo, who likes to make a hit with the girls, won't like it much. These two are much better fitted for a passionate and short-lived affair than the long haul of marriage. Let him whisk her away to the Himalayas for a couple of weeks, or go hunting for more Dead Sea Scrolls—it'll be terrific if exhausting both in and out of bed.

Leo could be the right man if Scorpio is willing to take second place in most things. But it is unlikely that she will be. He has to be the center of attention even when he gets into one of his despairingly lazy moods; then he expects solicitous attention day and night. This lady will get frustrated, but life won't be dull if she decides to give Leo a whirl around the block.

SCORPIO WOMAN—VIRGO MAN

Some people think this partnership can never succeed, but experience has shown that in a surprising number of cases accord is reached and the relationship becomes both rewarding and successful against the odds.

Perhaps the biggest problem is the Virgo critical attention. The Virgo man is a perfectionist and he expects things to work perfectly. They don't in most cases, and he gets frustrated. The Scorpio woman just can't believe that she is ever less than perfect, and her stubbornness is likely to prove a major stumbling block. He is a thinker and sometimes becomes fussy and silly over details, while she, although cautious, is a much stronger character and tends to see the larger picture.

Both work very hard, so poverty is not likely in their household. Indeed, work is sometimes raised almost to the status of a religion by these two, who believe in steady application rather than brilliant strokes of genius.

Sexually, the demanding and indeed voracious Scorpio may find Virgo too cold at times. If this happens, this sexy lady may look around for someone who can satisfy her, and Virgo will be dreadfully upset by what he will see as a betrayal of confidence.

Logically, Virgo will usually do the right thing. He won't really understand the mysterious side of Scorpio, her interest in the occult and the bizarre and the dark side of human nature. But he'll go along with this because he is a faithful, loyal sort. He is not too imaginative, but he is sensitive, particularly to criticism—one way to end this relationship fast is to criticize his dress sense and his appearance or suggest that he ought to bathe more often.

The curious thing is that although Virgo is often frustrated by mental and emotional things, Scorpio is likely to be frustrated by the physical aspect of life. It's all very frustrating! If this union is to succeed, there has to be a lot of give and take. He has to understand her emotional reaction to things, while she has to accept his cerebral approach to improving himself. He believes in education and improving his mind. The study of Etruscan pottery or Finnish dialects or Chinese art is crucially important to the Virgo nature.

It would be sensible to try to avoid meeting, because there could be a genuine attraction of opposites. But if fate steps in, then try to remember where the difficulties will appear and act accordingly.

SCORPIO WOMAN—LIBRA MAN

This is one of those on-off-on type relationship. Libra demands freedom to operate and won't accept the restrictions that Scorpio finds essential for real togetherness.

But he's damnably attractive and he knows it. Scorpio might decide she wants him right off, and she'll get him because once she makes up her mind, that's it; the poor guy hasn't a chance with this strong and determined woman. But he's a lightweight, charming, good-tempered, and rather sweet-natured.

Scorpio will certainly appreciate his winning ways—the champagne and roses he produces at the drop of a glove. But basically she wants total commitment from her man, and a Libran isn't likely to give it. She's too serious, mysterious, and emotional for him. His home is not very important to him, although he enjoys elegance and beauty as few others do. But he'll find it everywhere he goes, while the Scorpio woman needs comfort and security. And this applies to the finances, too. He'll happily blow money on luxuries, while given half a chance, she's a great provider and saver.

He needs plenty of mental stimulus and romance, while she might well decide that such things take second place to hard work, deep passion, and sex that means more than just a quick roll in the hay. This is a serious lady who will be intensely jealous of her man and his almost inevitable flirtations. He's certainly sensitive, but usually only when he's affected or his emotions are questioned. Not a promising combination for a meaningful long-term relationship. Things won't be boring, but they could be intolerable.

Scorpio should have a fun-filled flirtation with Libra and keep him as a loving friend. But she'll have difficulty keeping things on just that level. She'll want to analyze and understand how he thinks and functions, and when after about twenty minutes she understands everything about him, she'll wonder what it was that attracted her. He'll then do something absolutely charming and she'll fall for him all over again. He will have difficulty making decisions, but she'll happily make them for two or three or more, so he'll let her get on with it.

Don't assume that Libra is just a playboy; he truly appreciates beauty and art, but he cannot stand disharmony, and if a quarrel breaks out he'll mentally turn off and then depart in horror. It's easy to get rid of a Libran! He hates to be alone and he needs balance in his life. Scorpio could provide it—at a cost to her own sanity.

SCORPIO MAN—SCORPIO WOMAN

This will be quite a partnership, full of intensity and pain and ecstasy, but with luck it could be deep and satisfying and successful.

Scorpios are not always the nicest people, and they can hurt through words or their general attitude. There will certainly be emotional ups and downs, but it will take effort to keep them from being blown into more important scenes than they should be. Sexually, things will be fiery. Two possessive, determined people will love a lot and fight every now and then in dramatic fashion. There will probably be infatuation to start with, but whether that turns into real love depends on how mature they are. Both are going to have to make compromises because he wants to be the boss, while she won't want to give up an iota of her independence.

The Scorpio man's mistakes will be quoted back at him with relish. This woman will expect her man to be successful through hard, steady work rather than through some sudden stroke of genius. When he plays the heavy, she'll smolder and smolder and finally explode, but if she's sensible she'll limit her emotional outbursts to not more than ten a day!

There is great intensity about these two. They can enjoy life, but deep down they feel that life is about more serious things. Both have a lively temper and do not suffer fools gladly. She will fight every inch of the way when he orders her about. One comfort is that the finances are likely to be well organized because these two want a comfortable, welcoming home and are prepared to work very hard to get what they want.

Both are intensely jealous and have violent likes and dislikes. He'll be continually checking up on her, and she'll be calling up to find out whom he had lunch with, and a blond hair on his collar will require a very good explanation indeed. In all probability he's the most faithful guy around and she knows it, but she'll still secretly wonder if he's sneaking off to meet someone when he takes the dog for a walk. It can get a bit wearing, but Scorpios just cannot seem to help themselves.

If it all sounds a bit hopeless, it's not meant to—because this partnership is between two people who don't actually think alike but who certainly feel alike and understand each other's problems without having to utter a word. With a little give and take, it can be bliss all along the line. With a little too much rigidity on either part, it can be hell.

SCORPIO MAN—SAGITTARIUS WOMAN

A decidedly stormy relationship is in prospect here. Sagittarius is a great one for getting about, making friends, visiting old buddies. Scorpio views this with decided suspicion if not downright resentment.

This is an interesting woman, with a great sense of humor, lots of enthusiasm, and a roving eye. She doesn't worry too much about money or the future. She figures that something will turn up, and surprisingly it often does, because she's a lucky person. Scorpio likes to know exactly where he stands when it comes to finance, business, love, and everything else. He won't when this lady hooks him!

She'll drive him crazy, but he'll be fascinated with how she gets away with it. She may well be a good sportswoman, and sexually there won't be any complaints because both are adventurous and spontaneous. It's been suggested they might even try it on a bed of nails if one happens to be handy. It is to be hoped that life won't become a bed of nails for Scorpio, who will bite off more than he can chew if he decides this is the woman for him. She must have her freedom, and he just won't be able to understand it. After all, he's giving her everything. Well, perhaps not everything, but he is giving himself. Isn't it enough?

This is a masculine, strong, forceful man, intensely jealous and apt to believe the worst about his lover. A really jealous Scorpio is quite intolerable, so if this sort turns up, Sagittarius shouldn't even look at him, let alone smile. How to tell the difference between a nice Scorpio and a nasty one? The best way is to avoid them all. He's too persistent and interesting in a dark sort of way. OK, but the warning has been uttered.

The best thing to do is to find mutual interests. Anything will do as long as it's out of the home and promotes togetherness. They should make absolutely certain that vacations are taken together. And Scorpio would be wise to make sure that his best friend is a cross-eyed dwarf with one leg—and even then, he'd better keep a close eye on them. This is a bit strange because Scorpio is perfectly capable of seducing his lady's best friend and, when discovered, calmly announcing that it wasn't serious, he meant nothing by it, and anyway it was Sagittarius's fault entirely for not keeping him on a close rein. Is he selfish? Is he selfish! But once you've been close to a Scorpio, a lot of other relationships seem wishy-washy and a waste of time.

SCORPIO MAN—CAPRICORN WOMAN

This partnership is likely to produce a lot of strain and trouble, but once they're together it is unlikely that these two will part company no matter how difficult things get—life apart would be a lot worse.

This is a strong, intense, serious man. She is more detached, emotionally cooler, and perfectly capable of pointing out his errors and faults. Scorpio hates this—is he not perfect in every way? But with a little luck he'll only explode once a week. He's a jealous fellow who will make his woman's life a misery, although he will compensate by the way he turns her on. Sexually, these two go well together and there won't be many problems in the bedroom. When Capricorn broods, he'll remind her of the security she has being with him, of their possessions and his need to have her there. She'll probably cheer up, a bit anyway.

Sometimes this lady just won't understand what her slightly mysterious partner is up to and she'll feel especially vulnerable. She has a lot to give and she wants to give of her very essence. At times she might even seem to have a martyr complex, but mostly her sheer common sense sees her through. At least there should be few financial worries because both are good savers with due regard for the things that money can buy and a need for a comfortable if not elegant home. She will look after him very well because she seeks harmony. Yes, he'll want to own this woman, all of her, and she won't resent it as some signs would.

He's not the easiest man in the world to live with, but life without him can be intolerably boring for a woman who tends to rely on others to interest and amuse her, even though she is strong in that she expects her man to be successful and demonstrate this success by worldly things. Some might think there is a lack of subtlety in this partnership, but they do get on most of the time, provided Scorpio is not too unreasonable and is prepared to give a bit more of himself than his nature suggests is reasonable.

He'll always be imagining she has a secret lover or half a dozen. He might even go so far as to read her letters and then apologize, saying that he opened them by mistake. He does have more of a sense of insecurity than she does, but he hides it more successfully. As she gets older the Capricorn woman would be wise to avoid becoming colder and prouder and more insular than she is by nature. There are plenty of reasons why these two should avoid falling in love, but life is seldom simple.

SCORPIO MAN—AQUARIUS WOMAN

This is one of those fascinating partnerships that shouldn't work but does turn out well in a surprising number of cases.

Scorpio certainly appeals to the Aquarian woman. He's strong and a bit mysterious, demanding, jealous, and possessive. He is totally unreasonable at times, and this can be a recipe for disaster or she will find he means more to her than she ever imagined anyone could—even if at times she could cheerfully throttle him with his own necktie.

Aquarius is a much cooler, less emotional person. She has an excellent, logical mind and gets on with almost everyone. She has lots of friends and cares for them all, loves to visit and travel and share herself and her possessions with those she likes. This will certainly irritate her Scorpio partner, who expects her to be totally bound up with him and what he is doing, even if it is of no particular importance. At times he is a heavy number and she'll just turn off.

The more he blusters and complains and threatens, the more she will turn off and withdraw herself, until he gets the message. If he doesn't, she'll suddenly be off without a backward glance when she's had enough. She isn't too bothered about finance or power or the things money can buy. She's much more excited by ideas and potentials. She's always ahead of her time and often dresses in an unconventional but totally successful way. She won't look after the home nearly so well as this fellow expects—but she tries and is never vindictive. Some say that the Aquarian is too nice for this planet—with all that the word "nice" suggests.

She is cheerful, relatively easily pleased, and fascinated by new and original things and art forms. She has a passion to improve her mind by studying Urdu or ichthyology or Chinese history or vegetarian cookery—anything that is esoteric and probably useless. She has to be exceptional to put up with this guy, and in many cases he'll prove just too overbearing and she'll quietly pick up her couple of suitcases and vanish without tears or regrets.

In her way this lady is strong. Sexually and emotionally she won't be dominated, and this is one of the reasons Scorpio is attracted by her. He doesn't like a walkover; he likes a fight, even though he's getting far more than he bargained for when he tangles with this fascinating woman. One thing this pair must try to cultivate is a sense of humor, and really it shouldn't be too difficult.

SCORPIO MAN—PISCES WOMAN

This could be one of those extraordinary relationships that most of the rest of the world only dreams about. Pisces should certainly do more than dream about a Scorpio; she should rush out and find one, although because of her passive nature it is most unlikely she'll rush further than the front door.

Her dependence and her deep sexual need for gratification will really lift Scorpio's roof. This lady lives and breathes romance—true love and knights in armor and sultans on fiery steeds and all the rest of it. She's a sucker for the romantic gesture and the sunset and a man on his knees protesting undying love. Yes, she's moody and unpredictable and delightful and cloying and a bit crazy. She wants to be carried away and cosseted and taken care of forever.

She will not mind Scorpio's possessiveness and jealousy and dominant nature. She'll simply melt and melt until she becomes him, or he'll get so bored by all this passivity that he'll lose his temper—and she'll love him even more for it. It is not easy to imagine this pair unmarried; she certainly needs the security that he will provide. She'll keep the sort of spotless home he wants and look after the children superbly. Her intuition is uncanny, and she's probably psychic. She's the most feminine gypsy of an elegant charmer in the Zodiac. Looking after her man is a full-time job for her. She'll spend his cash like water at times, and although he'll curse, he'll give in and kiss her—after all, he can provide the money, can't he?

From time to time Pisces will suddenly demand that they move house, and they'll probably make a handsome profit on the transaction. She can get restless in this way, and he would be wise not to ignore her in such a mood. Her habit of surrendering every moment should not disguise the fact that she is one of life's survivors. This fact sometimes escapes those who consider Pisceans wishy-washy, weak, and ineffectual. Scorpio needs lots of love and understanding and above all sympathy, even when it isn't really deserved. He'll get what he wants from this woman. An abiding image might well be of a woman holding her man's head between her breasts—both motherly and sensual at the same time. He's not an easy man to understand, but Pisces is certainly his best bet to find paradise on earth. She's worth taking a lot of trouble over.

SCORPIO MAN—ARIES WOMAN

When raw energy meets a power structure, most people would prefer not to be around. The destruction may go on for a long time, but for sheer pyrotechnic splendor this partnership can't be beat.

It must be admitted that some Arians and Scorpios actually make a go of a passionate, stormy relationship that on the surface seems quite impossible. Aries is exciting, dynamic, bossy, careless of detail, and self-centered. Scorpio is dominating, possessive, jealous, critical, and determined to be boss. With an Aries woman there's no chance of his being the boss—but he'll keep trying. Boy, oh boy, will the sparks fly at times!

Harmony will not exactly be easy to obtain and maintain. The attraction will be powerful and sex will be pretty good, but the well-documented Scorpionic jealousy will infuriate this lady, who almost above anything else values her freedom and her strength. Certainly she lacks subtlety. She is liberated and will probably introduce herself to her Scorpio man by punching him in the stomach! "Hah, not as tough as they said," she'll then calmly announce as he doubles up. Arians hit hard even in fun.

Scorpio values his home and his environment, which he wants to see as an extension of his personality. Aries likes to get out and about and organize things and people—which she does quite well, incidentally. She's ambitious and smart and is likely to give the impression she knows everything about everything, even if she doesn't. She likes a word of congratulations and praise from time to time and might not get enough, but she won't take the sort of flattery a Leo thrives on.

Scorpio is a loyal guy, even though he's highly sexed, but his sarcasm won't cut much ice with this woman, who'll be too busy anyway to even notice that he was trying to be cutting about her domestic failings. He wants to possess her but he isn't going to, and this means that all except for pretty advanced characters are going to find it hard to maintain common ground. Both are workers and have more than abundant energy. But will this be enough? Scorpio wants to show his woman and his home off. Aries can't be bothered with such things. She's the sort who wins a tennis championship and then doesn't bother to collect her trophy, or who fights like mad for something and then, as soon as it is achieved, feels it has no value whatever. He's a complex, serious man and needs a more appreciative woman.

SCORPIO MAN—TAURUS WOMAN

A far from easy relationship between two complete opposites, but if it can be made to work, each has an awful lot to offer the other.

Scorpio tries to use his energies and his undoubted gifts to mold the world to his wishes. Taurus is much more able and willing to let the world be and to cooperate with nature and man to obtain what she wants. She needs the security of a strong man, and Scorpio is certainly that. He believes in the survival of the fittest, so he aims to be the fittest, and if he uses a few dirty tricks on the way—well, that's just playing the game the way he feels life expects it to be played. The straightforward Taurean will find it all a bit mystifying and unnecessary. She's not much more subtle than the Arian woman.

Scorpio is a perfectionist, but Taurus has no such thoughts. She's practical, sensual, and reasonable, emotionally dependent but strong in her way. She can take a lot of Scorpio's sarcasm and criticism and possessiveness, not to mention his insane jealousy. But even the worm turns.

Sexually, both have plenty of stamina and strength and there won't be any bedtime problems. Difficulties will arise in the living room or even more probably in the kitchen. Taurus is much happier spending than earning, while Scorpio is the reverse. Both are proud and very stubborn, particularly Taurus, so their relationship will not be marked by arguments so much as by prolonged and meaningful silences punctuated by screams of anguish. And yet, handled rightly, Taurus is one of the easiest people to live with, earthy, motherly, often devoted to artistic pursuits, particularly music, and a delightful if staid and traditional companion. She is romantic too, in a rigid sort of way. No Taurean could ever resist a great meal with wine and all the trimmings and a few violins playing just for her under a moonlit sky. Whatever else this turns out to be, it won't be a cold relationship. She needs a real man, and this deep, serious, slightly secretive and mysteriously motivated fellow is just that.

Scorpio expects his woman to respond to his feelings and thoughts before they are formulated. It probably won't happen, because this lady is not fast at responding, but she is sincere and honest in the relationship and certainly can be hurt. Some suggest that Scorpio could only be hurt by a couple of bulldozers working together, but this is unfair. OK, he's selfish and has quite a temper when crossed, and a Scorpio has been known to use his fists—but he *is* fascinating.

SCORPIO MAN—GEMINI WOMAN

Gemini can be an absolute charmer, but truth to tell she's too much of a lightweight for the formidable Scorpio man. She's likely to feel imprisoned if she enters a lengthy relationship with this sort of possessive and dominating lover.

She will be horrified by his jealousy and desire to take control and understand everything about her. She intends to retain her freedom of movement and expression. She likes company and good companions, and it is not unknown for Geminis to flirt. This will certainly infuriate Scorpio, who probably suspects the delivery boy and the bank manager anyway. It is unlikely that a true partnership can be achieved, although sexually they get along well enough. Gemini will be too light and humorous and scintillating at times, and Scorpio won't be impressed by her brilliant conversation, but he will try to please her. It isn't so much that he's faithful all the time as that he's determined and tenacious.

The Gemini lady has such a quick mind that at times she might even be surprised by it herself. She thinks so fast she might even appear to be emotional, but nearly always the effect is calculated. Yes, she'll change her wretched mind at the merest provocation and whim, and she loves to spend money of any denomination or currency. Her Scorpio partner will describe her as superficial to her face and she'll call him somber and greedy and an egomaniac. Neither will take much notice of the gibes, but that's a pity because there is some truth in them.

Certainly this lady can be like a breath of spring when she enters the dour (but not necessarily humorless) Scorpio penumbra. In the short term she could do a lot for him, help him get his desires and energies balanced, but don't take bets on a fifty-year marriage except for those who display zodiacally unnatural tendencies.

He's an exciting guy, there's no getting away from this. He does have a strange fascination for many women. But he'll expect total support for his battles from his woman, no matter in what sphere they are fought. Gemini is unlikely to feel that any battle is worth taking part in no matter what the prize. He needs a strong and peaceful, not to say placid, home life so that he can sally forth and fight the world. Alas, he won't find it if he joins up with a Gemini. One thing's for sure: This won't be a boring partnership—who knows, maybe sheer stimulus will prove sufficient in a minority of cases just to prove the astrologer wrong.

SCORPIO MAN—CANCER WOMAN

This is likely to be a harmonious and successful relationship between two emotionally oriented people who will understand each other well and relate nicely.

Quarrels are likely to be sudden and brief. The Cancer woman will look after her Scorpio man to the point of smothering him; she'll cook and cosset and worry about him. She'll be ideal for the Scorpio ego, and he'll never find a woman more prepared to put up with him. In return she wants to be loved, possessed, and dominated, and Scorpio is just the man to take her over completely. He will look after her and expect her total trust and commitment, which he will no doubt get.

This man works hard, he believes in success, and he will provide an attractive and relaxing home—not so much for his woman, but she will benefit from what he basically provides for himself. He's selfish and jealous even when there is patently no need to be, but he will make a genuine commitment to this woman. Sexually, he will bring out the best in her and she will become more passionate and expressive and willing to please. The only problem is that Scorpio will always hold a little of himself back. It may be a protective device, a defense against being hurt, or it may more likely be just the secretive and mysterious aspect of his nature showing. At times he will withdraw and Cancer will be hurt, but she's going to have to learn about this from experience.

There is likely to be an instant empathy between these two, a sort of intuitive bond that will grow over the years, because marriage is a necessity for this pair. This is a feminine woman who is romantic and can be a bit silly at times. Scorpio will rather enjoy this. He will occasionally jar on her sensibilities because he wants to run everything, take her over completely, and she is perfectly capable of cooking dinner or paying the electric bill without him breathing down her neck. He's going to look closely at any man who ventures into the house, but most of the time this lady won't mind. The beauty of this union is that the partners complement each other and with a little luck create a pleasing balance that everyone can see and share in. His masculinity and her coquettish ways are not offensive as they could be in another partnership, so perhaps the only other thing to watch is that they don't forget about the rest of the world and concentrate too much on each other. Too much proximity can put pressure on even the best relationship.

SCORPIO MAN—LEO WOMAN

This is going to be a real tempest of an affair, the sort of partnership that makes volcanoes look peaceful when they erupt! Leo is going to fight Scorpio every inch of the way, and in the end he'll probably be tempted to slug her.

The passion will almost be visible. They are physically attracted all right, but Scorpio will try to dominate, and Leo's self-respect will make her hit back. His overwhelming jealousy will infuriate her, and it's heavy odds on a short but decidedly lively affair rather than a solid long-term partnership.

Scorpio expects a lot in his partner, and this one is quite a woman. She dresses extravagantly and her home is likely to have what can only be described as touches of grandeur even in the most modest establishment. She loves to spend money and cut a dash—which she does splendidly—but he will be less than sympathetic if he is landed with the bill. He is not a stingy guy, but he likes to decide where the cash goes, and she's likely to continually defy him almost for the hell of it, even to the extent of buying things she doesn't really want.

Scorpio is never easy to get on with, and in all probability Leo just won't try. She's bright enough to realize when she meets another power structure that is as stubborn and weighty as her own. Two giant egos don't make for an easy union, even though a little outrageous flattery will get Scorpio almost anything he wants from this lady. He might even try a little cunning: "That other dress of yours, you know, the red one, looks fantastic. I'm not quite sure about the belt on this one." She'll bridle at having her taste questioned in the slightest degree, but there's a good chance the dress will finish up back at the shop, and next time out the red dress will be draped around her shapely form.

Scorpio sometimes has difficulty expressing his emotions and thoughts except physically. But when Leo flirts, he'll find a few choice words. He just cannot stand it. She'll possibly love the drama, but after a few times it will tire and she'll be rude. Bang! Crash! Scorpio has to have the power in this relationship—at any cost—and in many cases he'll get the power and find she's walked out on him.

Perhaps the difficulty here is that Scorpio wants to blend with a woman as he can with Cancer. There's no way that Leo—a loner—is ever going to blend in that way. She's too independent and proud and self-willed for this guy, and the battles will be just too wearing.

SCORPIO MAN—VIRGO WOMAN

This combination is likely to produce a difficult sort of relationship because both Virgo and Scorpio are critical and occasionally sarcastic, besides being perfectionists in their different ways.

They may well have quite a lot in common, but it will be hard to produce a proper relationship. Scorpio will dominate, while Virgo will hide her feelings. This complex, serious, hard-working man will find her appreciative of his sheer industry. She certainly admires efficiency, cleanliness, industry, and neatness. Both will be very careful with money, not to say downright tight-fisted. He will be jealous even though there is most likely to be no cause, and he won't get the sort of loving sympathy he expects when things go wrong. She'll probably take a careful look at the problem and announce that it was his fault all along.

Sexually, she may prove too withdrawn and not physical enough for him. She isn't cold, as some people think; it's just that things have to be right for Virgo, and then she's as passionate as they come. How often are they perfect? A surprising number of Virgos make good actresses. The Virgo woman seeks to create harmony and understanding but is not always successful because she tends not to give too much of herself. There's a critical restraint about her that can be rather off-putting.

This is a magnetic, attractive man, and Virgo isn't fireproof, so she may get hooked. But it will be a real union of opposites and it will take a lot of hard work to find common ground. Virgo does not want to fight—Scorpio does, and he never gives in. He's selfish and at times emotional. She's logical, sensible, practical, and often very charming. She'll never understand the jealous side of Scorpio, but then he doesn't either—it's just how he's made. Not that he'd have to worry about this lady's straying. When she makes up her determined little mind, she's faithful to almost ridiculous lengths. There won't be much coziness and rest about this partnership; it'll be more of a Scandinavian one in the sense of pale walls, frequent cleansing saunas, severe and practical furniture, and quite a lot of ice hanging around!

Both would be wise to give this one a try for a while before deciding it won't work. Which isn't to say it cannot work, just that life will be a lot more fun and a hell of a lot easier if Virgo can fall for someone else and Scorpio can persuade himself that the love of his life will be waiting just around the corner. Sounds brutal? Too bad.

SCORPIO MAN—LIBRA WOMAN

There's a lot going for this couple, but they could easily make a horrible mess of the partnership if they don't clearly understand each other's faults and virtues.

Scorpio is possessive and jealous and demanding and sexy. Libra seeks harmony and peace and affection. These two are likely to take their union seriously despite gibes that Libra is flippant, lightweight, and oversensitive. One danger is that after a while she will feel threatened by his instinct to possess and dominate and organize everything. This is a highly intelligent woman, but she'll run a mile rather than create a scene. She's likely to give in immediately and later snipe and subvert until she gets her way. Scorpio, power-mad though he is, has met a worthy opponent. He has illogical likes and dislikes, which will offend her, but he will care deeply for her and work extremely hard to provide her with a home and environment of the sort he feels she deserves. She enjoys luxury; he's not quite so sure about this, but her Cleopatra complex is not hidden. She is not likely to worry too much about money.

She enjoys sex very much and understands how to please her man. He is deeply passionate, so there are not likely to be any problems in the bedroom. Both are easily turned on. Mostly Libra is easy to get on with. She is a pleasing person with a nice appreciation of beauty and art. Scorpio is going to have to ease up and let her breathe. She'll be good for him if she's prepared to put up with him.

This is a romantic, sentimental lady. She won't get the murmured words of love she wants from Scorpio and may not get too many flowers or diamond bracelets either. However, the insurance policy is likely to be paid on time, and her car license will be up to date. That's a form of love!

This lady is dependent on her man, make no mistake about that. She believes truly in equal partnerships, equal shares, and could be hurt by Scorpio's withdrawn, slightly secretive side. Will it work? Yes, but it might be too late when this couple suddenly realize what they have lost. Libra is rarely without a man for long, and Scorpio seems to understand women as few others do. It would be a pity if these two parted without understanding each other's natures and making allowances for them. One more thing: Scorpio's tired, worldly-wise cynicism is not real, it's a coverup for his sensitive nature. He fears being hurt. She should help him.

SAGITTARIUS WOMAN—SAGITTARIUS MAN

This could be a very pleasing and a successful relationship provided it doesn't get just too chaotic. These two cheery, light-hearted, and fun-loving people value their freedom and will respect each other's.

Life will be pretty unpredictable, as will sex—it could happen anytime and anywhere. Both love to travel, experience new things, do exciting and stimulating things. Life could be pretty wearing, but Sagittarians are almost as good at bouncing back after disappointments as Arians are. Social life will certainly be hectic, with lots of friends and contacts, parties, and possibly quite a few lovers.

Both will find things in common, but it could also happen that these two drift apart—not intentionally, but because of the very volatility and number of interests they have. The Sagittarian man in particular takes chances, does outrageous things, gambles, and has the sort of lucky streak that makes things go right for him more times than he probably deserves.

There will be a touch of irresponsibility about some of the things this generous and outgoing couple does. There could be financial problems from time to time as a result. This could be one surprise neither will enjoy, although usually they love surprises. Plenty of imagination and humor make Sagittarians fun to be with. Sport could be important to younger Sagittarians, while older ones will yearn for the times when they were more active—even though they're probably doing five times as many things as most middle-aged couples.

The signs are good for a long-lasting relationship even though

Sagittarians can be remarkably disorganized. That's not quite true—they look disorganized, as do their desks, but they know just where everything is and from time to time come up with a remarkable stroke of brilliance that proves they are on the ball and not just meandering around as some will think.

Sex and the body are important to these two, who are physically oriented. In a way they'll be like two big kids who aren't going to grow up—but it's refreshing in a world like ours. The Sagittarian woman might try to persuade her man to stick to his job—after all, he's probably moved thirty-two times already in five years. They should tell each other frequently that love is vital and that love has struck—it'll probably be true anyway.

SAGITTARIUS WOMAN—CAPRICORN MAN

This is going to produce a lot of frustration and discontent before harmony is reached—if it ever is. These two see life in completely different terms. Capricorn is sensible, cautious, and practical and needs lots of love and understanding. Sagittarius is impulsive, lively, frank, outgoing, and a flirt.

She likes to spend and have fun. He prefers to save for a rainy day, even though he wants and appreciates quality things. It's like chalk and cheese when these two quarrel, as they surely will. And yet she can be a worrier. Nobody seems to know just what she worries about, but she needs the stability that this man can bring her. In many ways she will be happier if she can relate to him, understand his emotional needs, and enjoy home life more than tearing around the world with friends.

It won't help when he gets home from work and finds she's blown a week's wages on a crate of French champagne. Usually he has trouble expressing emotions, but he'll probably manage it when this happens, even though she'll tell him he's a bore and doesn't appreciate all she does for him. He is a serious and slightly gloomy guy at times—she can do a lot to help him cheer up, but she may already have left!

Sexually it won't be plain sailing. Sagittarius is good in bed, but Capricorn is perfectly likely to be thinking of something else, and she'll know. The fact that bills are paid on time and there is enough money for that holiday in Barbados and skiing in Switzerland may just not be compensation enough for the sheer boredom she is likely to feel at times. He can also be a bit bossy and try to organize his woman—and she doesn't want to be organized. In fact, she spends half her life avoiding being organized by other people. Yes, he's a bit intolerant and will speak his mind. He's often critical to a ridiculous degree, and of course this rubs off on those around him. It would probably be a good idea to let him criticize and speak his mind to someone else. If it's love, then it's going to be an uphill struggle, but good things sometimes fail to come easy.

Sometimes Capricorn will disguise his true feelings. He can be reserved and proud as he gets older. If she helps him crack through this shell he's busy building, he ought to be eternally grateful. Ought to be, but probably won't. Capricorn does have a tendency to take things for granted, unfortunately.

SAGITTARIUS WOMAN—AQUARIUS MAN

This relationship could prove surprisingly successful. The Aquarian man is unpredictable, eccentric, lovable, and at times as cool as October in Maine. But he is gentle, kind, and unselfish and perfectly likely to fall for this lady too.

He has a fine logical mind, sharp as a tack, but he isn't interested in power or making money. The Sagittarian enthusiasm and occasional strokes of brilliance could well endear her to this guy, who is one of the easiest in the Zodiac to get on with. They both love to travel, and new places, new ideas, and new experiences are meat and drink to this decidedly lively pair.

He doesn't want a dependent woman, and he certainly won't get one here; she has a mind and a will of her own. She isn't as tough as she makes out, but she enjoys life and living. At times Sagittarius will want consolation and love, and not just in bed. Aquarius could prove wanting at these times. Sexually there will be plenty of fun, though the relationship won't be too deeply passionate. Neither party is jealous or vindictive, and both will respect the other and seek a harmonious and equal partnership in the best sense of the word.

In fact, this relationship may well deepen in the way trees put down stronger and more permanent roots as time goes by. Money may be a problem because both love to spend and do so impulsively at times. But he will trust his woman—so she'd better not tell him about the handsome tennis instructor and the golf pro. He won't really want to know anyway, so why upset the poor guy even if only for an hour or two?

Aquarius would be wise to make an effort to tell this lady he needs and loves her. She'll be surprised and gratified, and it might just save the relationship. Remember that the Aquarian man thinks big; he's really a bit ahead of his time, dreaming of a perfect world where wars don't happen and everyone is nice. He won't worry about his home not being spotless or tidy all the time. Incidentally, he has an advanced social conscience and cares deeply for justice and the underdog.

At times this will not be a comfortable or cozy partnership, but apparently that's not how it is meant to be, so heed the warning. If Sagittarius wants passion and drama, then this is the wrong guy; but she shouldn't overlook his virtues in the quest for a little romance. He's worth taking some trouble over.

SAGITTARIUS WOMAN—PISCES MAN

This is potentially a disaster, but a few couples do get it together by dint of hard work and reliance on the physical aspect of the union.

Both can be enormously charming, but they are very different people. Pisces is all emotion, complex, intuitive, possibly even psychic, given to brooding. He wants to give himself totally. Sagittarius is lively, elusive, sociable, often superficial, busy, and decidedly optimistic, whereas this fellow can only be described as fatalistic and pessimistic.

He's a dreamer, not really strong enough to assert himself when she gets out of line, which she will probably do frequently. There are likely to be financial problems too. Pisces just doesn't seem able to understand that money has to be saved, although he is surprisingly good at collecting it from one source or another. Sagittarius just enjoys making a show. A new dress may well be more important to her than the week's shopping. Both love to travel and see exciting romantic places.

Sexually there will be passion and great moments, but both are unreliable and eventually she could feel hemmed in and put down by this man's dependence and even depression. It certainly won't be easy to find stable, solid common ground. In many ways he wants a mother figure, and she may not be prepared to play this role because she places great value on her independence. He has also been known to have affairs almost by accident. He can't resist the romantic gesture, and it can get him into deep trouble. He also withdraws at times into a whole world of his own, and this he guards carefully. He thinks in a slightly devious way, although he is rarely deliberately vindictive. But if he doesn't like someone, he can be decidedly off-putting, and that person will have no doubts about his feelings.

If Sagittarius is prepared to do more than half the hard work in this partnership, then it can certainly work, but it is asking a lot. This is an artistic man with a true appreciation of beauty, so he does have much to offer a woman, but he is not good at making decisions (to put it mildly)—although, moved by sudden whims and ideas, he may suddenly and willfully make an arbitrary decision that later both will regret.

The answer is for these two to gradually get to know each other and try to avoid an impetuous union. Sagittarius won't be easy to get to the altar anyway, so that's a good thing.

SAGITTARIUS WOMAN—ARIES MAN

This relationship is likely to prove successful for two very lively, outgoing, loving people with an urge to take the whole world on and beat the hell out of it.

Aries is dynamic, irritatingly boyish at times, energetic, warm, and enthusiastic. Sagittarius might just decide on the spot that this is the guy for her—at last she's found someone she can bear to be linked with. His ideas will sometimes founder because he loses interest and moves on to something else, but she won't mind too much because she's much the same, loves to move on, travel, experience new things, have a go at anything. It can be trying for their friends and relatives, but these two don't care too much about that.

Sex should be fine. Arguments are likely to erupt and then end rapidly. Aries will think this lady flirty and flighty sometimes, and she'll tell him his ego is too big and he's too self-centered. But if he does start to work for her or others in general, he'll be an even nicer guy. Both want their freedom. Don't expect meals to be on time. He'll order everyone around, but she'll chuckle and go her own way. When he gets irritated, she will point out his unreasonableness to him, and he'll grumble and resist and then accept graciously and be on the next project in no time. Neither is vindictive or selfish or unduly critical.

There'll be plenty of laughter and fun for this pair. In fact, there's every chance they won't like being apart because they find life so boring alone. Although he thinks he's romantic, Aries is about as subtle as a bear with a sore paw, but he does have other virtues. He's very honest, frank, and reliable, although it has to be admitted that he has an eye for the opposite sex. Sagittarius is probably not too far behind in this area either.

Financially things are likely to be chaotic unless he's an advanced sort of Arian. Both are extravagant and don't like to pinch pennies (neither finds bank managers especially endearing). Both are splendid hosts, and guests will get the best of everything whether the budget allows it or not.

There's a whole lot of world to be experienced and fought with—at least that's how this lively pair is likely to see it. Home life will suffer from this attitude. The thing to do is to make a real effort to do things together rather than apart, to work at togetherness.

SAGITTARIUS WOMAN—TAURUS MAN

These two may well be attracted, but it is likely to prove a difficult, highly frustrating, and unsatisfactory partnership in most cases.

Taurus likes to take the lead in everything. He's a bit slow, rigid, and greedy. He has a tendency to overeat, put on weight, and overindulge sexually. He can be damnably charming and courteous, and he has a genuine artistic sensibility and appreciation. He's sensible, practical, and realistic as well as being home- and luxury-loving. Sagittarius is much more frothy, lightweight in her responses, charming, and lively. She needs lots of stimulation and adventure, and has lots of friends and contacts and likes to visit them or have them around. She's going to find this guy just too much of a heavy number.

Certainly he would be good for her in the sense that he would provide an anchor for her, but he isn't going to be able to possess her and have her devote herself to him as he thinks she should. This will make him jealous, and she won't like that, to put it mildly. He is sensible with money, knows its value. She likes to splash it about a bit, to have fun and dress elegantly. He'll grumble about it but paradoxically likes to have her looking good and is proud to take her out. Sexually, Taurus will be too emotional in his responses and in his earthy requirement for plenty of action for the more mentally stimulated Sagittarian lady.

She is a busy lady, probably enjoys sports or walking or the like. He will prefer to laze in bed or in front of the TV with a novel and a box of chocolates. He doesn't like traveling nearly as much as she does. He can get really stuck in one spot or one job or one environment. It isn't exactly laziness; it's more a fear of change or anything that might disrupt his comfortable, well-understood existence. Life together will not be easy, so a brief romantic affair is to be recommended. If the relationship does settle down, there are likely to be recriminations and long drawn-out discussions into the night to settle problems. He wants his woman to live for him alone, while she wants to spread her virtue around a bit—and will certainly try!

There is a fair chance that she will drift into an affair with someone else, as much out of boredom as anything else, but Taurus will fail to see this and will interpret it as a direct threat to his manhood. He's proud, if not too bright.

SAGITTARIUS WOMAN—GEMINI MAN

This is one of those fascinating relationships that could be a terrific success or an unmitigated disaster because of the sheer volatility and excitability and changeableness of the partners.

Certainly there will be a terrific amount of fun and excitement, lots of people dropping in, and lots of visits. Both will be happy to lead very separate lives without trying to restrict each other, and there will be a tendency for jobs to change rapidly and erratically. Either or neither might decide to look after the finances, so they too are likely to be in a regular state of disarray, but neither will worry too much even when the creditors start moving the furniture. Both are light, optimistic, and cheerful.

These two will find it difficult to be compatible in the normal sense of the word. They won't meld together as a team, so sex is likely to be an instinctive and instantaneous thing rather than a regular, looked-forward-to experience as it is with some other couples. Lots of stimulation is needed by this pair, and a third party might just help to provide it.

The compatability will be a sort of magical delight at times, an impatient and charming and joyful togetherness when all the flowers will seem to be in bloom. It's not exactly romantic—more a case of everything becoming more real and meaningful. The partnership is actually likely to be a little crazy, but maybe that's the way it's supposed to be. Gemini in particular thinks so fast that he sometimes may appear emotional, but it isn't so. He changes so fast it seems that he is responding with his feelings, and he can even seem to get into an emotional tangle which is in fact a mental tangle! It can be all very confusing.

Brilliant ideas can flow from Gemini and be duly appreciated by Sagittarius. Will action follow the ideation? Once in ten times maybe, and that could prove enough to keep the finances just about stable. With a Gemini and a Sagittarian who are really relating, there will often be examples of intuitive communication beyond words, but conversation will also be tremendously stimulating. With noncompatible couples, the tension will be just too great and they should make tracks—separate tracks. Each will respect the independence of the other partner, but it would be wise not to give each other too much rope.

SAGITTARIUS WOMAN—CANCER MAN

There are too many fundamental obstacles here for this to be a comfortable, constructive, and enjoyable partnership. Cancer is probably too sensitive for the flighty, cheerful, optimistic Sagittarian, who loves to get out and about and enjoy herself with her many friends and contacts.

Cancer is all emotion. He's romantic to a fault, gentle, loving, and in need of reassurance—this he is unlikely to get from Sagittarius, whose idea of reassurance is a quick roll in the hay. She is charming and affectionate and pretty sexy too. She has no intention of devoting her life to Cancer's home and affairs. He can be a pretty tenacious, determined sort of guy and he does not expect her to be gadding about the countryside. He's cool and sensible with cash in most cases, while she tends to extravagance, so there will certainly be a few words about this.

Sexually Cancer is too sentimental (hearts and roses) for this lady, who believes in romance but prefers that *she* be the romantic one. She's rather selfish in many ways, and although they may reach sexual harmony after a while, it will always tend to tip one way or the other and he'll start sulking or get into one of his black moods, or she'll want a couple of rounds of golf and two or three hours of tennis before bed—not what he had in mind.

She loves to get around the world, visiting exotic and interesting places; he might stray three or four miles from home if pressed. Her

Sagittarian vitality will of course be good for Cancer, and in time he could even get her to enjoy a painting or poem or symphony. But in the end, an emotional man and a mental woman don't really meet, and a friendly, caring relationship would be much more sensible than what might at first promise to be a full and fruitful partnership.

Cancer is ambitious in that he expects to have to work to be successful, whereas Sagittarius has the curious ability to find success by sudden strokes of brilliance or intuition. He might well find this irritating. She will be hard put to stay long in any job and for that matter finds it hard to stay long with any guy—which doesn't mean that she won't try.

If it's love, then these two should be patient with each other. She should try to get him out of the house on weekends. Hikes in the woods, outings in the countryside, or sailing weekends—anything like that will do, for he is deeply responsive to beauty wherever he finds it.

SAGITTARIUS WOMAN—LEO MAN

There'll be a bit too much passion here, but that's a lot better than none at all, and it will help to cement a potentially excellent union.

Leo is dominant, egotistical, blustering, charming, exciting, and sometimes a bit like a big naughty schoolboy. He's just what Sagittarius needs. Emotionally and sexually these two will understand each other well enough. Both love life and cannot be bothered about trivial things that might interrupt their grand passion and their love of tearing around doing things!

These two are likely to have the same interests, whether art, music, booze, cars, or whatever, and although there is a risk that they'll rarely actually meet because each has so many interests, a typical Leo will lay down the law and the independent Sagittarian will take instructions because she can recognize the justice of what he says and will take trouble to safeguard and secure this relationship. He expects a nice home, and although she is not really interested in such things, she will do her best, even if she makes bad jokes about his cruelty and unfeelingness in tying her to the domestic routine.

Leo will be delighted by this vivacious lady—and marriage should be arranged. She will make him feel good and loving. She has plenty of vitality. He can become a little rigid as he gets older, so her youthful outlook and liveliness will do him a lot of good. And in return, Sagittarius gets the security she needs, even if she thinks she doesn't.

Sexually there'll be lots of passion. Not only will bedtime be good, but so will play and work and social time. These two are likely to be excellent hosts, even if the visitors aren't going to get much time to laze around and relax. Leo wants the very best for "his," and he expects his woman to take trouble with her appearance. Some Leos can be just too overpowering, but if flattered outrageously enough, they can even be taught to chuckle at their own dramatic gestures or laugh at their bombastic demands. This is a proud man, so she should take it easy on the criticism. Instead of saying he's got lousy taste in ties (which he probably has), she should suggest there's a fault in the weave. And she'd better not let him see her flirtations or he'll get jealous and pompous and stupid.

One thing about Leo—don't take him to sales. He doesn't really appreciate a bargain even if he pretends he does. He prefers to pay over the odds to get the very best. What price mink?

SAGITTARIUS WOMAN—VIRGO MAN

These two can make a go of things, but it won't be easy because they have very different temperaments and quite simply respond in different ways to the same stimuli.

Virgo is a careful—not to say finicky—sort of guy, rather cool emotionally and mentally oriented. He's a perfectionist in that he expects everything to run like clockwork and everyone to respond exactly as expected. Of course, things never do happen like this, so he is continually in a mild state of frustration with life and living.

Sagittarius is a worrier at times, a worker at others, and busy all the time in that she likes to get around and meet friends. He'll never quite know what to expect next. This would in fact be good for Virgo, because his organizing gifts are valuable to the world but can be irritating when he attempts to take over the home and everything else. In fact, Sagittarius will strenuously resist being a serf. She values her independence enormously and she won't hesitate to tell him so.

Virgo's decisions are activated by intelligence and logic, and he's good with money. He doesn't expect a windfall every so often, as Sagittarius does; he's prepared to work hard and steadily for his own and others' ends. In fact, he makes an excellent number two in any business but rarely gets to the number-one spot partly because he can become bogged down in details. Sagittarius acts from feeling and impulse, and she is right a surprising amount of the time. From the Virgoan point of view, her gambles have an irritating habit of proving successful.

All this creates an attraction of opposites, but it won't help true understanding. Sometimes Virgo will want to spend a quiet evening at home—he may even want to spend *every* evening quietly at home—and this won't go down well when Sagittarius gets her glad rags on and is all set for the party of the year!

Sexually Sagittarius is the livelier of the two and is more superficial in her approach to such things. Too often the Virgoan response will be boring to this lady. All things considered, it might be a good idea for these two to be good friends rather than lovers. Two more mature people will find it much easier to relate, although of course maturity may have nothing to do with physical age.

SAGITTARIUS WOMAN—LIBRA MAN

This relationship looks to be a good one. Libra will be most impressed by this lady's enthusiasm and sheer get-up-and-go. And she's likely to fall for him when he turns on the charm and whispers sweet nothings in her ear. In most cases she'd laugh at such things, but with this guy somehow it's different. He must have harmony in his life at any cost, and as she is relatively easy to get on with, these two are off to a good start. He wants to treat his woman as a complete equal, and this too makes a big hit with the independent Sagittarian woman.

It will be a tiring relationship because both have lots of friends and love to get out. Compared with some signs, their life together will have an element of superficiality about it. She is attracted by his elegance and rather sophisticated air. Finances are liable to be permanently strained because both tend to buy before thinking, and Libra might find that although he is reluctant to take responsibility, he has to take charge and balance the books. Decisions are often agony for him, but easy for her because she takes them in a completely irresponsible way.

Sex should be very good. Libra is a tolerant sort and he'll be amused by Sagittarius's exuberant antics. There'll be lots of fun in the bedroom and out of it. There will certainly be minor problems and lots of them, but they will probably pale into insignificance compared with the togetherness this couple can manage.

Romantic Libra understands women and is attractive to them, so Sagittarius shouldn't take his flirtations too seriously. Pretty women are meat and drink to him, but he'll be truly offended if she gets angry about his carrying-on. She is strong-minded (except that when it comes to money she can be self-indulgent) but selfish. Incidentally, he'll probably dislike quite a few of her friends because they aren't elegant or out of the top social drawer. But he'll expect her to applaud his choice of friends—after all, *he* chose them!

Libra is a diplomatic sort of man, is a good talker, and doesn't like drama and scenes, so if he's the one to play things down, keep it light and, like the bee to the flower, he'll be back for more.

SAGITTARIUS WOMAN—SCORPIO MAN

It is rarely safe for an astrologer to predict that a relationship will be a real disaster because there are always some couples who seem to make a great success of even the most unlikely relationships. However, these two certainly have the odds stacked against them. Scorpio is one man who gets horribly jealous, and this lady seems to be divinely ordained to bring out the absolute worst in him.

He will be attracted by her easy charm and way with both men and women, but if the partnership deepens, she is going to feel as though he wants to keep her locked in his private prison for the rest of her life. He wants exclusive rights to all of her, and Sagittarius is one who values her freedom, even if she's prepared to slip a slim gold band on.

She does sense his depth and his seriousness. His moods are indications of his emotional intensity, which is likely to hit her between the eyes at times. She wants to relate to him, but he doesn't make it easy; he's one of the hardest types in the Zodiac to get on with, although potentially one of the most rewarding. If only he were able to express his emotions to her in words—but most Scorpios seem to have extraordinary difficulty in even getting started on this.

Financially there will be problems because he likes things in perpetual apple-pie order, while she acts a bit like the wind when she's given a wad of money. He'll get angry (a real Scorpionic anger is something to view from a safe distance) and she'll call him a stuffed shirt and a monster and a lot more unsavory things. Sexually, life together, should be passionate, but she likes to keep things on a lighter, softer plane than he does. She isn't exactly without a temper herself, but hers comes and goes quickly. His builds up gradually like a thunderstorm and may induce weeks of brooding before the lightning starts to flash.

Don't get things wrong. Scorpio can be as charming as they come. He has an indefinable sex appeal, and although he will always be just a bit secretive, he can be a lot of fun—when he wants to be rather than when the circumstances necessarily warrant it. He can be devious and a trifle vindictive. The key to understanding him is to recognize his will to power. He has to be the boss at all costs. But instead of charging the gates with head down like an Arian, he'll dig a deep tunnel or two and infiltrate from the rear. He has lots of patience and determination and he can be a heavy number. If he sets his mind on a woman, she hasn't a chance, so flirt carefully.

SAGITTARIUS MAN—SAGITTARIUS WOMAN

Life is going to be pretty unpredictable for these two fun-loving people who both need their freedom yet respect each other's privacy and right to do his or her own thing.

There will be irresponsible things done by this pair, and their finances could be in a perpetual state of chaos. Both are generous and outgoing and not given to brooding about money, but there is a tendency for the Sagittarius man in particular to worry about other things, possibly his health, even though this would appear to be slightly out of character. He does have a lucky streak and is not averse to a little betting. He's more often than not a winner, and the same thing often happens in his work situation. He may appear to be a muddler and his desk is certainly likely to be chaotic, but he knows where everything is and doesn't like things moved. Every so often he'll come up with a brilliant idea, and it may even be intuitive.

The signs are good here for a long-term relationship because these two understand each other's need to get out and about, keep dozens of balls in the air at once, have lots of friends and contacts. Some Sagittarians are a bit superficial in their approach to life and flit from job to job and interest to interest. They tend to need and respond to stimulation and to enjoy the challenges that life tends to drop in their path. They're not so good at sustained work effort. Social life will indeed be hectic; a Sagittarian can be the life and soul of a party.

Both are optimistic and unpredictable. Sex is likely to be of the "happen when and where it will" variety. Life could be pretty tiring, but Sagittarians bounce back for more and always think that as one door shuts, another opens. Sex is important to this pair. The Sagittarius woman will almost inevitably find herself comforted by a bedding rather than a gentle talk. She'll probably enjoy sports and might even be better at them than he is. Both are likely to keep active well past the time when most couples take to easy chairs in Miami or settle for bridge or canasta.

It is possible for two Sagittarians to drift apart because each has an outgoing nature that allows almost excessive freedom to the other. It would be a good idea to try to create togetherness by doing things out of the house that interest and involve both partners—it doesn't really matter whether it's archery or yoga. Life apart is likely to be far less fun than life together.

SAGITTARIUS MAN—CAPRICORN WOMAN

It is by no means certain that this relationship will weather the storms of life—which is a slightly pompous way of saying that things ain't going to be too easy.

The restless and outgoing Sagittarian will have a difficult time relating to the more serious, practical, and cautious Capricorn woman, who is nevertheless likely to attract him because she will appear to rely on him. He rather likes to play the big shot. Later he is likely to find this irksome and to wish she were more independent. She is a serious lady in that she does concern herself with details in a way that he does not. But she worries about the finances in a way that he does not. She is not as selfish as he, but she can be overcautious, desperately romantic, and at the same time seemingly cold and calculating. She'll be horrified by the way Sagittarius seems to drift through life responding to situations as they occur, taking things as they come and more often than not coming out on top. She'd like to be like that but just cannot seem to take things so easily. Her efforts at fun can even look slightly desperate. A few drinks can persuade her to let her hair down, but next time she comes around she's back to "normal": "What party? Don't remember a thing."

Sexually she's too level-headed for Sagittarius and seems to need more affection than lovemaking. One moment she'll be decidedly passionate and the next worrying about the price of new curtains. She is unlikely to change his bad habits, but she'll try. She is likely to be faithful once she makes up her mind that it's love. A lot of Capricorn ladies seem to be able to sustain sexual relationships at a relatively superficial level for a long time without commiting themselves to anything further. This suits Sagittarius, and frankly it could be the best way for this twosome to carry on.

He will always be a roamer, either physically or in his imagination. He finds it difficult to resist a pretty face or figure. But she would be wise not to get jealous and critical, or more than likely she'll drive him away. He can't help flirting, but most times it doesn't mean very much.

There'll be quarrels when he wants to lash out with the cash and she decided that the budget won't allow it because she's saving. She may not be saving for anything specific—but it provides security, and that's terribly important for this lady.

SAGITTARIUS MAN—AQUARIUS WOMAN

This could be a good relationship provided Aquarius is able to get from her man a few tangible proofs of his love and need. Tangible proofs would come in the form of gold bars, sacks of diamonds, the deeds of houses, and other such trivia.

This lady is easy to relate to. She is independent, honest, often a bit kooky in the nicest possible way. She isn't ambitious or pushy. She likes to spend and she loves to get around to parties, have fun, go skiing, and all the rest of it. All this suits Sagittarius right down to the ground. That's his sort of life.

This guy delights her by suddenly suggesting they fly down to Rio. And even if the finances won't allow it, he'll come up with a suggestion that will delight her by its originality. Hamburgers in the sewers might be less than appealing, but it certainly could make a change! Sex will be interesting rather than madly passionate. Neither party is jealous or vindictive or mean or dominating. Each will appreciate the virtues of the other and will respect the other's right not only to his or her thoughts but to get out of the house alone from time to time. These two could casually drift apart without realizing it, but the union has a more than equal chance of becoming a deep and meaningful one.

The finances are likely to be in a permanent state of awfulness, so a friendly, understanding bank manager or two would be most useful. These two tend to think first and worry later. Aquarius might have to learn to worry a little about the cash or else those diamonds and gold bars will forever remain a dream and she'll always feel insecure. A couple of kids and her own growing bank account will do a lot for her morale—and might even reconcile her to Sagittarius's flirtations.

Both worry about the underprivileged, and she in particular displays an advanced social consciousness. She's really a most unselfish person who could well be a couple of hundred years ahead of her time. She can be rather reserved, but his humor and charm will quickly break that down and his warmth and real affection should do the trick. He might practice telling her that he loves her, and tell her twice a day for life. She'll always be slightly doubtful whether he means it or not, but it will at least add to her security. Every so often Sagittarius will show himself brilliant and intuitive. She should encourage him to show this side of himself more often.

SAGITTARIUS MAN—PISCES WOMAN

A decidedly thorny relationship that is more likely to be short and passionate than long and fulfilling. The Pisces woman is too much of a handful for this guy, who doesn't really want someone dependent on him all the time.

He seeks an equal partner, but she is pure emotion. Everything is related to her feelings. She loves intuitively and sometimes none too wisely. She gives herself totally, and she might well fall for the charming, boyish, dashing Sagittarian. He is, however, more likely to dash away after a while.

He is a playful, flirtatious guy. This lady doesn't want any of that. She's a sentimentalist, a romantic, a hearts-and-flowers lady, a lover. She is also the great dreamer of the Zodiac. She's a day and a night dreamer, quite possibly psychic, waiting for a knight in shining armor to gallop around the corner to carry her off. Sexually there will certainly be moments of deep passion and togetherness, but she is a timid, sometimes depressed, often up, often down person who needs either a strong man she can love and react against or someone like herself who will share her secrets and whisper sweet nothings in her ear.

She loves old things and frilly, gypsy-style dresses, but looks good in almost anything in a slightly old-fashioned way. She won't get enough attention from Sagittarius, and this could make her develop a martyr complex; she could become jealous when she sees him eyeing her friends. Financially things are likely to be far from easy. He likes to spend and she just can't seem to save. No one's perfect, but Pisces with her hothouse passions and deep emotions is quite a woman—too much for the relatively straightforward Sagittarian.

She is changeable too; emotions flash across her psyche like clouds in a storm. She's a beautiful, desirable lady but definitely difficult to live with. It would be a pity if she entered into this relationship without realizing that she could wind up lonely when her man gets out and about without really thinking about her. He's a lot of fun, adventurous. He'll probably adore his Piscean lady—most of the time; the rest he'll be far away recovering.

Pisces will keep her home spotless; she is very efficient around the house. She won't bother about her career when she settles down and she will expect to be provided for. Will Sagittarius do the providing? Probably not to her satisfaction.

SAGITTARIUS MAN—ARIES WOMAN

This could be a good relationship, full of fun and adventure and excitement, although there will be blowups every so often, to clear the air.

This lady is bossy, outspoken, and sometimes rude and infuriating. It has been suggested that Sagittarians would like to be Arians and Arians would like to be Leos. There's a grain of truth in this. The Arian lady could try to take over the relationship. This fellow just won't let her. Rather than quarrel savagely—she won't step back from a good fight, which frankly she enjoys—he'll walk away. He's no coward but he reckons life's too short to be disagreeable, and anyway there are lots more pretty girls around. He's a lucky guy, likes a gamble, and often pulls things off. Both these two can be selfish and petulant—a bit immature at any age—but life together could be such fun that they'll stick no matter what happens.

Sagittarius might well change jobs or occupations many times, but this won't worry Aries too much. She likes to keep busy herself. She prefers to work in short, incredibly concentrated bursts, while he flits from one thing to another. But both can be extravagant, so she would be wise to tuck a little money away and forget about it. If she should happen to persuade him to buy her the biggest diamond in the shop when things are going well, she'd be wise to hang on to it; it might be the only thing she has one day.

Sexually Sagittarius is a born philanderer without a trace of remorse. And Aries likes a rough and tumble. If they get it together in the bedroom, as they probably will, then the whole union is likely to be harmonic and pleasing. She's going to have to learn a whole new style of patience if she plans to stick with him, and she might be wise to start with the little things—like her big ego and her pride and the sergeant-major voice!

In many ways he is a nicer person than she is. He's easier to get on with, unself-consciously selfish, kind, and generous and he loves to be out with the boys (or girls). He likes a good time. She might find this a bit superficial. She won't see much of him at home no matter how charming or elegant their place is, but she'll be too busy to worry about this much. It will be a good idea if she manages to develop a profitable hobby or sideline. The cash will quite likely be needed when he puts their fortune into some outrageous speculation—which three years later makes them immensely and amazingly rich.

SAGITTARIUS MAN—TAURUS WOMAN

Don't take bets on this one lasting the course. Taurus is steady, a stay-at-home, a lover of comfort and luxury. Sagittarius is the original go-getter, irresponsible, charming, adventurous, and immorally flirtatious. He can't resist a pretty face, and from her point of view the pretty face had better be hers or else!

These two are just too different to make this one click in most cases. Taurus enjoys sex and plenty of it, while Sagittarius is more haphazard about everything. At times he'll be all over her and the next minute he won't hear of it. He likes to get out and about. Staying stuck in one place for more than fifteen minutes is death to a Sagittarian.

He makes a super pal for a Taurus, whom he will stimulate and cajole and infuriate by turns. But a longer stay? The outlook is not promising. She doesn't want to change emotionally. As they get older Taureans can become rigid and set in their comfortable, convenient ways. She could become critical and slow and boring. He won't put up with that kind of thing. The whole world is out there waiting for him; there are so many great places to visit, so many things to be seen . . . and so many women.

She'll probably try, but this essentially conservative lady is not going to be able to dominate this guy. She is by no means lazy; she's prepared to work, but it has to be for something practical like a new home or car or boat. He just likes to keep on the move. Sagittarius would be good for her in the sense that he'd persuade her to take up skiing or yoga, learn gourmet cooking, and study Chinese, and generally keep her on her toes and widen her horizons. But her idea of real fun is a box of candy, a log fire, sweet music, and a cuddle.

Sagittarius won't be easy to get to the altar. He'll probably discover he's supposed to be in Peking on the appointed day.

If it is love, these two should prepare for a big effort to achieve harmony. Both are going to have to make a lot of compromises. One thing's for sure, she'll do her best to fatten him up with her cooking. He won't mind that, but when she sees that he stays thin, she might take it as a personal affront.

Both can be charming and sincere and truly appreciate art and beauty, yet at the same time, with the best will in the world, not quite get it together. That's life.

SAGITTARIUS MAN—GEMINI WOMAN

This could be a successful long-term union albeit at times a strange one, or it could finish very quickly. It depends upon the maturity and tolerance of the partners more than with many other combinations.

Sagittarius is an exciting, interesting, stimulating guy to be with. He certainly has his faults, but with this lady they might well look like virtues! Gemini is a great communicator with an immensely quick mind, always attracted by new ideas. She can be practical when she wants, more so perhaps than the volatile Sagittarian, but both need lots of fun in their lives, lots of friends, lots of contacts. Both demand freedom and independence and are prepared to give it to others. He wants to do what he wants, while she has the curious tendency to do things she's been told not to. The changeable and at times stubborn Gemini nature is exhibited in this. Tell them not to smoke and they will, but if everyone around smokes, they won't.

Sex will be decidedly lively if unconventional. In many ways they are too restless for true compatibility, but if there are plenty of stimulating things to do together, then all could be well. Gemini should beware of being too critical but will really appreciate the unexpected ideas that this guy suddenly comes up with. No one gets bored when he's around. Sometimes Sagittarians make big promises that don't quite come true; they're irresponsible and at times selfish, but basically generous and well meaning. This will be a complex partnership that outsiders may wonder at. Mealtimes are likely to be chaos, particularly with the family. No one is likely to be on time and there's a fair chance it won't be clear who's cooking what. But Sagittarius is an easy sort of guy, and the intensity of some of the Geminian thought-patterns will be broken up by his good-natured humor. There'll be plenty of stimulus, but not too much peace, and plenty of imagination and imagining, for both believe in romance. He is a born flirter the way some men are born workers. He likes to feel good and to be with attractive people. But he won't try to mold Gemini in his own image, and this is an important plus for this pair.

Perhaps the biggest problem is the sheer volatility of it all. They might just bubble away from each other because there are so many exciting things to be done all around. One thing about this man is his honesty, and that shouldn't be underestimated.

SAGITTARIUS MAN—CANCER WOMAN

This partnership doesn't look too good for a long-time marriage but could be great fun for a week in Acapulco.

He will soon find her restricting and demanding and emotional. She'll decide he's irresponsible, flighty, and restless, and she certainly won't like his roving eye. She wants her man all to herself all of the time, and he wants to be out and about with friends, doing exciting, stimulating things that she will frankly find superficial.

These two couldn't be more opposite in their responses. Cancer needs loving care and security and plenty of reassurance. She's probably too sensitive for the frank, hard-hitting, no-nonsense type of Sagittarian one runs into and too sensible for the other type. There could be good sex, but really they'd make better pen pals than lovers.

Neither enjoys quarreling, and quarrels there will be. She wants him to look after the finances and he wants her to come out and enjoy them—as far as they'll stretch, that is. Cancer doesn't want to flirt or to battle with her man; she wants deep emotional empathy with him (kisses, in other words). She has a tendency to overact a bit, but Sagittarius, if it really is love, is a tolerant fellow who will put up with a lot more than many other signs would. There are going to be some nervous and nerve-wracking times for this lady. A comfortable home is important to her, and possessions, while not necessarily meaning a lot to her in the plural, tend to have sentimental or romantic associations, so she just can't part with them. She'll probably go berserk when Sagittarius throws everything out one afternoon when she's at her flower-arrangement class.

There's no doubt that this lady is attracted by such a charming, lively, caring man. He seems almost too good to be true to the unsure Cancerian. And that's exactly what he is—for her. They should have quite a few trial sessions before heading for the altar.

If the partnership is to work at all, Cancer must be willing to enjoy herself without recriminations or the feeling that she shouldn't be having fun and should be doing something more meaningful. Sagittarius must try to understand her sensitive and emotional nature. Incidentally, he is a bit of a gambler and, perhaps surprisingly, he does have a lucky streak, so she shouldn't thwart his instincts every time. If possible, these two shouldn't fall in love with each other.

SAGITTARIUS MAN—LEO WOMAN

This could prove to be a terrific relationship. Leo is more demanding than Sagittarius is, but if she can curb her jealous instincts, then all will be well.

Sagittarius will adore his beautiful, elegant, and at times bossy Leo. He'll laugh when she gets pompous and orders him about. There's no way this formidable lady is going to take him over, and if she's wise she'll soon get the message. There should be lots of passion, but they will respect each other, and this is important. He has a roving eye and makes little secret of it because he's an honest guy, so it's up to Leo to either keep him on the straight and narrow by cunning or turn a blind eye to his little naughtinesses.

He's an amusing, stimulating guy who loves to be out and about having fun. The clever Leo will not try to chain her man by grumbling at him or pointing out that it is his duty to provide bread and butter for his children, but will make him want to do it—and even provide the brood with champagne and caviar.

He is a great bouncer; knock him down and he'll be back with unquenchable and probably impractical ideas, so his woman had better keep at least one hand on the financial tiller if there are not to be serious cash-flow problems sooner or later. A few large diamonds tucked away somewhere will do a lot for her peace of mind. He will be good in that he'll keep her from getting too set in her ways (a risk that more mature Leos run). She likes comfort and elegance and the grand gesture and tends to make even the humblest dwelling better than most can. Sagittarius will certainly appreciate this on the rare occasions that he pops home to change his shirt.

Yes, he will flirt. He can't help it; it's in his blood. He'll enjoy sports, while Leo prefers to curl up on her elegant sofa with a romantic novel and listen to Frank Sinatra records. It is possible, however, that she'll be more successful in her career than he is, and this could certainly be a problem because he won't like that, even though he won't say no to the additional cash. A compromise here will depend upon the maturity—not necessarily in age—of the partners.

Sagittarius is a good-natured, optimistic guy, and he'll be good for Leo if she's prepared to put up with his unreliability and unpunctuality. She probably will do so because she thinks she's going to change him for the better. She won't be successful in most cases—but by then she'll probably be in love with him anyway.

SAGITTARIUS MAN—VIRGO WOMAN

Some relationships seem to be made in heaven, but this isn't one of them—and it's not likely to last too long on earth either. The difficulty is that these two are just too different. Virgo will be attracted by the hail-fellow-well-met attitude of this man, and he'll admire her neatness and practicality. But this is by no means enough for a long-term partnership.

Virgo is a nice person but she tends to be critical, and this won't go down well with Sagittarius. She always expects to be the only woman in her man's life, and unfortunately this one has a roving eye. He always seems to be surrounded by friends and likes to get out and about. He's the life and soul of parties and loves traveling. She'd just as soon stay at home with her hobbies and the children. She also needs financial security, while Sagittarius is a gambler. Admittedly he has a lucky streak, but really Virgo needs a man with a much more stable background.

If these two get married there are likely to be money troubles.

She believes in hard work producing financial security. That's just too boring for him, so his extravagance will deeply worry her. At times she'll enjoy traveling too, and she'll be an efficient traveler because she makes an ideal secretary. When she's around, the tickets are booked on time, the hotel reservations are made, and so on. So there is some common ground here.

Sexually he is much more adventurous than she is. She wants an affectionate man rather than a passionate one. But the myth about cold Virgos is not true; for the right man (and this is not he), she can indeed spread her wings. This lady is a thinker. At school she was likely to have been an excellent student, if at times she lacked drive. She will certainly be frustrated by any partnership with this charming, volatile guy.

Virgo needs to be needed and often told so. Sagittarius really only needs a part-time woman, so as a boyfriend he's ideal. Virgo would certainly get madly jealous, but this would in fact drive her man even further away. He does, however, want an equal partner in every respect, someone he can respect and who will make independent decisions. In many ways Virgo wants to take second place. If it is love and there's no one else in the offing, then these two have plenty of hard work ahead of them. They must learn to stay together, to do things together, and to build on the strong points, not pick on the weak.

SAGITTARIUS MAN—LIBRA WOMAN

These two could have a terrific relationship, but there is a possibility that it could degenerate into something very superficial.

Libra is flirtatious, charming, lovable, romantic, and physically oriented. Sagittarius is capricious, delightful, gallant, flirtatious, and physically oriented. Well, go to it! Sexually these two will bring out the best in each other; there'll be lots of fun and no need to quarrel. This is important because Libra seeks harmony everywhere and will go a long way to avoid a fight. And Sagittarius is too easygoing and kind to want to have an argument. He doesn't want to be criticized or browbeaten. He wants to be accepted for what he is, and he will respect his woman and treat her as an equal in everything. She finds this ideal because she's the original liberated woman.

In practice Sagittarius might just find himself jealous as she flickers her pretty eyes at his many friends. But most of the time he'll be as busy while she is enjoying herself. It would be a good idea to generate some common interests or this couple could just drift apart without meaning to.

With a little luck they could be firm friends as well as lovers. He'll have some crazy ideas, and she'll laugh at him and then give her encouragement. And she won't complain when everything goes wrong. Financially things are likely to be chaotic. Both live life to the hilt and spend beyond it, so one of them is going to have to learn to exercise a little restraint, even though it goes against the grain. There is always the possibility that this could be a dynamic and wild infatuation, so they should wait a while before exchanging wedding rings.

Sagittarius is a spontaneous guy, and this is one of his strong points. He doesn't worry too much about things; he smiles and comes up for air again before plunging into another aspect of life. He's likely to make even Leo gasp at the number of different jobs he manages to take. It must be admitted that some Sagittarian men are superficial and a bit juvenile, but it's unlikely that a smart and elegant Libran will be trapped by such a one—for long anyway.

Life together will certainly be stimulating and exciting. In fact, life with any other partner could be boring for each of them. They should stick together.

SAGITTARIUS MAN—SCORPIO WOMAN

This is certain to be a stormy and possibly short-lived relationship because Scorpio is intense, dramatic, and passionate, while Sagittarius is freedom-loving, easygoing, and sensitive to criticism.

The difficulty is that Scorpio lives life with an intensity that Sagittarius finds hard to take. He wants his independence, and she isn't likely to grant it willingly. He won't be dominated but he won't face up to the facts either. He wants to remain a carefree bachelor all his life. She wants a man she can depend on, one who can give her security and to whom she can relate at every level—she wants a lot!

Physically there may be a lot going for this pair, at least for a time. But he will be horrified by the brooding menace he sometimes senses in her, and when she does finally lose her temper, he's likely to head for cover rather than face the storm. She needs a man she can respect, so it might have been better if he'd stood up to her and given as good as he got.

Scorpio wants to possess and know everything about everyone, and of course that includes her lover. She will push and push until he becomes hers or he moves on. Not an easy position to put a man in. On the way there could certainly be ecstasy and joy. There won't be much joy over the finances. She's careful, to put it mildly, and he's extravagant. So Scorpio will probably have to take over the finances, even if they only get together for two weeks in Bermuda.

Scorpio is an emotional lady. Everything is fed through her intuitive and emotional apparatus, and she can get depressed. Sagittarius would be good for her in these moments because he doesn't like to see anyone in such a state. Both like to get out and about, but she is not likely to approve of his friends. In all honesty a short dramatic and enjoyable affair would be better for all concerned, and that might include several assorted husbands and wives.

Make no mistake—this partnership *can* work. Both are strong people in their different ways. He likes to roam but doesn't want his woman to, and she wants her man to be everything to her. Both are going to have to really struggle to make things work out, and this could create an even stronger bond. He is an independent one who doesn't want to be mothered, and she will have to learn this. He certainly needs encouragement, but he'll be difficult to change. They should go into this relationship with open eyes and separate bank balances.

CAPRICORN MAN—CAPRICORN WOMAN

There is every chance of this being a good partnership, but it is not one made in heaven, and the lovers will have to be prepared to make it a good relationship. Capricorns do perhaps need a little more imagination so that their romantic life will not settle into a boringly repetitious rut. Both will have to make compromises because neither is usually prepared to experiment or make a real attempt to enlarge his or her horizons.

These two will understand each other well enough, but they do take life awfully seriously and can become a bit boring if they are not careful. Capricorns are sensible, practical, realistic, and very cautious with money. They don't worship the stuff, but they do realize that it represents effort in our world, and they have a distinct tendency to tuck it away in odd corners and several bank accounts just in case a rainy day should come. Financially there won't be a lot to worry about with these two, but they'll do some worrying anyway because they can't help it.

Both believe completely in the virtue of hard work. Unceasing labors will bring their just reward, or that's how the Capricorn man sees things, and quite often he's dead right. His faithful lady nods her head sagely and happily counts their rising bank balance. She will make an excellent mother and wife (marriage has to happen for this pair simply because they would see anything else as second best and lacking security), and both will be proud of their spotless home and collections of goodness knows what. Capricorns tend to collect things; maybe it's all part of their search for security. There will be money for that vacation and the new car and so on—it all has to do with careful budgeting, something that is foreign to so many other signs.

Sexually this pair might well settle for comfortable familiarity rather than joyous passion. They can be a little pessimistic at times and also a bit gloomy. They both enjoy lovemaking but they are faithful, usually because they realize how inconvenient and unsatisfying affairs can be. There is a danger that the Capricorn man will become rather set in his ways as he gets older, and his female counterpart is not likely to do a lot to keep him young.

He's a strong man in his way, don't get that wrong. He is an upholder of laws and conventions and is likely to think the good old days were far better than anything happening now, and as for the younger generation. . . . Capricorns must work at keeping flexible and open-minded and bright. Sure, life's serious, but it doesn't have to be somber.

CAPRICORN MAN—AQUARIUS WOMAN

A far from easy relationship because the Aquarius woman tends to drift gently on the surface of life, while the Capricorn man just keeps on digging and digging into it. She's a more detached person who on the surface seems to lack some of the warmth of human kindness. Capricorn is sensible, practical, very hard-working, and dedicated to being successful. She's the sort of woman who will value his mind much more than his millions.

Aquarius isn't averse to a comfortable home life, but she isn't terribly keen on being dishwasher, bedmaker, and kitchen maid. This fellow does have a tendency to expect her to be all these things, and to be thrifty and frugal too.

There could be quarrels if he thinks she is not taking either him or his ambitions seriously enough. Her career will always have to stay in the background. He's sensible and sentimental (an interesting combination) and at the same time has a dash of romanticism in him, but he isn't nearly as sociable and fun-loving as she. She enjoys traveling, new experiences, and excitement much more than he does. She doesn't worry much about money and spends as she wishes without thinking about tomorrow. This will irritate Capricorn no end, as will her insistence on her personal freedom. She's a dreamer and she's curious, with a positive passion for improving her mind by the study of languages, sciences, and arts. She lives in the future, while he lives in the present or even the past. Thus there is not a lot of commonality here.

Affection is more likely than passion. The unconventional Aquarian lady doesn't like regular lovemaking in the same way at the same time and in the same place, while this is deeply comforting to Capricorn, who does, however, feel deeply about a lot of things. It won't be an easy partnership; a long cheerful affair would be the best bet.

One thing about him, he's determined, and Aquarius won't find it easy to shake him off if she decides to. Yes, he gets worried and depressed quite often, while she seems to sail blithely on. She could do quite a lot to help him in this area by keeping him on an even keel. He often sees the gloomy side of life and is pessimistic about success in any sphere, while all the time working hard to be successful. He can be critical too, but this won't cut any ice with this woman; she'll just carry on in her splendid detached Aquarian way.

CAPRICORN MAN—PISCES WOMAN

This is a fascinating partnership: the incredibly changeable Piscean with her deeply emotional response to everything and the practical, sensible Capricornian, who tends to think things out and then work hard to achieve his ambitions.

He can provide the security and reassurance that this remarkable lady needs, but she is not the easiest woman in the world to live with. She is charming, elegant, exasperating, and lovely and cannot make up her mind. She can be mortally wounded by a glance and turned on by another. She does not know her own mind and yet she is the most intuitive person in the Zodiac.

Sexually things could go very well indeed. Pisces wants to give herself and Capricorn is sexy and demanding. He is happiest when he's busy, so she would be wise to keep finding him little jobs to do. One thing, though, that Capricorn may never learn is that despite her sweetness Pisces has a gift for getting her own way, and she might just manipulate him very cunningly into the channels she wants him to go in. It's more a gift she has than any devious and wicked intent.

She will make her man the center of her existence, and this is precisely what Capricorn wants—an important point of contact between them. He will, however, have to learn to treat her more as an equal than he tends to do, or she could get depressed. She does in fact get depressed rather easily because she's so damned sensitive, but she always seems to survive.

She is a spendthrift, so this will also irritate the cautious and thrifty Capricorn. She seems to be careful with the cash one minute and then, when the mood takes her, she is crazily extravagant—but always charming. Then she'll burst into tears, and who could resist a Piscean weeping on his shoulder and holding his head on her breast (a favorite Piscean ploy that is usually successful)? Capricorn will never really understand how this lady thinks or feels, and when she goes silent he's going to feel very cut off and probably frustrated too.

Together Pisces and Capricorn can produce the two sides of a whole. She will provide the poetry and joy that is lacking in his life, while he will give her a firm foundation and the practicality that she so badly needs. If things don't work out, don't worry—Pisces will have another man looking after her within minutes; she's quite irresistible.

CAPRICORN MAN—ARIES WOMAN

There's more chance of these two having a loving affair than creating a real marriage. Capricorn is a romantic guy, but he's also cautious, slow, and sensible. No one ever said that about this lady. She has a driving style—she hates to be balked when she's made up her mind to do something. She has the constitution of a bulldozer, works very hard, and is about as sensitive as a bulldozer too.

Both are strong-willed and refuse to be ordered about. There will certainly be some first-class arguments if these two get together. There'll be lots of togetherness in bed, but in the living room there are likely to be problems—not least because Capricorn is a home-loving man and believes his woman should be too. In fact, Aries loves to get out and about, adores good parties, and thrives on meeting new and attractive men. She's a very sexy lady, and although Capricorn is equipped to look after her in that department, he will try to restrict her freedom. She'll kick over the traces and then anything can happen.

Sometimes this woman will be irritated by her gloomy man. She won't be terribly sympathetic when he's having one of his moods, but as she's a terrific optimist, she'll probably drag him out of his pessimistic thoughts willy-nilly.

This is an exciting, stimulating, slightly kooky lady; she's got terrific drive and determination, and she bounces back like a ball when things go wrong. She's ambitious and decidedly headstrong; she never knows when she's beaten. She cannot be bothered with details; she's blunt to the point of rudeness, and yet at heart she means well and is a romantic woman. Really she has to learn to loosen the reins a bit, not try to organize everything, and flow with life instead of fighting it, often when there's no need.

She will not like all the time Capricorn spends on his career, boosting his ego, becoming a success. She will expect him to want to be with her. In fact, she could be just too overwhelming for him— but given a bit of luck, she'll just be an ordinary Arian and not a super-Arian. She must understand his need for financial and emotional security and she must be prepared to give up a little of her pride and ambition and drive in the interest of creating a partnership.

This man has deep feelings, and mostly he's direct and honest, not prone to playing the field, although he does like pretty women. He'll shout and scream when this lady is extravagant, but secretly he'll admire her élan and her elegance and her sheer joy in life.

CAPRICORN MAN—TAURUS WOMAN

This looks like a good one. Both prefer to stay at home and cuddle rather than spend money having so-called fun. Security is important to this pair—a nice home and cash in the bank are of seminal importance. Taurus is a strong-willed lady with plenty of sex drive, and Capricorn is likely to take one look at her and decide she's the one. He'll still take a while to get around to proposing, but marriage it has to be.

He's an ambitious guy and he is going to want to be the boss. He's emotional and romantic in a slightly old-fashioned hearts-and-flowers way, but that suits this Taurean down to the ground. She'll feed him with goodies until he bursts, she'll adore him, and he'll be sensual and fulfilled. Most couples would find it all just a bit too much creamy-caramel-and-chocolate-eclair–style living, but Taurus and Capricorn can take a lot of that sort of togetherness.

Both are solid, dependable, conservative, devoted, and sentimental. They were lucky to find each other! It would be a great business partnership too, but don't expect too many moments of ecstasy—that sort of thing is likely to be mistrusted by this twosome.

On the outside there's a certain coolness apparent in this relationship, but it really is only skin deep. A few glasses of champagne and a tear-jerker of a movie are the best sport for this pair.

Don't assume however that this is just a superficial physical relationship. Capricorn is capable of deep emotional responses. Another sign might stretch him more, challenge him to grow spiritually, but even if communication is difficult at times, he will be dedicated and devoted to his family. He's more likely to prove his love than voice it. He needs the security that this woman can give him, the feeling that she's there to back him up and give him the stable home life he needs so badly if he's going to become a billionaire. In return he'll be there if and when the going gets rough. He's a tolerant man. The biggest danger is that this pair could become rather rigid in their views as they get older. It would be wise to get out and about more, travel, try to take in other opinions, and refrain from being dogmatic and having a fixed opinion on everything even if really neither know much about the subject.

At times Capricorn will be too cautious for this lady, and she'll get jealous, probably without reason. They should try to play this jealousy down—and count their blessings day by day.

CAPRICORN MAN—GEMINI WOMAN

Only the rare couple is going to make this partnership work. The volatile, changeable, stimulating Gemini woman is likely to find the Capricorn man too staid, too boring, too cautious, and too reserved. Frankly it'll be a miracle if they get to a second date at all.

These two really could not be more different. He's industrious and believes in success through hard work. She's a great communicator, a flirt, a bit superficial in some ways, but great fun. She loves to be the center of attention. If she really wants this guy, she's got a lot of hard work to do to get to grips with his deeper, more emotional response to the same set of stimuli. He is cautious; financially he demands security, a nice growing bank balance, a home where he can relax and putter about doing odd jobs. She tends to think about today and to hell with tomorrow—she might get hit by a thunderbolt, so let's have fun now.

Sexually there certainly could be plenty of immediate attraction, but it is likely to be short-lived. She's too capricious, to quick for him. In fact, Gemini thinks so fast she sometimes actually seems to be emotional. But she never is; she's cold and factual even if she kids herself at times that she's passionate. She's willful, charming, often genuinely delightful, but she needs continual stimulus and excitement of the sort that Capricorn is not likely to be equipped to provide.

She tends to make extremely rapid decisions, while Capricorn takes a long time to weigh things up. He's more possessive too, so if these two get together he's going to be continually jealous, even though that is not really in his nature to any marked extent. She will be irritated by his gloomy and pessimistic approach to some things. She's a perennial optimist who loves to laugh and indeed lives to laugh. She needs a lighthearted, jolly man who does crazy, impulsive things.

All this will appall a sober Capricornian. How can she possibly not take life seriously? After all, *he* knows life is a serious business. He's got plenty of problems, tends to worry over them, so certainly this lady could lighten his load—when she's around, that is.

In many respects these two would be good for each other; they could create a balance of opposites, and this is how a few couples do put things together and then keep them that way. Incidentally this woman can spend money with the abandon of a Piscean, even if a lot of the things she buys are for her lover or her friends. She's just a bit too selfish for this man, who longs to devote himself to an appreciative lady.

CAPRICORN MAN—CANCER WOMAN

This relationship is likely to be an enigma, not least to those involved in it. These two are complete opposites, and yet there certainly could be sexual attraction, and there is no doubt that the relationship could work out well.

The deeply sensitive Cancerian woman—emotional, wayward, easily hurt—is going to have to come to terms with this man's determination to be successful in his career. He believes in hard work leading to success, and she must learn not to be hurt if at times he seems to put success before togetherness. She seeks his attention. She recognizes that money is important and, if she's wise, will restrain her extravagant impulses. He in turn should work hard at telling her he loves her. That won't be easy for this man. He should also realize that Cancer needs a strong man and he should try to give her at least some of the attention she craves.

She will certainly look after her man when it comes to creature comforts, and he will appreciate this. Little luxuries and a cosy welcoming home are important to him. Beneath a less demonstrative surface this also is a man easily hurt, who needs the security of a steady, continuing flame of love and trust. At times he will become moody and withdrawn and unsure of himself, and Cancer has the ability to sense this. There can be many moments of shared joy and understanding without words, but it would be good for Capricorn to be persuaded that words have their place and should not be scorned as an inadequate medium to express his feelings.

If that all sounds a bit heavy, it needn't be. There'll be lots of fun, and Cancer can do a lot to ease her man up, to teach him to laugh and take things as they come. Sexually both can be a little shy, so real togetherness in bed is important to help them over the times when things don't seem to be going quite as smoothly as they think they should be. Capricorn does have a tendency to be demanding and jealous and possibly overbearing. This is something he must resist or the relationship will take a sharp downward turn, and that would be a great pity because these two have a great deal going for them.

Cancer has a tendency to daydream, to fantasize, but there is undoubted intuitive ability. This woman really does feel things rather than think them out. This won't always make for easy communication with the slower and more thoughtful and patient Capricorn man.

CAPRICORN MAN—LEO WOMAN

Leo extravagance could be a stumbling block because Capricorn will be hard pushed to recognize that it is merely an indication of a big heart and a loving nature.

This is a serious guy with a moody disposition who needs a secure home. He is not likely to approve of this flamboyant, sexy lady who likes men and the big gesture. He wants to take control of the relationship, but so does she. The result, fairly obviously, is conflict that could almost assume warlike proportions at times. The Leo woman is likely to deliberately do things to annoy her man and then refuse to recognize that she is being unreasonable. Both value security, for different reasons. For Leo it is a clear demonstration of power and success. For Capricorn it proves that he is on the right track and gives him the security he so badly needs. He indeed has a tendency to be overcautious. She is a perennial optimist who feels that life will be good to her—and she's usually right.

Capricorn may well admire her taste and yet be horrified by the way she spends to improve his home or dress up for him. He could perhaps do with a little more humor in his makeup or a little more lightness in his life style. Leo could do with a little less ego and a little less rigidity and selfishness. She *knows* she's right; Capricorn only *thinks* he is.

Sexually this woman wants more fireworks than Capricorn is likely to produce. She adores the unexpected, mystery trips, gifts for no apparent reason—she isn't going to get much of any of this sort of thing from a man who values consistency and order and law. But if she wants him, then this lady can twist him around her little finger. A sweet smile and a word of love, and he'd probably kiss her feet. If at times he starts ordering her about, she must learn to nod happily and then go her own way without ordering him about in turn or refusing point blank. As long as he's appearing to call the tune, Capricorn will be happy; the results aren't going to bother him too much.

Both know quality when they see it, so the home will be elegant. Leo will be very taken by a new exotic car. She wants proof of his love, and not just in bed. It may or may not be forthcoming—frankly, it depends on the mood she can create in her man. There will be diffcult days (to put it mildly), but togetherness is likely to grow as the years go by.

CAPRICORN MAN—VIRGO WOMAN

There's every chance of this being a good, stable relationship, for these are two people on broadly the same wavelength who will appreciate each other's virtues and strengths.

Virgo is sensible, cautious, continually frustrated by the fact that the rest of the world is not as efficient as she is. She believes in hard work, as indeed does Capricorn, so there is a strong bond here. Both need to be appreciated, and even if he should at times get a bit bossy, his pretty Virgo will soon sort him out. Both place great stress on their home and the secure base it provides for their forays into what they see essentially as an unfriendly world.

Virgo will look after the home extremely well; it will be spotless, and food will be good and elegantly prepared. But she doesn't respond too well to criticism, and Capricorn is rather prone to telling her and anyone else in earshot how the world should be run. He'd be wise to moderate this little character trait. But this is a highly intelligent lady who uses her excellent mind rather than her emotions. Some have suggested that she's a cold woman, but this is not quite true; she can be as sexy as they come if everything is perfect, and she has a natural respect and consideration for others that this guy is likely to stimulate.

The partnership could become one based more on deep affection than real passion, but since most other aspects of the union will work well, it probably won't matter all that much. Capricorn is a dependable, honest, if slightly gloomy guy. He takes life seriously, as does this woman. A cheery night on the town every so often would be a good idea to prevent a rigidity and a habitualness and a cosy convenience creeping gradually into the relationship.

Capricorn is, of course, ambitious, and Virgo will give him every possible support. She won't mind his missing meals or tearing abroad, provided she knows he's making a success of his job. She will have little to fear from his straying, but she could have a tendency to nag that he's likely to take in good part—initially, anyway, he'll regard it as a sign of love and caring. Later she might irritate him a little, but he's a relatively easy man to get on with, except when he's in one of his periodic morbid moods. Yes, he can become a snob, and this will certainly not be approved of by the more socially conscious Virgo, who will often take the part of the underdog or the oppressed. A pleasing, rewarding partnership for this lucky couple.

CAPRICORN MAN—LIBRA WOMAN

This will be a difficult, insecure sort of a relationship. It can work, but there will be some bad times for both partners before they reach any sort of harmony. And this business of a balanced harmonic relationship is absolutely crucial for Libra, who is charming, gay, elegant, fun-loving, beauty-loving, and often a bit lightweight in her responses.

Capricorn, on the other hand, is a serious, slightly gloomy type who will certainly not approve of her partygoing, her flirting, and her extravagance. He is a worrier, a worker, a critic, a man who demands quality and expects to have to work hard to be successful. He's ambitious. This lady flows through life, spends without a qualm, and doesn't worry much about tomorrow. She will need lots of assurance that her man loves and needs her, and she is not likely to get much of this from a man who is essentially a performer rather than a talker like her.

Sexually Capricorn will find this woman a stunner, but he's also going to find her too self-centered and selfish and perhaps unresponsive to his needs. Frankly, Libra is likely to start employing her considerable wiliness on any other handy males.

Really both are insecure and need a solid, comfortable home background, but the stronger Capricorn will find that his lady's insecurity shows in a nervousness and sometimes a rather high-strung way of living. She expects to be treated as an equal partner in every way, while he is more likely to want a little woman to hug him when he staggers home from work, and then rush in with his pipe and slippers. She's much more likely to be out when he gets home, even if she doesn't have a career that she has refused to give up just because he expects her to.

Capricorn is likely to be somewhat insensitive to the more subtle requirements of this woman, so this is going to be the sort of partnership sensible people avoid. However, love does not always obey the dictates of reason, so if Cupid strikes, be prepared for plenty of frustration and irritation on both sides. Life in a prison camp might be easier—but potentially marginally less rewarding!

Capricorn will be proud of Libra's looks and charm and in return could provide the security she needs—if only she will admit this to herself and then be mature enough to act accordingly. Three cheers for love.

CAPRICORN MAN—SCORPIO WOMAN

There will be difficulties, particularly for Capricorn, but there is every chance that this will be a fulfilling and satisfying relationship, not least in the bedroom.

Scorpio is likely to be attracted to this guy because of his air of reliability and steadiness. She herself looks uncomplicated and straightforward but is in fact a complex, emotional, deeply intense person who needs a great deal of love, who understands sex in all its aspects, and who is often very jealous. Fortunately, her jealousy—which undermines many relationships with other signs—is not likely to be too severely tested by Capricorn, who will be faithful and loving and forbearing.

She will be jealous in a way because he devotes a lot of his effort and time to his career and reaching the top in it, but at least she will know that he is working as much for her and any children they may have as for himself. At times she will positively demand his attention, and he'd better give it or else. Financial security is crucial for these two, but Scorpio is demanding and imaginative when it comes to sex. A happy love life will produce happiness for this pair in many other ways. There will be quarrels because Scorpios do feel even more intensely than Capricorns, who tend to hide their true depth of feeling—but togetherness is more likely to prove itself truly satisfying than either expects. If at times one or the other partner withdraws into him- or herself for a time and becomes moody or even broody, then that's the price they must pay for a passionate partnership rather than a placid one.

Scorpio has to have power; it's an elemental drive with her. She will decide whether her man spends time with her or not, and even if she grumbles, it is up to her to make the decision about how much of him she wants to see!

Both are disciplined, reliable, and industrious. No one starves when this pair is around. Sometimes she will feel that he fails to understand the depth of her feelings—she's right, he doesn't, but he tries. The best way to cheer him up is to seduce him, make love to him. He tends to forget his troubles when he gets a little physical exercise. A nice home with the little luxuries this man requires seems almost inevitable. At times he might seem a little stingy and then suddenly he hands his woman the keys to a new car. Living together for these two can be hard work—but it is worth it.

CAPRICORN MAN—SAGITTARIUS WOMAN

Frustration is likely to be one of the keynotes of this partnership. Sagittarius will refuse to be tied down by this more demanding man, while he will try to turn her into the person he wants—someone prepared to love and wait upon him and concern herself with every detail of his life. This is just too boring for Sagittarius, who likes to get out and about and isn't going to be tied down by anyone—particularly not by a boring old Capricorn.

Of course this is unfair, because Capricorn is reliable, steady, honest, and intensely hard-working. Unfortunately, Sagittarius is not likely to see it this way, and anyway they'll probably never get past their third date. She will either forget it or be so late that he gets the message there and then. If he doesn't, then love may be in the air and these two have got some hard work on their hands to produce a balanced and harmonious partnership.

Sexually Capricorn likes a passionate woman. Sagittarius is certainly extravagant and at times irresponsible and in her way passionate—but she isn't averse to spreading that passion around—which is a nice way of saying she likes men. She might just spend the housekeeping money on a crate of champagne and then be genuinely upset when he is furious and does not applaud her cleverness. "But darling, it was a bargain, reduced by thirty percent. What could I do? I thought you'd be so pleased." Capricorn will be gnashing his teeth and wishing he'd shacked up with the girl next door with the pigtails and walleye rather than the elegant Sagittarian. He doesn't find it easy to tell this lady he loves and needs her, which is probably fortunate—she might conclude he doesn't and go hunting somewhere else.

However, Sagittarius is an optimist, and this could be good for the rather gloomy Capricorn, who tends to see the pessimistic side of things even when he's doing well in his career and there is plenty of cash in the bank, as there probably will be. At times they will experience togetherness, but probably not often enough to make the relationship as satisfying as both want it to be; their natures are just too different. Incidentally, it's no use trying to boss Sagittarius around; she just won't wear it. She believes in equal shares in everything, and the well-known Capricornian bossiness will just be laughed at. And that ain't good for the Capricorn ego. It makes him even more insecure than he really is, although he tries to hide this anyway.

Life won't be easy for this couple—in some ways they are good for each other, but perhaps only in small doses.

CAPRICORN WOMAN—CAPRICORN MAN

This could be a good relationship, but don't expect bliss and joy. Two Capricorns are likely to understand each other well enough, but they do have a tendency to settle into a rut, and life could become both a bit serious and a bit dull.

Both are realistic and sensible, careful with money, and pretty ambitious. Capricorns believe in steady, hard work, but they will have to reach an understanding about career prospects. This woman will have to take second place to her man's ambition much of the time, but she may be doing well in her own career. She will make a good mother and homemaker, but there will be the occasional clash because both invariably think they know best. Capricorns can also be a little pessimistic and become withdrawn and proud as they get older.

Sexually they are likely to settle for comfortable familiarity, and fun could be hard to find, but of course there are consolations. They are likely to achieve a nice home and money in the bank, and they might even venture abroad for vacations, although Capricorns tend to think that a little too inconvenient or expensive.

Don't get the idea that Capricorns are difficult people, though at times they might get depressed. The Capricorn woman in particular might be better off with a more cheerful and outgoing partner, but at least she can be sure her male counterpart won't roam far from home. He is a man with a healthy sexual appetite, but mostly he is too sensible to start an affair, which he feels is too inconvenient. He might well become prominent in his profession, and it might be a good idea for his lady to persuade him to take the family out more often and be active in sports and a few community activities.

There is a danger that the Capricorn male in particular may become rigid in his views, set in his ways, a mutterer of clichés, a conservative in many things. He's a strong man and far from stupid, so with a little luck it can be explained to him and he might just see the sense of keeping a flexible and open mind about the many topics he is likely to pontificate on without truly knowing much about them.

This is not a combination made in heaven; it's one of those that can be made good. Capricorns have a lot going for them and should realize it, but they must also try at times not to be too intense, to keep things serious and yet not somber. A little more imagination is probably what these two need. Failing that, they should get drunk together once a month!

CAPRICORN WOMAN—AQUARIUS MAN

Not the easiest partnership, but certainly a fascinating combination with a lot of potential. Aquarius likes to get out and about and enjoy himself. He's kind, gentle, and fascinating. Some experts suggest that he's really on the wrong planet, but that's just the way he seems most of the time!

What he does have is a great talent for friendship, and he's great as a helper in a crisis because he genuinely cares about someone going through a difficult patch. He's not careful enough with cash for this lady, but because she will tuck some away there are unlikely to be any but temporary money embarrassments. Capricorn likes a steady, secure, well-ordered life, while Aquarius prefers the opposite—anything to avoid boredom, as far as he is concerned.

Perhaps strangely, he tends to be rather good at his job and demonstrates considerable efficiency and ability to engage everyone he comes into contact with and get them on his side. Capricorn is very ambitious for her man and herself, whereas he has hardly an ambitious or jealous bone in his body. He will, however, be impressed by her determination. He thinks big, but she'll be a very valuable sheet anchor for him when he decides it's time to save the world.

The freedom-loving Aquarian may find Capricorn a little dull in the bedroom, but then he is decidedly unconventional and often given to mystical speculations. He may indeed be a deeply religious man in an unconventional way. He isn't going to become a major tycoon and carry his woman to heights of financial or political glory. She'd like that, but she'll settle for slightly less . . . only slightly.

Oh, by the way, he is highly intelligent and at times very romantic. She likes the hearts-and-flowers bit, so this is a good meeting point. Will she be too boring for him? That depends on how much she is prepared to get off her bottom and join him in his fun activities or get him interested in skiing or skin-diving or yoga or chess. He's always thinking about the future, so find him some unusual or esoteric activity and he'll love it and whoever introduced him to it. One thing he might do is keep this lady from being so pessimistic, and that would be good. Each can learn from the other here, and quite a few Aquarians do whisk around the world working at this and that, even though Capricorn would think it all a little irresponsible. He doesn't worry about security, while she needs it very much indeed. Not an easy relationship, but potentially it could be a very rewarding one.

CAPRICORN WOMAN—PISCES MAN

This is likely to be a highly complex relationship, but it could prove successful in a minority of cases. Pisces is a curious mixture of the romantic, the weak, the sentimental, the sensitive, the charming, the mystic, and the impractical. Capricorn is sensible, practical, earthy, and not given to excessive emotional outbursts. At first glance they are as different as chalk and cheese. But opposites often do attract, and it is certainly possible for the virtues of both to be combined to offset the faults.

Pisces is a dreamer. He hardly manages to keep his feet on the ground at times. His emotions act on him in the same way the brain does on some others. He is changeable, spendthrift, gentle, unworldly, and at the same time often surprisingly successful. His intuition can only be wondered at sometimes, and he has a curious gift of being in the right place at the right time. He'll drive Capricorn wild, but she might just learn something from him.

Capricorn is certainly going to have to go more than halfway to keep this partnership going, but she may well decide that it is worth the effort. In bed she is likely to take the lead, and as Pisces is loving and has a deep wish to give of himself, this could be a most happy meeting ground.

He is likely to be the sort of man who prefers old houses, antiques, and frilly things (not necessarily for himself). He doesn't believe too strongly in the virtues of hard work, unlike his Capricornian mate. But he is sweet-tempered and it's awfully hard not to at least sympathize with him. He certainly needs a strong woman behind him, even though he's a good deal hardier than even he suspects. More Capricorns finish up in the mental hospital than Pisceans—perhaps they've all been looking after Pisceans!

One problem is that Capricorn needs reassurance and love, particularly if she is depressed, as she will be at times. Pisces might just not be there to hold her hand and assure her that everything is OK. Most of the time she will be doing the work of two, appearing twice as strong as she is while shrugging it off as if it were nothing at all. Incredible.

Pisces does have a slightly secretive side to his nature and at times just goes silent and cold. She'll get used to this even if she doesn't really know what is happening. He, too, gets black moods but usually he clicks out of them just when his lady is about to give up and go back to Mother. When things are going well, as they will be much of the time, life together could be great.

CAPRICORN WOMAN—ARIES MAN

This is a fascinating one. Capricorn is likely to be very impressed by this dynamic, passionate guy. She may well be impressed by the promise of security he seems to hold out—because she badly needs a stable, loving home life. But her commonsense attitude to life might just make her quickly realize that he is romantic, excitable, and too liberal with money.

What this means is that Capricorn is going to be torn between horror and admiration as she sees her Aries man tearing around. He's ambitious and so is she, but his ambition is not really channeled into making a fortune. He has to be meeting a challenge, to be out there taking the world on and winning. And he might just leave the spoils to someone else.

There will certainly be quarrels and disagreements, but they need not be serious ones. Sexually these two could well be compatible, even though Aries has a tendency to smile at pretty ladies. Capricorn could easily exhibit jealousy, but Aries will probably laugh it off and bring her a big bunch of red roses or some more original gift that she won't be able to resist. He'll change his job and seek new pastures whether they turn out to be greener or not, and she will be upset by this—but she will stick by her man. She believes in hard work, while he works hard in short bursts.

Socially he'll be good for her because he'll keep her on her toes, get her off her bottom and out of the house. Her home is very important to this lady, as is her family. They could meet at work.

At times Capricorn may become withdrawn, morbid, and self-centered, but Aries will take this in stride. There's no way he will be dominated by her, but he will appreciate the way she manages to put a little cash aside from time to time—it's all part of her security need. This relationship will never be dull, and this lady could prevent him from making serious blunders through overeagerness, while he will coax her into having more fun than she can imagine.

Capricorn tends to think things out and then act emotionally, a curious business when seen from the outside. Sometimes there's a sort of negativity about her. She wants to be sociable and often finishes up alone; she wants to have fun and doesn't manage it. She must come to terms with her neuroses, her fears, and learn to take each day as it comes. This is a clever lady, often good at a number of things. She sees no reason to compliment her Aries on things he isn't as good at as she, but she might be wise to do so—he's basically a simple, uncomplicated guy.

CAPRICORN WOMAN—TAURUS MAN

These two were probably made for each other. Physical attraction could be instantaneous, and as both would prefer to stay cosily at home rather than go partying, there'll be lots of cuddling and cooing.

Both are cautious with money and are sure that security, stability, and common sense are all-important. Capricorn will work hard for her man and her marriage (which seems inevitable for these two), while Taurus, although he is more lazy, will also knuckle down when he can see a positive gain ensuing. He may have artistic tendencies and will certainly expect his woman to look good, smell good, and cook well.

They may well have an interest in old *objets d'art* or in collecting—often with an eye to the profit that may accrue. The biggest danger—if that's the right word—is that they may finish up so contented and plump and satisfied that they'll never do anything together except eat out. Boredom and complacency could set in; even their sex life is satisfying and passionate.

Yes, these two are romantic in a slightly old-fashioned sort of way. Both have a real capacity for affection as much as for dynamic love. How could Taurus possibly resist his Capricorn lady's soulful eyes and tempting lips? Everyone is going to say this is an ideal match, and of course they'll be right. He has a sense of fun and humor too, so don't think their life together will be dour or somber all the time. He isn't too keen on strenuous sports, but that suits her fine. And at times he'll suddenly be wildly extravagant, but she will probably be the recipient of his kindness, so she needn't worry too much. She would be wise not to try to cut down on or criticize his little luxuries. He needs them to bolster his ego, and although he is certainly not a spendthrift, he likes to think he's living dangerously. Taurus has a great capacity for self-deception, and his lady had better realize this or she's not going to really understand what makes him tick.

By the way, Taurus can be unreasonably jealous at times. With this lady he's unlikely to have much reason for it, but it may come out in unexpected ways. She'd better not flirt too much when he's around or he'll suddenly act like a wounded bull elephant. And for goodness' sake, she should never let him know that he isn't the world's leading expert on the subject of his choice. The Taurean ego—lovely man though he is—can easily be wounded. Is he stubborn? He certainly is. Just agree with him!

CAPRICORN WOMAN—GEMINI MAN

A doubtful prospect except in the most unusual circumstances. These two are so different in their responses that it will be difficult to find a common meeting ground.

Gemini is just too lively, irresponsible, and changeable for this essentially serious lady, who needs plenty of reassurance and security and love and affection. A short affair might do no harm, but anything longer will be agony. Gemini makes decisions on impulse, while Capricorn thinks things out slowly and, although she can be emotional, does her best to make rational decisions.

He is a complex man, changeable, easily depressed, easily elated—and he is not a great budgeter, although he can be surprisingly efficient at work if he decides he ought to be. Gemini plays many roles and is good at most of them. He likes to get out and about, loves parties, flirts outrageously with every pretty girl, and hates being trapped in any situation—a marriage situation with a Capricorn would be a classic prison situation for him.

Sexually Capricorn will expect Gemini to do things her way, while he will expect her to adapt to suit him. He's too capricious and indecisive for her and he won't really appreciate her faithful, honest approach. He works hard at times and then lazes. Capricorn believes in steady, diligent work reaping its just reward in due course. That's plain old boring for Gemini. He needs a woman who'll give him as good as he hands out, not a sensitive lady cast in the traditional mold!

There is something essentially boyish about Gemini, and he may never grow up. This is part of his charm, but it can be distinctly wearing. Some suggest he is a Jekyll and Hyde character, but this is an oversimplification. He means well but is selfish and insists on doing things his way and going his own way. He likes sparkle and razzle-dazzle and is unlikely to appreciate the virtues of the more elegant and thoughtful Capricorn. Financially he'll be irritated by her safety-first approach, while she will wonder how he can be so irresponsible. Of course, any partnership can work, but for these two there will need to be a long period of adjustment fraught with frustration and almost despair at times. And then, two more mature people could have a workable relationship, she soothing his mercurial temperament and he encouraging her when things look bleak.

Capricorn tends to worry too much, and he'll help her loosen up. In return he would benefit from a stable home life—he enjoys a bit of mothering, as most men do.

CAPRICORN WOMAN—CANCER MAN

Cancer isn't the easiest man to live with, so this partnership is going to depend a lot on whether Capricorn is prepared to put up with his moods and sulkiness.

Capricorn is no angel; she has her dark moments. She's sensible and practical, and she needs plenty of love and security and reassurance that she is needed and appreciated. Cancer is just the sort of guy to provide all this because he is impressed by energy and common sense and he isn't too proud to bask in his woman's business success—or spend her money.

He is an intuitive and sensitive fellow who might well be attracted to someone who appears to promise him a solid base and a home. He's often dreamy and otherworldly and romantic. Capricorn might well upset him by telling him so. This might make him withdraw into himself and sulk. Financially, at least, there shouldn't be too many problems. Capricorn is a saver, a tucker away of money in odd corners and odd accounts. Cancer is more ready to spend, but he is surprisingly good at making money. There could be trouble if Capricorn tried to take over control of the relationship, and this could happen—he expects to be treated as an equal even if most of the time he doesn't act like one.

Sexually Capricorn may have to persuade herself to think romantically to safisfy this sensitive and perceptive man. It's no use counting sheep while making love with him, and expecting him not to notice it. A careful balance will have to be worked out, and this certainly will take time and patience.

It is possible that Cancer will just not be strong enough or tough enough to cope with this lady. He has a tendency to scuttle for cover like a crab when pressed, but this is not through cowardice. It's merely because he cannot bear discord or see why everyone should not live in harmonic friendship. He is easily hurt and may have learned to disguise his feelings merely to survive in our not-too-pleasant little world.

His home is as important to him as it is to the Capricorn woman, so this is a point of important contact. Capricorn is a sticker, a determined lady, and if it is love there will be no one more faithful than she. She will be critical—it is almost impossible for a Capricorn not to be—but she probably doesn't realize just how hurtful or critical she is. Mutual bliss may extract a high price in other areas for this pair; only they can decide if the price is too high.

CAPRICORN WOMAN—LEO MAN

This partnership is likely to be a terrific success or a disaster. Leo is certainly going to be attracted to this personable lady who exudes class. He cuts quite a dash too—money no object, the best of everything. Hi, big shot!

Capricorn likes being treated like royalty; she isn't quite convinced that fun is a thing one should have, but she'll go along with the King and his friends. She rather tends to believe one should work hard for the sake of working hard, whereas he believes work is to provide the wherewithal to enjoy himself.

Sexually Capricorn may not prove as outgoing as Leo would like; she might find him too sexy and too much of a big head. He is the greatest and needs to be told so. The more frequently he is outrageously flattered, the better. He knows it's outrageous, but he loves it anyway, and his woman had better learn quickly that the way to his heart and wallet is through a gracious compliment. He is a generous, kind guy and nothing will be too much trouble for those he loves or regards. He isn't likely to need to demonstrate much jealousy with Capricorn, because she's strictly a one-man woman—but of course it has to be a serious affair. Both are strong people in their different ways, so clearly those ways need to coincide. Leo can be led but not ordered about, and he certainly doesn't like being criticized, as this lady is prone to do, even though he probably deserves it.

There will be dramatic scenes for this pair, with Leo being dominating and bombastic and Capricorn being proud and stubborn. Friends and neighbors will be wise to insure property and persons if things really reach fever point. As a balance to this, Capricorn is trusting and determined, and if the union is working she'll be very supportive and even motherly if that is what he needs. She has a tendency to measure success by the size of the bank balance and her jewel chest, but with luck Leo might even satisfy her in this direction.

Capricorn rarely falls for a guy overnight, but Leo's overtures are often pitched at a level she well understands—long-distance calls from Tokyo and Buenos Aires, red roses, wine and beach houses (probably borrowed). From time to time he'll relapse into bouts of total laziness or depression, and although these are disconcerting, they seldom last long. Yes, he's temperamental, but he's all man. Life won't be easy, but Capricorn could do a lot worse. Both have to learn to give up cherished opinions and be a little more humble if they want to stay together.

CAPRICORN WOMAN—VIRGO MAN

There is every chance of a successful and enjoyable partnership in a slightly straight-laced penny-pinching sort of a way. It's not everyone's cup of tea, but then we're not talking about everyone—just two people in love, or contemplating love, because both tend to be cautious with their affections even if they are very attracted at first sight.

Virgo is sometimes called cold, but this is not really true; he is certainly reserved, but he has an advanced social conscience and is always ready to put himself out for someone in trouble. But he does discriminate between real hardship cases and phony ones. He tends to be critical and is more or less permanently frustrated because he expects everything to run perfectly and efficiently, and of course things seldom happen in this way.

Financially this is likely to be a particularly successful union. Capricorn is careful, knows the value of money, and tends to judge success by its practical and visible rewards. Virgo is also cautious when it comes to digging deep. Sex may well be good but is unlikely to dominate all the other togethernesses that life creates for these two. Don't expect fireworks in bed.

Both are workers, make no mistake about that. No other combination in the Zodiac will produce such a diligent pair, almost dedicated to hard work and the rewards that both believe will come from effort. In most cases one or the other will be successful in his or her profession, but there could be slight dissention when Virgo expects his lady to become a busy housewife. Not that she won't do that very well; the house will be neat, tidy, and spotlessly clean.

This is a disciplined guy who believes in improving his already sharp mind. He seems to need to amass information about all sorts of recondite subjects. The Capricorn woman is more likely to collect rare china or something else that provides her with security and genuinely interests her.

Both will appreciate the efforts of the other to make life more pleasant and convenient. There is a danger that their traveling will be done in books and their excitement come from the movies or TV, but these two are likely to prefer being together rather than apart. This is a partnership likely to last a lifetime and to deepen with the years, so life should be uncomplicated and pleasurable for this remarkably compatible pair.

CAPRICORN WOMAN—LIBRA MAN

This is likely to be a difficult relationship because Libra is a very sociable guy but Capricorn is much less interested in party-going. She's a much more intense and serious person, and it may well be that she will have to adapt to his way of life if she really likes him.

Libra has plenty of charm and he likes the girls. One thing he must always have is a harmonious relationship with his woman. Arguments are just not for him; he'll walk out. Capricorn also has a distinct tendency to be critical, and this isn't likely to go down well either. Sexually he would be good for her because he understands how to give pleasure and wants to please, but he may well be too self-centered and selfish. Marriage or a lengthy affair will be difficult even in the unlikely event that he has no other affairs.

He is a flirt, no two ways about it, and he isn't very interested in a nice home—he'd prefer a pad. He likes decorative ladies rather than good cooks and yet he has a social conscience that forces him—a man who'll walk a mile to avoid discord—to launch himself into the fray on behalf of someone he decides is being shabbily treated. He's no coward but he isn't quite as keen on hard work as Capricorn. She truly believes that industry will be crowned with success, and quite often it will be. He wants an equal partner, someone to share with, and he isn't averse to sharing her earnings either. Capricorn's ability to save and generate cash is likely to be severely tested at some stage of this relationship.

There are always some Libras and Capricorns who make a go of things, but they might well admit that it would have been useful to know beforehand what they were letting themselves in for. Too much closeness makes life more difficult for him instead of easier.

The Libra man finds it difficult to make up his mind. Perhaps this has something to do with his need to balance everything, whether it's emotions or ideations (it certainly isn't budgets), and this will irritate the Capricorn woman almost beyond belief. He'll cheerfully let his woman make the decisions, but in fact she would be unwise to do this too often because she might find herself stuck with making them all, and she won't relish this—particularly as he isn't going to smile cheerily if things go wrong.

There are always some Libras and Capricorns who make a go of things, but they might well admit that it would have been useful to know beforehand what they were letting themselves in for.

CAPRICORN WOMAN—SCORPIO MAN

Scorpio and Capricorn will have some desperately hard times, but they might decide it is even worse being apart. This is likely to be either a deeply fulfilling and successful affair or it could turn out to be a total failure.

Living with a Scorpio man will be no picnic. He hides his emotions, has firm views, and must be the boss. Capricorn will resist being taken over by this domineering man. And when she resists, he might get jealous and accuse her of loving someone else (which is ridiculous because she's a one-man woman). This jealousy is a Scorpionic trait that will cause almost any woman deep distress, but he just cannot seem to help himself. He will expect her to be totally devoted and wrapped up in him and his affairs. Most of the time she will accept this, but even the worm turns sometimes.

This isn't to imply that Capricorn is weak; she is definitely not, but she will go more than halfway to meet someone who loves and needs her. She requires security, and this is certainly something that Scorpio can offer.

Financially there are not likely to be any serious problems, because both are careful with money and want security. They could even become overcautious in this respect, missing out on a lot of fun because they think the nearest volcano (8,000 miles away) might erupt.

Sexually things could be very good. Both need lots of lovemaking, and in bed Capricorn will understand that Scorpio's possessiveness is one way he demonstrates his love. The sheer passion at times could become too much for anyone. Capricorn lives to give and Scorpio to take. It's all terribly intense and both will suffer. He doesn't really understand his own intense responses, so how can his woman possibly come to grips with them too? There is something slightly mysterious about him, and this attracts the ladies. But if he makes a commitment, he is likely to stick, even if at times he wishes he could just walk away.

There will be plenty of drama in this union. But don't worry, between the acts there'll be fun and pleasure and joy, and although things will get close to the breaking point, in most cases there will be just enough love between these two to prevent that final parting. Scorpio will always subconsciously be worried that Capricorn will leave him. She could help him a lot by reassuring him from time to time—provided, of course, that she's still around!

CAPRICORN WOMAN—SAGITTARIUS MAN

This partnership could work provided Capricorn doesn't become too irritated by Sagittarius' impulse to take a gamble from time to time. This impulse is not just confined to the ponies—he might risk their money, their house, their all on some extraordinary business project or accept a job in Peking on the spur of the moment without thinking about all the consequences.

Capricorn is going to need a lot of patience and understanding (not to mention love) when he starts flirting with her friends, comes home drunk at 2 A.M., and forgets her birthday. She hates insecurity, and that is certainly a state she will be in when this exciting, volatile, and charming fellow is around.

He likes constant change; he cannot stand to be in one spot for long, and he has lots of buddies and contacts. However, he will not be dominated by this lady. She has a strong character and will try, but no dice. If she persists in trying to tell him what to do, he'll be gone. He's an awfully difficult guy to change. He's extravagant and often rather irresponsible, while she is careful, cautious, and thrifty. Sexually he likes variety, while she seeks deep, passionate responses—she may not get them from her Sagittarius.

This is a real attraction of opposites, and each could help the other provided a little understanding and patience are exercised. He is seldom on time for a date; she always is. She is likely to be conservatively and elegantly dressed. He will turn up in sweater and gumboots straight from a fishing trip. He's a great talker, funny, fun-loving, a great partygoer. Capricorn's idea of fun is to curl up with her loved one on a big couch in front of a real tear-jerker of a movie with a bag of nuts, a box of chocolates, and several hankies.

She will create a secure and charming home because she badly needs some sort of security (particularly with this guy), and she'd be wise to insist on separate bank accounts and expensive jewelry that she can hock if need be. Financially she's going to have to take a strong hand, or the creditors will even make their way to Peking.

Sagittarius is rather difficult to get to the altar; he has dying relatives all over the place who need him. He does enjoy traveling and, strangely enough, he does have a lucky streak. He's the sort who walks out on his job without another to go to and then bumps into someone who offers him one at twice the salary. Capricorn will be horrified by the whole business, but her optimistic lover knows it's only part of life's rich pattern.

AQUARIUS WOMAN—AQUARIUS MAN

Aquarians are pretty easy to get on with compared with most people, and these two will be able to create a good partnership because they are mentally compatible and make ideal companions, even if affection rather than deep passion might keep the relationship going.

Both are so busy it's surprising they find time to meet at all, but with a little luck they'll travel and go partying together rather than apart. Some people think that the Aquarius woman in particular is a rather cold, detached person, but this is not really true. She simply does not suffer fools gladly, and she is likely to be as warm and loving with her man as anyone could wish. Both are perhaps too logical and sensible and reasonable to get totally involved in an emotional scene, but in a world like ours this might be a good thing.

The Aquarius man is not too good with the cash; he tends to spend it! And he'll certainly be aided and abetted by his lady love. One of them may have to suddenly be sensible when someone comes to take away the furniture. The Aquarius woman is not likely to be satisfied being only a mother and a housewife. She reckons there's more to life than diapers and vacuuming and cooking. Her man will see her point of view and encourage her to follow her career and involve herself in hobbies and interests. Both expect their union to be an equal partnership.

They are excellent hosts, love gossiping with friends, and are always available to help out those with problems or in distress. Both are curious about everything and like to swap ideas and speculations. There are so many exciting things to do and discuss in the world that

Aquarians are rarely if ever bored, except of course by domestic chores. Don't expect a spotless house and gourmet meals.

It is particularly interesting that both have a thing about education. They have a deep-seated need to improve and stretch their already excellent minds. Esoteric subjects, night classes galore, languages—are all deemed worthy of effort. Books, records, and gifts are all used by Aquarians to expand their own and others' horizons. What all this means is that two Aquarians will never have a dull relationship. They are quite likely to be artistic in some way and want to help humanity even if in general they cannot stand individuals (some of whom they adore).

AQUARIUS WOMAN—PISCES MAN

This is likely to be a thorny relationship because the Pisces man is going to need constant displays of affection, which the Aquarius woman may not be prepared to make.

Aquarius lives for and in the future, while Pisces is romantic and sentimental and lives in the past too often. He is a private person, easily bruised, deeply emotional, terribly sensitive, almost psychic in his responses, undoubtedly intuitive, and rather difficult to live with. He's changeable to an alarming degree, withdrawn one minute and silly the next, gay and happy, then withdrawn and gloomy as the emotions wash across his being.

Aquarius is likely to find all this just too wearing. She hates arguments. He's too selfish in many ways, and yet at the same time he wants a woman to whom he can give himself totally.

He might also be shocked by this lady's unconventional responses to things. She might dress in a truly elegant but slightly shocking way, she cares not a jot for power or prestige, and she doesn't worry about money. Pisces can be even more irresponsible than she when it comes to cash, so there could be constant money problems unless a really determined effort is made to save and not squander. Sexually there could be misunderstandings, so perhaps a long drawn-out affair would be more successful than a lifetime commitment.

One thing to remember is that Pisces is a dreamer, the great fantasizer of the Zodiac, ever given to romantic speculations. Aquarius is much more likely to dream about the perfect Utopia she reckons must be close at hand for all humanity. This is something she will work for because she tends to be more moved and excited by the great sweep of ideas rather than individual problems, even though she responds to injustice or hardship in a more practical way than might be expected. She is an honest person, frank and even brutal at times wth a word of criticism. Pisces is much more devious, quite prepared to lie to achieve his ends and feel no remorse about it. There's something slightly vague about him much of the time, and yet it is hard to resist his little-boy-lost act, which is in fact only partly an act.

He seeks experience; he's always ready to go out, loves parties and theaters and expensive hotels and restaurants, wallows in luxury. He hates or loves on impulse and is much stronger than even he thinks. He might just surprise himself by coming up trumps in a real crisis. Neither of these two is a coward, although they may think they are.

AQUARIUS WOMAN—ARIES MAN

This is likely to be a rewarding relationship, provided the Aries man is prepared to take charge of the financial arrangements. The Aquarius woman is going to be very taken by this man—his enthusiasm, his loyalty, and his sheer nerve in emergencies. He is as keen on new things and new ideas as she is. He can be selfish at times, but she can usually handle this.

There will be difficulties if either party tries to force the other to do something, but there is certainly compatibility, and the chances of this partnership working are high. He likes to get out and about, and almost certainly enjoys a sporting challenge, and he appreciates the independent way his Aquarian manages things if he is not around for a while. He's a great arguer, and his whole life will be dominated by meeting challenges. He might change jobs a lot, but he is not really interested in power or financial success. He's certainly not lazy, but his work must continually stretch him or he'll move on—expecting his Aquarian partner to follow. She'll usually be happy to do so because she, too, enjoys new places, new excitements, and new faces.

Together these two can explore new areas of human consciousness and push into uncharted territory. Sometimes, when it looks as though Aries is becoming a jack of all trades and master of none, the undoubted mental gifts of Aquarius can put him on the right track. This guy does have a tendency to ignore details and let someone else do the clearing up while he gets on with the planning, but he'll improve in this respect as he gets older. At times he takes dreadful risks without turning a hair.

Aries can be demanding and jealous while at the same time expecting to behave as he likes, but the tactful and logical Aquarius can point this out to him, and after he's exploded, he'll probably see the justice of her comments. It's a lucky Arian who finds an Aquarian lady prepared to take him on—and usually beat him!

It is quite likely that there will be instant attraction between these two, even if the meeting is decidedly unconventional. The elegant, civilized Aquarius lady could be swept off her dainty feet by this guy, who is just about unstoppable once he makes up his mind about what he wants. He tends to perform in short bursts rather than in long, steady stretches like Capricorns or Scorpios, but he probably gets more done in those bursts than anyone else in the Zodiac. If she keeps him stimulated and at the same time secure in the knowledge that he has a home to come back to, this will be a great partnership.

AQUARIUS WOMAN—TAURUS MAN

A wise Aquarian will run a mile when she sees a Taurean coming. But human beings are not always as sensible as they should be, so if the passionate, highly sexed Taurus man hooks himself an Aquarian lady, both had better be prepared for trouble.

Taurus doesn't want a buddy; he wants a mate to bundle with—often. Aquarius is slightly more discriminating, and she has too many interests outside the home for this guy, who expects her life to revolve around his own. There will be plenty of clashes and arguments. The home, a cosy fireside, good wine, good food, and luxury are what Taurus wants. This lady couldn't care less about such things; she wants stimulus and excitement. Her mind is far too good for Taurus, who thinks at the pace of a snail and feels (not to put too fine a point on it) through his sex organs.

Financially Taurus is a careful man who believes in the virtues of saving and banking and saving again. Aquarius will be irritated by this. She likes to have the security of a separate bank account and a few jewels, but once she has them she relaxes and forgets about money, spending it as she wants without bothering about the future too much.

If these two do get together, there is every chance that they will gradually drift apart, helped on by an occasional burst of jealousy from Taurus. Of course, this partnership can work, but frankly it will take the exceptional couple to go the distance. Communication is the problem here, as it usually is when partnerships begin to fail either at the personal or business level. These two are on different wavelengths most of the time. That's a pity because Taurus could bring Aquarius down to earth and she could open him up a little and prevent him from getting rigid as he gets older.

All this might make Taurus sound like a monster, but that is not the case. He's a civilized, charming, fun-loving guy with a distinct artistic bent, but he's likely to show his worst side once he's charmed Aquarius into a second date with him. He is patient and determined, so he could take some shaking off. It would be a good idea for Aquarius to make a brave attempt to shake off both him and his boring friends, who seem to be obsessed by cars, games, wine, food, and all the other things she is just not interested in. If Taurus really wants this lady, then he'd better start running a home for orphans or a soup kitchen for the indigent—she'll be very impressed and will pitch in like a shot.

AQUARIUS WOMAN—GEMINI MAN

This is likely to be a highly stimulating, unconventional affair, and there's a good chance it will work well. The excitable, versatile, charming Gemini man could make a big impression on the Aquarius woman. He's as sharp as a knife; his mind works even more quickly than hers. He hates to be tied down and changes from minute to minute, let alone day to day. He's crazy and terrific fun. Aquarius loves it, but in fact she feels more than he does, is far less selfish, and would be very good for him if she'll take a chance with him.

He tends to be critical and debate things, and these two could certainly become absorbed in each other in no time. Both have a deep need to learn and expand their consciousness, and this implies that jobs and situations can be and probably have been changed rapidly. The unwilling Aquarius may even be forced to take charge of finances, or there won't be any!

There'll be plenty of sexual excitement, with Aquarius probably making the running in the bedroom. No one gets bored when these two are around. The best way to keep Gemini happy is to play backgammon or chess or something more complex in bed with him. If

Aquarius can provide the stability that he needs, then they will be even more compatible than they would be anyway. Neither of these two is sentimental, and they aren't really romantic either, even though they think they ought to be. Neither cares a damn what relatives think or friends worry about, so they might well be quite happy with a long relationship without marriage. And if Gemini has a few little affairs on the side, Aquarius isn't going to be even particularly interested. At times this guy will act rather like a selfish child, so quite a lot depends on the woman in this partnership. She's the one who's going to have to decide how it is to work and, of course, whether or not she wants it to.

There will be a tendency for both to go dashing around the globe at a moment's notice, as both love new places and new scenes and new experiences. It would be wise to moderate this tendency in the interests of stability. Children are a great stabilizer for the Aquarius woman (in or out of wedlock), and despite his superficial nature Gemini is likely to take his responsibilities as a father very seriously. Whatever happens, the kids are going to have lively, delightful, irritating parents and they'll probably be the envy of all their school pals. One important thing is that these two will respect each other, always.

AQUARIUS WOMAN—CANCER MAN

The Cancer man is almost certainly too emotional and too passionate for the Aquarius woman. An affair might be good for both, but a longer-term relationship poses distinct problems that would have to be faced and overcome with a lot of understanding and effort.

Home is important for Cancer, as is sex. Aquarius, on the other hand, finds housework a bore. She's quite likely to have a successful career going (possibly more successful than her man's), and she'll be unhappy to give it up. He is a gentle, kind man but he is possessive and will expect her to gradually become deeply involved in him and his interests. She is much more likely to want to go her own way, demonstrate her independence, and go to parties. This doesn't mean she's superficial, just that she tends to slightly mistrust a situation in which togetherness is stressed. And she isn't very sympathetic to the sensitive Cancer's moodiness and sentimentality and romantic notions. He isn't the easiest man to live with, even though he has artistic gifts.

Aquarius is forward-looking, fascinated by new ideas and by the future. Cancer tends to look to the past for his inspiration. He probably likes antiques, and he'll be the first to weep at the movies. Aquarius thinks that's pathetic.

He's quite good with money, which is a plus, because Aquarius prefers to spend it rather than earn it. She can be sensible, but she likes always to have enough money to do what she likes when she likes. This gives her the security she needs, and then she won't worry. His security is to have a charming wife in a charming home looking after him, providing him with the little luxuries (not necessarily expensive ones) that he enjoys. It will certainly have to be love for Aquarius to stand for his sentimental and old-fashioned approach to women. She expects to be an equal partner in every way and won't put up with anything less. She's not really a feminist, because she knows there are more efficient methods of getting her way, but there is something slightly cold about her at times. She's tolerant and unselfish and easy most of the time, but occasionally he's going to wonder if she's really there or if in fact a robot has taken over.

Cancer is not likely to approve of her many friends and acquaintances; he might regard some of them as unsuitable, which will of course be considered a mortal insult by Aquarius if he should dare to utter his objections.

AQUARIUS WOMAN—LEO MAN

This is likely to be a stormy relationship; it can be an awful mess or it can be a success story. It all depends on the maturity of the partners.

Leo is a passionate, demanding, domineering, generous man. Aquarius is cooler, more mentally oriented, less of a show-off, socially conscious, sensible, and yet at times almost as extravagant as he is. Leos are more physical in their approach to life and can become rather rigid as they get older. If this relationship lasts, then the Aquarius woman will certainly prevent that from happening. She's a great one for collecting friends and acquaintances, and loves travel, exciting places, and new scenes.

The home is very important to Leo, who sees it as a projection of his often larger-than-life personality. He is dramatic and likes to feel important. The way to his heart is through outrageous flattery, which he sees through but enjoys anyway. Never tell a Leo he's wearing a scruffy shirt; he'll bridle as though he's been kicked in a tender spot. Aquarius is unfortunately not likely to go in for flattery; it's beneath her. She reckons she's too intelligent for such things, and she is. That's why she'll have problems with the more basic Leo. Sexually he tends to just grab like a greedy little boy—but it works in a lot of cases.

Leo cares about success in his job and good living. He needs to be the center of attention. The worst thing for a Leo is to be ignored. Basically he's conventional and traditional, while Aquarius is decidedly not so. She looks to the future and couldn't care less if she flouts convention in either her dress or her life style. She'll fascinate him and at the same time appall him. She is deeply concerned with education and the mind. Improving herself is almost a necessity for her. She possibly has a gift for languages and seems to learn things twice as quickly as her partner, although he is more determined and often more resourceful.

She won't be terribly interested in financial affairs, but she does need the security this man can provide. At times he'll be jealous even though he knows it's silly, and sexually he will be too forward and demanding for her much of the time, even though he can open her up and help her get rid of those nasty neuroses that cramp her style. Aquarius is sometimes, if not always, afraid of committing herself totally—something in her draws back from human contact into imagination or idea. These two should work at this relationship.

AQUARIUS WOMAN—VIRGO MAN

Some Aquarius-Virgo partnerships function well, but they are usually based on cooperation and affection rather than wild passion.

Virgo is a charming, frustrated, highly intelligent guy. He's an analyzer, one who likes to weigh things in the balance and work things out. He's an immensely hard worker who expects to succeed through his industriousness. He does perhaps lack a little imagination, favors the cautious approach, and thus sometimes gets bogged down in detail and doesn't quite make it to the top of his profession. The Aquarius woman will respect his quickness on the uptake and the excellent way he communicates, but she is much more interested in reforming the world than he is.

Virgo does tend to be a critic, and particularly in the home he could infuriate his Aquarian mate. She knows perfectly well she isn't the greatest housekeeper and cook in the world. Such things bore her; she'd rather have a career and outside interests. Indeed she could see the home as a mild prison. Virgo expects more from her than she is prepared to give in this area, and the same probably applies in bed too. He is sensible and practical and a great saver who knows the value of money. Aquarius likes to spend and doesn't worry too much whether there is enough cash around to balance the books. She'll leave that to her man, and she might be genuinely upset when she discovers she has badly overspent—again!

Aquarius expects to be an equal partner in everything in this relationship, but Virgo isn't so sure about that. He expects the whole world, and particularly the woman he is with, to perform with stunning efficiency at all times. Neither the world nor his Aquarian do perform in quite the way he expects, so he's continually in a state of irritated frustration. This lady wants her freedom, not some guy chasing her around giving her piddling little instructions about every damn thing.

It might be a good idea to have a friendly relationship rather than a sexual one, just for fifteen or twenty years, and then if things seem to be working out, head for the altar. After all, Virgo is a perfectionist. He will give his support to his woman's efforts to improve the world, simply because it makes sense to him. But he isn't going to feel the emotional responsibility she does. One thing about these two is that they both have open minds, ever ready to digest and use new ideas and methods. That is quite something.

AQUARIUS WOMAN—LIBRA MAN

These two are likely to be attracted to each other, and all the indications are that it will be a happy and long-lasting relationship based on trust and understanding.

The Libra man must have balance and harmony in his life. He enjoys himself a lot, flirts, and goes to parties much more than the Aquarius woman does, but he has a deep appreciation of beauty wherever he finds it—and he is so charming. He enjoys sexual games and little surprises, and Aquarius will happily fit in with his scheme of things even if at times it is a bit superficial. Both will enjoy little luxuries, concerts, travel to exotic places. Money is likely to be the biggest stumbling block to their joy. Aquarius isn't too good at saving, and Libra is a positive spendthrift. Twenty dozen roses and a crate of champagne may seem a necessity to him at times rather than a luxury!

Libra can be selfish and self-centered, while Aquarius gives much more of herself in a generous, free, easy way. They complement each other quite nicely a lot of the time. This lady is easy to live with as long as she is treated as an equal in all things, and this Libra is most certainly going to do because he genuinely believes in equality.

Aquarius has an excellent mind, which she enlarges by continuous study. She'll be out and about with her many friends, attending classes, learning more and more (often about things that no one else wants to know about), and he will be rather upset when he returns from work to find nothing on the table, the deep freeze empty, and his woman out. One thing's for sure, there'll be no cosy self-contented boredom with these two.

It must be admitted that Libra is attracted by the ladies, and they tend to fancy him. Aquarius, however, will take this in her stride, and she won't want to know about his little flings. He'll expect romance all the time, and when they are in their mid-eighties he'll still expect a cuddle and a kiss—but only twenty-seven times a day. This is an attraction based on a meeting of minds, but it would be wrong to assume that Aquarians are always cold and impersonal; they just like things—and especially bedtime—to be nice.

She should make a special effort to be elegant and witty and gay for her Libran. It won't be all that easy for her, because really she considers that sort of behavior superficial, but a few little sacrifices won't hurt too much. He believes the world is a happy, beautiful, holy place. Don't disillusion the poor mutt; after all, he's only a man.

AQUARIUS WOMAN—SCORPIO MAN

The Scorpio man is the complete opposite of the Aquarius woman in just about everything, and she'll soon find out what that means in practice. These two had better not make any long-term plans.

He is intensely jealous and demanding, while she is as free as the wind, easy and friendly. He'll go berserk—she'll go away. Aquarius will certainly be impressed by his strength of character, his intensity, his emotional fervor, and his passion. He tends to love or hate for intuitive reasons rather than logical ones, and she finds this difficult to understand. The more he tries to take her over and possess her, the more she will withdraw. She doesn't want to be his all; she wants a life of her own in thought, word, and deed. All this will create a sense of insecurity that just cannot last.

Of course, some remarkable couples will get it together, and in such cases the fighting qualities of this man and the generosity and kindness of this woman blend to produce an exceptional relationship. But this will be in a few cases only. He doesn't find it easy to talk things out as she does. He gives vent to his ideas and feelings in action, and that may well be in the bedroom. This is a sexy guy, and his very intensity could turn her off.

He also has a need for security, financial and emotional. Aquarius doesn't seem to worry about money; she just coasts along, spending as she feels like it. He'll decide she is irresponsible, and she'll think he's stingy. He expects his woman to be at home looking after him, longing for him to return to the nest. She expects to pursue her career.

It's no use. Aquarius just won't be controlled by this or any other man. And yet she is in reality so easy to get along with. It's almost as though Scorpio is set on destroying the relationship—he isn't; it's just his way. He is basically a faithful guy once he's made a commitment. Until then, or after it, wow! Aquarius isn't likely to bother too much either way, provided he doesn't admit anything in a fit of conscience. One advantage of living with this man is that he will create financial security, and this is something Aquarius needs.

Perhaps the crucial difference is that this woman thinks objectively; she puts space between herself and the event or action. Scorpio is quite unable to do this; he sees things in terms of black and white, yes and no. "Maybe" is a word he hasn't heard of. He could indeed be an exceptionally gifted man—and a great big pain at the same time.

AQUARIUS WOMAN—SAGITTARIUS MAN

It could be like living in the eye of a hurricane, always waiting for the top to blow off, but there's a very real chance that this will prove to be a fine, constructive, exciting, and definitely stimulating relationship.

Sagittarius is a busy man, and he's likely to be attracted by the independent, efficient way this woman goes about things. He respects her, treats her as a genuinely equal partner, and expects her to join him in his adventures. Money could be a distinct problem because he's prone to take crazy gambles, like risking everything on some outlandish scheme to mine gold in Madagascar or diamonds in Dalmatia. And, horrifyingly, there's a fair chance he'll make a billion!

His Aquarian partner, however, may have to step in and take control of the finances. He'll be quite happy, mainly because he won't be at home anyway. This guy is a great buddy; he has so many friends, so many contacts. Aquarius is no slouch when it comes to traveling, meeting her friends, and enjoying herself. He has the stronger sexual appetite, but don't think that this is a cold woman, as is sometimes stated; she is just rather particular. She will get irritated if he flirts too openly, so if he's wise, he'll be sensible and keep it under the covers.

These two can have a marvelous time sharing interests, teaching each other things they are good at, sports, games, mountaineering, collecting snuff boxes, learning obscure languages—the list could go on forever. These really are two fascinating people—not least to themselves. Yes, he has his faults, and one of them is that he cannot take life all that seriously, but there's no doubt about the mutual attraction. He will keep a dozen balls, a dozen projects, in the air at once. And if half fall down, the other half will stay afloat. Chaos, but organized chaos. He could even have a distinct spiritual side to his nature, even if he doesn't show it too often.

It might be a good idea to grab some of the cash and purchase a few gold bars when things are going well. He will be mildly grateful later when he's down to his last pair of underpants. But don't expect too much gratitude—it's all a game to this overgrown kid.

Aquarius is a lady who thinks big. She cannot help wanting to reform and save the world, but she isn't quite so good with smaller, more practical projects. With a little luck, Sagittarius will help out here, and he'll do a fine job too.

AQUARIUS WOMAN—CAPRICORN MAN

Not the easiest of relationships, but it can work if the will is there. The Capricorn man is cautious, slightly secretive, proud, and industrious. These are all things that the Aquarius woman really is not. She has many other virtues, but they are not necessarily the sort of ones that this fellow will approve of—which is a pity because she could be very good for him.

He's dependable and solid, and his career is important to him. He will certainly need all the encouragement she can muster, especially when he is in one of his dark moods. Her career will have to take a back seat if this partnership is to have the slightest chance of working.

Aquarius is sometimes regarded as eccentric. She is certainly determined to go her own way, have her freedom. He will object to this in no uncertain terms. She tends to think and plan for the future, while he looks to the good old days and is sentimental and romantic. She is quite likely to burst out laughing when he comes on strong. He'll be deeply hurt, right down to the roots of his Capricornian insecurity.

It is probably fair to suggest that Capricorn tends to concentrate his energies and attention, while Aquarius tends to diffuse hers. Thus he may appear to do more and be more successful, but in the long run, who knows? There will certainly be some quarrels but Aquarius will probably simply turn off. She cannot understand why he's complaining about the way she spends money. Doesn't he want her to look nice? Doesn't he like a nice home? One thing about this man is that he's determined. If he decides this woman is for him, then she's going to have a hard time dislodging him. He's a pessimist and a worrier too, so he'll also have a hard time. The smart Aquarian lady will twist him around her little finger with ease. The less smart Aquarian will decide that that sort of thing is beneath her. She'll be wrong.

Capricorn will hate her friends, complain about everything she does, and love her to distraction—it's his way of saying he cares. She'll decide it's all too much and pack up and leave. His caring is worse than most men's not caring!

Yes, there'll be plenty of headaches if these two decide to team up. A nice friendly affair would be a good idea, and then if by any quirk of fate everything is going splendidly, head for the altar—sometimes marriages really are made in heaven despite what the astrologer says. Aquarius is probably a hundred years ahead of her time, while Capricorn is fifty years behind his—the kids could be just about right.

AQUARIUS MAN—AQUARIUS WOMAN

There's no chance of this being a dull or boring relationship, and these two are perfectly well able to create an enduring and satisfying relationship even if it may not be a deeply passionate one.

Aquarians are easy to get on with. They can mate successfully with probably more other signs in the Zodiac than anyone else. But they do not suffer fools gladly and are sometimes prone to be too logical and sensible and practical and reasonable. Aquarians rarely lose their temper, though they may walk away and sulk for a few minutes. They're not particularly good with cash; they tend to spend it without worrying too much whether they can afford to part with it.

The Aquarian woman is certainly not likely to be satisfied with merely being a mother or a homemaker. She knows life holds more than that fate. She may want to continue with her career, and her Aquarian partner will understand and support her in this in the same way he will encourage her to broaden her mind and take up hobbies and interests. Car maintenance might be a good idea.

It isn't that she is inefficient—quite the opposite—or that she doesn't care; she quite simply expects to be an equal partner in every respect. Both are forward-looking, excited by new ideas, travel, enjoy parties and meeting friends and going to concerts and theaters, and even like a good gossip, although that scarcely fits in with their image as cold people. At times Aquarians can be detached, but this is not really coldness. Sexually these two are likely to be more affectionate and loving than passionate, and there isn't a jealous bone in their bodies. If either should stray or dilly-dally elsewhere there won't be repercussions. They are excellent hosts, curious, speculative, fascinated by big ideas, ever ready to save the planet rather than individuals.

Don't expect a spotless, antiseptic home. The important thing is perhaps that these two do more things together than they might have the tendency to do. There is always a small risk that they will drift apart without actually realizing what is happening. That would be a great pity for two such charming people who are always ready to help a fellow earthling in distress with money or time or effort. These are nice people, and they were lucky to find each other. Maybe it's a good thing in a world like ours that not everyone is emotional, but then again they are going to miss something in their relationship because of their low-keyed emotions.

AQUARIUS MAN—PISCES WOMAN

This is likely to be a difficult relationship because the totally emotional Pisces woman comes from a different world than the mentally oriented Aquarius man. She is totally wrapped up in herself, while he is forever helping others, trying to make the world a nicer and better place.

What this means is that togetherness will quickly degenerate into bickering and sulkiness. He's too detached, too sensible for this deeply sensitive and easily hurt woman. He is not interested in making money or being a great success in the world (although he doesn't mind spending cash). He's excited by ideas and the future rather than the present. Pisces is sentimental and very romantic; she lives in the past too much despite her little-girl charm and beauty. In all honesty it isn't easy being a Piscean in our aggressive age. She wants a man to look after her, and of course she won't be short of suitors—there are plenty of he-men around who want to do just that.

Aquarius isn't going to tell her he loves and adores her seventy-seven times a day. That's silly! Sexually, Pisces is a giver and wants to melt into her man. Unfortunately, Aquarius also tends to be a giver rather than a taker, so although bedtime could be fun and satisfying, the rest of the home life could be less than perfect. Perhaps a short love affair is the answer for this couple. A long one needs a lot of sympathy, hard work, and patience from both partners.

Aquarius uses his excellent mind to sift and sort what happens to him; he may well compartmentalize life. Pisces feels everything but can be frightened by her own intensity. She could do a great deal for this guy, helping him loosen up and enjoy art and poetry and music. He could provide her with a little more balance, and persuade her to daydream and fantasize less and think more logically.

Financially life may not be so easy. Pisces tends to buy on impulse, while Aquarius refuses to worry about details or count the cash. He's a great buddy and his cash is at the disposal of those who need it. There could be a lot of buddies who need it. In a real crisis, however, he will turn up trumps, perhaps to his own surprise. He's a gentle, kind man and she's sweet (in the real sense of the word) when she's not trying to play the femme fatale. One thing is certain: If these two do get together, no one's going to complain that life is humdrum or boring. This pair might be crazy but they are certainly fascinating. Fire and water don't mix—or do they?

AQUARIUS MAN—ARIES WOMAN

This is a fascinating partnership. It could be a total disaster, but strangely enough in a large proportion of cases it's going to work despite all the odds. The Aries woman is going to want to possess her man, make him fall madly, passionately in love with her. It just won't happen that way. He's too independent, too sensible to ever do such an outlandish and probably ultimately painful thing.

The Arian female, like her male counterpart, has to have a challenge or life isn't worth living. This guy is really going to be a challenge to her. She admires his superb mind, but she's going to feel she can't get close enough to him or get enough of him. He enjoys sex, and she certainly likes a frolic or two. She likes men—and he won't mind that too much; he knows he's got her hooked. If she threatens to push off, he'll say "Fine." If she loses her temper, he'll smile in a superior way and walk off. She can't win and it's going to drive her crazy until, like all good Arians, she faces up to the fact that not everything in the world can be gained by brute force or by demanding it. Aries is sometimes about as subtle as a bull.

Financially Aries may well have to take a firm hand. She can be extravagant, but at least she's interested in the family finances. He can't be bothered—it's almost an insult to worry him about money. After all, there's the whole world to save, sort out, make more efficient. He will, however, take it well when it's pointed out to him that he might try saving at home first.

Aries is egotistic, sometimes selfish, while Aquarius is not. He's a giver; he's detached from his ego, while she's interested in herself and her reactions. She can get possessive, her feelings can get out of control, but this is part of her responsive charm. No one falls asleep when this lady is performing. She enjoys working hard and rushing around, so don't try to stop her. She has immense stamina and works in short furious bursts. Both are prone to change jobs and situations rapidly. She needs a new challenge; he needs more scope for his ideas. He's going to be critical of her friends, her reading habits. He won't be an easy guy to live with, but then this lady doesn't want an easy, comfortable suburban existence. There's no doubt about it, this couple will stretch each other as few can do. There is genuine compatibility even if at times it doesn't seem like it. A little patience and understanding are all that is needed to make this union an outstanding and stimulating success.

AQUARIUS MAN—TAURUS WOMAN

If this partnership is going to work, then there will have to be a heap of compromises. The unconventional, freedom-loving Aquarian and the rather formal, straight-laced, old-fashioned Taurean are certainly going to have problems getting things together and then keeping them that way. In all honesty, the difficulties are going to be too much for this couple, except in the most unusual cases.

The highly sexed, passionate Taurus woman wants a mate, not a friend. Home-loving, bed-loving, and a one-man woman (at a time, that is), Taurus is going to find this guy's offhand attitude to sex and to her decidedly irritating (and that's putting it mildly). Neither is used to compromising and both usually get their own way, so stand by for fireworks. Security and possessions are of great importance to this lady. She respects law and authority and tends to think in straight lines. Aquarius gives not a fig for power or success; he works because it's what he enjoys doing and because he has an advanced social conscience. He has a far better mind than his Taurus mate and uses it to remarkable effect at times. He believes in education and expanding his mind in many ways. She tends to stick with the things she knows and understands and feels comfortable with.

Taurus is also a pretty jealous lady. This guy will drive her wild because she won't be able to pin him down, even though she's going to try pretty hard. When she explodes, he's going to walk away or mutter something about her being illogical and emotional. He can't be bothered with money, which is very important to her. The big problem here, as it is so often, is communication.

Aquarius doesn't see marriage as a tie, so he won't be tied down by it, which of course is not an ideal way to start a relationship with a traditionalist who also has a romantic and sentimental streak. She's going to decide this guy is a weirdo, fascinating in his way, but probably a bit nutty. He's going to find her fussy, rigid, and too difficult. It would be nice if they could be friends rather than lovers, but Cupid doesn't always oblige.

Most Aquarians do really want to change the world, while the Taurus woman now expects more from life than she might have done a hundred years ago, when she might have been tied to the kitchen, almost literally. He wants an honest response from his woman and he expects her to convince him of the necessity if she wants a fur coat or a new hat. He isn't stingy, but he is unpredictable. Be warned.

AQUARIUS MAN—GEMINI WOMAN

This is likely to be one of those very special, fascinating partnerships. It will either end fast or go on and on despite the inconsistencies and problems.

The Gemini woman will almost certainly be dominated by the Aquarius man, but it won't look that way, even to the partners themselves. Sexually there won't be any complaints, and this certainly isn't going to be a dull relationship of the diaper-changing, floor-cleaning type. Gemini won't put up with being turned into a drudge, and Aquarius certainly doesn't want that sort of woman. This lady thinks so fast she sometimes cannot follow her own flow of thoughts. Aquarius is no slouch in this direction either, and he has a breadth of knowledge and thought that will astonish her.

The main problem will be Gemini changeability and demand for continued and continuous stimulus and excitement. Aquarius could decide this is juvenile, and in that case she is going to have to convince him she's a basically serious person. He is perpetually curious about the way life works, and together these two can have a wonderful time asking all the questions no one else in the world has the time or the inclination to go into.

Both love to travel, go to parties, meet new people, and live it up, even though he's quite likely to say he despises luxury and such superficialities (the battle against superficiality is likely to loom large in the Aquarian canon). Gemini can be sensual rather than passionate, an imaginative rather than a great lover. There might be problems sometimes in completing tasks once begun, but no one ever called these two lazy; they are merely too busy to finish things. It would be a good idea if they could make a determined effort to do things together outside the home, to emphasize togetherness. Gemini is quite likely to drift into an affair or several affairs almost without meaning to, and he is quite likely not to be bothered. The danger is clearly that the relationship could disintegrate without either party's really realizing what is happening. One thing's for sure, these two will be equal partners in everything, and this is what they both want and expect.

At the intellectual level they will link splendidly. He won't be crazy about her friends, but he's a tolerant guy, relatively easy to live with. He's unselfish, hates arguments, and is reliable in crises. If he's a little distant at times, then that's too bad. In compensation he will adore his woman and always think the best of her.

AQUARIUS MAN—CANCER WOMAN

This is not an easy relationship. The Cancer woman is an intense, emotional person, passionate and demanding, sensitive and imaginative. The Aquarius man is the complete opposite.

He has a logical mind through which he sifts everything that is happening or is likely to happen to him, and he wants to improve the whole wide world and have everyone living happily and peacefully together. Cancer knows this isn't the purpose of life, but she isn't in fact quite sure what that purpose is. He certainly fascinates her because he is detached, unemotional, and at the same time charming. She gets hooked; in fact, his casual attitude toward sex mystifies and fascinates her. The partnership is likely to be very difficult, but of course it can work if these two are prepared to try to understand each other's very different responses to the same stimuli.

At times Cancer will wonder how Aquarius can be so unromantic. She'll decide he's so cold that ice wouldn't melt in his boots. But this is not fair; he can be as sexy as they come when everything is right and he feels in the mood. She'll probably wish he was in the mood more often. The one thing she must not do is start discussing something or present him with a problem he can get his elegant mind to grips with. Keep him quiet and loving!

Cancer is moody and difficult at times, occasionally jealous, sometimes critical. She has all the faults in modest proportions, and there is a fair chance she's artistic, with a deep sensitivity and appreciation of beauty that few in the Zodiac can even approach. He may decide it is his life's work to sort out all her problems and keep her neat and clean (emotionally). He'll probably fail to sort out all her muddles, but he'll have a damn good try. He seems to know everything, or at the very least he will, when given half an hour's notice, know everything. He will at times be astonished by this lady's intuitive brilliance. But when it goes wrong, he'll murmur, "I told you so," as he exits.

Cancer is sentimental and attached to her family and friends. She's a soft touch, whereas he decidedly is not. It's a pity these two find it so difficult to live compatibly together because they could teach each other a great deal about tolerance and beauty and logic and all the rest. If it is to work, then a great and supreme goal—whether to build a new pyramid or solve the world's food problem or found a new religion—is the best way to get and stay together. It could happen.

AQUARIUS MAN—LEO WOMAN

Two determined people can make this partnership successful, but there's a lot of hard work ahead of them. The Leo woman could find the Aquarius man too independent, too withdrawn and detached. He could find her overdramatic, quarrelsome, and pushy. It won't be easy to stay together.

Leo is rather more physically oriented than the more mental Aquarius. She is sexy, he is more affectionate, and both like their own way. She wants to be the center of attention whether at parties or at home. She's generous and a bit jealous and needs a strong man to tame her. Aquarius isn't likely to even try. He believes in equality in everything, and if she wants to do things her way, that's fine with him. She will resent what she sees as his lack of interest in her, which is in fact his respect.

There is a danger that this lady could get a bit rigid and set in her ways and opinions as she gets older. Aquarius is more humanitarian, socially conscious, and less interested in money and power. She expects her man to provide her with the money and power she is accustomed to—or if she isn't accustomed to them, then she reckons she ought to be.

There is a chance that Aquarius will find this lady slightly predatory, overwhelming, too demanding. If that is the case, he'll just cut off and go about his business. In fact, this more emotional woman could do a lot to loosen the logical mind he displays, and it could help to make an already nice man a very pleasant one to cohabit with. It's all a question of purpose. He is fascinated by new ideas and new gadgets; he has many interests and he does think big. Nothing less than changing the universe, never mind the world or galaxy, is good enough for him. Will he be successful? Who knows?

One thing about him is his unconventionality in dress and action. He finds traditions silly. Leo will see them as the essential fabric of society and feel threatened if he pooh-poohs them too much.

This will be a continually stimulating relationship. It could certainly end rapidly and dramatically, or it could soldier on through thick and thin. Life will be a challenge, but together it could prove very rewarding, provided they are determined to count the blessings and not be obsessed by the irritations. In a quiet sort of way, Aquarius expects a lot from a relationship, and so does Leo in a more vocal way. They should work at it.

AQUARIUS MAN—VIRGO WOMAN

This man could prove attractive to the Virgo woman, but these two might find life a lot easier if they can remain friends rather than lovers.

Both have an intellectual outlook on life. The sensible, practical, and sometimes critical Virgo is likely to find Aquarius just a bit too boring for her. He is not likely to be nearly as sympathetic as she expects when she comes for a little cuddle and some understanding. This lady is sensitive and very vulnerable despite the efficient and rather cold air she usually manages to project toward interested males. She has a good mind, but she tends to concentrate it. Aquarius also has a fine mind, but he tends to disseminate it. She'll work hard at making a better knitting needle. He'll be concerned that the inhabitants of Pluto might be short of calcium, or something like that.

At times Virgo's supercleanliness and efficiency will irritate Aquarius, and she in turn will get frustrated when he doesn't seem to appreciate her efforts to create a charming and neat home. She prefers to stay quietly at home, while he loves to travel, do stimulating things, and chat with his many friends. She might well feel a trifle resentful at the way he floats through life while she struggles to create a world as efficient as she is. These two should be able to talk, but there might not be so much action in the bedroom.

She knows the value of money and is good at saving it. He rather despises people who spend all their time "money-grubbing"; he doesn't like to have to count how much there is in his pocket or at the bank. A lot depends on Virgo's willingness to give more of herself than she may naturally feel inclined to do. A short affair might be easier on all concerned, and that includes the concerned relatives who wonder what these two see in each other.

These two might work things out, provided she realizes that people are important to him and he understands that things are important to her. His unpredictability is not easy to live with, and as he gets older he will work harder for his family than he might just for his wife or lover. It might in fact be a good idea if the clever Virgo uses a little of her smartness to pretend to be far less practical and capable than she really is. If she makes him think he is indispensable and the breadwinner, he will probably like the idea, even if the reality of doing things to earn money is not quite so appealing.

AQUARIUS MAN—LIBRA WOMAN

These two have a lot going for them and are likely to have many shared interests. This goes a long way to creating a real sense of togetherness for two essentially independent people who will certainly respect each other's privacy and treat each other as absolutely equal partners in the best sense of the word.

Both like to get out and about and love traveling and doing exciting and stimulating things. They might well meet at a party somewhere and carry on amid the social whirl. Money never seems to bother either of them, so funds could become decidedly short in record time. Sooner or later one of the partners is going to have to take a firm grip on the connubial purse and put his or her foot down when another crate of champagne is ordered.

The biggest problem might well be to find the time to get together. Deliberately shared interests might be a good idea. This is a broad-minded, reasonable, very nice man who is difficult not to like or get on with. At times he seems a bit detached and cold, but that's probably because he's thinking about some great universal problem. He doesn't suffer fools gladly, so it's a good thing the Libra woman is smart enough to seem to know a lot more than she probably does. All she really has to do to keep his attention is to keep asking him difficult questions.

Even if she doesn't know it, Libra's great theme is harmony. She longs for balance and harmony in all of life, and she seeks it wherever she can. She won't argue and criticize, and this suits Aquarius fine; the last thing he wants is to be nagged by his woman. The opinions of other people don't matter too much to this guy, although Libra is much more easily wounded. She does have a sentimental and romantic streak, but she is sensible up to a point. Sex is important to her, although it's probably fairer to say that she's impulsive and imaginative in bed.

Aquarius is a fine communicator when he wants to be. He'll be attracted to Libra because she usually looks good, but it's her joy in loving and living and her appreciation of beauty in its finest form that will truly attract him. Indeed, these two will find they have a great deal in common. Both want and give the truth, so don't expect too much flattery when they get together. Indeed this man is quite likely to be successful in a worldly sense without trying too hard to be so, but he values what he does rather than the financial return or power he obtains.

AQUARIUS MAN—SCORPIO WOMAN

Scorpio is going to get extremely frustrated if she falls for an attractive Aquarian. He doesn't like arguing, and he isn't very materialistic. This lady is combative, decidedly sexy, and very jealous, and she needs the security of a settled home environment.

This need for security is not likely to be met by Aquarius. He's a great roamer; he likes to visit new places and do new things. He can't be bothered with the humdrum things of normal existence. He isn't exactly romantic, but he does seem to live very much in the future and his imagination. This is going to irritate the practical, passionate Scorpio. She has an incisive mind and she will appreciate the breadth of his mental apparatus and his undoubted gifts. But she can be a very intense woman, and this won't suit him because he mistrusts emotional outbursts and isn't nearly as physical as she when it comes to the clinches.

She isn't going to take kindly to his involvement in the problems of others, his unquenchable interest and concern for people, and his ambition to improve the world. She believes improvement and charity should start at home. She's careful with the cash and she tends to like or dislike more or less on sight. There are bound to be many occasions when she feels bored and frustrated because either he isn't there or he isn't showing enough interest in her. Scorpio can be rather selfish and demanding. He is a much more cheerful, less intensely serious person. This difficulty of her possessiveness and his requirement of freedom and his detachment is likely to prove an almost insuperable stumbling block except in unusual cases. If these two can get it together, the relationship can be both extraordinary and very close, but even so there will be some sticky moments. Scorpio usually has a problem putting her feelings into words, which is probably why she uses her body and her emotions take such a beating at times. She does have quite a temper when it is aroused. Aquarius is truly a much nicer guy, unselfish, easygoing, socially conscious—but prone to take the easy way out in difficult situations.

This determined fighter of a woman never takes the easy way out. He is going to respect that and at the same time wish life could be a trifle more agreeable. The home is much more important to Scorpio who treasures ornaments and things as a reflection of her own personality. It would be a good idea for her to take an interest in his many activities, sports, and the like. She could prevent him from being a soft touch for the freeloader.

AQUARIUS MAN—SAGITTARIUS WOMAN

This looks like a good one. There will certainly be problems, but togetherness is likely to prove so much more rewarding than being apart.

Both the Aquarius man and the Sagittarius woman are social, like parties, going out, having fun. Neither seems to take the problems of life too seriously—and this, of course, could be one of the problems! Someone is going to have to look after the family finances and take a grip on things before someone comes to take away the stereo and the carpets. Both are strangely eccentric at times, with active minds that range at speed over a myriad esoteric subjects that would bewilder lesser mortals. This lady is an enthusiast and could be rather a worrier, but she is always fun to be with.

Aquarius wants a woman who is independent, and he'll certainly respect this one's ability to look after herself. It's equal shares for these two. Sagittarius doesn't like to spend too much time in the house, so the home could suffer a little. She has lots of friends and acquaintances and isn't above having a playful flirtation or indeed something more serious. He isn't likely to mind too much; he'll probably be at night school anyway. And when she really needs him— he won't be there. Neither has any hangups (or at least they're not visible—although of course all the best hangups are hidden anyway), and both seem to get along with anyone. They're both curious and, when called on, genuinely compassionate. One thing's for sure, there won't be any bored folks around when these two get together.

Life is likely to be one great big adventure for these two. Should it be a more serious business? Who's to say? Anyway Scorpio is going to hit it off right away with this charming guy, who intrigues her by his indifference one moment and his real interest and magnetism the next. Love will probably sneak up on these two as they are discussing the difficulties of flying from Mars to Jupiter or the optimum way of splitting the atom using just a computer. He doesn't suffer fools gladly, and this lady gives every appearance of knowing a great deal more than she probably does. She isn't averse to a little bluffing— all in a good cause, of course.

For this man life is a great big quest, though not for money or power or happiness or even love. He may never discover what he's searching for, but one thing is certain, this lady won't hinder him on his way and could be a considerable asset. If he wants to walk away, she might find herself more possessive than she thought she was.

AQUARIUS MAN—CAPRICORN WOMAN

On the surface this looks like a difficult relationship, but in fact these two can certainly make a go of things, provided Capricorn is prepared to make a special effort. She has a logical, practical mind and at the same time she's a romantic who needs to be frequently told that she's needed and loved.

Aquarius is unfortunately not much given to displays of emotion, and he isn't likely to be too sympathetic when he sees her getting morbid or depressed as she is likely to be at times. He doesn't seem to suffer such depressive symptoms and finds it difficult to understand how she can fail to see the bright side of a situation.

Sexually there are not likely to be many fireworks—probably not enough for Capricorn anyway. Aquarius is straightforward when he chooses to be, while she's more possessive and physically demanding. She is also rather traditional in her approach, whether it be flowers and candles or in the way she tucks money away for a rainy day or even a storm. She's a good anchor for Aquarius, much more ambitious than he is and almost certainly harder-working. She will be impressed by the intelligence that he displays at times, but she won't like the way he gets out of the home as often as possible (he's very sociable) and, as she sees it, neglects her. He isn't quite as well equipped as she is to meet the slings and arrows of life, but never underestimate this guy—he has a tendency to come up trumps in a crisis.

Capricorn will certainly have to take charge of much of the everyday functioning, though really she thinks he should be doing these things. But that's something she'll have to come to terms with if she wants to stay with him. He may go through quite a few jobs before he settles down, and this will irritate her, even if she manages to contain her highly critical instincts and gag herself too. He can't understand her need for security. But he'll make her life more friendly, cheerful, and fun. He's good for her even if true compatibility is hard for this couple to achieve.

It's quite likely he'll meet and fall for this lady when she's in trouble. He'll absolutely adore sorting things out for her, and she'll be so grateful she'll probably marry him on the spot. He's a generous guy who spends both money and effort to help others. He needs a little discipline, and she could bring it into his life, provided she doesn't overdo it and come to represent repression to him. She should try a little cunning with this guy—he's worth it.

PISCES WOMAN—PISCES MAN

This is likely to be a tremendously pleasing relationship for both partners, but it could degenerate quite rapidly because both are almost too sensitive, and this includes a failure to make decisions and sort out the family finances.

There will certainly be great harmony, but the Pisces woman in particular knows what hurts her man and might at times deliberately wound him. The mental and emotional togetherness is likely to be great, quite often reaching a psychic and intuitive level. Pisceans do want to please, and they give almost more than any other sign. Certainly they can become uncommunicative and go cold, particularly if they feel threatened in any way. In many ways the Pisces woman would be happier with a stronger man. But sexually these two will understand each other perfectly and more than likely become totally absorbed in each other.

The difficulty in this partnership is the emotional drain they are likely to make on each other, and they don't have all that much energy to spare. Someone once suggested that when two Pisceans get together it is like the blind leading the blind. There's a grain of truth in this because both can get into an awful emotional tizzy. Pisceans need security, not necessarily of a home, although this is important, but they need to be loved deeply and completely.

Decision making is painful for Pisceans. They tend to see sides of a situation that no one else has thought of. They are deeply romantic, sentimental, tradition-loving people. They like old houses and walks in the country, and can be jealous and demanding.

The other main thing to remember about Pisceans is that they are dreamers. They are the great fantasizers, forever expecting knights in shining armor or distressed damsels to pop up (or vice versa). Despite this, the Pisces man, to his own surprise, often tends to fall on his feet and may well do much better than expected in business, even though he's likely to drive his colleagues to distraction.

A Piscean relationship is dramatic, earth-shaking, and tortured at times—but at least life together won't be dull. It's hard to resist Pisceans' charm and friendliness. They mean well, but the results can be a total surprise to them and to those around them. It isn't easy being a Piscean, but the compensations are great.

PISCES WOMAN—ARIES MAN

It is generally agreed that this is likely to be an overwhelming relationship, at least for the Pisces woman. It could be love at first, or second, sight, as her sensitive nature latches on to his impulsive, dynamic potential. Sexually he will dominate, but this is what she wants.

The Pisces woman is very sensitive, not least to criticism, and the Aries man would be wise to bear this in mind. He can be decidedly insensitive as he tries to bludgeon her into submission with affirmations of undying love, presents, phone calls at three in the morning, and so on. The trouble is, he does get under her skin and she can't seem to do without him.

He will certainly be very good for this lady. Even if he doesn't pooh-pooh most of her mystic ideas, she'll sense a security and a protective aura that he spreads around her. Sex is likely to be sensational, and she'll feel secure in this area too. Yes, he does have a roving eye, but she is so fascinating and he cannot resist that tiny touch of mystery that gathers around her. He may never completely understand her, but that's really what he wants. This is a very feminine woman, changeable, intuitive, deeply emotional. At times he'll take her for granted or treat her like a little girl—she'll grit her teeth and put up with it because she loves him.

The Aries man is a terrific enthusiast; he moves at a great pace, but he'll come back to his Piscean woman not least because she's quite incapable of looking after the finances and he knows she needs him. This is a generous, unselfish man, a bit wrapped up in his own illusions. He has to learn to be more gentle and tender with this extraordinary woman. He must learn not to be quite so insensitive. He'll nearly always act first and think later, until he grows up. And that may never happen.

This will be a passionate, emotional affair however long it lasts, and chances are good that it will last. There will be difficulties in adjusting to each other, in understanding where the play-acting becomes real, where the pretended emotion becomes real. But these adjustments can be made because he hasn't the time to be less than sincere and she eventually learns that she has to be frank and simple and honest. The Aries man will adore his Piscean, and she'll find that she just cannot manage without him. Play this one by ear; don't try to work things out in advance or have expectations. It will turn out right.

PISCES WOMAN—TAURUS MAN

One of the nice things about the Taurus man is that he wants to look after someone, and as the Pisces woman really does want to be looked after—smothered in love, if not diamonds—then everything looks set for a very good relationship.

He's a simple sort of guy, likes luxury and comfort, his home, pipe and slippers. He will always see his Pisces partner as a fragile butterfly he has to protect from the big bad world. This suits her fine most of the time, and the rest she'll wander off for an afternoon's shopping and recharge her batteries. Sex can be overdone by these two, but he can be rather insensitive at times. She might indeed feel as though she's tangled up with a bull.

The Pisces woman is much more emotional, intuitive, sensitive, and easily hurt than the Taurus man even imagines. As long as he understands this and never takes her for granted, there should be few problems. It is unlikely that he won't appreciate his mysterious, enchanting, irritating Piscean. He can be incredibly stubborn once he's made up what he calls his mind, but he does love, there's no doubt about that.

Taurus can also be very jealous. He might try to bully the Piscean at times, but it won't work; he's a sucker for a weeping woman. However, he will sort the finances out because he's a practical and sensible fellow, just what the extravagant Pisces woman needs. He has a fear of not attaining financial security, and this will lead him to work hard both for himself and his woman. She'll be suitably appreciative, at least on the surface, because she knows it pleases him.

At times she'll long for a more romantic man rather than one who favors the grab 'em and bed 'em approach. But in case he sounds like a monster, it must be stressed that more than likely he has true artistic appreciation and needs beauty in his life, namely the Pisces woman.

If things get difficult the Pisces woman will simply slip into the day or night dream world that is never far from her anyway. He will probably fail to appreciate what is happening and, as he cannot bear to be ignored, will get irritable. If for any reason she decides that he is not for her, he'll take a lot of shaking off. She will, however, create a charming, spotlessly clean home for him and cook him delightful meals, probably daintily garnished with spring flowers. It's funny that some decide she's just too much trouble, but then the Piscean is the one who decides who and what she wants.

PISCES WOMAN—GEMINI MAN

This partnership could produce a short, fun-filled affair, but longer-term chances are not so good. Both have vibrant, intensely active minds, which will certainly create attraction, but the Gemini man likes to use his gifts to attract the ladies and the Pisces woman isn't going to stand for that.

Gemini likes to have his freedom. He won't be bossed or badgered, and as these two are changeable and moody and easily excited, there will be conflict all along the line. In a way both are unstable people who badly need a more stable partner to sort them out. There'll be physical attraction, plenty of ego on display from both partners, but they both need stronger people. Don't assume that these two are superficial characters. They're deep, enigmatic, charming, gentle, generous, and infuriating by turns. The Piscean is shy and withdrawn, delightful in her simplicity, and an enigma because of the complexity that lurks behind the exterior.

The big difficulty is that the Pisces woman is totally emotional, in touch with her feelings all the time, responding intuitively. Gemini is a thinker; he thinks so fast that he seems emotional but in fact he has a cold calculating mind of great efficiency that weighs and balances all the time, just like a massive computer—even though it goes wrong at times!

Pisces needs security both emotional and at home. Gemini doesn't really understand this. He needs excitement and stimulation. She is easily hurt by a thoughtless word. She's so sensitive that life is a continual round of joy and suffering. She can touch the heights and the depths almost in the same breath. Gemini is more selfish not least with money. At times he will be very generous, but this will usually have something to do with his own self-importance or be related to some advantage that will come about (at least he thinks so) from his generosity.

Financially there could be problems with the extravagant Piscean. This couple can't spend all the time in bed, and the bills only pile up if they are not dealt with. Of course, the relationship can succeed in exceptional cases, although frankly it will be a pretty nerve-wrenching business a lot of the time. Plenty of fantasy, yes. Dreams of wealth and power and Shangri-la. Impulsive outings, shopping trips, parties, and visits—but a lack of stability that will deeply disturb her. Both might accept flirtations and play down jealousy, but the way to Gemini's heart (if he has one) is to embrace and caress him.

PISCES WOMAN—CANCER MAN

These two are very compatible, romantic, and understanding, but the Cancerian moodiness and the inability of either to organize the finances will create difficulties.

Nevertheless, the many demands that Cancer makes will in most cases be met by the Pisces woman. Some Pisceans will find it all a bit too much and push off, but most are prepared to subordinate their own personality and wishes to their partners'. Both are almost too sensitive for our world and desperately need a happy stable home life. Can they provide it? Yes, but personal wishes and fantasies will have to put aside.

These two will genuinely care for each other. Sexually, Cancer is likely to make the running, but emotional needs will for the most part be satisfied and they are likely to spend a good deal of time in bed or in their bedroom. Cancer can be successful in his chosen career, which may often be artistic in some way, but he may also always feel that something is missing in his life that he finds it hard to define or even understand. Both tend to flow with life rather than fight upstream, so at times it might seem that not much is happening, but still waters do run deep.

Both can be lazy, luxury lovers, candlelight-and-wine people. The Pisces woman is a far better cook and homemaker than might be suspected, and the Cancer man will appreciate this. She wants to be looked after, and he'll do his best. There is real emotional under-standing and physical togetherness, but perhaps the mental relation-ship leaves a little to be desired. Both act out their fantasies, withdraw from the world at times, and get moody and difficult, but these phases won't last long. He expects her undivided attention, so there is an element of selfishness in him; but he is a pretty interesting guy and most of what he has to say is truly worth listening to. Fre-quent expressions of love and need are likely, and this will help to cement the relationship. There could even be overemphasis on small, unimportant details of life; they'll loom large for this pair, so that balance and harmony can be distorted in a strange way. But perhaps this is just another way of saying that each cares deeply about the other.

All in all, these two can expect a lifetime of joy and moonlight. If Cancer can't keep his Piscean lady, he has only himself to blame, because life has done its best to give him the world!

PISCES WOMAN—LEO MAN

This partnership is best avoided by all but the most exceptional couples. Fire and water don't mix, and neither do these two.

Leo will cosset his woman, provide her with the security she needs, and so on. But in practice he's quite likely to prove a tyrant, expecting constant praise and admiration, demanding much more from her than any woman is prepared to give. He tends to judge by surface show, and when she goes moodily around, grumbling and whining, he's going to get mad. There'll be romance to start with, but life can be awfully boring when a woman finds her partner im-mersed in becoming the world's most powerful man while she's ex-pected to sit at home making herself look pretty so he can show her off to boost his already massive ego.

If that makes Leo sound like a monster, he is, particularly where this woman is concerned. The truth is that she brings out all his worst qualities. He is a generous, loving, frank, self-centered, stimulating, and rather rigid guy. She is delightful, artistic, fey, gen-tle, poetic, irritating, and hopeless with money. They are not likely to get it together unless a miracle happens!

Leo has to remember that the Pisces woman is a deeply sensi-tive, intuitive, often spiritual person, very feminine, totally incapable of standing up to his brutal approaches. Water is not notably successful at challenging the hardness of steel—unless, and it's a big unless, the water has the time to wear away the steel, which it will.

The Pisces woman has the equipment to attract the Leo man. She's a consummate actress. Later he will genuinely appreciate her ability to look after the home, cook delightful meals, and entertain him with small talk. Later, after the bedding, he's going to start looking around for a more exciting woman, and that's the beginning of the end for these two. She'll put up with a lot, but not that. Leo likes to have an admiring circle; he's a real "ham," but he's good fun for all that. Tell him he's the greatest lover in the world, the wisest man, the wittiest companion, and he'll nod. Of course, it's all true, so why make such a fuss about it? Tell him the same thing a thousand times and he'll keep on nodding. Leo's are easy to handle, really. One comforting thought: The Pisces woman is tougher than she seems.

PISCES WOMAN—VIRGO MAN

Not an easy relationship by any standards. This man is cool when she is passionate, demanding when she shrinks, and yet she will see him as a sort of challenge—no one could be quite so independent and self-contained. She's right, of course, but in the process of discovering she's right, there's going to be a lot of frustration and pain and soul searching for the sensitive, loving, totally emotional Piscean. She'd be wise if possible to steer clear of this man despite his evident virtues.

He's very efficient, extremely good with money (makes an excellent accountant), cautious, sensible, and at the same time sensitive in his way. But he does tend to be highly critical of her, and this will hurt very much. He has great expectations, which the world continually torpedoes. He also works very hard indeed. He believes success will come from steady work rather than inspired actions, so he makes an excellent number two in a company even though he can get bogged down in details.

Pisces might in fact decide that Virgo is not capable of the depth of love that she demands, and it is true that he may put her second to his career or other interests. She won't stand for this. Sexually, he's not likely to satisfy her needs either. She acts impulsively and intuitively, while he considers all the angles first. Her extravagant tastes will turn him off, even though she will moderate them when told to. She just doesn't worry about money. Her partner has to provide, and always does. Pisces enjoys being looked after. Virgo will do this, but he'll also make sure she knows he's doing it.

Pisces is poetic, sentimental, loves old things. She's too romantic for someone who, although he may love flowers and mountains, isn't going to be content just to look at them. He'll want to know how the flower works and what rocks have built the mountain into the shape it is. It's all too much for her, but at least if these two do get together there'll be enough money to pay the bills and take that badly needed vacation. He is quite incapable of *not* taking care of everyone, but in this case the differences of temperament run very deep.

Pisces would be good to loosen up Virgo's tensions, to soothe his fevered brow and tell him everything is all right. He won't believe it, but he'll relax and maybe even nibble her ear. He lives by fixed rules and systems, and she doesn't.

PISCES WOMAN—LIBRA MAN

There will be tension and difficulties for this couple, but there is a good chance that the relationship will be successful. Libra is indeed a charmer and, like most charmers, is selfish and self-centered. But that's only half the picture—he also has a deep-seated need for balance and harmony in his life and in his relationships. This means that he backs away from quarrels and disagreements and tends to enjoy comfort and luxury.

Pisces could well be attracted to Libra; he knows how to treat a woman and has a genuine instinct for romance even if that response is superficial. Both have a tendency to get involved in others' difficulties, and as they are hospitable people this could well give Libra a chance to exercise what can only be called his roving eye. He likes women. She wants exclusive rights and won't accept that his flirting is not serious—hence disagreements which will irritate this freedom-loving man and encourage him to move further away from his loving Piscean. All very unnecessary, but that's life!

They relate nicely in bed, but the Piscean dramatic instinct, changeableness, and moodiness will be a major problem for a man who doesn't want any problems at home. The home, incidentally, will be kept spotless.

Both are dreamers. Pisces spends half her life in a long daydream (and the other half sleeping). Libra dreams, too—of beautiful women. She wants to be totally involved with a man who is totally committed to her. He wants an equal partner and wants to treat his woman as such. She needs a stronger man even though she will kick over the traces pretty frequently. He is good around the house and probably cooks better than she does. Financially, life will be difficult because she spends extravagantly while he does like to party. He needs lots of stimulus and brings fun into the lives of many. This usually costs money. If these two will make a special effort to play down their personal characteristics and appreciate each other's good points, they can create a curious but stable relationship. Otherwise, no chance.

Perhaps it is best to characterize the Libra man as a pleasure lover and a pleasure seeker. The Pisces woman sees much more to life and expects more. Fundamentally she's a serious "little girl" who gives much of herself and doesn't always get so much back. When she withdraws into herself and goes for long solitary walks, he should try to understand—the rewards are considerable.

PISCES WOMAN—SCORPIO MAN

In most cases this will be an absolutely stunning relationship. In a minority it will be a disaster.

The sheer sex energy developed would prostrate most people, but his driving demands will be more than met by her melting into his arms. He'll be like putty in her hands despite his domineering, stubborn, and intense nature. He's a strong man and just what she needs. He is also intensely jealous, and she'd better realize it soon— then life will be blissful. She'll certainly be needed and told so even though he's usually not too good with words, relying on his other physical abilities to get the message across.

His possessiveness can hardly be overestimated, but at least it does mean she will be looked after (which she wants desperately). The sooner this couple make it to the altar, the better. He isn't always easy to live with because of his power complex, but she'll calm him down, make him as sweetly reasonable as he's ever likely to be, and after he's exploded about her extravagance he'll be secretly proud of his beautiful Piscean.

At home he'll be gratified by the clean and comfortable and cosy atmosphere, and he likes antiques almost as much as she does. It isn't that she's so interested in the home; she just seems incapable of not making her nest elegant, and her children will be extremely well brought up. Her career goes by the board pretty rapidly, as may be imagined.

The linchpin of this partnership is the sexual and emotional relationship. She'll never stop being a dreamer, but he'll probably figure pretty large in those dreams. At times Scorpio is going to get bored and cast around, but fundamentally, despite his potent sexual drive, he's settled with this lady—after all, he chose her, or did he? When he's moody he needs cheering up, but she is quite likely to depress him even more by saying she understands. He will, in turn, be cruel and thoughtless and drive her to near desperation—and then make love to her all night until she's in ecstasy. All very wearing, but it's a nice way to go.

This remarkable lady will relate splendidly to his feelings most of the time, and although he'll never quite understand what really makes her tick, it won't matter. He's never quite as assured and confident as he seems, but she knows it. And even if everyone else thinks he's a bastard, she'll see the little boy inside and love him even more. This couple are not likely to do better if they're prepared for the pressure.

PISCES WOMAN—SAGITTARIUS MAN

There are a lot of forces working against this relationship, and a friendly affair would be a better idea than a lengthy partnership. Life, of course, doesn't always see it that way, so at least be prepared for some of the difficulties.

Sagittarius is an enthusiast. He likes to keep busy, balancing a dozen different projects, spending his energy and money without worrying about the future, living it up, having fun. Pisces finds this childish, to say the least. She will certainly be attracted by his infectious charm, but he does tend to spread it around a bit. Really he's a playful sort of guy. He's just not suitable for this emotional, sensual, and very sensitive lady unless she is prepared to make many compromises and frankly to come down to his simple level.

This doesn't mean Sagittarius is an idiot. Quite the contrary, he's sharp as a button, always looking out for number one, and always selfish. Pisces will never be able to trust him. He will be fascinated by the sheer complexity of her emotional apparatus. But he needs his freedom, room to be himself (whatever that is), and her jealousy will merely turn him off. He is a flirt, loves parties, and needs plenty of stimulus and fun. He works hard, but his efforts are often frustrated by his inability to keep at one thing for long. He's too much of a lightweight for the Pisces woman.

Sexually, these two will certainly have their moments, but her clinging demands could begin to bore the effervescent Sagittarian. He's not a sentimentalist or a romantic, although he tries to persuade himself that he is. And he is prone to take up ideas that cost money and don't work out. She isn't exactly cautious with cash either; she spends in a rather indiscriminate way, so the couple's finances are quite likely to be in a continuous state of disarray. He is generous at times and will satisfy her, but after he has explored life with his Piscean, he's ready to move on to greater challenges—or at least that's how he sees it. In fact, she's probably the greatest challenge he'll ever meet, if he only knew it.

Pisces needs security, a man to look after her, to lean on. This is decidedly not the man for that. He wants an equal partner and a woman who will challenge him and spur him on to greater things. He may become more responsible as he matures and the pressures of life force him to become more realistic and practical—but don't bank on it.

PISCES WOMAN—CAPRICORN MAN

This one can work out despite fairly evident differences of character that might initially upset the partners. Capricorn is a sturdy, practical sort, not much given to flights of philosophical fancy, but he's more sensitive than he pretends and he will truly appreciate his remarkable Piscean lady.

She will be exasperated at times by his failure to understand her emotional responses, and yet she will know she is deeply loved and needed. He will provide the security she needs, and she will bring a little fresh air and romance and joy into his slightly dull existence. There will be lots of minor misunderstandings, but the differences that these two clearly show can be used as the catalyst to link together into a splendidly durable union.

Capricorn tends to take things slowly; he doesn't rush into a relationship. He weighs the pros and cons and he is conscientious and intends to work hard at his career, even if that means neglecting his home life. His excuse will be that he's doing it for her, but that isn't really true; he's doing it because he thinks he ought to be at least moderately successful. And when he makes his fifth million and she demands to see more of him, he'll explain that things are not going too well at the Bangkok factory and he has to fly straight out there— he's got his responsibilities to the work force and he isn't going to shirk them. What can she say?

The Piscean is a complex lady, so one can't expect a stock response from her in any set of circumstances. She's going to get frustrated, but she'll work a lot of this out in her fantasies. Desert warriors will be waiting around the next bush to carry her off, debonair gamblers await her at the hotel, and so on. Strangely enough, such things do happen to her at times!

What it boils down to is that the Pisces woman is not going to have an easy time, but if she is determined that this man is for her, then she can make the relationship a success. He's more simple; he just wants a beautiful, loving woman waiting for him when he eventually gets home from wherever he's been. He tends to be faithful— affairs are too much trouble, too risky. One thing is certain: He'll adore this lady even if he can only see one side of her nature.

PISCES WOMAN—AQUARIUS MAN

Both have many virtues, but together these tend to cancel out, and if possible this link up should be avoided except by those determined that even the stars aren't going to influence their happiness.

Aquarius is a very independent, highly intelligent, emotionally rather cold guy. He is charming, interesting, gentle, and complex, but he isn't likely to match the Piscean ardor and determination to be permanently there in his thoughts and emotions. The Pisces woman has to be needed and deeply loved and told so both in words and actions.

Sexually, this union could be successful at first because both are inventive lovers and have vivid imaginations. But the problems will mount up, and Pisces will run for cover while Aquarius wonders what happened. He likes to get out and about with his pals, have a good time, travel the world. She longs for domestic bliss, a cosy fireside, and togetherness on the sofa. More than likely he'll want to play Scrabble when she wants to cuddle!

There will be a tendency for her to nag and scold and whine when she sees him worrying about everything else under the sun and moon except her. She is easily hurt, she's deeply sensitive, highly in-

tuitive, probably psychic. She will conclude he doesn't love her nearly so deeply as she loves him, and she'll probably have reached the
correct conclusion. He isn't materialistic, doesn't worry about money, but when he sees how extravagantly she spends, he'll probably
step in and take control.

The difference between them is that the Aquarian filters everything that happens through his excellent mind, while the romantic
Piscean lets everything hit her in the gut. She may well be more alive,
more vital, more changeable, more infuriating. She's certainly more
trouble! And he hasn't a clue to what she's on about most of the
time. He believes in manmade and created things and ideas, he believes in education as the key to the future, and he exercises his mind
in many directions. She believes in God as the key to the future. Both
are needed, of course, but will the twain come together in this relationship? Frankly the chances of these two lasting the course are
slim. Which doesn't mean that Aquarius is superficial or Pisces is a
shrew. Both are quite delightful in their different ways; it's not possible to say one is extroverted and the other introverted, although
there is a temptation to do this. They are too complex, unselfish, ever
ready to help the unfortunate—they should help themselves first.

PISCES MAN—PISCES WOMAN

Life is not going to be dull for these two. There will be great
togetherness, harmony, and love even though at times life will seem
tortured, painful, and dramatic.

Both partners understand each other so well that they could actually become too sensitive to moods and vibes that most people
wouldn't even notice—that's the penalty of being totally emotional,
totally Piscean. Neither finds it easy to make decisions, and both are
pretty bad with money. It comes and goes, and only the wind knows
where. If really pushed—as he will be if these two get together—the
Pisces man will finally make the cash decisions, but he still won't like
it.

At times this remarkable lady will deliberately go out of her way
to hurt her man, to get revenge for some imagined minor incident
or insult. Most of the time she will want to please, and her intuitive
and possibly psychic gifts will give her a remarkable ability to communicate with him. She'll go cold at times and wander off, but she'll
be back once her emotional nature is balanced again. She would be

happier with a stronger man because she wants to be looked after, but this particular partnership has an awful lot of compensations.

One thing to remember about these two is that they are dreamers. They spend most of their life fantasizing, in a world of their own peopled by knights and damsels, monsters and spaceships, and so on. They have a whole subliminal existence that others can only guess at. This makes them irritating, delightful, jealous, and often in a complete emotional mess. Sexually, things will swing. These two may never get out of bed. This sensual union could indeed go off the rails because they make a tremendous emotional drain on themselves and each other. The business of recharging the batteries is vital if they are to remain sane and relatively sensible.

The Pisces man is almost as romantic and sentimental as the Pisces woman. They are likely to love old things, like old houses; they respect laws and traditions; and they delight in talking about their schooldays or early life, to the total boredom of everyone else except other Pisceans, who keep seeing parallels in their own lives.

Pisceans are givers. This means that they want to give themselves totally to someone or something. It won't always be easy to have two givers in one household, but Pisceans somehow manage—and manage well.

PISCES MAN—ARIES WOMAN

This is undoubtedly a good partnership, although on the surface these two are very different characters. He will certainly fascinate this dynamic lady. She'll be tearing around as usual doing a hundred thousand things better than anyone else (or so she thinks) when suddenly a smiling Piscean will get in the way. She'll brush him off, but incredibly he'll still be there; but this time there'll be something slightly mysterious about his smile. The Aries is hooked and there's a fair chance she'll never recover.

This canny, intuitive, and gently charming man is going to need the strength and enthusiasm of an Aries woman. He'll happily let her make the decisions—which she is happy to do—until they get in the way of his plans and then he'll simply do things his way. She will feel most protective about her Piscean lover. She has quite a temper, and he will certainly make her wonder if she isn't living in a madhouse. His emotional responses will deeply try the efficient Arian impulses. She does need a lot of love and encouragement, and these she'll get—almost too much. She might even come to see Pisces as her jailer—that would be a pity, because he can do a great deal to make her understand harmony and beauty and to persuade her to be less selfish and self-centered.

Pisces does have the ability to act, so he can play the roles he thinks his woman wants. He's a giver, and this would be one aspect of the way he performs. He'll certainly idolize his Arian lady and dream about her day and night. He may get angry, but he'll never deliberately hurt her. He can say hurtful things and people of other signs would cringe, but the Aries woman won't even notice. Anyway he doesn't mean them; it's just that life gets on top of him and he needs comforting. Aries will fight many of the battles he should have been taking part in (and he might not even realize what has been going on). There's something feminine about this man, which doesn't mean he's a softie or a pushover. He takes life as it comes and tries to work with events, which of course is the complete opposite to the way this fighting lady performs. Sometimes she's about as subtle in her approach as a charging hippo—and might even look a bit like one too!

Pisces has a tendency to go out and drink with his buddies, to overdo things just a bit. Aries will let him know exactly what she thinks of this. Despite her previously active sex life, she is a puritan deep down. This is a splendidly complementary relationship that should not be missed.

PISCES MAN—TAURUS WOMAN

This partnership can be successful provided Taurus is prepared to accept that this man will not always be capable of organizing and dominating and making the decisions.

Pisces will apparently be ready to do her bidding, and she rather likes this. But soon she'll discover that he does things his way, does what he's told one minute and not the next. It's a bit confusing for the simple Taurean lady. She's practical, sensible, likes a nice efficient home, works hard, and occasionally collapses after bouts of total lethargy, overeating, overdrinking, and sensuality. Pisces is intuitive, gentle, needs lots of support, particularly in the bad times, but he is deeply sensitive, probably spiritual, a lover of beauty, delightful and irritating. He's a dreamer by day and night, a fantasizer of supreme proportions. Incredibly, his fantasies sometimes come true.

The Taurean's forthright approach to sex can be a bit too much for this romantic, sentimental man. He likes flowers and hearts and poems about undying love as much as he wants a woman caressing him. He's all man, but he's also very physical, and this includes a deep and genuine appreciation of beauty in any form.

The Piscean male overdoes things sometimes, whether it is drink or drugs or sex. It's a sort of release from the emotional tension he feels having to earn a living, support a family, and appear efficient and dynamic. Half the time he just wants to sit by a stream and write poetry and feel the wind in his hair. The other half he just wants to sit by the stream.

Taurus will happily make the decisions, organize the finances, move the furniture around, decide on the vacations, and then, if she is sensible, allow Pisces to make a few trifling decisions—and he'll be perfectly happy; the wine they drink is just as important to him as the town they drink it in. Pisces will always try to please his Taurus woman. He doesn't care about power or riches (although he can spend with the best of them), but he does like excitement and at times will take a real gamble, and probably win. In a pinch he will come out trumps almost to his own surprise. He thinks in subconscious universal ways, and the universal tends to look after its own. If that all sounds a bit complicated, it simply means that fate is on the Piscean's side—he doesn't have the equipment to fight life, so he works with it—perhaps subconsciously—to get his effect. Take a chance on this one.

PISCES MAN—GEMINI WOMAN

This is going to be a decidedly shaky union, to put it mildly. The Pisces man is several people rolled into one. He's practical and sensible and decisive one hour and indecisive, worried, unsure, and silly the next. The Gemini woman is also several people in one. She can be changeable, aggressive, charming, difficult, easy, and sexy all at the same time. These two will find that their relationship is like living on a volcano—at any moment an eruption could blot everything out. Obviously, the tension of waiting for such an outburst can be very corroding to any relationship.

These are two very attractive people. Gemini has an excellent mind, inquisitive, logical, often keenly thrusting. Pisces is all emotion. He responds intuitively, mystically. He likes or dislikes on sight, feels deeply, is too sensitive for his own good, and despite all his faults is so fascinating that Gemini cannot be blamed for being attracted to him.

She is going to start thinking that she's got mixed up with a sponge—an emotional sponge, sentimental, romantic, feeble. He is going to find the pizzazz of this woman terribly wearing. She never stops. He'll decide she's really a computer without an ounce of pity and humanity in her. And then this pair will suddenly pick up the pieces and it'll be great—for a time. They both have egos, don't ever doubt it, but both need stronger partners. They could have a sensuous and short-lived affair, but a longer-term commitment is going to be difficult.

Gemini has to understand everything that happens. She cannot believe anyone can act on impulse the way this Pisces man does. There'll be plenty of fun, but she will be upset when he suddenly withdraws into himself and becomes moody. In fact, he's recharging his batteries because he gives off a frightening amount of psychic energy. And of course he's a dreamer who finds everyday life much too boring to be bothered with. He isn't likely to get any better as he gets older, so it's no use her kidding herself about this.

The Gemini woman is quite aggressive, and she'll want to push her man on in his career. Pisceans are actually a lot more successful than might be expected, and this might surprise even them. They do have this rare ability to be in the right place at the right time when the breaks come, so it's a pity they aren't better at looking after the money when it does come.

PISCES MAN—CANCER WOMAN

These two are hardly likely to do better. There will be difficulties over money, his depressions, and other things, but really they are eminently compatible.

Both are imaginative, deeply sensitive, intuitive. It could well be one of those instantly super relationships that most people dream about. Both need emotional security, and this will need working on, but they will need each other desperately and tell each other so frequently. One danger is that this couple could become so caught up in each other that they'll shut the rest of the world out as they cuddle close around the dying embers of the fire. Ah, romance! These two are sentimental, romantic, silly at times. He possibly overindulges at times, but she'll accept it—as long as she's invited along to overindulge too.

Sexually, the Cancer woman is more demanding than the Pisces man, but there won't be any complaints even if they overdo things. On the physical level there is no difficulty, on the mental level there are no problems, because neither thinks much anyway (and when they do, it's illogically), but emotionally there'll be fireworks of all sorts—for good and ill. Both enjoy a glass of champagne, a love poem, roses, and a crescent moon. Pisces is a great wooer, so the courtship should be sensational. She just won't be able to resist his ardor; she won't be able to bear being parted from him for a moment.

Home life will be fun, important to both. They'll cut off and go cold at times and no amount of cajoling will bring them back to everyday life, but it won't be for long. Everyone will love this pair even though there's a little too much of the family and friends bit at times. They are quite incapable of telling anyone to push off except in the most trying circumstances. Financially, the Cancer woman is going to have to take over, however distasteful this is to her. The Piscean is quite incapable of worrying about the finances and he spends on the spur of the moment. He recognizes quality and is prepared to pay for service, so let's hope he has rich parents. In large things like investment in a new house he may prove quite brilliant, so perhaps his smaller money failures will be forgiven him by his admiring Cancerian.

This will be a complex union; it's no use pretending it will be straightforward. Half the time the lovers won't know their own minds and emotions, and the other half they'll experience bliss.

PISCES MAN—LEO WOMAN

This won't be a cosy relationship. The Leo woman may well decide that the Pisces man badly needs her and devote herself to organizing and protecting him. She'll get a shock when she next meets him and he's dynamic, positive, and impressive. Unfortunately, he wavers between extremes and it's going to drive the purposeful and rather bossy Leo wild.

Pisces certainly does need a woman like this. He's a great talker but not so good at doing. He'll promise her the stars, romance her, adore her, and then go out with someone else. The Leo woman won't stand that for ten minutes; she'll be off and well out of it. Pisces unfortunately lives in a fantasy world populated by dragons and ghosts and ladies in distress. He does tend to project these dreams into his life. It's fascinating but wearing to live with such a man.

She is outgoing, while he is introverted, much given to emotional crises and questioning why things happen as they do—even though she never listens to the answers! Pisces cannot understand why life seems so uncomplicated to the generous, fun-loving Leo woman. She in turn cannot see why he makes such a fuss and gets into such a state over unimportant things. When he gets into one of his depressive moods, she's likely to say exactly the wrong thing to try to cheer him up and then wonder why he howls like wolf.

Sex is important to this couple, although they approach it from different ends of the spectrum. She grabs, while he sidles up and gently insinuates himself. If she is prepared to accept a weaker man as a lover, then this can be a good relationship because she'll learn something about giving and taking, harmony and beauty. Most Leo women are not willing to do this and would be well advised to make a friend of the Pisces suitor, resist his amorous blandishments, and avoid a good deal of personal distress over a long period. Easier said than done with this guy, but at least she's been warned.

Leo has quite a temper and it will show from time to time—a nasty shock for the Piscean who thought she was all warmhearted generosity. The Leo woman does have a tendency to get rigid and set in her ways even at a relatively young age. The important thing for Pisces is a charming, peaceful, home atmosphere. He likes to have his admiring friends around—admiring his wife, that is, and of course she loves it, but he only wants to see a few people at a time. She is a great partygoer who loves to hold court and monopolize attention. In all fairness, she often looks terrific, and he will be delighted by this. He isn't a jealous fellow.

PISCES MAN—VIRGO WOMAN

These two are opposites in the Zodiac and opposites in most things. She's too reserved and he's too disorganized for this to be anything but a relationship of convenience. It's true love? OK, there are always exceptions, but call us back in twenty years' time.

Pisces is likely to decide that his pretty Virgoan is too cold, too critical, and prone to find faults even when he's doing his best. She is going to regard him as an emotional dustbin, and there's just enough truth in that to really hurt. He does bruise easily, and despite his evident charm, his deep sensitivity, and his real willingness to please, he's too vague, too changeable for her.

Pisces tends to act impulsively and intuitively, while Virgo carefully weighs things and only then makes up her mind. This is why she has a reputation for coldness; it isn't true, and she can be as sexy as they come, but she does like conditions to be right before she makes a commitment. She is in a continual state of mild frustration because the world never seems to be quite as efficient as she herself is. Perhaps this is something she'll learn to live with, though experience suggests she's never going to be quite rid of this curious character problem.

Virgo is a quiet, rather shy woman. She is a beauty and an excellent catch—for someone else. She needs affectionate warmth and security to blossom in. She isn't likely to get the security she needs with a Piscean around. He needs a stronger partner to organize him. She'll certainly try to do this, but she does see the other person's point of view too much. This is not the way to treat Pisces. And she certainly will not approve of his overindulgence. There's something slightly puritanical about this woman, and she won't have a lot of sympathy for his intuitive and spiritual flights. It's a pity, for she could learn quite a lot if she had a little more patience.

If Cupid does call, then Virgo will have to organize the family finances, something she is rather good at anyway. Pisces is not noted for his financial prudence, while she makes an excellent accountant and bookkeeper. Sexually, Virgo might well resist what she sees as importunate demands but then submit with the sort of resigned air that will finally break up the partnership. There's a lot of hard work in store for these two if they plan to make this relationship work. Do remember that Pisces is a dreamer, a fantasizer, something rather alien to the Virgoan way of thinking.

PISCES MAN—LIBRA WOMAN

These two are not really compatible, but it can work out if Libra doesn't expect to have a man she can lean on and Pisces doesn't get too weak and emotional and generally willowy.

Pisces is a sensitive, charming, romantic, sentimental fellow, and he'll make this woman feel good. She wants to be an equal partner; she demands a harmonic delightful relationship but doesn't much care for his extreme emotionalism. They will relate well sexually, there's no doubt about that. Libra loves to be courted, and the Piscean will play it for all he's worth. He's a great actor, but he will mean a lot of what he whispers in her shell-like ear. Both enjoy luxury and could overdo things at times, but at least they both know the score.

Pisces can become depressed about his role in life. He's fundamentally a serious fellow, while Libra is more lightweight, more out for a good time. She wants to share things, while he is more secretive. He tends to store up his beautiful experiences, and communication is not really his strong point except when he's after a woman!

The difficulty with Pisces is that he's a dreamer, a fantasizer, a man perpetually living in two or three different worlds. Everyday life is just not exciting and interesting enough for him, although he creates his fair share of dramas. She tends to have more practical dreams about people she knows or boyfriends she has discarded. Libra would be happier with a stronger man, and Pisces certainly needs a woman he can lean on much more. He leaves an awful lot to his partner, and his total emotionalism and intuitive brilliance are not always compensation for her having to make all the decisions and look after him.

Libra can get a bit lazy at times or may even have a minor revolt when her partner can't make up his wretched mind about something. This partnership is likely to be one of those in which the partners cannot make up their mind whether they would be better off together or apart. And quite honestly it will be very much up to them to make that decision even if it takes fifty or sixty years to come to a conclusion. If they opt for togetherness, then it's going to be a case of not looking back, counting the blessings, and taking each day as it comes. There is no point in thinking that these two will go in for financial planning. Pisces is a spendthrift, and Libra cannot resist beautiful clothes, beautiful places, and, for that matter, beautiful people. Things won't ever be easy—they seldom are when the furniture has been sold—but at least they won't be boring.

PISCES MAN—SCORPIO WOMAN

This is likely to be a dramatic and successful partnership between two deeply emotional people who will at times be irrational but are likely to fall in love and never recover!

The secretive, intense, sexy Scorpio woman will be enormously excited by this man. He isn't strong enough for her, but she won't mind making the decisions, controlling the finances, and generally organizing life. He's a dreamer, passive, sensual, sentimental, romantic, delightful. She can be cunning, dominant, incredibly jealous, and demanding. Her jealousy might make her a bad bet for many, but the Piscean will probably give her little to complain of. He doesn't mind being spied on and dominated—he knows this means she loves and needs him. And when he does get a wistful look in his eye and starts leering at other women, she'll give him a swift clip on the ear and drag him back to her lair. It won't really be like that, but the scenario isn't as far-fetched as might be thought.

Sexually, there will be deep physical passion. Pisces will positively blossom, and they may never get out of bed. Explosive rapture is possible for this pair. The sooner they get married, the better. Scorpio will soon start in to try to discover everything about her man—it's her way—but she will never completely succeed and therefore she'll always be interested. The reason she won't succeed is that he himself doesn't understand why he is the way he is. Emotional chaos is the only phrase to use to describe the way he responds to stimuli.

Deep Piscean depression can be deepened even further if the Scorpio woman starts being critical, as is her wont. And his dreamy moods will irritate her. It might in fact be a good idea if he stayed at home and she went out to work. She is immensely ambitious, and he isn't bothered about power or influence, although he likes to spend as though he had millions. However, she will soon take charge of the finances and occasionally let him have a little pocket money.

Don't assume that Pisces is lazy; he works as hard as anyone when the mood takes him and then relapses into lethargy of his own special type, even if it looks to everyone else as though he's as busy as ever. He is often more successful than even he expects in making big money—to the fury of the Scorpio woman, even though she will benefit. He isn't always weak either; he changes from day to day, if not from minute to minute. This will be a fascinating union.

PISCES MAN—SAGITTARIUS WOMAN

The relationship between a sexy, flirtatious woman who nevertheless has her virtues and a deeply sensitive man who wants a loving, dedicated woman to take him in hand is not very promising.

Only the exceptional couple is going to make this one work for more than a few weeks, even though it might be fun trying.

One difficulty would be financial. The reckless Piscean would find the Sagittarian spending what little money he has left over on theater tickets, new dresses, and other extravagances. She's open, honest, and not really happy about making decisions. She's immensely optimistic, but even that quality could be somewhat dented by the Piscean gloom and despondency that will occasionally descend. It would be great if these two had immensely rich parents who also happen to be very generous.

Sexually, there may well be good moments, but the Sagittarian woman likes to get out and about, while the Pisces man wants to wallow in luxury at home—not a promising start, and both are quite likely to start looking elsewhere for solace and understanding. As she becomes more independent, he will at first become more emotional and demanding and then, when she is bored, he will be deeply mortified. Both are possibly interested in the occult and the mystic, but the rent still needs to be paid, alas. Pisces won't be able to resist her, and she'll be very taken by him. Oh, well, life likes to play games sometimes.

Sagittarius wants to get married and yet wants her freedom. Pisces always wants to get married and then wishes he hadn't. It's all very confusing. One thing is for sure, she will have to make the big effort if she wants this partnership to be a creative and lasting one. There will be an appreciation of beauty from her but it won't be nearly so deep as his empathy with sunsets, kittens, swaying trees, and yachts. She likes to have her many friends around; he will be charming but distant and wish they were all dead. He has vast energy one day and is completely exhausted the next.

As Sagittarius gets older, she will probably find that she is much better with money than she thought she was, and if Pisces is still around he'll begin to see it too and congratulate himself on a wise choice of partner. If she can channel his abilities into some artistic backwater, he'll be happy and she'll also be left alone more and will find she can be more loving and sympathetic when he comes running to her for encouragement or caresses.

PISCES MAN—CAPRICORN WOMAN

This partnership will be complex and difficult. Capricorn is practical and sensible, and does not suffer sentimental fools gladly.

She'll probably decide that her Piscean man is just too much trouble—one minute he's the he-man hero and the next he's a helpless infant. And yet he has many virtues—most of which she won't appreciate.

She finds emotional people inconstant and unreliable, and she hates this. She needs security and love, and although Pisces will certainly make her feel desirable and appreciated, it won't be enough to ensure a long-lasting and satisfying relationship. Pisces will bring a breath of romance into her dull life—at least that's how he sees it—but he's too moody and changeable and intuitive and sentimental for the Capricorn woman, who is made of sterner stuff. If these two do live together, Capricorn will do her best to run his disorganized life, but she won't be particularly sympathetic when he gets depressed.

Sexually, they could go well together because he's a fine actor and when she is happy she gives much more of herself. There are times when he will delight and enthral his Capricorn lady, as indeed he would almost anyone. Even the mildly pessimistic Capricorn woman loves having him around—some of the time!

Financially, he'll drive her crazy. She's a great saver-for-a-rainy-day, cautious with the cash. He spends as the mood takes him and worries about it later. He is certainly extravagant. She knows quality and likes to run a tight ship. In fairness it must be said that he will work hard for his family, but he does tire easily (he lacks stamina) and will probably come home to collapse, have his fevered brow stroked, and bemoan his fate.

Capricorn is certainly an ideal lady to lean on in a crisis. She summons up strength from her boots and keeps on going when most have fallen by the wayside. She's perhaps too proud to give in. It probably sounds as though this is going to be a rather one-sided relationship, when it comes to working at the partnership, and that is true. And yet at times there will be genuine togetherness if she's bold enough to take him on. She would of course be wise to see him as a major liability, but it's well known that love is blind, and lovers have been known to make crucial decisions for ludicrous reasons.

PISCES MAN—AQUARIUS WOMAN

It would be nice to suggest that this partnership is likely to be a great success, but honestly it looks as though the problems will prove too much for these two, except in unusual cases.

Aquarius is detached, while Pisces is committed and involved. She is unemotional, while he weeps and gnashes his teeth. She thinks things out, while he responds intuitively and without calculation. He is gloomy and depressed, while she is regal. And so on. And yet both have a genuine gift for friendship. The difficulty is that he needs mothering and cosseting, and that's the last thing she intends to do.

But he likes capable, sensible women and he can be great fun. He relishes every stimulating and exciting experience, loves parties, possibly overindulges, and certainly enjoys himself flirting. She regards all this as juvenile; there are much more important things to do, such as saving the world, or even the galaxy. She tends to think better in cosmic terms than individual ones—which doesn't make her any the less feminine or fascinating. She has an excellent mind and believes in education. He believes in emotion!

He expects to be placed at the very center of her world, and he is due for a shock if he gets involved with this elegant lady. She believes in equal shares, and she expects him to take an equal share. Most men are expected to make more than fifty percent of the decisions, but not this one.

Financially, Pisces is a nonstarter, and the Aquarian woman prefers not to have to think about the family purse. However, if forced to, she will take charge and do an efficient job. Basically he's too self-centered for her, and she'll soon find it out if she takes a chance on him. She tends to live for the future, while he spends a lot of romantic time and energy thinking and living in the past. Aquarius and Pisces do really seem to be traveling along the same road—but in opposite directions. It would be sensible to shake hands, sit down, and have a cup of coffee and then say good-bye. In some ways the most irritating thing will be that just as Aquarius has made up her mind that he's a wishy-washy weakling, he'll prove himself strong, capable, and manly—before going wishy-washy again. It's all too much for her sensibly balanced emotional and mental structure. She'll push off—or she'll find that he's a major challenge and that, despite the unhappiness, loneliness, and possible separate beds, he is in fact going to be her life work. And if she should succeed, she'll have created a truly wonderful union.